RACE AND EDUCATION

RACE AND EDUCATION
The Unending Controversy

By

LAURENCE R. MARCUS, Ed.D.

New Jersey Department of Higher Education

and

BENJAMIN D. STICKNEY, Ed.D.

Pikes Peak Board of Cooperative Services

CHARLES C THOMAS • PUBLISHER

Springfield • Illinois • U.S.A.

Published and Distributed Throughout the World by
CHARLES C THOMAS • PUBLISHER
2600 South First Street
Springfield, Illinois 62717, U.S.A.

©1981 by CHARLES C THOMAS • PUBLISHER
ISBN 0-398-04515-1
Library of Congress Catalog Card Number: 81-4742

Library of Congress Cataloging in Publication Data

Marcus, Laurence R.
    Race and education.

    Includes bibliographical references and index.
    1.   School integration — United States — History.
    2.   College integration — United States — History.
    3.   Segregation in education — United States — History.
    I.   Stickney, Benjamin D.   II.   Title.
    LC214.2.M37   370.19'342   81-4742
    ISBN 0-398-04515-1   AACR2

Printed in the United States of America

S-R-1

PREFACE

While this book has consumed a major portion of our time during the last few years, our interest in the black educational experience and the problems of black America stretches back to our youth. Having grown up in Miami and greater Boston, respectively, we experienced the disgrace of the legally segregated South and the hypocrisy of the critical North. During the 1960s, we participated in demonstrations that provided support for the changing order in which segregation laws fell by America's wayside. In the wave of idealism which accompanied that era, we each decided to make our individual contribution to the solution of poverty and racial injustice. One of us joined the Peace Corps and served as a teacher in Nigeria; the other spent time working with youthful offenders through the Commonwealth Service Corps, the Massachusetts equivalent of VISTA. By the time we met in graduate school at the University of Massachusetts in the early 1970s, one of us had worked as a teacher in the inner city schools of Miami's predominantly black Liberty City section and those of Washington, D.C., as well as having taught at the collegiate level. The other had served as a social worker and a university administrator. Both of us have been active on affirmative action committees at our institutions. Our doctoral research focused, respectively, on the effectiveness of compensatory education programs and affirmative action programs.

Since that time, we have each maintained our research and professional interest regarding the promotion of equality through education. Throughout our careers, we have known large numbers of high potential, but low achieving black students. We were heartened when we saw America make a commitment to them, but were saddened a few years later when that commitment was pulled back.

Unfortunately, too many of the students whom we taught in the latter part of the 1970s did not understand that overwhelming barriers still exist for America's minorities. They believed that an end to segregation laws meant an end to discrimination, that the legacy of the past has been overcome through the initiatives of the 1960s and that it is individual ability and drive that now determine achievement. While we wish that persons holding those beliefs were correct, we understand that America is not yet the Great Society.

We decided that our most effective contribution to the extension of equality at this point in America's history and our own professional development would be the writing of a book that would examine the legacy of centuries of racial injustice and the problems which confront blacks at all levels of the educational system today.

The research, the discussion and the writing of this volume have been truly enjoyable. The process was made much easier as a result of the encouragement of our families, friends, and colleagues. We wish to thank those who spent time reacting to early drafts of portions of the book, particularly Doctor Arthur Jensen of the University of California, Berkeley, Doctor Katherine Hecht, formerly of the United States Office of Education, and Doctor Ann Weinheimer, currently with the United States Department of Education, who, although they may or may not agree with our analyses and conclusions, provided us with helpful feedback. Further, we wish to acknowledge the contributions of Ruth Pasola for her help in the preparation of the proposal for the book and of Lorraine McNichol and Mae Smith for their invaluable assistance in the preparation of the manuscript.

Laurence R. Marcus
Benjamin D. Stickney

INTRODUCTION

Perhaps no American domestic issue has ignited greater controversy among more people for a longer period than race and education. As one civic institution capable of influencing nearly all American youth, the schools have often been put at the forefront of the fight to secure equality for blacks. Accordingly, more Americans may have come face to face with the United States racial trauma through experiences with public education than through any other means. During the last thirty-five years, the schools have been viewed as playing a primary role in righting the racial wrongs of more than 350 years. Given the degree of racism and segregation throughout most of our history and the absence of any national mandate on the means by which schooling could remediate for such injustice, it is hardly surprising that race and education continue to provoke such passion.

This book is less a description of the emotions produced by race and education than it is an accounting of why the controversy arose, when it began to surface, and why it promises to continue during the remainder of the twentieth century. Mainly, the volume is a chronicle of the black educational experience in America, a story that merits telling and retelling because of the unique history of blacks in this country. The book also includes a critical research analysis of many educational programs for underachieving students, in which blacks have been enrolled in disproportionately high numbers. We feel it is not only important to offer a concise description of such events as the legal battle over desegregation, the implementation of Head Start, and the racial hostility in Boston, but to give the reader an overview of the research on the effectiveness of those educational strategies that promised to provide greater equality of educational opportunity.

EDUCATION, INCOME, AND RACE

Before going any further, it is appropriate to address two important questions:

1. What relationship does education have with greater earnings and occupational status for Americans?
2. Why is it important to offer a racial analysis of the inequalities in educational opportunities and income in America?

Education and Income

Perhaps the most comprehensive assessment of the impact of background on income and occupational status can be found in a book appropriately entitled *Who Gets Ahead*, authored principally by Harvard's Christopher Jencks.[1] Published in 1979, the work summarizes the analyses of eleven surveys of several population samples at various ages. Because the surveys included a paucity of data on women, Jencks chose to limit his analyses to males. The book's findings are also restricted by the fact that it contains no sample data after 1974. Despite these limitations, Jencks still builds a rather compelling argument for the significance of education. Schooling was found to be related to greater earnings and higher status occupation, even after controlling for family background and academic ability.[2] Education appears to pay greater dividends, however, at the college level than at the secondary school level. Finishing high school instead of elementary school is associated with an estimated 15 to 25 percent increase in earnings, while a college degree is associated with a projected 30 to 40 percent earning advantage over a high school diploma.[3] These estimates are somewhat lower than those of the United States Census Bureau. According to the Bureau, the value of the bachelor's degree is evidenced by the fact that those with the four year degree will earn 50 percent more than those with high school diplomas while those with only some college will earn only 14 percent more than high school graduates.[4]

According to Jencks, *et al.* "The earnings advantage of college graduates derives largely from the fact that they enter higher-status occupations than other men. This is not so true of secondary schooling... Unless high school attendance is followed by a college education, its economic value appears quite modest."[5]

Their data also suggest that blacks benefit less than whites economically from a high school degree, but that a college diploma is more profitable for blacks than for whites.[6] Therefore, it would appear that any significant reduction in the inequality of earnings must involve a more equitable access to education, particularly higher education.

However, greater access to schooling means a good deal more than desegregation and the existence of open enrollment community and four year colleges. Equality of opportunity must go hand in hand with other strategies to equalize educational achievement. On the various aptitude and scholastic measures, the average black child does not perform as well as the average white child. In the basic skills area, black children tend to learn reading and mathematics at a slower rate than white children, which means that most blacks fall further and further behind the national reading level during their years of schooling.[7] A child who is two years behind at the end of the sixth grade may be four years behind upon graduation from high school, and it is doubtful whether an eighth grade reading level adequately prepares a person for a successful stay in an institution of higher education. Consequently, special classes may be necessary to accelerate the scholastic growth of many black children.

Jencks *et al.* report that measured "academic ability predicts educational attainment at least as well as socioeconomic background" and that most of this relationship is independent of family background.[8] Therefore, students with greater ability may tend to stay in school longer and enjoy greater earnings and higher occupational status. Jencks and his associates also note, however, that there is little evidence that "brightness" in itself is the critical variable and that years of schooling may tell us more about chances for economic and occupational advantage than measured intelligence. It was found that persistent slower learners who stayed in school and eventually achieved reasonable mastery of the material fared about as well occupationally as more rapid learners.[9] Accordingly, if programs such as Head Start could permanently increase measured ability or if programs such as

Title I reading could give so-called disadvantaged children adequate preparation for college, low income black children would
probably stay in school longer and thus enjoy greater earnings
and occupational status. The highly motivated pupil who enters
college reading at the eleventh grade level may graduate and
eventually learn as much as his more academically advanced
counterpart who had attained that degree of reading proficiency
in the eighth grade. On the other hand, the high school graduate
student who has progressed no further than an eighth grade reading level will find college an extremely difficult, if not unsur-
mountable challenge. One of the important problems we face is
that black children throughout their years of schooling typically
score about a standard deviation lower than white children on
ability and achievement tests, which means that 30 to 50 percent of
the black population may be four to six years behind the national
average at the end of twelve years of schooling.[10] As long as these
substantial achievement inequities exist between blacks and whites
it is highly unlikely that simply equalizing educational opportunity through desegregation and expanded higher education will
lead to greater equality of learning. Consequently, many educators long ago developed and continue to advocate special instructional strategies for underachieving children to help eliminate or
at least narrow the academic gap between the economically
advantaged and disadvantaged in general and between whites and
blacks in particular.

Race in Particular

It has been argued recently that one must look more to class
discrimination than racial discrimination for an understanding of
the remaining inequities separating blacks and whites in America.
Political scientists such as Nathan Glazer and Edward Banfield
have suggested that socio-cultural differences, rather than race *per
se*, explain most of the current discrimination targeted at blacks,
and that white racial prejudice will subside considerably as a
greater percentage of blacks enter the American middle class.[11]
This position has gained further support from a book entitled *The
Declining Significance of Race* by William Wilson, published in 1979.

Sociologist Wilson contends that "the recent mobility patterns of blacks lend strong support to the view that economic class is clearly more important than race in predetermining job placement and occupational mobility." He argues further that "... the black middle class is enjoying unprecedented success in finding white-collar jobs in both the corporate sector and the growing government sector." [12]

Without getting into the debate over how substantial the economic gains of blacks have been and the causes of discrimination in employment, it is important to point out (as does Wilson) that educational and social policies have done little or nothing to enhance the economic opportunities of the black lower class and to remember as well that the black underclass would not be nearly as large today if race had not been an important factor in determining education and occupational opportunity. Furthermore, one cannot explain the racial differences in measured academic aptitude and school achievement by looking solely to traditional socioeconomic indices. Blacks and whites have had different histories in this country, which may have much to do with the fact that blacks perform lower than whites scholastically, after controlling for socioeconomic status. Given the dehumanizing experience of blacks in our 350 year history, it would be surprising indeed if blacks performed as well on mental and achievement measures as their economically equal white counterparts. But while affirmative action and mastery of the basics have championed the opportunities of blacks from middle class backgrounds, lower class blacks have generally benefited very little from more egalitarian employment policies [13] and have typically acquired few of the academic skills conducive to educational longevity and thus greater occupational economic opportunity. [13]

As a group, blacks continue to suffer from economic and occupational disadvantage. According to the United States Bureau of the Census, in 1977 the median income for whites was $16,470 and for blacks was only $9,563. In that same year, roughly 29.0 percent of all blacks earned less than $6,191 (the official poverty level figure) as compared with 8.9 percent of the white population. In 1978, unemployment percentages were twice as high for nonwhites (13.1%) than for whites (6.2%), and a significantly greater percentage of whites (64.1%) had managerial and white-collar jobs than blacks (39.8%). [14]

During the 1960s, more technical, managerial, and white-collar jobs opened to blacks than ever before. However, while many blacks made it into the middle class, the progress was short-lived. The 1970s saw a severe decline in the rate of entrance into the professions. [15] In fact, while the ratio of black family income to that of white families rose from 51.8 percent in 1961 to 60.9 percent in 1969, it fell to 57.1 percent ten years later. Even more disturbing is the fact that the 1979 figure is less than two percent higher than it was at the end of World War II. [16] Reflective of this decline was the addition of a half million blacks to the poverty ranks between 1974 and 1977. [17] While that period saw an increase in the proportion of white families earning more than $15,000 per year, it saw a decline in the proportion of black wage earners in that category. [18] A recent report issued by the National Urban League indicated that many blacks are in the throes of an economic depression of the likes of that of the 1930s. According to the Urban League, 24 percent of black heads of household were unemployed in the last quarter of 1979, a level three times the national jobless rate. [19] In many cities, the unemployment rate for black youth has hovered around 50 percent for the last few years. [20]

Many researchers have shown a direct tie between parental income and educational achievement. Among these are Samuel Bowles and Herbert Gintis, who point out that children from families with low incomes are less likely to be graduated from high school and, if they make it to college, are more likely to attend a community college rather than a baccalaureate level institution. In fact, those from high socioeconomic background are more than four times as likely to attend college as those from low socioeconomic backgrounds. [21]

Thus, there is a clear cycle of low income and underachievement, a cycle in which race plays an important part. Those who graduate from college earn more than those who do not. Further, their children attend college in higher proportions than do the children of others. Blacks are disproportionately underrepresented in the ranks of the college graduates, as well as the middle and upper socioeconomic groupings. Their children, then, are less likely to graduate college and to get professional jobs. Professor Wilson may be overoptimistic in his belief that race is a declining determinant in what most of us consider success.

Black America is not unaware of the trend toward more, not less, inequality. A 1978 New York *Times* poll indicated that the proportion of blacks who believed racial prejudice and discrimination would eventually end declined twelve points since 1968 to 37 percent, while the proportion believing that prejudice would always exist rose to 53 percent.[22] Secretary of the United States Department of Health and Human Services, Patricia Harris cited the belief among blacks that America has lost its concern for its disadvantaged as one of the primary causes of the riot in the Liberty City section of Miami (which resulted in eighteen deaths and $100 million in property damage).[23]

In summary, as long as there are substantial racial differences in income, occupational status and academic preparation in America and as long as the schools are viewed as a principal means for reducing or eliminating these inequities, it is important for the literature to include analyses of inequality of opportunity (both educationally and economically) along racial lines.

OVERVIEW OF THE CHAPTERS

This volume offers an analysis of race and education first by addressing the desegregation struggle, second by reviewing the most common instructional alternative for many blacks (compensatory education), and third by summarizing opportunities in higher education. Part I, "The Desegregation Struggle," includes three chapters. The first traces the educational history of blacks from the earliest days of slavery to World War II. Chapter 2 focuses on the legal battles to overcome the legality of segregated schooling, culminating in the historic 1954 *Brown vs. the Board of Education* Supreme Court decision. The third chapter discusses the desegregation struggle first in the South and then in the North from 1954 to the present period. Part II, "Compensatory Education and Beyond" begins with a summary of the rationale for, and early implementation of, compensatory education programs such as Head Start and Title I remedial reading, and continues in the fifth chapter which reviews the research on the effectiveness of these programs. The research review goes on in the following chapter as the data on desegregation's influence on achievement and a controversy over busing is scanned. However, most of Chapter 6 is devoted to critiquing the herediatarian hypothesis that black and white differences in achievement are caused principally by black and white differences in innate ability. Part III, "Higher Education" includes the seventh chapter which addresses the legality and the political controversies surrounding affirmative action. Chapter 8 focuses on the black experience in universities and colleges and examines the future of traditionally black colleges. Finally, Chapter 9 attempts to tie it all together and offer some policy recommendation and generate some hypothesis for future scrutiny.

REFERENCES

1. Jencks, C. *et al.*: *Who Gets Ahead? The Determinants of Economic Success in America.* New York: Basic Books, Inc., 1979.
2. Ibid., pp. 187–188.
3. Ibid., pp. 187–188.
4. Bowles and Gintis, H.: *Schooling in Capitalist America, Educational Reform and the Contradictions of Economic Life.* New York: Basic Books, 1976, p. 217.
5. Jencks, op cit., pp. 188–189.
6. Ibid., p. 187.
7. Coleman, J. *et al.*: *Equality of Educational Opportunity.* Washington: U.S. Government Printing Office, 1966, p. 220.
8. Jencks, op cit., p. 104.
9. Ibid., p. 114.
10. Coleman, op cit.,
11. Wilson, W.: Reviews the declining significance of race in america. *The Review of Black Political Economy,* 9(4):453–459, 1979.
12. Wilson, W.: *The Declining Significance of Race.* Chicago: University of Chicago Press, 1978, pp. 52, 199.
13. Ibid., pp. 88, 109.
14. *U.S. Bureau of the Census, Statistical Abstract of the United States, 1979.* Washington, D.C.: U.S. Government Printing Office, 1979, pp. 396, 449, 463.
15. Anderson, B.: Economic progress. in Williams, J. (Ed.): *The State of Black America.* New York: National Urban League, 1980, p. 7.
16. Kusnet, D.: Black Depression. *The New Republic,* 181(20):16, 1979.
17. Watson, D.: Through the Academic Gateway. *Change Magazine.* 11(7):26,1979.
18. Kusnet, op cit., p. 16.
19. *Chicago Tribune.* August 3, 1980.

20. Two Societies, America Since the Kerner Report. The *New York Times*, March, 1978, p. 2.
21. Bowles and Gintis, op cit., p. 31, 33.
22. Two Societies, op cit., p. 2.
23. *Chicago Tribune*, August 3, 1980.

CONTENTS

RACE AND EDUCATION

PART I

THE DESEGREGATION STRUGGLE

CHAPTER 1

IGNORANCE IS NOT BLISS

"From every mountainside, let freedom ring!" So ends one of the best known of America's patriotic songs. To those who landed at Jamestown and Plymouth, to those who cleared through Ellis Island, to those who come today, "America" has meant "freedom," whether it was religious, intellectual, or economic freedom that they sought. Such has not been the case for the great majority of America's black immigrants—those who reached our shores in manicles and within the sights of muskets and the reach of whips held by whites who sought to profit from their sale as laborers. The first recorded mention of black presence in what was later to become the United States was chronicled by, the early Virginia explorer and settler, Captain John Smith, who noted the purchase of twenty blacks from a Dutch trader; it is not clear, however, whether they were slaves or indentured servants.[1] Virginia county court records, dating back to the 1640s, reveal the sale of blacks for periods of a lifetime but make no reference to slave status. Perhaps the first archival evidence of American slavery can be found in the register of a 1643 transaction in which Governor Leonard Calvert of Maryland procured seventeen "Negro slaves" from ship owner John Skinner in exchange for "certain estates."[2]

SLAVERY IN COLONIAL TIMES

Until 1810, when by Constitutional compromise the importation of slaves was ended, millions of blacks were legally introduced to this country; however, the exact number is in dispute. Historian J. D. Fage believes it unlikely that there were more than 6 million West Africans involved in trans-Atlantic slavery; 4.5 million coming between 1701 and 1810.[3] Meier and Rudwick, on the other

hand, believe that as many as 50 million people may have been
lost to Africa as a result of slave raids. Of this number, they believe
that only 15 million reached the New World. The British, alone,
transported 2 million to their North American and West Indian
colonies. [4]

Most of the African slaves had originally made their homes on
the western shore of the continent from Ghana to the Cameroons,
a part of Africa with a rich tradition prior to European coloniza-
tion. The culture of the people who inhabited that part of the
world, though different from that in Europe, was far from uncivi-
lized. In fact, as early as the seventeenth century, Timbuktu boasted
one of the great fountains of knowledge in the Muslim world, the
University of Sankore. [5] However, the Dutch, Portuguese, Spanish,
British, and French chose not to recognize this rich cultural tradition in order that they might satisfy the need for a cheap labor
supply for New World mines and plantations.

To keep the blacks in a state of slavery required that they be
kept in a state of ignorance, that they be kept away from the
intellectual tradition that many colonists carried across the Atlantic
and that would eventually result in the secession of the colonies
from England. There were, however, several factors that worked
against this conspiracy to keep literacy from blacks. First was the
desire of the slave owner to maximize his profit. To do so necessitated that some slaves be taught skilled trades such as carpentry,
blacksmithing, and other such occupations that required their
knowledge of reading and computation. Further, there was the
calling among the Christian slave-holding class to bring religion
to their servants (although most of the original slaves were
already religious, following either Islamic or tribal religious
customs) as a way to guarantee their own salvation as well as that
of their chattel. Many colonists believed that such efforts would be
wasted since they believed that blacks had no souls. Nonetheless,
to them, a religious slave meant an obedient slave. Thus, some
slaves were taught to read the Bible and were baptized. This raised
a serious issue since prevailing British law did not allow Christians to be held as slaves. The matter was resolved when a declaration by the Bishop of London, along with actions taken by colonial
legislatures, abrogated this long held more. [6]

The slaves, themselves, desired literacy because they associated it with being "quality people." House servants found it necessary to learn to identify the various newspapers that their masters requested. Foremen had to learn enough to keep a log of the day's work. Others were driven by their own intellectual curiosity. Many slaves seized every opportunity to receive instruction. Some did so by learning from their children who had been taught by playing school with the children of their owners. One example of such an instance was found in the household of South Carolina Supreme Court Justice John F. Grimke whose daughter Sarah wrote that as a child, she and her sister Angelina had taught their slaves: "The light is put out, the key hold secured, and flat on our stomachs before the fire, with spelling books in our hands, we defied the laws of South Carolina."[7]

Virginia's lawmakers first passed a statute concerning slaves in 1660,[8] and then, two decades later, enacted one intended to prevent black insurrections, which was the result that those opposing the education of blacks feared most. That law proclaimed that "the frequent meeting of considerable numbers of negroes . . . is judged of dangerous consequence" and provided a penalty of thirty lashes of the whip to offenders.[9]

Such an insurrection occurred in South Carolina in 1739. In the wake of the deaths of twenty-five whites, the legislature adopted the first of the slave codes, "An Act for the Better Ordering and Governing of Negroes and Other Slaves in This Province." The ordinance defined as "Negro" anyone who had a black mother. These persons were not permitted to travel freely throughout the state. They were denied the use of guns, were forbidden from commercial occupations, and were not allowed to operate boats. Such private rights as the ability to beat a drum and the prerogative to drink liquor were denied. Not only were blacks who were convicted of assaulting a white person or of raping a white woman subject to the death penalty, but capital punishment was also the retribution that slaves were to receive for refusing to submit to the interrogation of any white person who approached them.[10] Further, South Carolina's slave code required a state of compulsory ignorance for its blacks:

And whereas the having of slaves taught to read and write or suffering them
to be employed in writing, may be attending with great inconveniences;
Be it enacted, that all and every person and persons whatsoever, who shall
hereafter teach, or cause any slave or slaves to be taught to write, or shall
employ any slaves as a scribe in any manner of writing whatsoever, hereafter taught to write; every such person or persons shall, for every offense,
forfeit the sum of one hundred pounds current money. [11]

Similar slave codes were enacted in most of the colonies—even
Connecticut passed one in 1715. [12] Their prevalence and harshness
led Thomas Jeffeson to include them among the grievances against
King George III that were penned into the early drafts of the
Declaration of Independence. However, a compromise, which guaranteed the unanimous vote of the Continental Congress in favor of
the resolution, removed mention of slavery from the document.

The French colonialists were more humane in their treatment
of blacks than were the British. Under their Code Noir, freed
blacks were to be treated as anyone who was born free. Further,
slave owners were required to teach their slaves to read in order
that they might become good Christians. (In 1716, the Jesuits took
control of a number of plantations in the French colonies and
increased the educational opportunities available to the slaves
who worked for them.) Unlike their British counterparts, the
French were forbidden from destroying slave families by selling a
spouse or any of their young children. Additionally, they were not
allowed to torture their slaves, nor were they permitted to let them
go ill-fed or ill-clothed. And, they were required to care for their
"old and decrepit slaves." [13] But, while the French were more
humane, it must be remembered that they, too, were participants
in an ugly institution.

While antiblack attitudes and legislative restrictions retarded
the schooling of blacks in the Southern British colonies, they did
not remove all of their opportunities for literacy. In addition to
the informal examples of instruction previously cited, there were
also established schools for blacks. One such institution was found
in Goose Creek Parish, S.C. in the early eighteenth century. The
teacher, Episcopal minister Samuel Thomas wrote, "I have here
presumed to give an account of one thousand slaves . . . [who] are
desirous of Christian knowledge and seem willing to prepare

themselves for it, in learning to read, from which they redeem the time from their labor."[14] Another school, this one in Charleston, S.C., was run by the Society for the Propagation of the Gospel, an arm of the Episcopal Church. The Society purchased two slaves and taught them to be teachers. In 1744, classes began for sixty young slaves. The school was to exist for some twenty years; however, the enforcement of the colony's antiliteracy statute shortly led to the replacement of slaves with free blacks.[15]

The Quakers were major contributors to the education of Southern blacks. They believed their efforts to be payment of the "just debt" that they owed to the blacks for having participated in the institution of slavery.[16] As early as 1672, Virginia attempted to stop the Quakers by making it illegal for them to bring blacks into their religious services. Quaker schools were also established in North Carolina beginning in 1731, and, similarly, that colony passed restrictive ordinances against the Friends in order to squash their efforts to assist blacks.[17]

EDUCATION IN ANTEBELLUM AMERICA

With the American Revolution came a wave of hope and an improvement of conditions for blacks. In the South, free blacks began to initiate instructional programs. In 1790, the Brown Fellowship Society of Charleston opened a school. It was followed some twenty years later by the Minor Society, which taught poor and orphaned blacks. One of its graduates, Daniel A. Payne, carried on the tradition in 1829 when he founded his own school. In Baltimore, the Sharp Street Methodist Church and AME minister, Daniel Coker, both were running schools by 1800, and two decades later adult blacks were studying Latin and French in evening classes.[18]

Conditions in the District of Columbia and its surrounding area were also favorable. The Roman Catholic influence in Georgetown made the District a center for integrated education: "So liberal were the white people of this town that colored children were sent to school there with white boys and girls who seemed to raise no objection." Neighboring Alexandria, Virginia also had integrated schools.[19] In 1807, three blacks, none of whom could read and write, built a school for blacks in the District and hired a white teacher. Another black school was opened there in 1818 by the Resolute Beneficial Society. [20]

Educational opportunities were not, by any means, universal. South Carolina, for instance, prohibited the education of slaves in 1740 and, then, following the slave insurrection led by General Gabriel in Virginia in 1800, did the same for free blacks. Judge St. George Tucker spoke for many when, in response to the revolt by Gabriel, he stated "Our sole security then consists in their ignorance of this power (doing us mischief) and their means of using it ... Every year adds to the number of those who can read and write; and the increase in knowledge is the principal agent in evolving the spirit we have to fear." [21] Laws against blacks became harsher as the nineteenth century got older. Louisiana prohibited the migration of free blacks into that state in 1814 as a block against the incitement of slaves. [22] Five years later, Virginia forbad slaves from assembling for the purpose of learning to read and write; offenders would receive a penalty of up to twenty lashes. Similarly, North Carolina sentenced free blacks to receive thirty-nine lashes and assessed whites $200 fines if they violated the state's compulsory miseducation statutes. [23]

The Southern fears of the power of education were vindicated again in 1822 when blacks in Charleston, led by Denmark Vasey, an educated black from Santo Domingo, revolted after reading of the antislavery debates that accompanied the Missouri Compromise. [24] A more important revolt led by Nat Turner occurred nearly a decade later. In response, Georgia, Virginia, Mississippi, and North Carolina enacted strict laws prohibiting the assembly and education of blacks. Penalties included whippings for blacks and fines and imprisonment for whites. Even more insidious, the Mississippi ordinance also required that "within 90 days every free negro or mulatto in the State, under the age of 50 years and over the age of 16 years to remove and quit the State and not to return on any pretense" under penalty of sale into slavery. A law of the same nature was passed in Missouri; it gave free blacks three days in which to leave the state unless they received a license permitting them to stay. [25]

The border states of Maryland and Delaware also responded in fear to the possibility of slave uprisings. While they did not move to prohibit the education of blacks, they sought to keep them under the watchful eye of whites. Delaware forbad groups of twelve or more blacks from meeting beyond midnight except under the direction of three whites. Further, it did not allow a free black to hold a religious meeting unless authorized to do so by a judge or justice of the peace upon the recommendation of five "respectable and judicious citizens."[26] Similarly, Maryland forbad the congregation of blacks for religious purposes unless the services were conducted by white clergymen. So strict was an 1835 Maryland law against the publication and distribution of antislavery material that "an old newspaper used for wrapping purposes often visited upon its possessor the severest troubles."[27]

Despite the efforts of most slave owners and Southern legislators, the education of blacks was not squelched. Some whites disregarded the law and taught their slaves; some taught only the slave children that they fathered. Literate blacks secretly taught their fellow bondsmen. Further, some slave children (including Frederick Douglass) were taught by their white playmates. The number of literate slaves was, however, not high. For example, C. G. Parsons found that only 5,000 of the 400,000 slaves in Georgia in the 1850s could read and write.[28]

In 1850, 4114 free blacks attended public schools in the sixteen slave states. However, free blacks often sought education in defiance of the law. One school run by a Mrs. Deveaux was successfully kept in secret operation in Savannah for thirty years preceding the Civil War. Beginning in 1837, free blacks in Fredericksburg, Virginia petitioned the legislature for a school. Once their request was denied, they emigrated to Michigan.[29] However, a school, led by the father of Richard DeBaptiste, later eluded Fredericksburg police surveillance and resulted in the education of many of the remaining blacks.[30] Secret Sabbath schools also provided educational opportunity as did vocational apprenticeships.

Education in the antebellum South was not only poor for blacks, but it lagged behind the North in the education of whites. While over 18 percent of whites in nonslave states were in school in 1840, only 5.72 percent of their counterparts in slave states were similarly occupied. The North had a population twice as large as the South, but had three times as many schools and six times more books in libraries, which outnumbered those in the South twentyfold. [31] Plantation owners obviously thought that an investment in slaves and production was worth more than an investment in education.

Surprisingly, perhaps, there were more educated blacks in the South than in the North as late as 1840. However, on the eve of the Civil War, a different situation existed. By 1860, there were fewer than 3700 blacks in Southern schools (only seven in Georgia and two in Mississippi) compared to nearly 29,000 in the North, primarily New Jersey, Ohio, New York, and Pennsylvania. [32] [33] The educational opportunities for blacks in the North were not as great as some would have us believe, however.

A 1784 Rhode Island law requiring the teaching of black children went unheeded. [34] In New Jersey, however, a 1788 statute mandated the teaching of slaves prior to their emancipation; subsequently, schools were opened in Burlington, Salem, and Trenton, all in the slave-holding southern portion of the state. By 1801, most towns in New Jersey included blacks alongside of the white children in the schools. [35] Separate schools, however, were the predominant pattern in the North. In Newport, Rhode Island, in 1807, the black African Benevolent Society reopened a school originally established for blacks in 1763 by a white Episcopal cleric. In Boston, most blacks were unwilling to stand the abuse they received in the majority white schools. Thus, in 1798, Prince Hall, a black, opened a school in his home. It remained there until 1806 when it moved to the African Meeting House where it flourished for nearly three decades. [36, 37] It was not until 1820 that the City of Boston opened the Smith School, a publicly funded school for blacks; by 1828, Boston had three such schools. [38]

In New York City, a white abolitionist group, laboriously named the Society for Promoting the Manumission of Slaves and Protecting Such of Them as Have Been or May Be Liberated, opened the New York African Free School in 1790. Its student body grew from 40 to 130 by 1801. After 1814, the society built six additional schools including one which served 500 pupils. Incorporated into the curriculum were such subjects as reading, writing, advanced composition, mathematics, geography, astronomy, navigation, sewing, and knitting. The society, aware of the desire of its students for good jobs, ran a placement center for its graduates. In 1832, control of the society passed to its black membership who subsequently replaced the white teachers with blacks.[39] Two years later, the African Free Schools became part of the New York City public school system.[40]

As was the case in Boston and New York, the availability of public education for blacks in the North lagged behind that for whites. By 1830, most Northern states provided free, tax supported instruction for white children. Ohio, Michigan, Wisconsin, and Iowa did not do so for blacks for several more decades; Illinois and Indiana were several years further behind. In most instances, even these schools were segregated. New York statutes allowed school boards to decide whether or not to segregate, while those in Ohio and Pennsylvania mandated such treatment if twenty or more black children lived within the school district.[41] [42] The Quaker State was the center of much abolitionist activity but the democratic fervor did not extend as far as integrated, public schools. In Philadelphia prior to 1860 there were fifty-six private black schools. Blacks, however, had no access to public high schools. Perhaps the most important black high school was the Quaker-supported Institute for Colored Youth (ICY), which began as an agricultural school in 1839. After 1849, it adopted a new approach. The students were apprenticed to black mechanics during the day and attended classes in the evening. The curriculum was academic in nature since the school's trustees hoped to develop it into a first class university offering courses in law, medicine, literature, and theology. In 1852, the school took a step in that direction by opening a new day school. By 1857, trigonometry, higher algebra, Latin, and Greek were added to the course offerings. (Collegiate status was not attained until after the turn of the century.[43, 44])

Not all schools fared as well as the ICY, especially when compared to white schools. A New York Tribune editorial in 1859 noted that:

> The school houses for whites are in situations where the price of rents is high, and on the buildings themselves no expenditure is spared to make them commodious and elegant . . . The schools for the blacks, on the contrary, are nearly all, if not all, old buildings, generally in filthy and degraded neighborhoods, dark, damp, small and cheerless, safe neither for the morals nor the health of those who are compelled to go to them, if they go anywhere, and calculated rather to repel than to attract them.[45]

The city spent $1600 per white student on school buildings to every dollar spent for blacks. [46]

Blacks did not easily accept such treatment. Opposition to segregation led to successful school boycotts in Nantucket, Salem, and Boston (in Massachusetts) and in Rochester, Buffalo, and Lockport (in New York). Antislavery societies and the presence of an educated black elite were important to those efforts. [47]

Integrated schools were found in the 1830s and 1840s in Cleveland, Ohio, and in a number of Massachusetts cities including Cambridge, New Bedford, Worcester, and Lowell. In Canaan, New Hampshire in 1835, whites burned the Noyes Academy, a school which served twenty-eight whites and fourteen blacks.[48] Harrassment in Hartford schools led blacks to demand separate schools; whites were quite willing to be accommodating. [49, 50]

Pre-Civil War Legal Decisions

Blacks in Boston responded to school segregation in a rather different manner than did their counterparts in other areas of the country. From the earliest days of the all-black Smith School, its pupils were accorded second class treatment. They were not allowed to march with white children in the annual Independence Day parade, nor were they permitted to attend the city-wide awards ceremony for students who won academic competitions. Further, they were subjected to a white principal who believed blacks to be the intellectual inferiors of whites and who treated them accordingly. [51] In 1849, Benjamin Roberts sued the City of Boston on behalf of his daughter Sara who had to walk past five white elementary schools in order to reach the run down and educationally inferior Smith School. Roberts wanted his daughter to be able to attend the neighborhood school, which had been reserved for whites. His case was argued by the white abolitionist Charles Sumner, assisted by Robert Morris, a black attorney. [52] They contended that the segregation of black children served to "brand a whole race with the stigma of inferiority and degradation." Classification for purposes of school assignment should support an educational purpose and should not be done along racial lines. They went on to cite their belief that a segregated black school could never be the equal of a white school due to the stigma surrounding it. Not only does such a practice injure black children, but it hurts white children as well: "Their hearts, while yet tender with childhood are necessarily hardened by this conduct..." The argument presented by Sumner and Morris proved to be unpersuasive. In early 1850, the Massachusetts Supreme Court ruled against Roberts and accepted the practice of segregation so long as the separate schools were equally provided for.[53] This first use of the often to be repeated "separate but equal" doctrine was not well received by the citizens of Massachusetts. (Several years later another black lost a similar case in Boston.) Roberts spearheaded a petition drive that led to the passage of a law in April, 1855 prohibiting school assignment based on race. Shortly thereafter, the Smith School was closed.[54]

On the heels of Roberts came the *Dred Scott* case in which a slave held in free territory claimed that he was a free citizen. Speaking for the United States Supreme Court in this polarizing case, Chief Justice Roger Taney held that blacks "had no rights which the white man was bound to respect."[55] Scott, then, was not a citizen but remained a slave.

THE CIVIL WAR YEARS

Prior to the Civil War, blacks, North and South, suffered educationally, sometimes by law, sometimes by practice. In 1860, only 1.8 percent of the blacks aged five to twenty were in school, this compared to 56 percent of the whites; only about 5 percent of the slave population was literate.[56] The prevailing tenor of the times, according to Goodwin, held that "no white can do a wrong to a colored man, and no colored man willingly does right to anyone."[57] Even the great educator, Horace Mann, believed that "in intellect the blacks are inferior to the whites, while in sentiment and affection the whites are inferior to blacks."[58] This stereotype of the intellectually feeble yet cheerful black held for generations.

The desire for education on the part of the blacks in the South was never snuffed out. In the wake of the victorious Union armies came a host of white, Northern-based freedmen's aid societies with food, medicine, and schools for the newly liberated blacks. The protection of the Union troops was crucial to the continued activity of these organizations since opposition from white Southerners was everpresent. The schools were so popular that, for example, nearly the entire black population of Charlottesville, Virginia engaged themselves in instructional activities.[59]

By the war's end, massive amounts of private money flowed south through the benevolent societies. In 1863, alone, the Quakers provided $20,000 and an additional $19,000 in clothing. The National Freedmen's Relief Association had provided $200,000 for educational programs by the time of the Confederate surrender. The American Missionary Association (AMA), originally established in 1846 by the American and Foreign Anti-Slavery Society, but later an arm of the Congregational Church, contributed $240,000 during the war years. Other important participants in this effort included the Contraband Relief Association, the Union Relief Association, the Contraband Committee of the Mother Bethel Church, the Freedmen's Friend Society of Brooklyn, and the African Civilization Society. In all, there were sixty-five benevolent groups (not all of which were white, as evidenced by the activity of the African Methodist Episcopal Church). Financial records remain for only sixteen organizations; they indicate that in the twelve years following 1862, a total of $3,933,278 was spent in support of the development of free blacks in the South.[60,61]

For a period after the Civil War ended, conservative white Southerners retained control of their state governments. W. E. B. DuBois later noted that "opposition to Negro education in the South was at first bitter, and showed itself in ashes, insult and blood; for the South believed an educated Negro to be a dangerous Negro. And the South was not wholly wrong."[62] On the individual and collective front, whites attempted to intimidate blacks. Former slave Peter Woolfolk wrote in April, 1865 that Richmond landlords threatened to evict black tenants if they sent their children to school.[63] The following year, the Ku Klux Klan was formed in Tennessee and quickly spread across the South carrying with it a reign of terror aimed at the subjugation of blacks. On the legal front, the legislatures in the former slave states quickly enacted Black Codes, similar to the old slave codes. Most defined as black anyone with at least one black great grandparent. These codes sought to bind blacks to their old plantations by requiring them to sign year long contracts in order to be given employment. These contracts forbid them from quitting their positions and obligated them to sunrise to sunset working hours. Even worse, blacks who desired to move away from their plantations were liable for a charge of vagrancy and a subsequent fine that could be paid on their behalf by any land owner who could then force them to work off the fine. On the positive side, the codes gave blacks the statutory right to own property, make contracts, and have a fair trial, but the benefits were few since the statutes also provided the death penalty for any black convicted of having sexual intercourse with a white woman and whippings for those who assaulted their employers. Often the codes restricted blacks to employment as servants, farmers, or unskilled laborers.

RECONSTRUCTION AND THE FREEDMEN'S BUREAU

Congress sought to implement a Reconstruction program that attempted to stop the legal and extralegal behavior that kept blacks from enjoying their freedom. Fearful that the Supreme Court would rule the Civil Rights Act of 1866 unconstitutional, Congress sought to guarantee citizenship and equal protection of the laws to blacks by passing the fourteenth amendment. The fifteenth amendment provided blacks with the constitutional right to vote.

For the short run, the establishment of the Freedmen's Bureau in early 1865, and the subsequent extension of its purview to education in 1866 were the most important of the Congressional initiatives. An arm of the War Department, the Bureau's charge was to provide and equip school buildings and to accord protection to teachers and students; funds for these programs were obtained by selling Confederate lands. Freedmen's Bureau Commissioner, General O. O. Howard, stated his belief that "education underlies every hope of success for the freedman."[64] A Congregationalist, he was supportive of the AMA and helped that organization establish itself as the leading provider of education for Southern blacks. The Bureau initiated 4239 schools, hired 9307 teachers, and provided instruction for 247,333 children and adults.[65] By its closing days, it

had spent $5,145,124 on schools. The freedmen, themselves, pro-
vided an additional $1.7 million through tuition, taxation, and
church donations.[66] In fact, the State Superintendent of Education in North Carolina, F. A. Fiske, reported that, in many instances,
blacks "even taxed their credit in the coming crop to pay the bills
necessary to keep up the school."[67] DuBois, looking back on the
activities of the Bureau, noted that its "greatest success . . . lay in
the planting of the free school among Negroes, and the idea of
free elementary education among all classes in the South."[68]

Several factors accounted for its success. One was the genuine
idealism and social concern and excellent training of those who
came from the North to teach Southern blacks. Another was the
desire of blacks to learn and to make sacrifices so that school
attendance was possible. A third factor was General Order Number 44, which permitted the Freedmen's Bureau to detach troops to
prevent the intimidation of students and parents and, thus, to keep
schools open.[69] Finally, the Radical Reconstruction plan adopted
by Congress in 1867 provided for the dissolution of the conservative Southern state governments, and led to their replacement with
governments made up of blacks, liberal Southerners and Northern carpetbaggers.

Changes occurred throughout the region. The revised laws in
Alabama (1867) provided that "every child between the ages of six
and 20 years shall be entitled to admission into and instruction in
any free school." However, a statute passed later in the same year
allowed the establishment of separate schools for blacks "whenever as many as 30 pupils in sufficient proximity for school purposes claim the privilege of public instruction, and the fund for
that purpose is sufficient to support a school for four months in
the year."[70] State law in Arkansas permitted the rental of abandoned
plantations provided that certain conditions were met, including
one that mandated "for every lot of 500 acres so leased, the employment of at least one teacher for the freedmen who cultivated
them."[71] In Florida, a state that did not receive great attention
from philanthropists due to its relatively sparse population, a
statute was passed established public schools for blacks. To finance
these schools, students paid fifty cents per month in tuition charges
and "all male persons of color between the ages of 21 and 45" were

taxed one dollar per year.[72]

In the South, economic hard times followed the Civil War, and whites who would not have previously considered doing so became teachers of blacks. Georgia State Superintendent of Education, G. L. Eberhart reported in 1867: "At the beginning of the current school year scarcely any white persons could be found who were willing to disgrace themselves by 'teaching niggers'; but as times grew hard . . . applications became so numerous . . . Not a few appeared to think that 'anybody can teach niggers'."[73] The effect was the establishment of additional schools, yet one must wonder whether or not the concern that a teacher should have for a student was present in those classrooms and whether the children were well served.

A summary of the data provided in 1871 by M. B. Goodwin in his *Report of the Commissioner of Education on the Improvement of the Public Schools in the District of Columbia* indicates that progressive movement in the education of blacks in sixteen former slave holding states was uneven. In 1866, there were 87,565 blacks in school. In the following year, there were 119,062, but in 1868 enrollments declined by nearly 10,000 students. Similarly, the amount of money spent on the schooling of blacks declined from $680,814 in 1867 to $533,792 the following year; per capita expenditures declined from $5.85 to $5.01. Alabama and Mississippi fostered the least favorable financial climate, providing $1.89 and $1.48 respectively, per capita. Alabama also saw a 50 percent decrease in black enrollments from 1867 to 1868. By contrast, $10.89 per student was spent on the education of blacks in West Virginia.[74]

The late 1860s, then, saw quantum gains for blacks in the educational area. While less than two percent of the black population aged five to twenty was in school at the beginning of the decade, 9.2 percent were attending in 1870 (over half of the comparable white population was similarly engaged.)[75] That year, Mississippi finally opened a public school system. Also, in 1870, South Carolina saw a near doubling over the previous year of both black enrollment and the total number of schools in the state.[76]

EROSION OF BLACKS' RIGHTS

Once the Freedmen's Bureau withdrew from the South, the pressure was put on the black community. Conservatives began to regain power in the Southern legislatures and began to turn back the clock. In 1873, for instance, the black schools in Alabama were temporarily closed since sufficient funds were not allocated to them. The violent tactics of the white supremacist groups, such as the Ku Klux Klan, the White Leagues, the Red Shirts, and the Redeemers, resulted in the closing of some schools and the burning of others. Congress responded by passing the Civil Acts of 1870 and 1871 (the latter one was known as the Ku Klux Klan Act) as a means toward protecting the voting rights of blacks and toward protecting them from private and public intimidation and harrassment. [77]

Such statutes were rendered useless when, in 1876, the United States Supreme Court ruled in *United States v. Cruikshank*. That case stemmed from an assault by whites on a black political meeting in Louisiana. Two of the attackers were convicted and subsequently appealed. The Supreme Court held that the fourteenth amendment prohibited states from denying blacks their rights, but that the amendment did not prohibit private individuals from so doing. Thus, those federal laws that sought to implement the fourteenth amendment did so unconstitutionally if they attempted to regulate the behavior of private citizens. [78] Thus, the road was cleared for those who sought to repress blacks through violent means.

Radical Reconstruction ended in 1876 when a deal was made that resulted in the election of Rutherford B. Hayes to the presidency. The Hayes-Tildon race was not decided by the voters since neither candidate had the necessary majority of electoral votes. Neither was it decided in the House of Representatives where the members split evenly in their preferences. But, it was uniquely resolved by a special commission in which the *quid pro quo* for the election of Hayes was the removal of the troops from the South and the return of the state governments to the conservatives.

Without the watchful eye of the federal government and the Union Army, the Southern states moved little by little, but deliberately, against the blacks. Nevertheless, by 1880, nearly one-third of school aged blacks were attending classes in segregated schools throughout the South.[79] [80]

Weinberg believes that the last two decades of the nineteenth century were an educational catastrophe for blacks. By the end of that period, the black school aged population grew by 25 percent, but the proportion attending school fell below the level of twenty years earlier.[81] One example of the shoddy treatment received by blacks was evident in 1890 by the failure of Congress to pass a bill that would have provided federal funds for an eight year war on illiteracy; states with the highest illiteracy rates (i.e. the South) would have received the lion's share of the money. Southern senators, realizing the potential for blacks, voted no.[82] Another example was seen in Kentucky where, in 1882, the state was providing $1.40 per capita in state funds for white schools but only $0.11 per capita for black schools. That year, in *Commonwealth v. Ellis*, separate but equal schools were ruled acceptable in the Kentucky courts. In compliance, the legislature passed a measure providing for the equal distribution of state aid to education on a per capita basis. However, the measure did not affect the allocation of the largest proportion of school funds, those raised by local taxation. Black parents brought the matter of the inequitable school financing to the Federal District Court, where they were able to show that the town of Owensboro budgeted $700 to provide 500 black children a three month school year while $9400 was provided for a nine to ten month school year for 800 white children. In *Claybrook v. City of Owensboro* (1883), the Federal District Court ruled that funds must be distributed on a fair and equal basis, but that it was not necessary for the black and white per capita shares to be precisely the same.[83] [84]

Other court cases proved to be equally as unfair to the cause of blacks. The Civil Rights Cases (1883) all illustrate this point. In overturning a Civil Rights Act concerning access to public accommodations, the Supreme Court pulled the federal government back from its support of blacks by stating: "When a man has emerged from slavery, and by the aid of beneficient legislation has shaken off the inseparable concomitants of that state, there must be some stage in the process of his elevation when he takes the rank of a mere citizen, and ceases to be a favorite of the laws, and when his rights as a citizen or a man, are to be protected in the ordinary modes by which other men's rights are protected."[85] Buoyed by these victories and aware of the failure of the federal government to intervene on behalf of the black population, the Southern legislatures began to rewrite their constitutions and, in the process, did what they could to write out the black vote. The Mississippi constitution of 1890, for instance, required that voters pay a poll tax, be literate and be able to interpret passages in the state's constitution to the satisfaction of the registrar of voters. The catch was that even the most educated, wealthiest black was not able to satisfy the registrar; 123,000 blacks lost their franchise. South Carolina enacted a literacy and property tax requirement. Other states followed Louisiana's lead in establishing a "grand-father clause" requirement; those whose grandfathers had voted in 1867 were eligible to vote, others were not. Since few Louisiana blacks had the right to vote at that time, black voters in that state decreased from over 130,000 in 1896 to 5320 in 1900. The United States Supreme Court, in *Williams v. Mississippi*, held such practices to be constitutional since the laws on their face treated blacks and whites the same.[86] [87] The Court was not willing to look beyond the obvious smoke screen.

Separate but Equal

The knockout punch came shortly thereafter in an 1896 case concerning interstate travel, but which had a profound effect on the future of education and every other facet of American life for the next half century. In 1869, Louisiana had enacted a law that forbid racial segregation on any train and coach that came into the state. Eight years later, in the case of *Hall v. DeCuir*, the United States Supreme Court nullified that statute, saying that Congress was the only body which could regulate interstate travel.[88]

A decade later, Southern legislatures began to take a different approach to passenger seating on public transportation. Beginning with Florida in 1887, most states below the Mason-Dixon line required the separation of the races on the railroads; either blacks and whites were to ride in different cars or, if in the same car, to be in different sections. In every instance the states made it clear that whites and blacks were to be treated equally in their separate accommodations. Louisiana's law of 1890, "An Act to Promote the Comfort of Passengers," was not appreciated by its black population nor by the East Louisiana Railway. To the blacks, the law meant second class status. To the company, the law meant more cars, extra conductors, the possibility of trouble on board, and lower profits. Thus, in 1892 in hope of having the law overturned, an incident was arranged whereby Homer A. Plessy, a person who had a black great-grandparent, boarded the "whites only" part of a train and was arrested after refusing to move.[89] A local judge in New Orleans, John H. Ferguson did not accept Plessy's plea that the fourteenth amendment prohibited laws of the sort that caused the arrest. The matter reached the United States Supreme Court in 1896 as *Plessy v. Ferguson.*[90]

Justice Henry Billings Brown, writing for the majority of the Court, affirmed Ferguson's decision and upheld the law. He stated that the separation of blacks and whites was constitutionally acceptable as long as they were treated equally. He noted that: "The object of the [fourteenth] Amendment was undoubtedly to enforce the absolute equality of the two races before the law, but in the nature of things it could not have been intended to abolish distinctions based upon color, or to enforce social, as distinguished from political, equality, or a commingling of the two races upon terms unsatisfactory to either." He cited the school segregation case of *Roberts v. City of Boston* as an example of the established tradition of the separation of the races for "their comfort, and the preservation of the public peace and good order." To the argument that segregation resulted in second class citizenship for blacks, Brown wrote that Plessy was not correct in his view that the law "stamps the colored race with a badge of inferiority. If this be so, it is not by reason of anything found in the act, but solely because the colored race chooses to put that construction upon it."

The only Justice to dissent was John Marshall Harlan, who saw the Louisiana law for what it was, a measure "not so much to exclude white persons from railroad cars occupied by blacks, as to exclude colored people from coaches occupied or assigned to white persons." He believed that the statute provided the "guise of giving equal accommodation" but that it really was intended to support white supremacy. He held that "in the view of the Constitution, in the eye of the law, there is in this country no superior, no dominant ruling class of citizens . . . Our Constitution is color-blind . . . All citizens are equal before the law." He lamented that, despite the elimination of slavery by the thirteenth Amendment, it would once more be possible for the states "to place in a condition of inferiority a large body of American citizens," and that it was again permissible for "the seeds of race hate to be planted under the sanction of law."

Nevertheless, "separate but equal" was now constitutionally permissible. State constitutions were amended and laws were adopted which, for all Southern states, required segregation and, for many Northern and Western states, made the practice permissible. *White Only* and *Colored Only* restaurants, theatres, hotels, drinking fountains, neighborhoods, beaches, ticket windows, and baseball teams were allowed, and "Jim Crow" became a way of life in much of America. Even the federal government sullied itself in 1913 when President Woodrow Wilson moved white and black government employees into separate facilities.[91] The Post Office Department, which between 1825 and 1865 had denied blacks the opportunity to deliver mail, was the first federal agency to segregate.[92]

The practice of segregation in education was upheld by the United States Supreme Court shortly after its ruling in *Plessy*. The background of the case of *Cumming v. Richmond County Board of Education* is similar to that for black education throughout the South in the days between the close of the Civil War and the turn of the century.[93] At the outbreak of the Civil War, there were only 386 blacks in Augusta, Georgia, but after the war the black population grew rapidly.[94] In 1867, the black community there was given control of the eleven schools established by the Freedmen's Bureau. It was not until 1873, however, that the financing and management of any of these schools came under public jurisdiction. By that time, Georgia law permitted separate but equal education. Slightly more than half of the 900 students in the public elementary schools were black, and their schools were in better condition than those for the white children. The Richmond County School Board turned its attention to the improvement of the white schools and, in the process, decided to move into the area of high school education. In 1874, they agreed to subsidize the tuition of white boys who attended a private high school. Two years later, a public high school for white girls was opened. It was not until 1880 that blacks, arguing for their rights to equal education, were able to send their daughters to Ware High School, a public high school for black girls. In 1891, the school was temporarily closed but reopened after black parents agreed to pay an annual tuition of $10. By 1894, Ware still only offered eighth and ninth grade education, while the white high schools provided a tenth grade as well. Upset that only half of the salary for Ware's sole teacher was paid from public funds and that the School Board was not willing to finance the school properly, the black parents stopped making tuition payments. White opponents believed it unnecessary to support the public black secondary school, since, they claimed, Augusta's three private high schools for blacks adequately met that community's needs. In 1897, Ware High School was closed. However, the county still financed the high school for white girls, and still subsidized the tuition for white boys attending the private high school. The black parents sued. The School Board, citing a lack of funds, claimed that its action was not a prejudicial one but was necessary if it were to continue the black elementary schools. Blacks argued that the white high school should be closed until the fiscal crisis passed and then both high schools could be reopened.

Writing for the unanimous Supreme Court, Justice Harlan, reversing his own position taken in *Plessy* several years earlier, found in favor of the School Board. He stated that: "The education of the people in schools maintained by state taxation is a matter belonging to the respective states, and any interference on the part of Federal authority with management of such schools cannot be justified, except in the case of a clear and unmistakable disregard of the rights secured by the supreme law of the land." Apparently, then, "separate but equal" applied to what a school board said that it would like to provide rather than what it was actually providing for blacks. The decision, the Court's first ever in regard to education, was taken as vindication for the practice of school segregation and for reduced support to black education.

THE INFLUENCE OF THE PHILANTHROPISTS

One of the primary areas of support for black schools came from a group of philanthropic foundations. Recall the role of missionary societies in the education of blacks. Not only did they establish elementary schools during and after slavery, but by 1915 they had begun over 100 secondary schools and institutions of higher education, which at that time were serving nearly 7800 high school students and over 2500 college and professional school students. Nearly 33,000 black teachers had been trained as a result of the efforts of the missionary groups. By 1900, most of these societies were in severe financial straits. In their wake, a group of industrial philanthropists rose to prominence. [95]

One of the earliest was the Peabody Fund, directed by Doctor Barnas Sears, former president of Brown University and former Secretary of the Massachusetts Board of Education. Sears, an opponent of integrated education, allocated funds only to racially separate schools. [96] In 1871, the Fund determined that it cost less to educate blacks than it did whites, thus black schools received a per capita amount only one-third of that given to white schools. [97]

Other important philanthropic groups included the John F. Slater Fund, the General Education Board, the Anna T. Jeanes Fund, the Phelps-Stokes Fund and the Rosenwald Fund. The amounts of money funnelled through these organizations was impressive. John F. Slater, a Connecticut textile manufacturer, provided $1 million in 1882. The General Education Board, established in 1902 by John D. Rockefeller, collected $53 million from leading industrialists in its first seven years alone. Between 1913 and 1932, the Rosenwald Fund provided grants that helped 883 counties in 15 Southern states build nearly 5400 schools, industrial education shops, and teachers' homes. Up to the early post-World War II period, it had donated over a half-million school books. Further, the Fund supported black universities in the District of Columbia, Atlanta, Nashville and New Orleans to the tune of $1.5 million. In all, the philanthropic foundations supplied black schools more than $134 million, which generated another $100 million in matching donations and public funds. [98, 99]

There was, however, a cost associated with the receipt of this support. The major foundations were all controlled by interlocking directorates whose members included the country's most important industrialists and bankers, a group convinced that the most appropriate form of education for blacks was one geared toward the training of manual laborers rather than professionals. [100] They also believed that the economic revival of the South was dependent upon the existence of a properly trained supply of black laborers, particularly in the area of agriculture. [101] During the 1880s, the concept of industrial education was well accepted in white high schools in communities throughout the country. The nation was experiencing the Industrial Revolution and it made sense to train factory workers, mechanics, etc. However, industrial education meant something different for Southern blacks. The Peabody Fund under Sears strongly advocated educational programs that would produce black agricultural workers. The successor to Sears, Jabez Curry, a Southern patrician, did not believe that blacks could benefit from education, but saw vocational education as being in the best interests of the South. [102] By narrowing black educational horizons, the Southern *status quo* could be maintained.

The Slater Fund believed that it would be decades, perhaps even centuries, before blacks would become the equals of whites. In its view the most appropriate form of education for blacks, then, was one that stressed moral development and training in farming and the skilled trades. Since the trustees of the Slater Fund virtually captured the black public schools in the South, their philosophy regarding black education became the predominant one among school policy makers. Not only was it supported by the other philanthropic groups, but it also was popular among Southern whites who recognized it as a way to keep blacks working with their hands rather than gaining professional skills and, thus, to relegate them to a continuing subordinate role. [103, 104]

In many instances, industrial education meant the removal of traditional courses and textbooks from the schools and their replacement by subjects and materials focused on rural life. For instance, under the "curriculum integration" program promoted by the Negro Rural School Fund and the Jeanes Fund, courses would be developed around projects in the community. Thus, in an area where poultry was important, it would be the focus of all educational activity. Vocabulary words would include the various breeds of chickens and poultry diseases; animal husbandry and local growing conditions would provide the basis for science and geography, and; the teaching of mathematics would be geared toward animal and feed weight ratios, the calculation of the necessary area per chicken for greatest egg and weight yield, etc.[105] Literature, history, the arts, languages, etc., were not included in the curricula of these schools.

THE WASHINGTON-DUBOIS CLASH

The founders of most of the important philanthropic groups were influenced, either in the initiation of their activity or in the implementation of their educational philosophy, by Booker T. Washington, the best known black of his day and a leading proponent of industrial education. Although he is remembered as its most important advocate, the belief in the propriety of that form of education for blacks predated Washington. In 1794, the American Convention of Abolitionist Societies felt that it was best to educate blacks in "those mechanic arts which will keep them most constantly employed and, of course, which will less subject them to idleness and debauchery, and thus prepare them for becoming good citizens."[106] A half century later, when some whites were supporting an education for blacks that would prepare them for a return to Africa, Martin Delany countered, "What we need most . . . is a good business practical Education." Another black, the first to be admitted to practice law before the U.S. Supreme Court, John Rock, disagreed with both positions, claiming that blacks needed education that promoted, rather than limited, their life chances.[107] While Frederick Douglass believed that blacks should have the opportunity to receive a higher education, he had concluded by 1853 that blacks would not have immediate access to the professions and, thus, should move "through the intermediate gradations of agriculture and mechanic arts." He favored industrial schools, but not those where books served as the vehicle for learning. He argued for schools "where colored men could learn some of the handicrafts, learn to work in iron, wood and leather, while incidently acquiring a plain English education."[108]

One of the most important advocates of this approach was General Samuel C. Armstrong, who, in 1868, founded Hampton Institute, a college for blacks. Through his widely circulated newspaper, the *Southern Workman*, he contended that "proper" Reconstruction of the South would not occur until the black voters and politicians were removed from the process since he believed them to be immoral, irresponsible, and ignorant. It was the responsibility, he argued, of the superior white race to rule the darker races until the latter had become civilized. Although they were mentally capable, their earlier paganistic practices had left them morally feeble. Thus, until this deficiency was overcome, it was inappropriate for blacks to venture into areas such as politics or the professions where a strong moral foundation was required.[109] Thus, at Hampton, Armstrong sought to build strong moral and Christian principles in his students. The intent of the Hampton curriculum was four-fold: to develop the students to be of service to themselves and to whites; to reinforce the dignity of human labor; to develop a personal sense of responsibility in each student, and; to infuse manual training into every aspect of the curriculum.[110]

Armstrong asked conservative white school officials to recommend potential students to him, since he only wanted "worthy colored youth," those who would not be rebellious and who would accept his approach to education. His *Southern Workman* was required in all reading classes so that his moralistic, hard work, subordination to whites philosophy was continually reinforced among the students. Since most of Hampton's graduates eventually became teachers (in 1900 only 50 of the 656 students were in programs other than teacher education), this message was carried back into the black schools throughout the nation. As Armstrong said, "Let us make the teachers and we will make the people." His teachers would not be "polished scholars" but "guides and civilizers whose power shall be that of character and example, not of sounding words."[111]

One of those teachers that Hampton produced was Booker T. Washington. Born a slave in Virginia four years before the outbreak of the Civil War, Washington went to Hampton at the age of sixteen and was taken under Armstrong's wing. That he had accepted Armstrong's point of view became evident in his establishment of

Tuskeegee Institute in Alabama on the Hampton model. A racial accommodationist, he said what whites wanted to hear and, as a result, was asked to speak throughout the South. His fame spread beyond that region after his speech before the Cotton States and International Exposition held in Atlanta in 1895. He had been invited there to demonstrate that racial progress was occurring in the South, and he did not let his hosts down as he called upon blacks to remain in the hospitable South. He reminded whites that by helping their black neighbors, they would be helping the South to prosper. "It is at the bottom of life we must begin, and not at the top," he told his audience. "The wisest among my race understand that the agitation of questions of social equality is the extremest folly, and that progress in the enjoyment of all the privileges that will come to us must be the result of severe and constant struggle rather than artificial forcing ..." He noted that most blacks were faithful and unresentful to their white employers, and that "the opportunity to earn a dollar in the factory just now is worth infinitely more than the opportunity to spend a dollar in an opera house." In the portion of his speech which drew the most attention, he called upon blacks to accept segregation in return for economic opportunity: "In all things that are purely social we can be as separate as the fingers, yet one as the hand in all matters essential to mutual progress."[112-114]

Washington was a person dedicated to his ideals and should not be viewed as one who had sold out to the white power structure. He truly believed that blacks who worked hard would make progress and, over time, would be accepted by whites. He was taken seriously by many well meaning people, both black and white, since he, himself, was a living example of his own philosophy. His following was not limited to those in the field of education. For example, Presidents Theodore Roosevelt and William H. Taft consulted with him on all matters affecting blacks and on appointments of blacks to key government positions.

There were, however, those who used his words to justify their own racist beliefs. University of Virginia faculty dean, Paul Barringer, expressed to the Southern Education Association in 1900 his belief that intellectual education was inappropriate for blacks since they were a "source of cheap labor for a warm climate; everywhere else, [they are] a foreordained failure."[115] The Southern white leadership also took advantage of Washington by pointing to his description of the role and future of the black without remembering that his treatise included a role for whites in support of black development. For instance, in 1901, the Governor of Georgia stated, "I do not believe in the higher education of the darkey. He must be taught the trades. When he is taught the fine arts, he is educated above his caste, and it makes him unhappy."[116] Georgia certainly did not rush to teach the trades to its black youth.

Many educators followed Washington's lead because they accepted his point of view. One such case was Philadelphia's noted Institute for Colored Youth. The school's Quaker trustees had been convinced of Washington's position by the mid-1890s and permitted the opening of an industrial component alongside the predominant Academic Department. In 1899, Washington criticized the primacy of its liberal arts curriculum by citing "the pitiable or the ludicrous ambition of young colored men to become 'professional' men when in many cases it must have been evident . . . that there could hardly be success for them." The following year, the industrial program began to take precedence, and, in 1901, ICY's principal, Fanny Jackson Coppin, resigned after losing her quest to keep the school focused on the liberal arts. Shortly thereafter, the Academic Department closed.[117]

Washington was not without his critics. The United States Commissioner of Education, William T. Harris, was one. He favored intellectual rather than industrial education as the best guardian against black reverting to their "former stage of spiritual life." He recognized that "with the advance of civilization and the development of machinery, the proportion of manual laborers in every community is steadily diminishing, while the proportion of the directors of labor and other brain workers is correspondingly increasing." Similarly, Professor William E. Hutchins of Biddle University noted, "If there is industry in the South, the Negroes have it. What they want is education. What can you teach colored women about washing clothes."[118]

Washington accused his critics, particularly the educated black elite, of being able to understand only theories and ideas; he believed them to have lost touch with the problems confronting the average black.[119] He included in that category his most articulate and ardent foe, W. E. B. DuBois. A dozen years younger than Washington, DuBois was born to free parents in western Massachusetts. He did his undergraduate work at Fisk University, a black institution in Nashville, and received his doctorate from Harvard. He also studied at the University of Berlin. A sociologist, essayist, and activist, DuBois, though a contemporary of Washington, was a person of a different generation, one whose ideas are more accepted in the latter half of the twentieth century than they were at its beginning.

For many years, DuBois and Washington debated, both face to face and in writing, the merits of higher education versus industrial education for the black population. In his classic work, *The Souls of Black Folk*, written in 1903, DuBois noted Washington's belief that "the picture of a lone black boy pouring over a French grammar amid the weeds and dirt of a neglected home soon seemed to him to be the acme of absurdities," but, he pondered, "one wonders what Socrates and St. Francis of Assisi would say to this."[120] He stated that "it is now the fashion of today to sneer at [the college educated] and to say that with freedom Negro leadership should have begun at the plow and not in the senate."[121] He believed that the brightest blacks thirsted for more than manual labor. He asked, rhetorically, ". . . by refusing to give this Talented Tenth the key to knowledge, can any sane man imagine that they will lightly lay aside their yearning and contently become hewers of wood and drawers of water?" He was convinced that it was impossible to "induce black men to believe that if their stomachs be full, it matters little about their brains."[122] Not only that, but the black race needed its own professionals: ". . . college men are slowly but surely leavening the Negro church, are healing and preventing the devastations of disease, and beginning to furnish legal protection for the liberty and property of the toiling masses. All this is needful work. Who would do it if the Negro did not? How could Negroes do it if they were not trained carefully for it?"[123]

DuBois had no doubt that Washington had been betrayed by his policy of accommodation. "As a result of this tender of the palm branch, what has been the return? In these years there have occurred: 1. The disenfranchisement of the Negro. 2. The legal creation of a distinct status of civil inferiority for the Negro. 3. The steady withdrawal of aid from institutions for the higher training of the Negro." Washington's doctrine "tended to make the whites, North and South, sluft the burden of the Negro problem to the Negro's shoulders . . . when in fact, the burden belongs to the nation." [124]

Not only did DuBois attack the voice of industrial education, but he also attacked those colleges that had adopted it as the main thrust of their curriculum. Speaking before the faculty of Hampton Institute in 1906, he said, "If . . . we simply are trying to follow the line of least assistance and teach black men only such things and by such methods as are momentarily popular, then my fellow teachers, we are going to fail and fail ignominiously in our attempt to raise the black race to its full humanity and with that failure falls the fairest and fullest dream of a great united humanity." [125] Before this audience, which was not likely to be enthralled with his remarks, he boldly accused Hampton of being at "the center of this . . . educational heresy." [126] In 1924, speaking at Fisk on the thirty-fifth anniversary of his own graduation and on the occasion of his daughter's graduation from that institution, he lamented that Fisk had not taken "an honest position with regard to the Southern situation" and that it now professed "that the only thing required of the black man is acquiescence and submission." [127]

Later, DuBois began to say kinder things about industrial education without, however, backing away from his belief in higher education. In 1930, he received an honorary doctorate from Howard University and, in his address, allowed that "Negro industrial training in the U.S. has accomplishments of which it has a right to be proud . . . It has helped bridge the transition period between slavery and freedom . . . On the other hand, it has tempered and rationalized the inner emancipation of American Negroes." [128] A decade later, he reflected on the pattern of education he had seen at the turn of the century and what he had thought about it (though, perhaps, had not said so as not to deflect his argument):

It was in a sense logical and sincere and I would have said in 1900 that I believed in it, but not as a complete program. I believed that we should seek to educate a mass of ignorant sons of slaves in the three R's and the techniques of work in a sense of the necessity and duty of good work. But beyond this, I also believed that such schools must have teachers, and such a race must have thinkers and leaders, and for the education of these folk we needed good and thorough Negro colleges. [129]

Myrdal, in his classic study, *The American Dilemma*, written in the early 1940s, found that DuBois's fears had proven true. His research revealed that "by and large, in spite of all the talk about it, no effective industrial training was ever given the Negroes in the Southern public schools, except training for cooking and menial service." He noted that true vocational training never became more than a slogan. [130]

SEPARATE AND UNEQUAL

Unfortunately for blacks and for America as a whole, the country, particularly (though not exclusively) the South, was not ready for an approach to education based on DuBois's philosophy. Most of the sons and daughters of slaves and their children and grandchildren were provided a third rate, industrial education, if they received an education at all. Between 1900 and 1940, the proportion of white youth enrolled in school grew slowly from 53.6 percent to 71.6 percent. During that same period, the 31 percent of the black school aged population attending school grew to 64.4 percent. While black enrollments lagged behind those for whites, they continued to grow against stiff opposition, some of it presented by state and local officials who did not want to spend much on the education of blacks, some of it presented by the hooded terror of the Klan. Between 1883 and 1903, 3,000 blacks were lynched. [132] 1896 was a horrifying year; one black was lynched every 56 hours. [133] By 1922, the twentieth century had seen 1563 illegal hangings, and, between 1918 and 1922, there had been thirty-four blacks burned at the stake. [134] Prior attempts to pass antilynching and antiterrorist legislation continually failed in Congress, and blacks learned that to assert their rights could have disastrous consequences since the sanctity of black life was not highly regarded in many parts of the nation.

Neither was the desire to dedicate much in the way of public funds to the black American. In 1910, blacks in the South averaged only seven years of schooling, as opposed to the 9.7 year average for whites. At that time, there was not even one eighth grade in that region to serve rural black children. By 1929, only 6 percent of the high schools in the South enrolled blacks despite the fact that in some states black high school aged students outnumbered whites. Further, the eleven states of the old Confederacy spent an average of only $2.90 per capita for black schools in 1910, while they spent $9.45 per white child. By 1916, blacks in those states had lost $0.01 per student in expenditures while whites gained $0.87. For the entire Southern region, per capita spending in 1915 was $10.82 for whites, but only $4.01 for blacks. By 1930, the amounts were $42.39 and $15.86 respectively; the gap in Florida was nearly $68 and in South Carolina, ten times as much was spent per white child than per black! (Only one of those states, Kentucky, spent more per child on blacks.) Similar discrepancies can be found in teachers' salaries. In 1910, white teachers averaged $60.60 per month while their black counterparts were paid only $32.67. The year the Stock Market crashed, the salaries of white teachers had risen to $118.01, but black teachers still lagged behind at $72.78. In South Carolina, the gap was the largest; white teachers received more than three times the salary of black teachers. It could be argued that the salary differential existed since blacks had a shorter school year (the average Southern black grammar school graduate had spent nearly fifty-eight months in school in 1930; those who graduated from neighboring white schools averaged eight additional months in class), however, that would be a specious argument since talented whites had many options open to them while talented blacks did not.[135, 136, 137] Thus, a high supply and a low demand, sprinkled with a little racism, resulted in low salaries for black teachers. (Blacks were similarly treated in most, if not all, occupations, North and South.)

DuBois described the school where he first taught in Tennessee, years before the period under consideration here but no different from what was found elsewhere in the South in the first three decades of this century.

> There was an entrance where a door once was, and within, a massive
> rickety fireplace; great chinks between the logs served as windows. Furni-
> ture was scarce. A pale blackboard crouched in the corner. My desk was
> made of three boards reinforced at critical points, and my chair, borrowed
> from the landlady, had to be returned every night. Seats for the children —
> these puzzled me much. I was haunted by a New England vision of neat
> little desks and chairs, but, alas! the reality was rough plank benches
> without backs, and at times without legs. They had one virtue of making
> naps dangerous — and possibly fatal, for the floor was not to be trusted. [138]

The federal government did little to change this. During the
Great Depression, the Public Works Administration (PWA) and its
successor, the Works Progress Administration (WPA), constructed
public buildings throughout the country. An examination of
expenditures for school building construction in Mississippi between
1935 and 1937 reveals that the New Deal did not break with the
tradition of doing the minimum for black education — $8 million
was spent for new schools to serve whites while only $400,000 was
spent for schools for black children. [139] Of the total amount spent
in sixteen Southern states by the PWA for new schools, approximately $84 million went to white schools and approximately $7
million to black schools. [140]

When he visited a one room school in rural Georgia, near
Atlanta during the 1940s, Myrdal found a disturbing example of
the success of the Southern strategy of providing blacks with a
substandard education. In the dilapidated building, originally
constructed with money from the Rosenwald Fund (and in better
shape than many black schools), were students from age six to
seventeen. The teacher, not far beyond her teen age years, told
Myrdal that she had only received a high school education herself.
When he questioned the students, he found that:

> No one could tell who was President of the United States or even what the
> President was. Only one of the older students knew, or thought he knew of
> Booker T. Washington. He said that Washington was 'a big white man' and
> intimated that he might be the President of the United States. This student,
> obviously a naturally very bright boy, was the only one who knew anything
> about Europe and England . . . No one had heard of the N.A.A.C.P. . . . Asked
> if they knew what the Constitution of the United States was and what it
> meant to them, all remained in solemn silence, until the bright boy helped
> us out, informing us that it was a 'newspaper in Atlanta'.
> When telling such a horror story it must, at once, be added that it is not

typical, though a large portion of rural Negro schools are at, or near, this cultural level.[141]

And no wonder. At the time Myrdal conducted his research, he found that the average school term for whites was 167 days but only 146 for blacks, and only three to four months long in rural districts. In the Southern elementary schools, each black teacher taught an average of forty-three students; only $17.04 was spent for each child per year. In fact, the higher the black population in an area, the lower the amount spent per child. By contrast, white teachers taught thirty-four students in schools supported at a level of $49.30 per child. While only 6 percent of the white teachers had not, themselves, gone beyond high school, the same was true for nearly one-quarter of all black teachers.[142] Thus, black teachers were under-trained, over-worked, and under-funded, and their students were at a severe disadvantage.

INEQUALITY IN THE NORTH

Though far from ideal, conditions in the North were substantially better. The great migration of blacks to the North and to the cities began to occur prior to World War I. Those who moved did so in hopes of finding better jobs and equal treatment. To a certain extent, that proved to be true, but, as the numbers of blacks grew in Northern cities, so did their problems. Generally, in the North during the early part of the twentieth century, *de jure* segregation in the schools was a thing of the past; most students attended schools in their neighborhoods. However, that was not always the rule. In 1925, Burlington and Gloucester counties in southern New Jersey still maintained dual school systems in all grades, while every city and town in the state from Princeton southward, including Trenton (the state capital), enrolled black and white elementary students in racially separate schools. In 1939, a legislative study concluded that conditions had worsened over the last several years.[143]

In many Northern cities, the black community, unhappy with the public schools, turned to the local YMCA for lectures and courses focused on black history, individual and community development, and black social and political advancement.[144] Courses often sought to train blacks for specific jobs available in the city, but the Ys also provided such avocational offerings as music and such practical offerings as household management.[145]

Most Northern blacks, however, received their educations in the public schools. Educational conditions in Philadelphia, New York, and Chicago were probably representative of those in major Northern cities with increasing black populations.

In Philadelphia, the black population grew from 4.45 percent of the city in 1900 to 11.2 percent in 1930. Just before the start of the twentieth century, there were nearly four times as many blacks in integrated schools as there were in the six all black schools; however, many of the mixed schools were nearly all black. Black protest concerning *de facto* segregation in the schools began in 1908, despite the fact that the black community was not universally opposed to all black schools since they provided job opportunities for black teachers, a group which was permitted to teach only in schools with overwhelmingly black student bodies. (Until 1937, there were two lists from which prospective teachers were drawn in the City of Brotherly Love—one white, one black.) The Philadelphia *Tribune*, a newspaper serving the black community, argued in 1912 for integrated schools in an editorial which read, "It is the school room where children are educated either to despise colored people or respect them. The separate school house...gives children the wrong kind of education for future citizenship."[146]

As Southern blacks moved into Philadelphia during World War I, the black community began to polarize. Long time residents blamed the newcomers for the crowded classrooms, the increasingly segregated neighborhoods, and the growing white resentment toward blacks. But, as the black population grew so did the numbers willing to challenge poor school conditions. The NAACP became more aggressive in the 1920s, confronting the Board of Education on the use of IQ tests for student placement and participating in a partially successful school boycott resulting from the reassignment of 300 black students from integrated to racially separate schools.[147]

In the latter part of the Roaring Twenties, in what was to be only one of the many legal challenges to Philadelphia's failure to provide integrated education, a black man sued the city school board for sending his six-year-old son past an all-white school, two blocks from his home, to an all black school several blocks further away. The superintendent's office assured the man that it was over-crowding, not race, that had resulted in the assignment. Noting that it was the black school that was so strained that classes were taught in the halls, the man demanded the right to send his child to the closest school. The local court found on behalf of the Board of Education.[148] The time was not ripe in Philadelphia for court-ordered desegregation.

In New York, the black population increased more dramatically than in Philadelphia. By 1920, the black community in New York was the largest in the country and, twenty years later, had grown to over a half million people. In 1921, a district school superintendent in Harlem reported that seven of every eight children recently arrived from the South were at least one year behind New Yorkers of their own age, and that three of every eight were more than two years behind. As more black people moved into the city, school conditions for blacks worsened. Not only were classes over-crowded, but racially biased texts were introduced into the faltering curriculum. As in Philadelphia, black teachers and administrators were not found in most city schools. However, unlike Philadelphia, the black community in New York was well organized, and benefited from the presence in the city of the NAACP's national headquarters.[149]

The organization sought to improve black school attendance by striking out against parental apathy; approximately 38 percent of the 16,000 school aged blacks were not enrolled in 1936. Once the Committee for Better Schools in Harlem became active, four new schools were built in the community prior to World War II. Attention was drawn to school district gerrymandering, which promoted segregation, and to the inadequate curriculum in the predominantly black high schools.[150] Yet, for years to come, most blacks remained in segregated, academically undernourished, crowded schools.

To many Southern blacks, Chicago was to be the fulfillment of a dream. The black population grew from less than 2 percent of the city in 1900 to nearly 7 percent thirty years later.[151] Despite the 1917

United States Supreme Court ruling in *Buchanan v. Warley* that
ordinances that established segregated neighborhoods were not
constitutional, the Chicago Real Estate Board sought to evade the
law by establishing neighborhood improvement associations to
keep neighborhoods white, by making it standard practice to allow
the black neighborhoods to grow only one block at a time, and by
having clauses forbidding the future sale of a home to blacks
written into deeds. (This practice spread nationally during the
following decade.) Thus, nearly all of Chicago's black population
was forced to reside on the city's South Side. [152]

This was not without its beneficial side effects, however, since
the community was then able to elect blacks to the state legislature, to the city's board of aldermen and to Congress. While this
resulted in blacks securing city jobs in proportion to their numbers in the population, it did not give them access to the Board of
Education, a body named by the mayor. It was not until 1939 that a
black was appointed to the school board. The white school board
hired a largely white group of teachers who were not wholly
supportive of the notion of developing the full potential of black
children. One teacher, interviewed by the Chicago Commission on
Race Relations which had been formed in the aftermath of the
1919 riot, stated, "Colored children are restive and incapable of
abstract thought; they must be constantly fed with novel interests
and given things to do with their hands." This point of view was at
variance with the intellectual needs of those students who were
found to favor the academic curriculum over one geared toward
working with their hands. [153] [154]

Opposition to school segregation and unequal treatment began
in Chicago as early as 1903. Nevertheless, in 1930, twenty-six
schools were in excess of 85 percent black. In all, nearly 28,000 of
the 37,000 black students were in segregated schools, and many
mixed schools had segregated classes. Per capita expenditures
were 6 percent higher in white schools, double the gap of ten years
earlier. Slightly more than 2 percent of the city's teachers were
black, and of the 345 principals only 1 was black. [155] A study
undertaken the following year indicated that 39 percent of the
schools that had over 85 percent black enrollment needed replacement, while only 26 percent of the rest of the city's schools were in

such a state of disrepair.[156] In 1933, thirty-five elementary schools, mostly located on the South Side, had classes as large as fifty to sixty students and were on double sessions. This practice did not end until 1944.[157] Thus, it is clear that blacks who moved north did not find the hospitable conditions that they hoped would greet them.

Eternal Hope

Unfortunately, an examination of the history of black education from slavery through the first half of the 20th century does not reveal the sort of change that one would expect over a period of more than 300 years. Surely more blacks were attending schools by that time, but the median years of schooling for blacks was still only 5.9 while for whites it was 9.3. Only 14.4 percent had graduated from high school and only 4 percent had attended college.[158] Without doubt, black hopes were continually thwarted, as members of the white community conjured up new ways to keep blacks ignorant. Even worse, those practices were supported by a national government whose Supreme Court permitted legally segregated schools and imbalanced school expenditures, whose Presidents had not undertaken serious efforts to insure that the "equal" part of the "separate but equal" equation was kept in balance, and whose Congress had refused to enact voting rights laws, antilynching laws and antiilliteracy laws. But, black America did not lose hope that conditions would improve, and, in the 1930s, it began an assault on segregation that would force change to occur.

REFERENCES

1. Jordan, W.: Modern tensions and the origins of American slavery. In Haynes, R. (Ed.): *Blacks in White America Before 1865*. New York, David McKay Company, 1972, p. 105, 113.
2. Ibid., pp. 109–110.
3. Fage, J.: Slavery and the slave trade in the context of West African history. In Haynes, R. (Ed.): *Blacks in White America Before 1865*. New York, David McKay Company, 1972, pp. 56–57.
4. Meier, A. and Rudwick, E.: *From Plantation to Ghetto, An Interpretive History of American Negroes*. New York, Hill and Wang, 1966, pp. 33–34.
5. Ibid., p. 9.

6. Woodson, C.: *The Education of the Negro Prior to 1861*. New York, Arno Press, 1968, p. 4.

7. Bullock, H.: *A History of Negro Education in the South from 1619 to the Present*. Cambridge, Harvard University Press, 1967, pp. 9–10.

8. Jordan, op cit., p. 105.

9. Goodwin, M.: *History of Schools for the Colored Population*. New York. Arno Press, 1969, p. 307. (This was originally published in 1871 as the *Report of the Commissioner of Education on the Improvement of Public Schools in the District of Columbia*.)

10. Fleming, J.: *The Lengthening Shadow of Slavery, A Historical Justification for Affirmative Action for Blacks in Higher Education*. Washington, Howard University Press, 1976, p. 9.

11. Weinberg, M.: *A Chance to Learn: A History of Race and Education in the United States*. New York, Cambridge University Press, 1977, p. 13.

12. Fleming, op cit., p. 10.

13. Woodson, op cit., pp. 20–23.

14. Ibid., p. 26.

15. Ibid., p. 34.

16. Perkins, L.: Quaker benificence and black control: The institute for colored youth 1852–1903. In Franklin, V. and Anderson, J. (Eds.): *New Perspectives on Black Educational History*. Boston, G. K. Hall and Company, 1978, p. 19.

17. Woodson, op cit., pp. 45–46.

18. Meier and Rudwick, op cit., pp. 85–86.

19. Woodson, op cit., pp. 108–109.

20. Meier and Rudwick, op cit., p. 86.

21. Woodson, op cit., pp. 118, 156–157.

22. Ibid., p. 160.

23. Fleming, op cit., p. 13.

24. Bullock, op cit., p. 13.

25. Carruthers, I.: Centennials of black miseducation: A study of white educational management. *Journal of Negro Education*, 46(3):297, 1977.

26. Woodson, op cit., p. 165.

27. Goodwin, op cit., pp. 308–309.

28. Woodson, op cit., p. 215.

29. Weinberg, op cit., pp. 15–18.

30. Woodson, op cit., pp 217–218

31. Fleming, op cit., p. 23.

32. Weinberg, op cit., p. 16.

33. Woodson, op cit., pp. 235–236, 238.

34. Weinberg, op cit., p. 23.

35. Woodson, op cit., pp. 74, 100.

36. Meier and Rudwick, op cit., p. 84.

37. Woodson, op cit., pp 95–96.

38. Weinberg, op cit., p. 24.

39. Woodson, op cit., pp. 97–99, 148.
40. Fleming, op cit., p. 30.
41. Meier and Rudwick, op cit., p. 86.
42. Weinberg, op cit., pp. 25–26.
43. Woodson, op cit., pp. 269, 273.
44. Perkins, op cit., pp. 19–23, 38.
45. Meier and Rudwick, op cit., p. 86.
46. Fleming, op cit., p. 25.
47. Weinberg, op cit., p. 27.
48. Fleming, op cit., p. 30.
49. Weinberg, op cit., p. 21.
50. Meier and Rudwick, op cit., p. 87.
51. Weinberg, op cit., pp. 24–25, 28–29.
52. Kluger, R.: *Simple Justice, The History of Brown v. Board of Education and Black America's Struggle for Equality.* New York, Alfred A. Knopf, 1975, p. 93.
53. Meier and Rudwick, op cit., p. 88.
54. Fleming, op cit., p. 25.
55. Blaustein, A. and Ferguson, C.: *Desegregation and the Law: The Meaning and Effect of the School Desegregation Cases.* New Brunswick, N.J., Rutgers University Press, 1957, p. 84.
56. Myrdal, G.: *An American Dilemma, The Negro Problem and Modern Democracy.* New York, Harper and Row, 1969, pp. 887, 942.
57. Goodwin, op cit., p. 312.
58. Weinberg, op cit., p. 31.
59. Ibid., p. 38.
60. Bullock, op cit., pp. 26–27.
61. Meier and Rudwick, op cit., pp. 141–143.
62. DuBois, W.: *The Souls of Black Folk.* New York, Dodd, Mead, and Company, 1961, p. 24. (A)
63. Bullock, op cit., p. 43.
64. Ibid., p. 24.
65. Carruthers, op cit., p. 299.
66. Bullock, op cit., p. 27.
67. Goodwin, op cit., p. 369.
68. DuBois (A), op cit., p. 24.
69. Howard, V.: The struggle for equal education in Kentucky, 1866–1884. *Journal of Negro Education, 46(3)*:309, 1977.
70. Goodwin, op cit., pp. 323–324.
71. Ibid., p. 327.
72. Ibid., pp. 337–338.
73. Ibid., p. 340.
74. These figures were calculated using data found in Goodwin on the following pages: 325, 327, 336, 338, 342, 349, 352, 356, 359, 360, 368, 387, and 400.
75. Myrdal, op cit., p. 942.

76. Bullock, op cit., p. 54–55.
77. Wilkinson, J.: *From Brown to Bakke: The Supreme Court and School Integration: 1954-1978.* New York, Oxford University Press, p. 979,15.
78. Kluger, op cit., p. 74.
79. Myrdal, op cit., p. 942.
80. Fleming, op cit., p. 50.
81. Weinberg, op cit., p. 47.
82. Fleming, op cit., p. 60.
83. Howard, op cit., pp. 323–326.
84. Weinberg, op cit., p. 47.
85. Chambers, J.: Implementing the promise of *Brown*: Social science and the courts in future school litigation. In Rist, R. and Anson, R. (Eds.): *Education, Social Science and the Judicial Process.* New York, Teachers College Press, 1977, p. 35.
86. Kluger, op cit., p. 83.
87. Bullock, op cit., p. 71.
88. Bullock, op cit., p. 67.
89. Kluger, op cit., pp. 89–90.
90. *Plessy v. Ferguson*, 163 U.S. 537 (1896).
91. Kluger, op cit., p. 111.
92. Goodwin, op cit., p. 321.
93. *Cumming v. Richmond County Board of Education*, 175 W.S. 528 (1899).
94. Patton, J.: The black community of Augusta and the struggle for Ware High School 1880–1899. In Franklin, V. and Anderson, J. (Eds.): *New Perspectives on Black Educational History.* Boston, G. K. Hall and Company, 1978, p. 45.
95. Anderson, J.: Northern philanthropy and the training of the black leadership: Fisk university, a case study, 1915–1930. In Franklin, V. and Anderson, J. (Eds.): *New Perspectives on Black Educational History.* Boston, G. K. Hall and Company, 1978, p. 98–99. (A)
96. Fleming, op cit., pp. 56–57.
97. Carruthers, op cit., p. 300.
98. Anderson, J.: The Hampton model of normal school industrial education, 1868–1900. In Franklin, V. and Anderson, J. (Eds.): *New Perspectives on Black Educational History.* Boston, G. K. Hall and Company, 1978, p. 84. (B)
99. Bullock, op cit., pp. 84, 122, 124, 139, 141–143.
100. Carruthers, op cit., p. 300.
101. Anderson (A), op cit., pp. 100–101.
102. Fleming, op cit., p. 57.
103. Meier and Rudwick, op cit., pp. 178–179.
104. Bullock, op cit., p. 158.
105. Bullock, op cit., p. 137.
106. Woodson, op cit., p. 77–78.
107. Weinberg, op cit., pp. 29–30.

108. Woodson, op cit., pp. 301, 303.

109. Anderson (B), op cit., pp. 63–66.

110. Bullock, op cit., p. 32.

111. Anderson (B), op cit., pp. 61, 69–70, 72.

112. Kluger, op cit., pp. 85–87.

113. Bullock, op cit., p. 81.

114. Meier and Rudwick, op cit., p. 180.

115. Kluger, op cit., pp. 105–106.

116. Bullock, op cit., p. 94.

117. Perkins, op cit., pp. 35–37.

118. Bullock, op cit., pp. 77–79.

119. Dennis, R.: DuBois and the role of the educated elite. *Journal of Negro Education*, 46(4):392, 1977.

120. DuBois (A), op cit., pp. 32–33.

121. Dennis, op cit., p. 392.

122. DuBois (A), op cit., pp. 78–80.

123. Ibid., p. 77.

124. Ibid., pp. 38, 43.

125. DuBois, W.: *The Education of Black People: Ten Critiques, 1906–1960*, Aptheker, H. (Ed.). Amherst, University of Massachusetts Press, 1973, pp. 10–11. (B)

126. Ibid.

127. Ibid., pp. 42, 49.

128. Ibid., pp. 61, 68.

129. Ibid., p. 5.

130. Myrdal, op cit., p. 899.

131. Ibid., p. 942.

132. Kluger, op cit., p. 84.

133. Peltason, J.: Fifty-eight Lonely Men, Southern Federal Judges and School Desegregation. New York, Harcourt, Brace and World, 1961, p. 248.

134. Weinberg, op cit., p. 56.

135. Bullock, op cit., pp. 123, 173, 178, 180–181.

136. Kluger, op cit., p. 109, 168.

137. Weinberg, op cit., pp. 58, 66.

138. DuBois (A), op cit., pp. 47–48.

139. Weinberg, op cit., p. 63.

140. Myrdal, op cit., p. 343.

141. Myrdal, op cit., pp. 902–903.

142. Ibid., pp. 319–320, 339–340, 948.

143. Weinberg, op cit., p. 75.

144. Franklin, V.: In pursuit of freedom: The educational activities of black social organizations in Philadelphia, 1900–1930. In Franklin, V. and Anderson, J. (Eds.): *New Perspectives on Black Educational History*. Boston, G. K. Hall and Company, 1978, p. 114.

145. Williams, L.: To elevate the race: The Michigan Avenue YMCA and the advancement of blacks in Buffalo, New York, 1922–1940. In Franklin, V. and Anderson, J. (Eds.): *New Perspectives on Black Educational History*. Boston, G. K. Hall and Company, 1978, pp. 139–141.

146. Mohraz, J.: *The Separate Problem. Case Studies of Black Education in the North, 1900-1930*. Westport, Conn., Greenwood Press, 1979. pp. 7, 87–91.

147. Ibid., pp. 109–110, 113–114.

148. Ibid., pp. 116–118.

149. Weinberg, op cit., pp. 71–73.

150. Ibid., p. 74.

151. Mohraz, op cit., p. 18.

152. Weinberg, op cit., pp. 70, 77–78.

153. Mohraz, op cit., pp. 21–22, 75, 81.

154. Homel, M.: The politics of public education in black Chicago, 1910–1941. *Journal of Negro Education, 45(2)*:182–183, 1976.

155. Mohraz, op cit., pp. 98, 131, 137.

156. Homel, op cit., p. 180.

157. Weinberg, op cit., p. 70.

158. Bullock, op cit., pp. 73–75.

CHAPTER 2

THE SECOND DECLARATION
OF INDEPENDENCE

The struggle to end *de jure* segregation in education is essentially the story of the NAACP, the courts (particularly the United States Supreme Court), and scores of brave people who dared to defy a bigoted white establishment by bringing suit to secure what they implicitly knew to be their constitutional right to an equal education. It was based on a strategy which took over twenty years to be played out. However, the gears were set in motion several decades in advance.

The National Association for the Advancement of Colored People (NAACP) was founded in 1910 as an outgrowth of a group begun five years earlier by W. E. B. DuBois. Known as the Niagra Movement (due to the location of its meetings), all sessions were held on the Canadian side of the Falls since hotels and other facilities there were equally open to blacks. At its peak, the Movement had 400 members. At the second annual meeting held in August, 1906, the group declared war on illiteracy among blacks in the South: "We want our children educated... We want our children trained as intelligent human beings should be... They have a right to know, to think, to aspire."[1, 2]

This focus on education was carried forward by the NAACP on the belief that an uneducated black populace compromised the general welfare of the country.[3] The concept of a mass movement of blacks and whites to combat discrimination gained strength, particularly after the NAACP began its publication of *The Crisis*, which was edited by DuBois. The young organization won its first case before the United States Supreme Court in 1915.[4, 5] It received a financial boost in 1929 when it received a grant from the Garland Fund of $100,000 (much of which was subsequently lost in the

47

Great Crash of 1929). The money was to support taxpayers suits to force the equalization of schools in seven Southern states.[6] Under the direction of Howard Law School's Charles Houston, the thrust of this activity was changed to begin an attack on "separate but equal" schools by demonstrating that they were not equal. The NAACP hoped that the cost of equalization would be so burdensome as to prompt the school districts, as well as the higher education systems, to merge the racially dual systems.[7] Houston transformed Howard Law into a laboratory for civil rights advocacy that was to produce many of the attorneys who would participate in the forthcoming litigation.[8]

THE EARLY CASES

By 1935, 113 school segregation cases had made their way into the courts in twenty-nine states and in the District of Columbia. The constitutionality of the practice was challenged unsuccessfully in each of the forty-four instances in which it was raised.[9] One reason often cited was the United States Supreme Court's ruling in the 1927 case of *Gong Lum v. Rice*.[10] Martha Lum, a Chinese-American, attempted to enroll in a white school in Mississippi, but was not permitted to do so. Since there was no separate school for Asians, she was assigned to an all-black school. Her father brought suit in a Mississippi court claiming a violation of his daughter's fourteenth amendment rights. They lost. That state's Supreme Court subsequently heard the case and ruled that "The legislature is not compelled to provide separate schools for each of the colored races, and unless and until it does provide such schools, and provide for segregation of the other races, such races are entitled to have the benefit of the colored public schools . . . If the plaintiff desires she may attend public schools of her district, or if she does not so desire, she may go to a private school."[11]

Thus, the Mississippi Supreme Court held that only whites could attend the schools set aside for whites and that everyone else had to attend the schools established to keep black children separate from whites, or they could choose to attend a private school. The United States Supreme Court later agreed that it was not an infringement of the rights of a Chinese-American to be assigned to a black school. The Court acknowledged that most of the previous controversy and litigation was focused on the establishment of separate schools for whites and blacks, but it did not believe that "...the question is any different, or that any different result can be reached...where the issue is as between white pupils and the pupils of the yellow races. The decision is within the discretion of the state in regulating its public schools and does not conflict with the Fourteenth Amendment." The Court did not mention in its ruling that application of the separate but equal doctrine to education was still valid, but it certainly seemed to imply that it had no problem with those who would broadly interpret *Plessy*.[12]

The NAACP's first successful challenge to racially segregated schools came in the mid-1930s in the border state of Maryland. In January, 1935, Donald Murray, a member of a prominent black family in Baltimore and a graduate of Amherst College in Massachusetts, was denied admission to the University of Maryland Law School and was told to apply to Howard Law School in nearby Washington. Murray sued.[13] During the district court trial, the attorney representing the University agreed that, as a black, Murray was not eligible for admission. Since Maryland had no law school for blacks, he would have to leave the state if he wanted a legal education, and the state would assist him in this endeavor by providing tuition aid.

Representing Murray, Charles Houston and Thurgood Marshall introduced testimony by a member of the scholarship commission who noted that there were currently 380 applications for the 50 grants of $200 each available to blacks for out-of-state study. Thus, Marshall argued, Maryland was not living up to its obligation under its separate but equal law. The judge agreed and ordered Murray admitted to the heretofore lily-white University of Maryland Law School.

Despite the fact that Murray began classes in the fall of 1935, the University sought to overturn his admission in the Maryland Court of Appeals. But in January, 1936, that court found that since Maryland had only "one existing law school, the petitioner, in our opinion, must be admitted there." They also ruled that the ordering of separate schools for blacks was not a proper remedy since Murray deserved equal treatment immediately. The court noted its belief that "compliance with the Constitution cannot be deferred at the will of the state." The University did not press the matter any further and the case was dropped.[14] The first segregation barrier had been broken, but the decision applied only to Maryland.

The issue of the use of out-of-state scholarships for blacks as a means to foreclose the possibility of their enrollment in a state university was finally joined at the level of the United States Supreme Court in 1938 in the case of *Missouri ex rel Gaines v. Canada*.[15] Two years earlier, Lloyd Gaines, a graduate of the all-black Lincoln University (Mo.) had applied to the University of Missouri Law School. At that time, there were only forty-five black attorneys in the state and there was no black law school. Gaines was denied admission due to the Missouri statute that provided for the support of black Missourians "at the university of any adjacent state to take any course or to study any subjects provided for at the state university of Missouri and which are not taught at Lincoln University." The state would provide grants to pay "reasonable" tuition charges at the out-of-state institutions.

Chief Justice Charles Evans Hughes saw the validity of Gaines's claim: "That for one intending to practice law in Missouri there are special advantages in attending a law school there, both in relation to the opportunities for the particular study of Missouri law and for the observation of the local courts, and also in view of the prestige of the Missouri Law School among the citizens of the State, his prospective clients." Speaking for the six to two majority, Hughes disagreed with the state court, which had stressed the "advantages that are afforded by the law schools of the adjacent states, Kansas, Nebraska, Iowa, and Illinois, which admit non-resident negroes. . . ." He retorted: "We think that these matters are beside the point. The basic consideration is not as to what sort of opportunities other states provide, or whether they are as good as those in Missouri, but as to what opportunities Missouri itself furnishes to white students and denies to Negroes solely upon the ground of color." Thus, the Court ruled that Missouri must provide Gaines within the state "facilities for legal education substantially equal to those which the State there afforded for persons of the white race."

The Court, then, had finally begun to establish the minimum

standards for equality in education. [16] [17] However, the decision was tactfully worded so as not to challenge Missouri's "state's rights" position since that would have raised the ire of the South. The decision did not specifically state that Gaines must be admitted to the University of Missouri Law School, only that he must be educated in Missouri. The state chose not to admit him to its white university but instead to establish a separate but equal law school for blacks. The NAACP quickly challenged this solution fearing that the new school would be less than equal. However, their client disappeared shortly thereafter and was neither seen nor heard from again. [18]

The quest for school equalization continued during the 1940s. By 1942, the NAACP had won a number of court cases where black teachers had been paid salaries far below those of the white teachers in the same school district. However, such victories affected only the district under suit. During the next six years, the NAACP won twenty-seven more cases—still only a small dent in the 11,173 school districts that either required or allowed segregation. [19] [20]

It took until 1948, ten years after *Gaines*, for another case to reach the United States Supreme Court. [21] This one, too, concerned a black applicant who had been denied access to a state law school had been reserved for whites. While the excuse used by Missouri in the *Gaines* instance was that of the availability of out-of-state tuition aid, in the instance of Ada Sipuel, it was that Oklahoma would soon be establishing a law school for its black citizens, and, thus, there was no reason why Sipuel should not wait. The state, however, did not want to open the school until there were enough black applicants to justify the expense. The Oklahoma court which originally heard the case saw no problem with such an approach, neither did the Oklahoma Supreme Court.

Sipuel did not want to wait any longer than she had already and, thus, appealed to the U.S. Supreme Court. Arguing her case, Thurgood Marshall reminded the Court of its earlier decision in *Gaines*, that the state must provide in-state graduate education for its black residents. However, he went one step further by making the argument that "there can be no separate equality," that Sipuel's legal education should occur at the University of Oklahoma. It took the Court only one weekend to reach its collective mind, indicative of its desire that Oklahoma stop procrastinating. [22] It ordered that "the State must provide [a legal education] for her in conformity with the equal protection clause of the Fourteenth Amendment and provide it as soon as it does for applicants of any other group." But, the Court only agreed with the first part of Marshall's argument. It gave the State the choice of admitting her to the University of Oklahoma until such time as a black law school was opened, or of ceasing admissions at the white law school until a black one was opened. Thus, it allowed the continuation of the separate but equal approach.

The Oklahoma Regents acted quickly to avoid desegregation by establishing a black law school in a roped-off section in the State Capitol. Sipuel was its only student. She went back to court, claiming that Oklahoma was attempting to evade the Court's order since, surely, it was not an "equal" law school which had been made available to her. In a seven to two decision, the Court held that its order had been followed, particularly in view of the fact that the question of whether or not the new school was an equal one was not at issue in its earlier ruling. [23] Thus, Oklahoma and the rest of the Border and Southern states were still able to maintain separate educational facilities, though it was evident that they were in no way equal.

In the late 1940s, the proportion of whites attending high school was four times that for blacks. Even worse, one-quarter of the black population was functionally illiterate. Further, the seventeen states that required segregated schools spent $86 million on higher education for whites and only $5 million for blacks. [24]

Never out of ideas on how to avoid desegregation, fourteen Southern governors met in 1948 to chart a course they hoped would head off further cases such as Sipuel's. They sought to avoid the expense of each state's establishment of professional and graduate programs for blacks to match those available to whites within the state. Their Southern Regional Education Plan would provide shared facilities open to black students from participating states. Educational costs would be borne by the states in proportion to the enrollment of their citizens. The plan, however, never got off the drawing boards and, thus, was never subjected to the *Gaines* test. [25]

Much to the chagrin of those governors and to the people who voted them into office, the Supreme Court waited only two years, after telling Ada Sipuel Fisher that the quality of her legal education was not an issue before the Court, to consider what was required to constitute an "equal" education. The case originated in 1946 when Heman Marion Sweatt sued the University of Texas Law School for denying him admission based on his race alone. A Texas district court judge ruled that either he be admitted or that a law school be established at Prairie View A & M University for blacks. The state chose the second option, opening a law school with essentially no library and only four part-time faculty. Sweatt went back to court. As his second case was working its way up the judicial ladder, the Texas legislature established a new Texas State University for Negroes and appropriated $100,000 to go toward the development of a good law school for blacks. Sweatt was still not satisfied and, in 1950, the matter found itself before the United States Supreme Court. [26]

In its unanimous decision, the Court examined the quality of the law school to which Sweatt was denied access and compared it to that of the black law school. It noted that the school at the University of Texas had sixteen full-time faculty and three who taught on a part-time basis; some of this group were nationally recognized legal scholars. The school also had 850 students, a library with 65,000 volumes, a law review, and moot court facilities. The Court knew that Texas could take pride in that school since, "It may properly be considered one of the nation's ranking law schools." On the other hand, it found that the school at Texas State had only five full-time faculty, twenty-three students, a library of only 16,500 volumes, and a moot court. It had no law review and was not accredited. The Court said it could not agree that the two schools were substantially equal. While it stopped short of defining *equality*, it noted that "The University of Texas Law School possesses to a far greater degree those qualities which are incapable of objective measurement but which make for greatness in a law school."

Arguing for Sweatt, Thurgood Marshall hoped this case would be the one where the separate but equal approach would be declared unconstitutional. At his urging, Thomas Emerson of the Yale Law School submitted an *amicus* (friend of the court) brief signed by 187 law professors from throughout the nation. The brief stated that blacks had had their equality before the law removed at the time that the Court ruled in the *Plessy* case, despite the fact that "the Equal Protection Clause makes racial classifications unreasonable." It urged the Court to overturn the *Plessy* doctrine.

Sweatt proved to be the first instance of Marshall's use of social science data to support his case that segregation could not be justified on the basis of any inherent differences between whites and blacks. He attempted to show that segregation was a psychologically and sociologically destructive factor in American life.[27] The Court, however, was not ready to tackle the segregation issue. It recognized that "broader issues have been urged for our consideration but we adhere to the principle of deciding constitutional questions only in the context of the particular case before the Court;" i.e., has Sweatt been denied access to a good law school in favor of a less elite law school based solely on his race? The Court noted its "traditional reluctance to extend constitutional interpretations to situations or facts which are not before the Court" and held that "much of the excellent research and detailed argument" was unnecessary to the resolution of the case. The end result, then, was that the University of Texas had to admit Sweatt to its law school, but the South was not forced to close its "separate but equal" schools.

On the same day that the Court ruled in *Sweatt*, it also rendered its verdict in the case of *McLaurin v. Oklahoma State Regents for Higher Education*.[28] George McLaurin was a sixty-eight-year-old black educator who sought to enroll in a doctoral program in the School of Education at the University of Oklahoma in 1948. He was not admitted and thus had brought suit in federal court. A three judge district court panel had ruled similarly to the United States Supreme Court in the *Sipuel* case, and, subsequently, the legislature agreed to allow the admission of blacks to white colleges if the black institutions did not offer the academic program sought by the black applicants. However, any blacks admitted to white institutions were to receive their educations on a segregated basis. Thus, McLaurin had to eat at a separate table in the dining hall, had to study at a special desk in the library and had to receive his instruction in a railed area within the classroom marked "reserved for colored." He went back to the federal district court and argued that such treatment pinned upon him "a badge of inferiority." The court did not find any conflict with the separate but equal doctrine so McLaurin and his attorney, Thurgood Marshall, petitioned the Supreme Court for relief.

And relief is what they received. The Court unanimously found that "the restrictions placed upon [McLaurin] were such that he had been handicapped in his pursuit of effective graduate instruction"; that they impaired his "ability to study, to engage in discussions and exchange views with other students, and, in general, to learn his profession." Not only did McLaurin suffer, the Court deduced, but those whom he would teach would also suffer from the shoddy treatment accorded him. The Justices recognized that McLaurin might not be in a "better position when these restrictions are removed, for he still may be set apart by his fellow students." However, the Court said, "This we think irrelevant. There is a vast difference—a Constitutional difference—between restrictions imposed by the state which prohibit intellectual commingling of students and the refusal of individuals to commingle where the state presents no such bar." Despite the fact that the Court could not blunt individual racism, it could block racially-based state prohibitions on intellectual interaction.

Together then, in *Sweatt* and in *McLaurin*, the Court came as close as it could to barring separate but equal without so doing. In *Sweatt*, it ruled that an inferior school would not satisfy the *Plessy* doctrine. It was clear that it would be exceedingly difficult for an underfunded, inadequately staffed and ill-equipped black graduate school to be shown the equal of its well established and well respected white counterpart. Thus, unless the Jim Crow states were willing to invest major sums of money into the black institutions, they would be forced to admit them to the white ones. And, once having admitted blacks, they were bound by *McLaurin* not to discriminate against them. While the Court left *Plessy* intact, it began to put serious pressure on the South.

THE SCHOOL DESEGREGATION CASES

Attention turned away from graduate schools to the elementary and secondary schools. The NAACP brought five cases through the judicial system to the United States Supreme Court in the early 1950s. These cases, known as the School Desegregation Cases, included one from the northern state of Kansas, *Brown v. Board of Education of Topeka*, one from the border state of Delaware, *Gebhart v. Belton*, one from the Deep South (South Carolina), *Briggs v. Elliott*, and one from the upper South (Virginia), *Davis v. County School Board of Prince Edward County, Virginia.* [29] The fifth case, *Bolling v. Sharpe*, concerned the District of Columbia. [30] Together these cases included all grade levels. By consolidating all five, each one with its different circumstances, the Court was moving to an "all or nothing" ruling on school segregation. Thus, when the Court ruled on May 17, 1954, its decision was of immediate importance to the seventeen Southern and Border states (as well as the District of Columbia) that required segregated schools and to the four states (Arizona, Kansas, New Mexico, and Wyoming) that permitted them on local option. Of the nation's school children, 40 percent were enrolled in those schools. [31]

Before moving to the arguments at the Supreme Court level, it is useful to examine the background of each case. *Briggs*, the first of the cases to reach the Supreme Court, concerned the schools in Clarendon County, South Carolina. Kluger has noted that, for blacks, life there "was nothing short of economic slavery, an unbreakable cycle of poverty and ignorance." [32] The county was 70 percent black, yet 85 percent of the land was owned by whites. Most blacks were tenant farmers—poor, uneducated tenant farmers. Only one-third of the black families earned more than $1000 per year. Most had never even reached the fifth grade, and those who did received inferior educations. In the 1949–1950 school year, Clarendon County spent over four times as much on the education of white children as it did for blacks. The sixty-one schools that served over 6500 black students were blighted. They had a combined property value of nearly $0.5 million less than the twelve schools that served nearly 2400 white students. A further sign of inequality was found in the fact that the average white teacher made two-thirds more salary than the average black teacher.

Led by the Reverend Joseph A. DeLaine, the black community sought to better their lot in the schools. [33] Twenty parents coalesced to sue on behalf of their sixty-seven children. (Many, including DeLaine, lost their jobs and their credit.) Since the suit was filed as a challenge to the constitutionality of the state's segregation laws, a three judge panel heard the case in federal district court. The law required that "separate schools shall be provided for children of the white and colored races, and no child of either race shall ever be permitted to attend a school provided for the other race."[34] During the trial, the attorney for the school board acknowledged that the black schools were not the equal of the white ones and asked for a reasonable period of time to bring them up to par. Thurgood Marshall argued for the plaintiffs that the only constitutional solution was for their children to be admitted to the white schools. The panel ruled (two to one) that the proper place to consider the discontinuation of segregation was in the state legislature, not in the court. Said presiding Judge John Parker, "We think . . . that segregation of the races in the public schools, so long as equality of rights is preserved, is a matter of legislative policy for the several states, with which the federal courts are powerless to interfere."[35] The Court gave the school board six months to equalize the county schools.

In Kansas, segregation was allowed in the elementary schools in cities with populations of over 15,000. (Kansas City was the only city allowed to segregate its high schools.) In 1951, there were eighteen elementary schools for whites in Topeka and four for blacks. Oliver Brown had been refused permission to register his daughter, Linda, at an all-white school seven blocks from home. Instead, she was required to enroll in a black school a longer distance away, one which necessitated her walking across a dangerous railroad switching yard in order to meet her school bus. In February, 1951, Brown and other black parents, on behalf of their children, sued to overturn the law that permitted such inequities to exist. They were represented before a three judge federal panel by Robert Carter, an NAACP attorney, who presented an argument similar to that presented in *Briggs*. However, as in the other case, the judges were not convinced that segregation was a violation of the equal protection clause of the fourteenth amendment. They concluded "that in the maintenance and operation of the schools there is no willful, intentional or substantial discrimination."[36] Thus, the *status quo* could be maintained.

In April, 1951, poor educational conditions led Barbara Jones, a student at the overcrowded, all-black Moton High School in Prince Edward County, Virginia, to initiate a student strike at the school. [37] Moton was obviously inferior to the two high schools enrolling white students and, the students were upset over the county's failure to provide funds for a new high school for black students. Their school had no science facilities, no cafeteria, a weak library and an inadequate shop. It had no lockers, no showers, and inadequate toilet facilities. Its curriculum was weaker than that at the white schools. Its auditorium was, in reality, a large hallway. Its best paid teacher earned a lower paycheck than the worst paid teacher at the neighboring white high school.

The student strike led to the involvement of NAACP attorneys Oliver Hall and Spottswood Robinson. A month later, the inequality of the school was brought before the federal district court in Richmond. Again, the NAACP sought to overturn the school segregation laws that had precipitated the unequal conditions. Testimony presented before the three judge panel indicated that Moton had an inferior physical plant and a weaker academic program than the white high schools, and that its teachers were less experienced. Attorneys for the school district pointed out that, subsequent to the filing of the suit, the county had provided funds for a new black high school. The Virginia Attorney General, Lindsay Almond, participating on the defense team, told the judges that Virginia would close its schools before it would desegregate them.

That course of action would not yet be necessary, however, since the court did not overturn the segregation statutes. It cited data that indicated that in 63 of the 127 school districts, blacks and whites had equal facilities, and that in nearly half of the already equal districts approved building programs would make the black schools better than the white ones. It did find that Prince Edward County was one of the districts where schools were not equal, and it ordered the school board to upgrade the black schools "with diligence and dispatch." A deadline of September, 1953 was set for the opening of a new black high school. [38]

Delaware's location as a Border State might lead one to believe that it was more progressive than its neighbors to the South. However, it was one of the states that never ratified the thirteenth, fourteenth, and fifteenth amendments (though once accepted by three-quarters of the states those mandates were equally applicable in that state). Segregation was as legal there as it was throughout the South. What resulted from the Delaware school desegregation case was, however, radically different than that which occurred in the other three states discussed thus far.

There were two cases, *Belton v. Gebhart* and *Bulah v. Gebhart*; they were subsequently combined and reached the U.S. Supreme Court as *Gebhart v. Belton*. The first case concerned the reservation for white students of Claymont High School, located in a Wilmington suburb. Black students were forced to ride a school bus to Howard High School in Wilmington. The quality of the teachers, curriculum, facilities, and student activities was demonstrably greater at Claymont. The second case developed in another Wilmington suburb, Hockessen, where a black woman sued over her daughter's inability to ride a "whites only" school bus that passed her house on its way to a whites only school. Instead, she had to drive her daughter to a one room schoolhouse reserved for blacks.

The judge of the Delaware Chancery Court, Collins J. Seitz, visited the schools in question and must have found sharp differences because he judged the white schools to be "vastly superior" to the black ones. In April, 1952, he found that "state imposed segregation in education itself results in the Negro children, as a class, receiving educational opportunities which are substantially inferior to those available to white children otherwise similarly situated."[39] Since the plaintiffs had been able to demonstrate that their schools were not equal, they were "entitled to have made available to [them] the state facilities which have been shown to have been superior."[40] Seitz stated his hope that the U.S. Supreme Court would overturn *Plessy* once and for all.

Needless to say, the cases were appealed to the Delaware Supreme Court. Four months later, that Court concurred with Seitz's ruling. Thus, finally, there was a ruling against school segregation by a court of law, and that ruling was subsequently upheld by the state's highest court. The NAACP's hard work had finally borne fruit.

The final case to be joined in the School Desegregation Cases was that of *Bolling v. Sharpe*. Because the case concerned the District of Columbia, the assault on segregation was not based on the equal protection clause of the fourteenth amendment; that amendment affects states only. Since the District of Columbia is under federal control, *Bolling* was based on the violation of the due process clause of the fifth amendment.

As with *Davis*, the momentum leading to this case developed as a result of a school boycott, this one led by a black parent, Gardner Bishop. [41] The NAACP's Charles Houston became involved but illness forced him to turn the matter over to James Nabrit. Bishop's community mobilization led to an ill-fated attempt to have eleven black children transferred from the forty-eight-year-old, poorly equipped Shaw Junior High School to the recently opened John Philip Sousa Junior High School, which had been reserved for whites. Despite the fact that it could be demonstrated that the black school was inferior to the white one, that issue was not raised when *Bolling* came before Judge Walter Bastian in United States District Court. Instead, Nabrit focused only on the point that educational rights are fundamental and, under the due process clause, may not be unreasonably restricted—further, that segregation was an unreasonable restriction not warranted some eighty-five years after the end of slavery. Judge Bastian found the School Board's arguments more compelling and ruled negatively in this case.

In October and November, 1952, the United States Supreme Court granted *certiorari* (that is, accepted) the five School Desegregation Cases. *Briggs*, *Brown*, and *Davis* had worked their way up through their respective Circuit Court of Appeals, and *Gebhart* came from the Delaware Supreme Court. However, *Bolling* was still pending before the Circuit Court of Appeals when the Supreme Court invited a petition from the plaintiffs to skip that level and appeal directly to the highest court. In so doing, the Court seemed to indicate that it wanted to meet the issue of segregated schools head on, and that it considered the matter to be more than a legal problem but a compelling social problem. [42]

With Chief Justice Fred M. Vinson presiding, the United States Supreme Court heard oral arguments on the five School Desegregation Cases over a three day period in December, 1952. Other members of the Court were Hugo L. Black, William O. Douglas, Felix Frankfurter, Robert H. Jackson, and Stanley F. Reed (all appointed by President Franklin D. Roosevelt) as well as Harold H. Burton, Tom Clark and Sherman Minton (who, along with the

Chief Justice, were appointed by President Harry S. Truman).
Among that group, Black, Clark, and Reed were Southerners.

SOCIAL SCIENCE DATA

During the course of the oral arguments, much attention was
focused on the testimony of social scientists that had been presented
at the lower court hearings. It was part of the NAACP's strategy to
employ social science data to demonstrate that segregation *per se*
had a harmful effect on black children. By so doing, they hoped
that they would be able to ward off any attempt to continue the
separate but equal doctrine. No amount of money added to upgrade
segregated schools, they argued, could ever compensate for the
damage that segregation had on black children.

At the lower court hearings, the NAACP had called a series of
expert witnesses, all university faculty members and researchers,
in order to introduce the results of studies which supported their
case. Attorneys for the respective school boards sought to discount
this testimony with experts of their own. To introduce such evidence was a controversial move, though Judge John Minor Wisdom has noted that "Sociology has always played a part in the
decision-making process, although frequently it comes wearing a
mask—sometimes as public policy or common knowledge, sometimes legislative or constitutional facts. In these instances, the
judge unwittingly may be functioning as a sociologist without the
benefit of witnesses and solid empirical data."[43] The NAACP had
unmasked the role of the social scientist and had directly placed
the evidence before the courts.

In the *Briggs* case, Thurgood Marshall had called on a black
social psychologist Doctor Kenneth Clark, who along with his
wife, Mamie, had previously conducted research concerning the
effect of segregation on the self-image of black children. Beginning in 1940, they had collected data using their "doll tests."[44] In
Clarendon County in the days before the trial opened, Clark
conducted the same tests on sixteen black children from the ages of
six to nine years old. The children were presented two dolls that
were identical except in color. Ten children said that they pre-
ferred the white doll over the black doll. When asked which doll

was the "nice" one, nine picked the white doll; when asked which one looked "bad," eleven selected the black doll. While each child was able to identify the black doll as black and the white doll as white, seven chose the white doll when asked to identify the one that looked most like themselves. Clark found these results to match those of his earlier tests with other children. [45]

He also reported his findings on a test that involved the use of crayons. One of the girls, "a dark brown child of seven," was asked to color a drawing of herself. She "picked a flesh color, pink, to color herself. When asked to color a little boy the color she liked little boys to be, she poked all around the 24 crayons and picked up the white crayon." [46]

Clark concluded that "These children in Clarendon County, like other human beings who are subjected to an obviously inferior status in the society in which they live, have been definitely harmed in the development of their personalities; that signs of instability in their personalities are clear, and I think that every psychologist would accept and interpret these signs as such." [47] He had no doubt that segregation caused the black child to have "basic feelings of inferiority, conflict, confusion in his self-image, resentment, hostility towards himself, [and] hostility toward whites." [48] He had found that these children often cope with this conflict by escaping or withdrawing.

Doctor David Krech, a University of California and Harvard psychologist, had carried the argument one step further by testifying that by the time a child, who has grown up in a segregated community, reaches age twelve, that child "will probably never recover from whatever harmful effect racial prejudice and discrimination can wreak." [49]

In the *Brown* case, Ohio State University psychologist, Horace English, former president of the American Association for the Advancement of Science, had presented testimony to the fact that there was no evidence to indicate that one's race had any relationship with the ability to learn. However, he pointed out that "segregation definitely depresses the Negro's expectancy and is therefore prejudicial to his learning." [50]

In the *Davis* case, Isidor Chein had reported on his survey of 849 psychologists. (Among the 517 who responded, 8.4 percent were

Southerners.) In response to the question, "Does enforced segregation have detrimental psychological effects on members of racial and religious groups which are segregated, even if equal facilities are provided?" 90 percent answered that it did; only 2 percent thought not. Even among the Southern respondents, 91 percent said yes. An overwhelming proportion (83% of the total and 84% of the Southerners) also thought that there was a detrimental effect on the group that enforces the segregation.[51]

When *Gebhart* was being argued in the Chancery Court, Frederic Wertham, a psychiatrist, had entered more saddening data into the record. He had interviewed a small group of Delaware children, black and white, and found that black children came to believe that segregation is punishment for some evil committed by their race. He concluded from his study that "The physical differences in these schools are not at all really material. . . . [If] the state of Delaware would employ Professor Einstein to teach physics in marble halls to these children, I would still say everything I have said goes: It is [the] fact of segregation . . . that to my mind is anti-educational."[52]

The district courts had each treated the detailed social science data differently. In the South Carolina case, the court had said that it could not tamper with the law based on the theories of a few sociologists. In the Kansas case, the court had accepted the arguments that segregation affected the self-image and motivation of black children, but it still found segregation legal. In the Virginia case, the social science data had been totally ignored, but in the Delaware case, it had served as the bedrock upon which the desegregation order was based.[53]

Once all of the cases were simultaneously before the Chief Justice Vinson's Court, there was the opportunity for further consideration of the scholarly evidence. Some of this was done in the oral presentations made by the NAACP attorneys, but they also submitted a 4,000 word brief written by Kenneth Clark with the assistance of Isidor Chein and New York University's Stuart Cook, and signed by thirty-five well known social scientists, including Gordon Allport, Otto Klineberg, and Robert Merton. The brief noted that a child "May be able to cope with ordinary expressions of prejudice by regarding the prejudiced person as evil or misguided; but he cannot readily cope with symbols of authority, the full force of the State — the school or the school board, in this instance — in the same manner."[54] It concluded with a reaffirmation of the belief that the response of a black child to official prejudice is a psychologically detrimental one.

The attorneys for the defense obviously did not allow such testimony to stand unchallenged. In each case, the defense attorneys presented their own expert witnesses in an attempt to prove that black children did better under segregation than they would do in direct competition with white children. Perhaps the most eloquent denunciation of the NAACP's social science data came from John W. Davis who argued South Carolina's side in the Briggs case.

Davis was a well respected national political figure, having served as President Wilson's Solicitor General. In 1924, he had run as the Democratic candidate in the presidential election won by Calvin Coolidge. He later served as the Ambassador to England. When the steel companies sought to enjoin President Truman from taking over their mills, Davis gained further attention and prestige by successfully arguing their case before the Supreme Court.

In his pleadings before the Court in the Clarendon County case, Davis challenged the credibility of Thurgood Marshall's expert witnesses:

"I do not impugn the sincerity of these learned gentlemen and lady. I am quite sure that they believe that they are expressing valid opinions on the subject. But there are two things notable about them. Not one of them is under any official duty in the premises whatever; not a one of them has had to consider the welfare of people for whom they are legislating or whose rights they were called on to adjudicate. And only one of them professes to have the slightest knowledge of conditions in the states where separate schools are now being maintained."[55]

He was directly critical of the testimony presented by Kenneth Clark since Clark's data indicated that black children in the North had worse self-images than those in the South. "Now these latter scientific tests," Davis noted, "were conducted in non-segregating states, and with those results compared, what becomes of the blasting influence of segregation to which Dr. Clark so eloquently testifies?"[56] (Of course, as has been discussed in the preceding chapter, while the North may not have permitted *de jure* segregation, there is no doubt that most black children attended segregated schools there. Thus, Clark's findings are understandable: what must a black child think of himself/herself when the law does not require segregation, but it exists nonetheless?)

Davis went on to cite the writings of W. E. B. DuBois to support his case that black children do better in separate schools. Said DuBois, "We shall get a finer, better balance of spirit, an infinitely more capable and rounded personality by putting children in schools where they are wanted, and where they are happy and inspired, than in thrusting them into hells where they are ridiculed and hated."[57]

At least one observer has seen the irony of this quotation being presented to the Supreme Court by Davis, since it is clear that DuBois wanted an end to the use of race as a basis for decision-making. Yale Kamisar has pointed out that DuBois, in the same work quoted by Davis, went on to note that "there is no room for argument as to whether the Negro needs separate schools or not. The plain fact faces us, that either he will have separate schools or he will not be educated."[58]

Kenneth Clark later discussed the importance of social science data to the arguments before the respective courts in the School Desegregation Cases. He indicated that by providing evidence concerning the damage inherent in segregated education "The social scientists made it possible to avoid the need to obtain proof of individual damage and to avoid assessment of the equality of facilities in each individual school system. The assumption of inequality could now be made wherever segregation existed."[59]

OTHER ORAL ARGUMENTS BEFORE THE COURT

The oral pleadings before the Court did not focus solely on the social science data. The *Brown* case was the first to be argued. NAACP attorney Robert L. Carter put forth the contention that underlay his case, "That no state has any authority under the equal protection clause of the Fourteenth Amendment to use race as a factor in affording educational opportunities among its citizens."[60]

Carter nearly had no opposition. An election in Topeka replaced three conservative school board members with liberals, and the newly constituted board voted not to defend the suit before the Supreme Court. However, that Court ordered the state's attorney general to proceed with the case.[61] Kansas Assistant Attorney General Paul E. Wilson based his case before the high Court on the fact that the federal district court had found the physical facilities and curricula in the white and black schools were substantially equal; thus, separate schools met the test under *Plessy*. Justice Felix Frankfurter asked Wilson, "Suppose this Court reversed the case?" Wilson showed that his defense of his state's practices was not a passionate one when he said, "In perfect candor, I must say to the Court that the consequences would probably not be serious."[62]

In the arguments during *Briggs*, the Justices were tough on Thurgood Marshall. He was interrupted 127 times by questions or comments from the bench. On the other hand, his adversary, John Davis, was only interrupted eleven times. That is not to say that the Court was being unfair to Marshall; probably it wanted to be sure that his arguments could withstand strong challenges, since it was his case which was the one in opposition to the established precedent. In some instances, the interruptions were supportive. For instance, Marshall pondered whether South Carolina would surreptitiously defy the Court if desegregation were ordered. Justice Frankfurter stopped him and said, "... nothing would be worse, from my point of view, than for this Court to make an abstract declaration that segregation is bad and then have it evaded by tricks."[63]

This statement by Frankfurter did not put to rest the possibility of defiance. In the *Davis* case, J. Lindsay Almond, arguing on behalf of the Prince Edward County Board of Education warned that the tradition of segregation was "deeply ingrained" in the people of Virginia, and that if that tradition were to be deposed it would "make it impossible to raise public funds through the process of taxation ... to support the public school system of Virginia." He went on that, "it would destroy the public school system ... as we know it today. That is not an idle threat."[64]

Most of the arguments in defense of segregation were not as menacing. In *Briggs*, for instance, Davis argued for the *status quo*.

He found the classification of students by race to be perfectly normal and acceptable. "I am unable to see why a state would have any further right to segregate its pupils on the ground of sex or on the ground of age or on the ground of mental capacity. If it may classify for one purpose on the basis of admitted facts, it may, according to my contention, classify it for other."[65] Milton Korman, Assistant Corporation Council for the District of Columbia, contended in *Bolling* that separate schools were "Not set up to stamp these people with a badge of inferiority. . . . There was behind these acts a kindly feeling; there was behind these acts an intention to help these people who had been in bondage."[66]

Marshall, in *Briggs*, countered such a position by stating his opinion that the only defense for the use of race as the determining factor in school assignment "is to show that Negroes as Negroes—all Negroes—are different from everyone else."[67]

The Truman Administration finally took a stand on the issue of segregated schools by filing an amicus brief written by the Assistant Solicitor General, Philip Elman, and the Attorney General, James McGranery. It supported the position for desegregation. However, it attempted to show the Court how it could so rule without overturning *Plessy*: in South Carolina, Virginia, and Delaware, blacks could be admitted to the superior white schools until such time as the black schools were made equal; in Kansas, even though the district court found that equal facilities existed, the Supreme Court did not have to limit the requirement for equality to physical facilities alone, and could order blacks into the white schools until the curriculum was equalized; in the District of Columbia case, the matter could be sent back to the district court, which could find that Congress had never intended the schools there to be segregated. The brief went on to argue that if the Supreme Court did choose to rule that "separate but equal" was a contradiction in terms, it did not have to order the immediate abandonment of segregation, but could adopt a phased approach.[68]

THE COURT ASKS SOME QUESTIONS

The Court spent six months pondering the arguments and briefs presented in these cases. From the information that scholars have been able to piece together, the Justices probably stood six to three in favor of outlawing segregation in the schools when they convened on June 8, 1953. [69] However, rather than to announce a decision, the Chief Justice Vinson asked each side to prepare briefs and oral arguments on five questions that the Court felt important to the resolution of the cases. The Justices wanted to know what evidence existed to show that Congress and the state legislatures that ratified the fourteenth amendment did or did not understand it to abolish segregation in the public schools. If they had not understood it to do so, could future Congresses do it or could the judiciary do it? Assuming that segregation was found to be unconstitutional, how should desegregation be accomplished? The Court invited the United States government to participate in the oral arguments that it scheduled for October 12, 1953. (Reargument was subsequently postponed until December.) [70]

Some Court observers viewed this "intermediate order" as an indication that the Justices were deadlocked. However, some took it to mean that the Court was preparing to outlaw segregated schools, and that it wanted to give the South some time to adjust. Many Southerners felt that the delay provided them with a final chance to equalize the black schools as a means of staving off desegregation. [71] In any event, it allowed many of the nation's schools to open the 1953–54 academic year as they had closed the preceding June — separate and unequal.

Before the rearguments could be heard, Chief Justice Vinson died, and President Dwight D. Eisenhower nominated California governor Earl Warren to be the new Chief. Although Warren was not confirmed by the Senate until March 1, 1954, he presided over the Court when it opened in the fall of 1953. [72]

Thurgood Marshall convened a group of historians to prepare the NAACP's brief. He warned them that "what looked like a 'golden gate' might turn out to be a booby trap with a bomb in it." [73] He feared that the evidence might not be as compelling as he would like. Nevertheless, the brief he submitted to the Court argued that the fourteenth amendment intended to destroy all color and caste legislation in America. The case was based on the abolitionist background of the framers as well as of those who controlled Congress. It cited the debates preceding the passage of the Civil Rights Act of 1866 in addition to those offered during the consideration of the fourteenth amendment.[74] Said New Jersey Democrat Andrew Jackson Rogers in 1865, "Under this Amendment, Congress would have power to compel the states to provide for white children and black children to attend the same schools."[75] Congressman Thaddeus Stevens had argued that it would allow Congress "to correct the unjust legislation in the states, so far that the law which operates upon one man shall operate equally on all.... Unless the Constitution shall restrain them, these states will all, I fear, keep this discrimination and crush to death the hated freedman."[76] In the upper chamber, Senator Howard had held that the amendment abolishes "all class legislation in the states and does away with the injustice of subjecting one caste of persons to a code not applicable to another."[77]

The NAACP brief contended that all of the readmitted Confederate states and nineteen of the twenty-two Union states that ratified the fourteenth amendment understood it to forbid school segregation.[78] (The Attorney General of the United States, Herbert Brownell, submitted a 600 page brief which essentially agreed with the NAACP. However, it avoided a direct call for the outlawing of segregation.)[79]

The lawyers for the school boards countered that twenty-three states did not have that understanding at the time of ratification; fourteen never even discussed the issue. In fact, nine northern and western states permitted separate schools at the time of the amendment's passage.[80] Congress had even permitted segregated schools in the District of Columbia, and it never acted to keep the Representatives and Senators from states which permitted segregation from taking their seats in Congress.[81] Thus, the segregation proponents argued that "It is not within the judicial power to construe the Fourteenth Amendment adversely to the understanding of its framers, as abolishing segregation in the public schools." And, even if it were, "Each case of such segregation must be decided upon the facts presented in the record of that case; and unless the record establishes by clear and convincing evidence that school segregation could not conceivably be warranted by local conditions" segregation cannot be abolished.[82]

Thus, it was not possible to reach a clear resolution concerning the intent of the framers and ratifiers of the fourteenth amendment. The Court was back where it had left off one year earlier. It had before it one argument that said that the *Plessy* doctrine of separate but equal had been a valid decision. It had another that held that *Plessy* was wrong, that separate never could be equal. Not until May 17, 1954, did the Supreme Court reveal its collective thoughts on the matter.

A LANDMARK DECISION

In the five months following the close of the rearguments, speculation concerning the Court's impending decision was rampant. At one extreme was the belief that the Court would find that "substantial equality" either existed or that it did not in the respective cases; thus, the Court would avoid ruling on the separate but equal premise underlying the practice of dual school systems. At the other extreme was the thought that the Court would overturn *Plessy* and would order immediate desegregation. There was, of course, in the discussion a myriad of compromise decisions between the two extremes.[83] Warnings flowed north from several southern governors. South Carolina's James F. Byrnes and Georgia's Herman Talmadge both proclaimed their willingness to close the public schools rather than to integrate them if the Court ruled an end to segregated schools.[84]

This threat foreshadowed the events of the next decade since the Court, in an opinion written by the new Chief Justice, proclaimed that "In the field of public education the doctrine of 'separate but equal' has no place."[85] Warren had worked effectively to insure that the opinion was a unanimous one since he believed that on an issue as divisive as this was, the Court needed to speak with a single voice. He also wanted the decision to be one the average person could read in its entirety; thus, it was short and was written in language addressed not to the lawyers but to the people.[86] [87] This prompted some observers to react with disappointment, since they believed the *Brown* decision to be a great one but the written opinion to be something of an anticlimax.[88]

The opinion, which covered all four state cases, briefly reviewed the history of denial of education to black Americans, the arguments concerning the intent of the fourteenth amendment and the court cases from *Plessy* to *Sweatt*. The Court then declared "We cannot turn the clock back to 1868 when the Amendment was adopted, or even to 1896 when *Plessy u. Ferguson* was written, we must consider public education in the light of its full development and its present place in American life throughout the Nation. Only in this way can it be determined if segregation in the public schools deprives these plaintiffs of the equal protection of the laws."

In so stating, the Court broke with its principle of *stare decisis* (that is, a reliance on past cases and existing interpretations) and opened the way for a new method of judicial determination — the examination of a situation in light of modern thinking.[89] Usually when the Court departs from its previous rulings, it either notes that the earlier decision (in this instance *Plessy*) was erroneous or that it was inconsistent with later decisions. However, at no place in the opinion did the Court say that *Plessy* was a misinterpretation of the Law of the Land. It had become bad, in part, because the importance of public education had grown.[90]

"Today, education is perhaps the most important function of state and local governments. Compulsory school attendance laws and the great expenditures for education both demonstrate our recognition of the importance of education to our democratic society . . . In these days, it is doubtful that any child may reasonably be expected to succeed in life if he is denied the opportunity of an education. Such an opportunity . . . is a right which must be made available to all on equal terms."

Warren then acknowledged the damage done to black children by virtue of being segregated: "To separate them from others of similar age and qualifications solely because of their race generates a feeling of inferiority . . . in a way unlikely ever to be undone." He went on to state that "whatever may have been the extent of psychological knowledge at the time of *Plessy u. Ferguson*, this finding is amply supported by modern authority." Here, Warren (via the now famous Footnote 11) made reference to seven social science works, and said, "Any language in *Plessy u. Ferguson* contrary to this finding is rejected." Cited were the following: Kenneth Clark's *Effect of Prejudice and Discrimination on Personality Develop-*

ment (1950), which held that racial attitudes are "relatively set" by the sixth grade and that "Negro children reveal most vividly and often the feelings of insecurity resulting from anticipated rejection or insult from white children"; *Personality in the Making*, edited by Helen Leland Witmer and Ruth Kotinsky (1952), which stated that black children were "ambivalent in their feelings about themselves and the group to which they belong, on the one hand accepting derogatory stereotypes of the Negro and, on the other, feeling inferior and resentful about being so classified"; the survey of social scientists conducted by Max Deutsher and Isidor Chein which had been entered in testimony in the *Davis* case; a follow-up to that study written by Chein; Theodore Brameld's "Educational Costs," which cites "the cost in delinquency, crime, [and] poor relief" of denying the Black the "right to the kind of education he desires and deserves"; E. Franklin Frazier's classic, *The Negro in the United States*, which indicated that segregation has meant inferior schools, inferior teachers for blacks, and has "caused a high rate of illiteracy to continue among Negroes"; and, finally, Gunnar Myrdal's epic study, *An American Dilemma*.[91]

The use of these seven social science sources as part of the basis for the decision was most controversial. However, it had the impact of demonstrating the predominant social science understanding that the achievement differential between whites and blacks was not genetically based but was a factor of environmental conditions, among which one of the most important was school segregation.[92] It led directly to the Court's statement that "Separate educational facilities are inherently unequal," and that "by reason of the segregation complained of, [the black children] are deprived of the equal protection of the laws guaranteed by the Fourteenth Amendment."

While the social science data was important to Warren's opinion, it would never have been sufficient to rule out segregation.[93] As William Doyle later put it, the grounding of the *Brown* decision "is that the isolation of an entire people is constitutionally wrong—is repugnant also to our most fundamental belief, to our fundamental notion of democracy."[94]

While the equal protection clause of the fourteenth amendment was the basis for the four state cases subsumed under *Brown*, that amendment applied only to the states, not to the District of Columbia. Thus, in a separate ruling in the *Bolling* case, the Court relied on the fifth amendment for its finding that "Segregation in public education is not reasonably related to any proper governmental objective, and thus it imposes on Negro children of the District of Columbia a burden that constitutes an arbitrary deprivation of their liberty in violation of the Due Process Clause."

The Court did not simultaneously issue an enforcement order to desegregate any of the schools affected by the School Desegregation Cases, but instead cited "the great variety of local conditions" which "presents problems of considerable complexity" to the formulation of a final resolution. Thus, it ordered all parties to propose appropriate solutions in briefs to be filed by October 1, 1954. It also invited the Attorney Generals of all states that permitted or required school segregation to submit briefs.

While most of the public reaction to the decision followed the Court's subsequent enforcement order (which came a year later), the media did not wait that long to express its editorial sentiment. At one end of the spectrum was the New York *Times*, which described *Brown* as a "monumental constructive stride in constitutional law and fundamental justice." That view was also held by *Life Magazine*, which observed that the Supreme Court had "at one stroke immeasurably raised the respect of other nations for the United States." At the opposite extreme were views such as that of the Washington *Star*, which condemned the decision as "a blow to fundamental American institutions." Staunch segregationists like Mississippi's Senator James Eastland also spoke out. He felt that "the Court [had] responded to a radical, pro-communist political movement."[95]

Brown II

On April 11, 1955, the parties appeared before the Court for oral arguments concerning enforcement of the *Brown* decision. Kansas, Delaware, and the District of Columbia all cited the desegregation progress made within their respective borders and, thus, held that no enforcement order was necessary. South Carolina argued that the white people of Clarendon County would not send their children to schools with blacks and pointed to New Jersey, a state more receptive to integration than South Carolina, but one which, as late as 1951, still had three segregated districts despite a law to the contrary. Similarly, Virginia predicted that "in the lifetime of those of us hale and hearty here," there would not "be enforced integration of the races in the public schools" of Prince Edward County.[96] Supportive briefs and oral arguments were presented by Arkansas, Florida, Maryland, North Carolina, Oklahoma, and Texas. Texas said it for all of the South, "It is our problem—let us solve it."[97]

The NAACP, on the other hand, argued for minimal delay in bringing about full compliance to a program of integration. They held that "gradual adjustments" would not protect the rights of those being denied an equal education, and that their clients and all other blacks so disadvantaged "should forthwith be admitted to schools of their choices."[98] To the argument that black children are not educationally competitive with whites and thus should not be rushed into classes with them, Thurgood Marshall countered "What we want from this Court is the striking down of race . . . the question is made about the educational level of children . . . so what do we think is the solution? Simple. Put the dumb colored children in with the dumb white children, and put the smart colored children with the smart white children—that is no problem."[99]

The Court's opinion was handed down on May 31, 1955.[100] Known as "*Brown II*," the unanimous enforcement order reiterated that "racial discrimination in public education is unconstitutional" and stated that "all provisions of federal, state, or local law requiring or permitting such discrimination must yield to this principle." However, "full implementation of these constitutional principles may require solution of various local school problems." Local opposition, though, would not be tolerated: "It should go without saying that the vitality of the constitutional principles cannot be allowed to yield simply because of disagreement with them." The cases were remanded to the supervision of the respective federal district courts to assure that school authorities admitted the black plaintiffs "to public schools on a racially nondiscriminatory basis with all deliberate speed."

It was this phrase, "with all deliberate speed" (a term of legal art rooted in the eighteenth century), that set the tone for what was to happen. [101] By not setting a specific date by which desegregation must be implemented, the Court was seeking a compromise that would allow progress to be made, but at a pace acceptable to the fifty-eight federal district judges serving the segregated states, persons who understood the feelings of the local white communities since they were a part of them. The Supreme Court obviously believed that moderate Southerners would rule the day and would move deliberately toward fulfillment of the Court's mandate. [102]

Sadly, none of the children involved in the *Briggs* and the *Davis* cases ever attended an integrated school. [103] When *Briggs* returned to the jurisdiction of Judge John Parker for enforcement, he held that "the Constitution does not require integration. It merely forbids discrimination." [104] The obligation of the school board was merely to remove the prohibition against blacks entering white schools. Thus, tokenism, at best, was to be the rule in Parker's district. Harry Briggs graduated from an all black high school in 1960. [105] It was not until 1965 that a black went to school with a white in Clarendon County, and, by 1979, the school district was virtually all black. [106] The states of Kansas and Delaware had made good starts toward desegregation, but after *Brown II* they slowed down their activity. In both instances, the plans submitted to the courts in late 1955 by the respective school boards were found to be "good faith" efforts and thus desegregation was permitted to proceed slowly. [107] Twenty-five years after the Supreme Court ruling, Linda Brown Smith, by then a mother of two children in the Topeka schools, led a group of blacks back into federal court, claiming that Topeka's schools remained racially imbalanced. [108] Prince Edward County and most of the rest of Virginia openly resisted desegregation for as long as they could. Only in the District of Columbia was desegregation appreciably implemented for the 1955–56 school year. [109] Among the other segregating states, the western states of Arizona, New Mexico, and Wyoming quickly ended the practice; Maryland, Missouri, and West Virginia began desegregation, and; Tennessee developed a desegregation plan. The rest held back for some time. [110]

While ten years before the *Brown* ruling only about one-third of the nation favored desegregation, by 1956 the proportion had increased to nearly 50 percent.[111] However, racism still pervaded American society. Kenneth Clark noted that people attempted "to use the *Brown* decision as a form of therapy, to free American whites and Negroes from the depths of this disease."[112] *Brown* was viewed positively by many Americans. Jack Greenberg, one of the NAACP attorneys involved in the School Desegregation Cases, reflected that it "proved to be the Declaration of Independence of its day."[113] But, like the original Declaration, the opposition did not merely surrender. It was seven years between the signing of Thomas Jefferson's document and the signing of the treaty guaranteeing American independence. It has been more than a quarter century since *Brown*.

REFERENCES

1. Kluger, R.: *Simple Justice, The History of Brown v. Board of Education and Black America's Struggle for Equality*. New York, Alfred A. Knopf, 1975, p. 118.
2. Fleming, J.: *The Lengthening Shadow of Slavery, A Historical Justification for Affirmative Action for Blacks in Higher Education*. Washington, Howard University Press, 1976, pp. 81–82.
3. Rosen, P.: *The Supreme Court and Social Science*. Urbana, University of Illinois Press, 1972, p. 122.
4. Fletcher, J.: *The Segregation Case and the Supreme Court*. Boston, Boston University, 1958, p. 2.
5. *Guinn v. United States*, 238 U.S. 347(1915).
6. Kluger, op cit., pp. 165, 173.
7. Meier, A. and Rudwick, E.: *From Plantation to Ghetto, An Interpretive History of American Negroes*. New York, Hill and Wang, 1966, p. 215.
8. McNeil, G.: To meet group needs: The transformation of Howard University School of Law, 1920–1935. In Franklin, V. and Anderson, J. (Eds.): *New Perspectives on Black Educational History*. Boston, G. K. Hall and Company, 1978, p. 164.
9. Kluger, op cit., p. 210.
10. *Gong Lum v. Rice*, 275 U.S. 78 (1927).
11. Spurlock, C.: *Education and the Supreme Court*. Urbana, University of Illinois Press, 1955, p. 187.
12. Wasby, S., D'Amato, A., and Metrailer, R.: *Desegregation from Brown to Alexander, An Exploration of Supreme Court Strategies*. Carbondale, Southern Illinois University Press, 1977, p. 29.
13. *Murray v. Maryland*. 182 A. 590 (1936), 169 Md. 478 (1937).
14. Kluger, op cit., p. 242.
15. *Missouri ex rel Gaines v. Canada*. 305 U.S. 337 (1938).

16. Rosen, op cit., p. 125.
17. Chambers, J.: Implementing the promise of *Brown*: Social science and the courts in future school litigation. In Rist, R. and Anson, R. (Eds.): *Education, Social Science and the Judicial Process*. New York, Teachers College Press, 1977, p. 37.
18. Wasby et al., op cit., pp. 51–52.
19. Bullock, H.: *A History of Negro Education in the South from 1619 to the Present*. Cambridge, Harvard University Press, 1967, p. 217.
20. Kluger, op cit., p. 412.
21. *Sipuel v. Oklahoma State Board of Regents*, 332 U.S. 631 (1948).
22. Wasby et al., op cit., p. 52.
23. *Fisher v. Hurst*, 333 U.S. 147 (1948).
24. Kluger, op cit., p. 322.
25. Miller, L.: *The Petitioners, The Story of the Supreme Court and the Negro*. New York, Pantheon Books, 1966, p. 336.
26. *Sweatt v. Painter*, 339 U.S. 629 (1950).
27. Rosen, op cit., p. 131.
28. *McLaurin v. Oklahoma State Regents for Higher Education*, 339 U.S. 637 (1950).
29. The four state cases were collectively decided by the Supreme Court as *Brown v. Board of Education of Topeka*, 347 U.S. 483 (1954).
30. *Bolling v. Sharpe*, 347 U.S. 497 (1954).
31. Blaustein, A. and Ferguson, C.: *Desegregation and the Law: The Meaning and Effect of the School Desegregation Cases*. New Brunswick, N.J., Rutgers University Press, 1957, p. 6.
32. Kluger, op cit., pp. 6–9, 16.
33. Ibid., p. 28.
34. Friedman, L. (Ed.): *Argument: The Oral Argument Before the Supreme Court in Brown v. Board of Education of Topeka, 1952–1955*. New York, Chelsea House Publishers, 1969, pp. 36–37. This volume is an edited transcript of the oral arguments presented by all parties in *Brown* and *Brown II*.
35. Friedman, op cit., p. 40.
36. Blaustein and Ferguson, op cit., p. 46.
37. Kluger, op cit., p. 593.
38. Friedman, op cit., pp. 70–73.
39. Blaustein and Ferguson, op cit., pp. 48–49.
40. Kluger, op cit., p. 569.
41. Ibid., p. 650.
42. Wasby et al., op cit., p. 65.
43. Wisdom, J.: Random remarks on the role of social science in the judicial decision-making process in the school desegregation cases. In Levin, B. and Hawley, W. (Eds.): *The Courts, Social Science and School Desegregation*: New Brunswick, N.J.: Transaction Books, 1977, p. 137.
44. Rosen, op cit., p. 183.
45. Kluger, op cit., pp. 415–416.

46. Fletcher, op cit., p. 57.
47. Ibid., p. 57.
48. Ibid., p. 55.
49. Ibid., p. 58.
50. Kluger, op cit., p. 523.
51. Carmichael, P.: *The South and Segregation*. Washington, Public Affairs Press, 1965, p. 121.
52. Kluger, op cit., p. 563.
53. Rosen, op cit., p. 136.
54. Ibid., p. 138.
55. Friedman, op cit., p. 58.
56. Ibid., p. 59.
57. Ibid., p. 61.
58. Kamisar, Y.: The school desegregation cases in retrospect. In *Argument: The Oral Argument Before the Supreme Court in Brown u Board of Education of Topeka, 1952-1955*, pp. xxvi–xxvii.
59. Clark, K.: The Social Scientists, the Brown Decision and Contemporary Confusion. In *Argument: The Oral Argument Before the Supreme Court in Brown u Board of Education of Topeka, 1952-1955*, p. xxxvii.
60. Friedman, op cit., p. 14.
61. Kluger, op cit., pp. 692–693.
62. Friedman, op cit., p. 29.
63. Ibid., p. 48.
64. Ibid., p. 99.
65. Ibid., p. 51.
66. Ibid., p. 133.
67. Ibid., p. 63.
68. Kluger, op cit., pp. 706–708.
69. Wasby et al., op cit., p. 78.
70. Friedman, op cit., pp. 177–178.
71. Wasby et al., op cit., p. 79.
72. Kluger, op cit., p. 875.
73. Wolf, E.: Courtrooms and classrooms. In Rist, R. and Anson, R. (Eds.): *Education, Social Science and the Judicial Process*. New York, Teachers College Press, 1977, p. 97.
74. Fletcher, op cit., p. 20.
75. Blaustein and Ferguson, op cit., p. 59.
76. Fletcher, op cit., p. 25.
77. Ibid., p. 27.
78. Zeigler, B. (Ed.): *Desegregation and the Supreme Court*. Boston, D. C. Heath and Co., 1958, p. 70.
79. Kluger, op cit., pp. 823–824.
80. Zeigler, op cit., p. 71.
81. Harris, R.: The constitution, education and segregation. In Zeigler, B. (Ed.): *Desegregation and the Supreme Court*, Boston, D.C. Heath and Co., 1958, p. 75.

82. Zeigler, op cit., pp. 71–72.
83. Leflar, R. and Davis, W.: The Supreme Court Cases. In Zeigler, B. (Ed.): *Desegregation and the Supreme Court*, Boston, D.C. Heath and Co., 1958, p. 65.
84. Spurlock, op cit., p. 210.
85. *Brown v Board of Education of Topeka*, 347 U.S. 483 (1954).
86. Wilkinson, J.: *From Brown to Bakke: The Supreme Court and School Integration: 1954–1978*, New York: Oxford University Press, 1979, p. 30.
87. Craven, Jr., J.: The impact of social science evidence on the judge: A personal comment. In Zeigler, B. (Ed.): *The Courts, Social Science and School Desegregation*, Boston, D.C. Heath and Co., 1958, p. 153.
88. Harris, op cit., p. 83.
89. Irion, H.: The constitutional clock: A horological inquiry. In Humphrey, H. (Ed.): *School Desegregation: Documents and Commentaries*. New York, Thomas Y. Crowell Company, 1964, pp. 49–50.
90. Harris, op cit., p. 82.
91. Carmichael, op cit., pp. 111, 119, 131, 136.
92. Rosen, op cit., pp. 186–187.
93. Wisdom, op cit., p. 142.
94. Doyle, W.: Social science evidence in court cases. In Rist, R. and Anson, R. (Eds.): *Education, Social Science and the Judicial Process*, New York, Teachers College Press, 1977, p. 13.
95. Blaustein and Ferguson, op cit., pp. 6, 8, 12.
96. Kluger, op cit., pp. 916, 924–926.
97. Ibid., p. 927.
98. Blaustein and Ferguson, op cit., p. 169.
99. Friedman, op cit., p. 402.
100. *Brown v Board of Education of Topeka*, 349 U.S. 294 (1955).
101. Freund, P.: Understanding the school decision. In Zeigler, B. (Ed.): *Desegregation and the Supreme Court*, Boston, D.C. Heath and Co., 1958, p. 85.
102. Peltason, J.: *Fifty-Eight Lonely Men, Southern Federal, Judges and School Desegregation*. New York, Harcourt, Brace and World, 1961, p. 18.
103. Miller, op cit., p. 351.
104. Peltason, op cit., p. 22.
105. Ibid., p. 16.
106. New York *Times*, May 18, 1979.
107. Fletcher, op cit., p. 79.
108. New York *Times*, November 30, 1979.
109. Miller, op cit., p. 353.
110. Spurlock, op cit., pp. 218–219.
111. Wolf, op cit., p. 99.
112. Clark, op cit., p. xl.
113. Wasby et al., op cit., p. 93.

CHAPTER 3

TOO MUCH DELIBERATION,
NOT ENOUGH SPEED

A society that for centuries had devoted much of its energy toward keeping its black population in a peasant caste was not about to yield readily to the will of the nine men who made up the Supreme Court. Much of the initial criticism of the *Brown* decision focused on the Court's apparent reliance on social science data rather than on the law. While there were those who lamented that the constitutional rights of blacks seemed to rest on the "flimsy foundations" of data "no more scientific than the evidence presented in favor of racial prejudice," there were others who attempted to remind America that "Hitler was always able to commandeer social scientists to support Nazi theses."[1, 2, 3] Most Southerners believed, as did Peter Carmichael, that the *Brown* decision was "not founded on law, since there is no applicable [federal] law saying that separate schools are unequal."[4]

Those who make and enforce the law were equally as outspoken. The theme of outside agitation was a common one, and those favoring a change in the Southern *status quo* were called "socialists" or "communists." In fact, the Attorney General of the State of Georgia attacked the decision as being based on the writings of such enemies of democracy.[5] The belief that the Supreme Court's ruling was illegitimate led Senator James O. Eastland of Mississippi to proclaim to his constituents, "You are not required to obey any court which passes out such a ruling. In fact, you are obliged to defy it."[6]

And defy it they did, not only in Mississippi but throughout the South. Antidesegregation referenda were passed in Georgia, Louisiana, and Mississippi in 1954 and two years later in Alabama, North Carolina, and Virginia.[7] Between 1954 and 1958, eleven Southern states enacted 145 statutes designed to thwart the *Brown* ruling.[8] Georgia, Alabama, Virginia, and Texas all attempted to revive the principle of "nullification"; the claim, lost in the Civil War, that a state could void a federal requirement within its borders.[9] The South Carolina legislature, for instance, held that the states never gave the federal government the power to prohibit separate but equal education, and, thus, "The State of South Carolina as a loyal and sovereign State of the Union will exercise the powers reserved to it under the Constitution . . . to protect its sovereignty and the rights of its people" to maintain segregated schools.[10] The measure passed by the Virginia General Assembly claimed that "the Commonwealth is under no obligation to accept supinely an unlawful decree of the Supreme Court of the United States."[11] Subsequently, a special commission established by that legislature to study the meaning of *Brown* concluded "that grave violence is done to the structure of constitutional government, and ominous precedents are set . . . when the Court's action is accepted without sincere and continuing protest."[12]

At the Congressional level, all of the Southern senators except Majority Leader Lyndon B. Johnson of Texas, Albert Gore, and Estes Kefauver (both of Tennessee), as well as 101 Southern Congressmen (all but twenty-three from that region), signed what came to be known as the Southern Manifesto.[13] Drafted by Senator Sam Ervin, best remembered for his role as Chairman of the Senate Watergate Committee, the resolution proclaimed that "the decision of the Supreme Court in the school cases [is] a clear abuse of judicial power" since "the original Constitution does not mention education" nor does any Amendment. It went on to note that the decision created: "Chaos and confusion in the states principally affected. It is destroying the amicable relations between the white and Negro races that have been created through 90 years of patient effort by the good people of both races. It has planted hatred and suspicion where there has been heretofore friendship and understanding."[14, 15]

Without a doubt, such a statement by so many members of Congress served to blunt any action that an already reluctant President Eisenhower was likely to take to enforce the wishes of the Court. It also gave heart to those who felt resistance was justified by any means. In rationalizing the violence that accompanied desegregation in one town, an attorney referred to the Manifesto: "What the hell do you expect these people to do when they have some 90 odd congressmen [saying] you're a southern hero if you defy the Supreme Court."[16] The extralegal activities of the Ku Klux Klan once more became a fact of Southern life, and a new organization, the White Citizens' Council, appeared in communities throughout the old Confederacy. The first Council was established less than two months after *Brown* in Indianola, Mississippi. Three years later it boasted a large membership including 80,000 in Mississippi and 100,000 in Alabama.[17] Composed of the leading community figures, these locally based groups served to blunt any school committees which felt compelled to comply with federal court desegregation orders. Their literature was often inflammatory and accused integrationists of being communists and, even worse, Jews![18] [19] Together, the Klan and the Councils served as a powerful block to blacks and their white sympathizers.

EARLY PROGRESS

However, in the post-*Brown* era, blacks were not as willing to endure the pain of racial injustice in the schools as they were before.[20] They kept up the pressure through the courts, and, slowly, change began to take place, despite the reluctance of many state court judges and some federal judges in the Southern districts to carry out the *Brown* mandate.[21] [22]

By fall, 1955, the District of Columbia, two school districts in Arkansas, nine in Delaware, one in Maryland, two in Missouri, two in Texas and one in West Virginia had removed restrictions against the education of whites and blacks in the same school. In the latter state, all of the districts which had both black and white children were desegregated shortly thereafter.[23] Washington, Baltimore, St. Louis, Wilmington, Louisville, and San Antonio were the first important cities to abandon their segregation policies. By September, 1956, there were over 700 districts that had moved toward the removal of racial barriers. Nearly all were in the Border states, Oklahoma, and western Texas.[24] [25] However, Alabama, Florida, Georgia, Louisiana, Mississippi, North Carolina, South Carolina, and Virginia still maintained strict segregation in all of their school districts.

It should be noted that, in many instances, desegregation was of a token nature; only a few black students were enrolled in formerly all-white schools. While these school districts may have removed the official racial status of their schools, they employed a variety of means to keep black and white children separated. The most common were "freedom of choice plans" where students could choose to enroll in any school they desired. However, no whites ever chose a black school and there were almost never any seats available for blacks who chose to enroll in a white school. In other instances, the gerrymandering of school attendance zones resulted in one-race schools. Another policy, which was racially neutral on its face but which had a segregatory effect was known as the "pupil placement program." Students were placed in schools according to the ability of the school to meet their educational needs or match their psychological profiles. Not surprisingly given the history of these districts, blacks and whites somehow were never found to have compatible needs and were, thus, placed in separate schools.

Benjamin Muse, a former member of the Virginia Senate and a racial moderate, wrote that the reluctance to desegregate was stirred by three fears: first, the belief that integration was a communist plot to undermine America; second, that racial contact in the schools would lead to interracial marriage and ultimately to racial amalgamation; and, third, that a well educated black would provide competition to low income whites for jobs.[26] Thus, resistance was tenacious. (A study by Melvin Tumin indicated that it was the young, poorly educated, underincome white who resisted desegregation most strongly.[27])

In the relatively few districts that did move to desegregate in the early years after *Brown*, most did so in an orderly fashion. However, serious violence did break out in a small number of instances, most notably in Milford, Delaware; Sturgis, Kentucky; Mansfield, Texas; and Clinton, Tennessee. In the case of Clinton, whites were frenzied, in the fall of 1956, by KKK organizer Asa Carter and by John Kasper, an avowed segregationist from New Jersey who travelled throughout the South to deliver his message. The enrollment of twelve blacks in the previously lily-white high school led not only to cross burnings and rallies, but to the deployment of 633

battle-equipped National Guardsmen who, with fixed bayonets
and supported by seven tanks and three armored personnel carri-
ers, dispersed a mob of 1000 angry whites. Shortly thereafter, the
home of a black family was bombed, and a white minister who
walked to school with six black children was severely beaten. Two
years later, Clinton High School was blown up by persons who
still held to the past. [28] (One irony of this situation was that Kasper
was able to escape conviction, as he was in other instances which
were similarly ugly. Congress did not move to enact a law intended
to stop those who travelled across state lines to incite lawlessness
until more than a decade later when it did so to retard the spread
of the Black Power movement.)

Little Rock

Perhaps the most notorious outburst of that period concerned
the desegregation of Central High School in Little Rock, Arkansas
in 1957, an instance which eventually reached the United States
Supreme Court. [29] Three days after the Court ruled in *Brown*, the
Little Rock District School Board stated that it would comply with
the landmark ruling. A year later, it approved a desegregation
plan that was to begin in the fall of 1957 at the high school level.
According to Superintendent of Schools, Virgil T. Blossom, seventeen black students were carefully chosen, based on their mental
ability and past records in school, to enroll in Central High. [30] By
the time that classes began in September, 1957, only nine of the
original seventeen were still interested in being among the first
blacks to join the student body at Central. Prior to the opening of
school, the local White Citizens' Council placed ads in the newspapers citing all of the evils that desegregation would bring:
integrated dances, integrated showers and rest rooms, integrated
field trips and club activities, and integrated love scenes in student
dramatic performances! [31] The evening before the opening, Governor Orville Faubus, originally elected as a moderate, appeared
on television to announce that he had activated the National
Guard since he believed that order could not be maintained if
desegregation occurred; the Guard was to be outside of the school
to preclude entrance by the nine black children.

On the morning of September 2, a hostile white crowd hurled insults at the black children as they approached the school. One of them, Elizabeth Eckford, recalled that day. She had been covered with spit and had been the object of vocal abuse but "wasn't too scared because all the time I kept thinking that the guards would protect me." When she neared the soldiers, they raised their bayonets and moved in her direction. Simultaneously, the crowd seemed to collapse on her, someone yelled, "Lynch her, lynch her." Eckford turned back toward the guardsmen but saw that they were not committed to her safety. Somehow she made her way to a bus stop bench. From the crowd came, "Drag her over to this tree! Let's take care of this nigger." Before that virulent American could have his way, a white woman hustled Eckford onto a bus and sat with her as the bus drove from the scene. [32]

On September 14, the Governor met with the vacationing President Eisenhower in Newport, Rhode Island, and Faubus agreed to follow the directive of the federal district court judge who was studying the occurrances of the preceding weeks. [33] That judge subsequently found that the desegregation of the high school would have occurred peacefully, but had been "thwarted" by Faubus's use of the National Guard. Outside the courtroom, a leader of the segregationist Mothers League of Central High School proclaimed defiantly, "I don't give a damn what that stupid little judge says, my children are never going to school with monkeys." [34] Three hours later, Faubus withdrew the troops but called upon the blacks to "refrain from seizing upon that right to [attend Central] until such time as there is assurance that it can be accomplished in a peaceful manner." [35]

Nevertheless, on September 23, the black students entered the high school. An uncontrollable white mob attempted to gain entrance to the school in order to remove the blacks. In protest against the desegregation, the white students walked out of the school. For safety purposes, it became necessary to withdraw the black students.

President Eisenhower, in the first show of federal force to promote the promise of *Brown*, gave the Secretary of Defense authority to enforce the orders of the district court judge. He nationalized 10,000 members of the Arkansas National Guard, and authorized the Secretary "to use such of the armed forces of the United States as he may deem necessary."[36] One thousand paratroopers from the 101st Airborne Division were quickly brought into the city. Faubus referred to these troops as "occupation forces."[37] Their presence enabled the black children to return to Central High School for the remainder of the school year.

The school board returned to federal court in the spring and asked a different judge for a stay of the desegregation order for a period of two and one-half years in order to quell the problems of the preceding academic year. The judge concurred, but the case was immediately appealed. The Supreme Court, in a special late-August session called so that a decision might be reached prior to the opening of the fall, 1958 school year, promptly heard oral arguments in the case of *Cooper v. Aaron.*

When it ruled, the Court (in a decision signed by all nine Justices — something unprecedented in the Court's history) stated its belief that the school board had acted in good faith throughout the period since it initially announced its intention to comply with *Brown*, but that "the actions of other state agencies responsible for [the noncompliance] compel us to reject the Board's legal position." The Justices went on to hold that the constitutional rights of the black students "are not to be sacrificed or yielded to the violence and disorder which have followed upon the actions of the Governor and the Legislature." In a concurring opinion, Justice Felix Frankfurter went further: "Violent resistance to law cannot be made a legal reason for its suspension without loosening the fabric of our society." Thus, the *Cooper* decision set a precedent requiring the state to provide protection for individuals attempting to exercise their constitutional rights.

The aftermath of the decision did not, however, live up to its expectations as Faubus closed all three Little Rock high schools rather than desegregate them.[38] The following summer he declared that it would take federal force "using live ammunition" to desegregate the high schools. But then a series of Labor Day bombings raised the consciousness of reasonable citizens of Little Rock and the avid segregationists began to lose ground.[39] Eventually, the schools reopened on a desegregated basis. Sadly, no one was ever prosecuted for their acts of violence during this several year period.[40]

Massive Resistance

Violent outbursts were by no means the norm in the South's effort to maintain segregated schools. In Virginia, for instance, a campaign of "massive resistance" orchestrated through legislative and gubernatorial acts was successful for many years in holding back the tide of equal educational opportunity. Virginians, by and large, believed that the Supreme Court had violated the state's rights principle which had theretofore existed in America. James J. Kilpatrick, then editor of the Richmond *News Leader*, best captured this sentiment in an editorial written in 1955: "[The Supreme Court] repudiated the Constitution, spit upon the Tenth Amendment, and rewrote the fundamental law of this land to suit their own gauzy concepts of sociology. If it be said that now the South is flouting the law, let it be said to the high court, You taught us how."[41]

In a special twenty-seven day session in 1956, the Virginia legislature enacted twenty-three measures aimed at thwarting school desegregation and at ridding the state of the NAACP. One important statute provided that in the event of the enrollment of any child in a school established for the other race, "such school is closed and removed from the public school system," though its teachers and principals would continue to be compensated. Students who chose to attend private schools would be assisted with public funds.[42] Proponents of this approach hailed the "freedom of choice" made possible by these measures; they rejected the notion that public taxation in support of private schools is a denial of the right of the people to control that which they collectively fund.[43] More on their minds was the keeping of their school-aged white children away from black children.

In August, 1958, twenty-two black high school children in Warren County applied for admission to the public white school. It was not long before they had the backing of a federal court order. But, Governor Lindsay Almond (who had earlier argued on Virginia's side before the Supreme Court in the *Davis* case and who, in his speech on the occasion of his inauguration as governor proclaimed, "Against these massive attacks [on Virginia's sovereignty], we must marshall a massive resistance") ordered the school closed. He subsequently did the same in Charlottesville and Norfolk. [44] In January, 1959, the State Supreme Court of Appeals and the federal district court both found the law permitting such actions invalid, and the schools were subsequently reopened on a desegregated basis. [45]

The Virginia legislature was quick to respond. It repealed the compulsory school attendance requirements and provided tuition assistance directly to students who chose to enroll in private schools. [46] Several months later, the Fourth Circuit Court of Appeals ordered the Prince Edward County schools to desegregate by September, 1959. Recall that these schools had been the subject of one of the cases decided at the same time as *Brown*. In the four years since the enforcement order (*Brown II*), not one black had attended school with a white in that county. Rather than permit that, the county supervisors closed the schools and reduced taxes by over 50 percent. The Prince Edward Education Foundation opened six "private" elementary schools and two high schools to serve the white population. Their students received tuition grants of $125 to $150 from the state and another $100 from the county. Parents also received tax credits for their contributions to these schools. Once more, the black community took the county to court.

Until 1963, most of the black children stayed home. That year the Kennedy Administration helped to establish a school for blacks. At first, attendance was below expectations. Many parents, too poor to afford school clothes for all of their children, sent them to school on alternate days so that they could share the clothes. When school officials recognized the source of the low attendance, they were able to distribute enough clothes to raise the participation level of the children. [47]

It was not until 1964 that the matter was resolved by the United States Supreme Court. [48] J. Segar Gravatt, attorney for the county, claimed that the "freedom of choice" plan was intended not to avoid integration but to promote liberty. Chief Justice Warren asked whether "Those little colored children who have been without education" had freedom. Gravatt replied, "They've had liberties." Warren repeated, "No, have they had freedom?" Gravatt answered in the affirmative whereupon Warren shot back, "Freedom to go through life without an education." [49] The Court, in a decision written by Justice Hugo Black, found that Prince Edward County had had sufficient time to desegregate its schools, but instead chose to be obstructionist. It struck down the practice of providing tuition grants and tax credits to support private schools in lieu of public schools, and ordered a reopening of the public schools equally accessible to children of all races. For blacks in Prince Edward County and throughout Virginia, progress had been slow and the struggle hard, but after 13 years of litigation, the school doors began to open.

The schools were equally impermiable elsewhere. Rulings such as the one by the Florida Supreme Court which held that "all deliberate speed" did not require action so soon, provided support for deliberate delay.[50] By the time John F. Kennedy assumed his presidency, Mississippi had yet to desegregate a single school, but continued to claim that it was providing equal schools despite the evidence that four times as much was being spent per white student as per black. Alabama and Louisiana also maintained lily-white schools. In eight other Southern states, less than 7000 of the nearly two million black pupils were in desegregated schools. By the time that *Brown* was ten years old, less than one-tenth of 1 percent of black students in the Deep South attended classes with whites.[51, 52]

DESEGREGATION GOES TO COLLEGE

At the collegiate level, within three years after *Brown*, token desegregation had come to 52 percent of the formerly all-white public colleges in the South, but Florida, Georgia, Mississippi, and South Carolina remained totally closed to blacks.[53] [54] In February, 1956, Autherine Lucy briefly attended the University of Alabama but was suspended "for her own safety" when a mob of 1000 students gathered on campus. Subsequently, she was ordered readmitted by a federal judge, but was immediately expelled for having accused the University of complicity in the mob action. The University was not finally desegregated until June, 1963, when President Kennedy issued a proclamation ordering Governor George Wallace to obey a court order which had admitted two black students to the Tuscaloosa campus. Deputy Assistant Attorney

General Nicholas Katzenbach accompanied the two students to campus. Symbolically, Wallace, himself, blocked the doorway as the students attempted to enter. Kennedy then federalized the Alabama National Guard, and, later that day, the students re-appeared with 100 guardsmen. Wallace, again in the doorway, read a statement of protest, but stepped aside and allowed the students to enter. [55]

While few incidents in recent times have been as dramatic as that scene in which a most defiant state's rights governor yielded to the power and authority of the federal government, an earlier incident at the University of Mississippi in Oxford did more, perhaps, to shape the thinking of the American people. [56] When James Meredith attempted to enroll there in 1961 he needed the support of 320 federal marshalls. A massive riot involving thousands of whites ensued. Ironically, the mob was led by former General Edwin Walker who had been in command of the federal troops sent to Little Rock several years earlier. A federalized National Guard contingent as well as regular Army troops were brought in. By the time the rioting had ended, two persons had been killed and 375 injured (including 166 marshalls, 29 of whom had been shot). Within a few days, 30,000 troops had been deployed in Oxford. Many remained on the scene for nearly two years. [57]

THE CIVIL RIGHTS ACT OF 1964

The ugliness of the response of Mississippians to the enroll-ment of Meredith, as well as similar outbursts when blacks in that state and other Deep South states attempted to assert other rights (i.e. Birmingham and Selma, in particular), were seen on television and, thus, engraved a sharp image in the minds of most Northerners and Westerners. They gave impetus to the Civil Rights Act pro-posed by President Kennedy. [58] However, it was not until after Kennedy's assassination that the bill was finally passed by Congress. Signed on July 2, the Civil Rights Act of 1964 was an omnibus bill that owed its strength to President Lyndon B. Johnson who was able to maneuver it nearly intact through a Congress that was being immobilized by a Southern filibuster. [59]

The Civil Rights Act included sections on voting rights, desegregation of public facilities and public accommodations (including restaurants, hotels, and theaters), and equal employment opportunity. Title IV concerned the desegregation of public education and gave the Attorney General the power to bring suit in federal court against offending school districts. That section of the bill, however, did not: "... empower any official or any court of the United States to issue any order seeking to achieve a racial balance in any school by requiring the transportation of pupils or students from one school to another or one school district to another in order to achieve racial balance...."[60] Thus, Congress had stated its belief that desegregation of schools was required but that the use of busing to bring about full integration was not. (The Supreme Court would have more to say about this matter.)

Title VI required nondiscrimination in any program which received federal funds—and most public schools and colleges as well as many private ones receive federal dollars. Any such program found to be discriminatory could have its federal funds removed and could be made ineligible for federal money until such time as it corrected the problem.

Thus, the Civil Rights Act provided a double blow to school systems for which there was evidence of a public policy promoting the continued maintenance of racially identifiable schools. The Commissioner of Education could withhold federal funds and the Attorney General could bring suit in federal court. The intention here was to relieve black parents and black organizations of the financial obligation of bringing costly and drawn out litigation concerning their constitutional right to an equal education. The wealth and power of the federal government were henceforth officially in the fray.

The Barriers Begin to Fall

In the decade following the implementation of the Civil Rights Act, the Justice Department initiated 500 school desegregation suits, and the Department of Health, Education, and Welfare brought 600 more actions.[61] HEW issued guidelines that called for all grades to be desegregated by the fall of 1967. Once in place, these guidelines brought about more desegregation in four months than had occurred as a result of federal court activity in the preceding ten years. In fact, the color barrier in those districts with the strongest resistance to desegregation was, at least in a token way, broken within a year. Even in Virginia, two years of enforcement of the Civil Rights Act resulted in the admission of one-quarter of the state's black pupils to schools formerly reserved for whites.[62] [63] However, advances that went beyond tokenism required court action and were painstakingly slow.

Several important cases were decided by the United States Supreme Court in the late 1960s and early 1970s. One by one, they removed the obstructions to desegregation that had been put in place by resistant school boards and legislatures. In the first of this series, *Bradley v. Richmond School Board* (known as *Bradley I*), the Court said that "delays in desegregating school systems are no longer tolerable."[64] It quickly put this finding into practice when it overruled "grade a year" desegregation plans.[65]

Three years later, in 1968, the Court finally struck down the "freedom of choice" approach to desegregation.[66] In the oral arguments during the case of *Green v. County School Board of New Kent County* (Virginia), Chief Justice Warren asked the lawyer for the school board, "Isn't the net result [of the freedom of choice plan] that while they took down the fence, they put booby traps in place of it?" Thurgood Marshall, who had been appointed to the Supreme Court by President Johnson, followed by asking, "Assuming a Negro parent wants to send his child to the . . . previously white school and his employer said, 'I suggest you do not do it,' would that be freedom of choice?"[67] The answers were apparent since the freedom of choice plan had resulted in 85 percent of the black students remaining in all-black schools. The Court ruled that this passive approach was no longer acceptable, that school boards had an "affirmative duty to take whatever steps might be necessary" to end segregation. In the unanimous opinion written by Justice William Brennan, the Court stated that "the burden on a school board today is to come forward with a plan that promises realistically to work, and promises realistically to work *now*." Freedom of choice, in and of itself, was not an acceptable approach. In a companion case from Tennessee, the Court ruled that a "free-transfer" plan, which assigned a child to a given school but permitted subsequent transfer to any other school on a space available basis, was equally unacceptable since it, too, failed to bring an end to the dual school system. [68]

Thwarted by the Supreme Court, segregationists sought to bring pressure upon the Executive Branch to delay the enforcement of desegregation orders. In one such instance, President Nixon sought to promote his "Southern Strategy"—the attempt to move the traditionally Democratic South into the Republican fold—by responding to the wishes of Senator John Stennis of Mississippi; Nixon had his HEW Secretary write to the chief judge of the Fifth Circuit Court of Appeals stating that immediate desegregation would result in "chaos, confusion and a catastrophic educational setback."[69] That court granted a three month delay of a Mississippi case, forcing the NAACP to raise the matter with the Supreme Court. For the first time in years, the federal government was openly on the side of the Southern intransigents.[70] However, the Supreme Court was not influenced and, in *Alexander v. Holmes County Board of Education*[71], overturned the Fifth Circuit and ordered a Louisiana school district to desegregate within eight weeks.[72]

As a result of these actions, the intent of the Supreme Court became clear to the Fifth Circuit. In the next nine months, that Circuit issued 166 desegregation orders. By 1971, 44 percent of the South's black school children were attending schools that were majority white.[73]

On April 20, 1971, the Supreme Court, led by its new Chief Justice Warren Burger, issued another in its series of school-related rulings.[74] This case, *Swann v. Charlotte-Mecklenburg Board of Education*, was to become a benchmark case, one whose impact is being felt across the country today. It was here that the Court first discussed the question of busing as a desegregation tool.

In the school district that encompasses both the city of Charlotte, North Carolina and the surrounding Mecklenburg County, 71 percent of the students were white and 29 percent were black. Nearly nine out of every ten blacks in this, nation's forty-third largest district, attended schools in the city, and the majority of these were enrolled in all-black schools. The local federal district court, unsatisfied with the school board's desegregation plan, appointed Doctor John Finger to prepare one for the court. Under the order finally rendered by the district court, nine black inner city elementary schools were grouped with twenty-four white suburban schools; blacks in grades one through four and whites in grades five and six were to be bused to produce a set of elementary schools were from nine to 38 percent black. Attendance zones for the junior highs and high schools were also altered in order to produce schools which, as closely as possible, would reflect the overall racial makeup of the system.

The Supreme Court, in its final unanimously decided school desegregation case, upheld the order of the district court. In so doing, it accepted the use of mathematical ratios as a part of the school board's plan: "School authorities . . . might well conclude . . . that in order to prepare students to live in a pluralistic society each school should have a prescribed ratio of Negro to white students reflecting the proportion for the district as a whole. To do this as an educational policy is within the broad discretionary powers of school authorities; absent a finding of a constitutional violation, however, that would not be within the authority of a federal court." But, the Charlotte-Mecklenburg School District was one that had been previously segregated by law and the dual system had never been effectively dismantled. Thus, a constitutional violation was present and court-ordered ratios were possible here. The Supreme Court did note, though, that every school need not exactly match the district-wide ratio and that "some small number of one-race or virtually one-race, schools within a district is not in and of itself the mark of a [segregated] system." However, it stated that "awareness of the racial composition of the whole system is likely to be a useful starting point in shaping a remedy to correct past constitutional violations."

The Court upheld the pairing and grouping of schools in distant noncontiguous parts of the district to be acceptable: "All things being equal, with no history of discrimination, it might well be desirable to assign pupils to schools nearest their homes. But all things are not equal in a system that has been deliberately constructed and maintained to enforce racial segregation." This conclusion led the Court to hold that "desegregation plans cannot be limited to the walk-in school," and that school authorities could be required by the courts "to employ bus transportation as one tool of school desegregation," buses which would transport whites to formerly black schools and blacks to formerly white schools.

Thus, the *Swann* decision permitted the use of mathematical ratios, the pairing and grouping of schools, and the use of busing. It did not, however, require that every school in the district be involved in the plan.

The decision came as a surprise and a disappointment to millions of Americans who had expected the Burger Court to depart from the tradition of the Warren Court. The New York *Times* reported that "Chief Justice Burger has served notice to those inside and outside the [Nixon] Administration . . . that he does not intend to allow the Supreme Court to be undercut or influenced by political pressures in the area of civil rights."[75]

The realization that the days of dual public school systems in the South were all but over led to the establishment of as many as 2500 private schools dedicated to a white-only education.[76] In Memphis, for example, the forty-one private schools in 1970 had grown to more than 125 five years later; enrollments more than tripled to over 37,000.[77] The arguments that the parents of these children maintain against busing and in favor of the neighborhood school ring hollow when it is understood that high proportions either ride a school bus each day, take public transportation to and from school, or are driven in the family automobile or via carpool.[78] Obviously, it is not the bus but the blacks that serve as the *raison d'etre* of these schools. Since 1972, the Internal Revenue Service has attempted to force the segregationist academies (as they are known) to comply with federal nondiscrimination mandates or lose their status as tax-exempt institutions.[79] Many of these schools are sectarian and, thus, claim that the IRS is interfering with their right to the free exercise of religion. Several brought the IRS to court, but, in 1977, lost their case.[80] Nevertheless, they continue to stand firm. One such institution, Bob Jones University in Greenville, South Carolina, not only lost its tax exemption but also lost the right for its students to collect benefits from the Veterans Administration.[81]

The impact of the establishment of the segregationist academies has only been slight, however. A national survey of those school

districts that enrolled at least 1500 students and had at least 5 percent minority enrollment revealed in 1977 that the South had the
lowest levels of segregation among school systems across the country. Only 2.5 percent of the districts in the Southeast were highly
segregated, compared to 6.8 percent nationally, and 85.3 percent
had low levels of segregation compared to 79.2 percent nationally.
(In 1968, the Southeast had the worst statistics in the country.[82])
This dramatic change was the result of the federal activity which
was focused on that part of the country, perhaps at the expense of
attention to other parts of the nation.

FOCUS ON DE FACTO SEGREGATION

Thus, it was reasonable that the attention of HEW and the
courts turn northward and westward. School districts in those
areas were not segregated by state law as was the case in the
Southern and Border states, but segregation developed nonetheless as has been discussed in an earlier chapter. It was generally
accepted that this *de facto* segregation was the responsibility of
housing patterns and not the result of actions taken by public
officials. Farley's study of the nation's largest cities is revealing.
He assigned each city a segregation index (on a 0 to 100 scale)
according to the percentage of whites or blacks who would have to
move from their own neighborhood to another one in order that
each neighborhood in the city would reflect the city's overall
racial makeup; he used the same approach to describe the segregation in the schools. Using the 1970 census, he found that the
neighborhoods in New York City were 77 percent segregated;
using 1972 enrollment figures, he found that the schools there to
be 54 percent segregated. In Los Angeles, the indices were 91
percent and 87 percent, in Chicago 93 percent and 93 percent, in
Philadelphia 84 percent and 81 percent, in Detroit 82 percent and
78 percent, in Boston 84 percent and 74 percent, in Cleveland 90
percent and 92 percent, in Pittsburgh 86 percent and 74 percent,
in Minneapolis 80 percent and 71 percent, and so on.[83] Thus,
there was a strong relationship between highly segregated neighborhoods and highly segregated schools.

The nation's neighborhoods did not develop along racial and

ethnic lines by accident. Until 1948, the official policy of the Federal Housing Authority encouraged residential segregation.[84] Also, as has been discussed in relation to Chicago's South Side, realtors continually engaged in practices designed to keep the races in separate neighborhoods. A 1971 study by the Maryland legislature indicated that racial steering and "blockbusting" was intense throughout that state and had been a major factor in Prince George's County, a Washington suburb that resisted meaningful school desegregation until 1973. There was nothing subtle about the practice as was evident by the inclusion in the newspaper real estate ads of such wording as "whites only" or "colored home."[85] A 1978 study conducted by the United States Department of Housing and Urban Development indicated that only one out of every four blacks is given the same choice as a white person when attempting to rent an apartment. Additionally, HUD found that two of every three blacks confront discrimination when seeking to buy a house.[86] Such discrimination is evident throughout our nation's suburbs where the number of blacks living there is far lower than the number of blacks who could afford to live there. In Chicago, only one-sixth of blacks with sufficient incomes were suburbanites; in Philadelphia only one-third, and in Boston one-fifth. In more than half of the suburban communities surrounding Detroit, there were fewer than five black families.[87] [88]

Thus, residential segregation in the North and West, both within the cities and between them and their suburbs, continues to be strong. This has led many living in those areas to believe that the use of the neighborhood school approach was not one that was intended to be invidious and, thus, does not require any correction other than that in which residents might choose to engage. Southerners have decried the hypocrisy of those who denounced racial segregation in the old Confederacy but countenanced it in their own communities.[89] Not all Northerners, however, supported the existence of dual school systems where they lived. By 1963, there was active and organized pressure from blacks and whites for desegregation programs in sixty cities in the North and West.[90] New Haven actually began implementation of a voluntary desegregation plan in 1964 on the belief that "racially unbalanced schools are educationally unsound."[91] Unfortunately, though, this was not the norm, and it was necessary for court action to be initiated elsewhere. In New Rochelle, New York, a federal judge warned that "compliance with the Supreme Court's edict was not to be less forthright in the north than in the south." He ordered that desegregation occur by the 1961–1962 school year.[92] Similarly, HEW sought to bring pressure to Northern school districts in the 1960s. Under the provisions of the 1964 Civil Rights Act, $32 million in federal funds was temporarily held back in Chicago in 1965 since 95 percent of that city's black children attended segregated schools. Under intense political pressure, the funds were restored. Subsequently, the U.S. Commissioner of Education and the Assistant Secretary of HEW both resigned.[93]

ALTERNATIVES TO BUSING

For a time, the pressure to desegregate Northern and Western school systems subsided. As it did, the community control movement began to gather momentum. It was spurred on by the general demand in the 1960s for greater citizen participation in the political and governmental processes. What whites were demanding in the suburbs, blacks were beginning to demand in the cities.[94] Further, many blacks began to conclude that desegregation would not be a reality and, thus, began to question the desirability of continuing to tilt at that windmill. They began to believe that it would require strong parental involvement in order for their children to become well educated. Said the Congress of Racial Equality: "Whether or not a given school is inferior or superior has nothing, as such, to do with whether or not it has an admixture of racial and/or ethnic groups, but has everything to do with who controls that school and in whose best interest it is controlled."[95]

The community control movement reached a climax in New York City in 1968. In the late 1960s, the New York schools were majority black and Puerto Rican yet there were only four black principals and twelve black assistant principals, indicative of the fact that minorities had little control over the schools.[96] Under an experimental program, a community school district was established in the Ocean Hill-Brownsville section of Brooklyn, one of the worst slums in the country. At the time, the United States

Department of Labor estimated that a family of four needed an income of at least $10,000 in order to maintain a reasonable standard of living; in Ocean Hill-Brownsville, over half of the households had incomes of less than $4000. Of the district's 100,000 students 73 percent were black; 24 percent were Puerto Rican. Sixty percent were at least three years behind in basic skill achievement; the high school drop out rate was over 70 percent.[97] The new Community School Board, seeking to bring to the schools teachers who would improve those dismal statistics, fired thirteen teachers and six supervisory personnel in May, 1968. A week later, 350 union teachers in the district went out on strike to protest the action. The issue was not resolved by the conclusion of the school year, and, when the next school year began, a brief city-wide school strike occurred. Two more strikes occurred, each longer than the preceding. Finally, in order to reduce the friction, the state entered the fray.[98]

The study issued by the state indicated that decentralization in and of itself could not solve the problem of poor education in New York City's schools.[99] Under the recommendations presented, the community control program was essentially gutted and the Ocean Hill-Brownsville district was abolished. The districts were made much larger, so large in fact that each district was larger than most city school systems: systems the local black communities claimed were so large as to deny them any control over the schools affecting their children. Community control fell over the crucial issue of hiring. While the movement still had its supporters, attention slowly began to shift back to desegregation plans.*

Although whites and blacks in most Northern and Western cities did live in separate neighborhoods, it was readily demonstrable that the school board in nearly every one of those cities had done something beyond the strict use of the neighborhood concept to keep whites and blacks in separate schools.[100] The first *de facto* segregation case to reach the Supreme Court was that of

---

*The issue of who controls the schools in New York was again joined a decade later, again over the issue of hiring. The Chancellor of New York City schools suspended the ability of the community school districts to hire their own teachers, claiming that too many persons had been hired (*New York Times*, January 24, 1979). Twenty-eight of the thirty-two community school boards planned a court challenge (*New York Times*, January 25, 1979).

Keyes v. School District Number 1, Denver, Colorado. [101] In a decision written by Justice William Brennan, the Court acknowledged that Denver had never operated its schools "under a constitutional or statutory provision that mandated or permitted racial segregation in public education." Nonetheless, it found that the school board had "by use of various techniques such as the manipulation of student attendance zones, school site selection and a neighborhood school policy, created or maintained" segregated schools throughout the city. The Court went on to conclude that the neighborhood school policy, which on its face appeared to be neutral, had resulted in the "deliberate racial segregation in the schools attended by over one-third of the Negro school population." Thus, segregation in Denver was, in fact, not *de facto* but was *de jure*. Under the *Keyes* doctrine, then, any school system whose segregation could be shown to be the result of school board actions was as liable to court remedy as any school system in the Southern and Border states.

With such a clear message, many cities attempted to implement voluntary desegregation plans. A common feature of most was a provision for "open enrollment." The premise here was to provide students the right to transfer to other schools; blacks would, it was thought, choose to transfer to predominantly white schools. Problems associated with this approach when used in the South have been discussed. In the North, even when spaces were available and free transportation was provided, no more than 15 percent of the black parents exercised this option for their children. More common, unfortunately, was its use by white parents seeking to remove their children from integrated schools. [102]

Another approach, based upon the open enrollment concept, has been that of "magnet schools." Historically, American schools have been comprehensive in their curricular offerings. Specialized schools in some of the larger cities were, alternatively, made available to the most gifted students, i.e. Bronx High School of Science, Boston Latin School, etc. The magnet school concept sought to provide average students with a variety of curricular options by offering specialized schools that focus on such subjects as science, the fine arts, or languages, or which apply different philosophies to learning such as the Montessori approach, the ungraded classroom approach, or the military school approach. These schools, it was hoped, would be so special that whites and blacks would both find them desirable. By admitting applicants in accordance with a plan for racial balance, such a system could voluntarily desegregate the district's schools. [103]

In no place was greater commitment made to this approach than Cincinnati, a system which was 51 percent black and 49 percent white. The magnet plan had some positive effects. In the 1975–76 school year, it attracted back into the public schools over a thousand white students who had previously enrolled in parochial and private schools. [104] It resulted in nearly two-thirds of those schools which were 90 percent or more one race at the plan's start to move marginally closer to racial balance. However, 20 percent of the city's schools remained 90 percent or more one race. [105]

The evidence from across the country has indicated that magnet schools alone are not sufficient to desegregate the schools, though they can be an effective part of a broader program. [106] In Milwaukee, for example, a federal judge found in 1978 that a fifteen school magnet plan had not produced the desired city-wide result. He ordered stepped-up efforts. [107] In Seattle, an unsuccessful voluntary desegregation program based on magnet schools was transformed by the school board into a mandatory plan involving the grouping of schools which were less than 34 percent or more than 54 percent minority. (Seattle became the first major American city to implement a mandatory plan without a court order or HEW pressure. [108])

Philadelphia's magnet plan, although not in effect for too long, is currently under pressure. A city with a minority enrollment approximately two-thirds of the total, Philadelphia was ordered by the Pennsylvania Human Relations Commission in 1968 to prepare a desegregation plan. It not only dragged its heels, but under Mayor Frank Rizzo, dug them in. In February, 1979, it began a thirty-three school magnet program that had the support of much of the city as an alternative to "the uninviting prospect of city-wide busing." [109] Desegregation (defined in Pennsylvania as 25% to 75% white or black enrollment) occurred in only 14 percent of the schools. In April, 1980, the Human Relations Commission informed the city that not enough progress was being made and

that court action was likely unless the school board were to adopt
year-by-year goals aimed at desegregating two-thirds of the system's 230,000 students by June, 1982. [110]

BUSING

It was the spectre of court-ordered busing that led those cities to
attempt voluntary magnet plans. The school bus has been on the
scene for a long time. In 1869, Massachusetts first authorized the
expenditure of public funds to transport children to and from
school; by 1919, all forty-eight states had such laws. Now, 43
percent of all school children ride the school bus each day; another
22 percent regularly use public transportation. [111] The reality of
residential segregation requires busing to achieve any semblance
of racial balance; no other technique has achieved what busing
has. [112] Since *Swann*, busing orders have been common. However,
busing for racial balance has increased in the number of students
bused to and from school a mere 5 percent. [113] (It is true, though,
that their destination may be different than before.) The United
States Department of Transportation has estimated that less than 1
percent of the annual increase in students bused is attributable to
desegregation, while 95 percent is due to population growth. [114]

Generally speaking, busing for purposes of racial balance has
been highly unpopular. National polls between 1959 and 1975
showed decreasing opposition to integration in the schools. However, in April, 1972, Harris Poll found only one of every five
Americans favoring the use of busing to promote racial balance;
73 percent were against its use. While a poll conducted by the
United States Commission on Civil Rights taken in November,
1972 showed the public in support of busing 43 percent to 31
percent, most polls have shown the public to be consistently
opposed to busing since 1972. [115] [116] One Alabama resident spoke
for many by saying, "If a kid's got to ride a bus 50 miles to get to
school, I'm in favor of it. But I'm not in favor of carrying them one
mile to achieve integration!" [117]

Orfield believes that busing has been an explosive issue because
schools are the largest and most visible of public institutions, and
school assignment patterns can be changed rapidly and without

the consent of the parents or the local school board. [118] Others, however, believe it has less to do with the issue of local control and more to do with racism and the economic fears of the working class and lower middle class. [119] [120]

One frequent complaint about busing is that it is a costly venture whose funds would be better spent on improving educational opportunity in neighborhood schools. This argument has proven specious upon examination. A study of seventeen school districts including Nashville, Richmond, and Charlotte, indicated that the share of the school budget devoted to transportation increased only marginally after the desegregation orders; at most, the proportion rose only 2.2 percent. [121]

Other arguments in opposition have focused on the fear that white children bused to formerly all-black schools will receive a poorer quality of education than is offered at the white neighborhood school. This fear has also proven groundless. The data on achievement indicates that white students do not fall behind. (This topic will be discussed in greater detail in a later chapter.)

One of the biggest fears of parents is that their children will be physically harmed either as a result of antibusing demonstrations or of hostility toward their race in the new school. Due to the widespread attention paid to the violence that has occurred in some school districts, it is difficult to convince parents that their fears are not likely to be realized. People remember the ten school buses that were blown up in Pontiac, Michigan, and the white mobs in Little Rock, Boston, and Louisville. What they do not recall is that the public outcry, while often a cathartic one, usually disappears quickly. [122] A 1973, United States Commission on Civil Rights study of ten communities found that violence had occurred in only four of them and that it was very short-lived in three of those. [123] Another study conducted by the Commission in 1976 showed no disruption in twenty-seven of twenty-nine districts studied. [124] In its report on the decade of desegregation from the mid-1960s to the mid-1970s, the Commission concluded that serious disruptions had occurred in fewer than one-fifth of the districts which enrolled at least 1500 students, at least 5 percent of whom were minority. Many people would be surprised to learn that the same national survey indicated that opposition to desegregation by white parents declined from 59 percent prior to the local plan being put into effect to 18 percent after; in districts under court order, the decline in opposition was equally as dramatic—from 78 percent to 26 percent.[125] Studies of Charlotte-Mecklenberg and Berkeley, California confirm this finding.[126] [127]

Nonetheless, opposition in the political arena has been consistent since the early 1970s. Neither geographic region nor ideological persuasion has been a definitive predictor of Congressional sentiment on the matter.[128] In fact, antibusing feeling has been so strong that beginning in 1966, Congress passed an annual string of measures intended to restrain school integration.[129] Included was a rider attached in 1972 to the Higher Education Amendments ordering that lower court busing decrees be stayed pending final resolution at the appellate levels;[130] and stipulations in the 1974 Elementary and Secondary Education Act that require federal courts to look at all alternative means before ordering busing, and which require that children not be bused beyond the school closest to their home.[131]

Executive support for busing waned after Lyndon Johnson left office. President Nixon's early efforts on behalf of delay have already been mentioned. His statements in the wake of the *Swann* decision proved to be confusing. He first stated that busing was the law of the land and would be enforced by the Executive Branch. Shortly thereafter, the Administration announced that it would not authorize the expenditure of federal desegregation funds to support court-ordered busing programs.[132] In the 1972 election, Nixon sought to capitalize on antibusing feelings by making his opposition to busing a campaign issue. The Democratic candidate, George McGovern, a liberal, tried to minimize discussion of the issue in order not to lose votes.[133] Once having won reelection, Nixon ruled out the use of the powerful weapon provided by Title VI of the Civil Rights Act of 1964—the withholding of federal funds to programs which discriminate against minorities. Thus, even the most committed HEW officials were hampered, and HEW involvement under Presidents Nixon and Ford began to focus on equalizing educational opportunity in neighborhood schools rather than on forcing the desegregation that the Supreme Court had earlier said was the only path to equal education.[134]

Things improved under the Carter Administration. HEW was pressed into actively pursuing school desegregation in forty-four districts by an order of Judge John J. Sirica. HEW Secretary Joseph Califano and Attorney General Griffin Bell once again placed the two most important federal enforcement agencies into the camp of those demanding school desegregation.[135]

Metropolitan Busing

Unfortunately, however, that came at a time when antibusing sentiment had entrenched itself in many of our nation's suburban areas. At first, suburbanites favored busing; it did not affect them since few minorities lived in suburban communities. The growth rate of the minority population in the suburbs has been so slow that it would take five centuries (at the rate of change that occurred between 1960 and 1970) for their presence there to be proportionate to their national share of the population.[136] Any serious effort to speed up the process of minority suburbanization is likely to meet with serious community resistance.[137] Since there does not appear to be any massive white return to the cities and little opportunity for blacks to leave them, the cities and their schools are likely to become increasingly minority.[138] In fact, approximately half of the nation's minority school children currently live in the twenty-nine largest school districts, where minority enrollment averages 60 percent. In only eight of these districts is there a white majority in the public schools.[139]

Thus, if there is to be any meaningful desegregation in most of those cities, it will be necessary to develop city–suburb busing plans. While this raises the hackles of many suburbanites, there are cogent reasons for adopting metropolitan desegregation programs. One is that several voluntary efforts (admittedly small ones involving the busing of blacks to white suburban schools) have proven to be successful. Educators in Rochester, New York; Hartford, Connecticut; and Boston, for example, concluded that both white and black children had benefited from the cross-district programs.[140] Boston's METCO program, which began with 220 students in 1966, involved the busing of over 3,000 blacks from Boston to 185 schools in thirty-seven suburban cities and towns. If the college-going rate is an indication of success (85% of the 194 METCO graduates in 1978 went on to college), then the program has been an unqualified success. [141]

Much attention has been paid to the fear that desegregation will result in massive white flight from the cities. While this is a topic that will be examined in a later chapter, it should be noted here that the loss of whites in desegregated districts which include the city and the surrounding communities, i.e. county districts like Charlotte-Mecklenberg, is not large. [142] It follows that, if there is no place to which whites can move to avoid busing, they will not move when a plan is put in place. This argues, then, for metropolitan approaches.

Detroit, a city whose schools are 90 percent black, is one place where such an approach was appropriate unless desegregation was to be defined as each school having one white youngster for every nine blacks. Recognizing the hollowness of such a definition, Federal District Court Judge Stephen Roth ordered the Detroit school district to be merged with fifty-three districts in three suburban counties. Under Roth's plan, fifteen new districts were created, each with some Detroit schools and those of two or more suburban communities. As one might have quickly deduced, the order was rapidly appealed.

To the dismay of proponents of desegregation, the Supreme Court decided to draw the line at the city line. [143] In the 1974 case of *Milliken v. Bradley* (*Milliken I*), a divided (5 to 4) Court held that "the notion that school district lines may be casually ignored or treated as a mere administrative convenience is contrary to the history of public education in our country." Noting the American tradition of local autonomy regarding the schools, the Court went on: "Before the boundaries of separate and autonomous school districts may be set aside by consolidating the separate units for remedial [desegregation] purposes or by imposing a cross-district remedy, it must first be shown that there has been a constitutional violation within one district that produces a significant segregative effect in another district. . . . [W]ithout an interdistrict violation and interdistrict effect, there is no constitutional wrong calling for an interdistrict remedy." Thus, since the school boards in Detroit's suburbs had not been responsible in any way for the segregation in Detroit's schools, a metropolitan solution was not constitutionally required. In Detroit and similar cities, it is unlikely that black children will ever attend integrated schools.

(A subsequent court ruling concerning that city revived the notion that the urban schools should be made equal to the schools in the surrounding suburbs. The State of Michigan was required to share the cost of programs intended to counteract the effects of long term segregation. When the decree in this case, *Milliken II*, was upheld by the Supreme Court, it marked the first time that remedial education programs were ordered as part of a desegregation ruling. [144])

The Supreme Court has consistently applied its *Milliken I* rule. For instance, in 1974, it refused to accept a case concerning city-suburb busing in the Louisville area. [145] During the legal battle following an appelate division upholding of a metropolitan approach, the Louisville school board dissolved itself, and, under Kentucky law, Jefferson County assumed responsibility for public education. Thus, since the city had relinquished its authority to the county, the Supreme Court refused to upset an order to develop a county-wide desegregation program.

It upheld such an approach concerning Wilmington, Delaware, and the surrounding New Castle County area. [146] In 1975, the Court let stand the finding by a three judge panel that a 1968 statute that exempted Wilmington (with its 80% minority member school population) from a statewide school consolidation program involving eleven districts had a segregative effect. Since a share of the blame for the segregation in Wilmington lay outside of the city, a metropolitan solution was appropriate. Busing involving 21,500 students began in September, 1978, and was implemented smoothly and without incidence of violence. [147] Despite this, antibusing advocates continued their legal efforts to retain separate city and suburban districts and, thus, to avoid the busing of white children into Wilmington. However, in April, 1980, the Supreme Court again declined to take their case. [148] Presumably that action ended the battle to desegregate the schools in Wilmington, a battle which, essentially, first reached the Supreme Court in *Gebhart*, one of the companion cases to *Brown*.

While the *Milliken I* rule has been used to justify metropolitan busing in Louisville and Wilmington, it has also been used as a basis to deny such plans in cities where there was no official action which kept the city district black and the suburban districts white. One such case, recently affirmed by the Supreme Court, concerned a lower court's rejection of the consolidation of Atlanta's predominantly black school system with nine predominantly white surrounding school systems. [149]

Surely other cases will reach the Supreme Court. One may concern Houston, the sixth largest district in the nation. [150] Its schools are 46 percent black and 28 percent Hispanic. The city has a magnet plan that attempts to attract suburban whites to the Houston schools in order to promote desegregation. However, in an effort to insure that effective desegregation occurs without delay, a suit, involving Houston and twenty-two surrounding school systems, has been filed.

Boston

Busing came to Boston in a way that shocked most Americans. The fact that Boston is known for its contributions to American culture and learning and to the American democratic ethos, and the fact that it is widely regarded as one of the strongholds of liberal political thought all combine to produce the belief that Boston is a state of mind, the embodiment of American progressivism and dignity. Add to that equation the fact that no major American city, not even Boston, is free from ethnic isolationism and racial xenophobia, and the product is one that can shake the confidence of those who believe in the ability of America to fulfill its promises about equal opportunity and domestic tranquility. The desegregation of Boston's public schools was so traumatic that its story must be told as a warning to the millions who live in cities where the script for desegregation is still emerging.

The decent and forward looking people of Boston established the nation's first public school system several hundred years ago. Its racial progressivism had given the city a position of leadership in the abolitionist movement. In the wake of the *Roberts* decision, Boston, in 1855, became the first city to outlaw racial segregation in its schools. [151] For centuries, the descendents of the Pilgrims and the Puritans maintained positions of power in banking, commerce, education, and politics. Known as Boston's Brahmins, they began to lose their hold on the city's government in the late 1800s, as the Irish Catholic community began to grow in size and solidarity. The antipathy between the English and Irish in the Old World crossed the Atlantic with those who sought better lives in America. Both here and abroad, the religious differences between the groups led to dissimilar outlooks on life which caused friction between them. But, even more, the emnity in both situations had to do with ruling class–working class distrust. When the Irish moved to the verge of political domination in Boston, the Brahmins, still in solid control of the legislature, transferred a number of crucial powers from the city to the state in a successful effort to retain a certain level of influence over the city. Also, at the turn of the current century, they replaced ward representation (in the name of "good government") with city-wide elections (actually to forestall the Irish take-over). [152]

As the Irish population in the city grew, however, it was the Irish who benefited from this latter move. At the time when school desegregation was being debated, they had a solid hold on most elected and appointed political positions as well as throughout the civil service and teaching ranks. Nowhere was this more visible than in the Boston School Committee, which between 1960 and 1974 had seated seventeen different persons—fifteen Irish Catholics, one person whose mother was Irish and father Jewish, and one Yankee. It was not until 1975 that an Italo-American was elected and not until 1977 that a black (the first since the early days of this century) was chosen. [153] [154] [155]

Boston is a highly ethnic city. More than one-third of its population is either foreign born or the offspring of at least one foreign-born parent. Add to this mostly European ethnic population a black population in excess of 16 percent and a small but growing Hispanic population, and the seeds are present for disharmony. [156] The city's neighborhoods are by no means a melting pot. Most blacks live in Roxbury, the South End, Mattapan, and portions of Dorchester and Jamaica Plain. Hispanics live in the South End. Italians live in East Boston and the North End. The Irish live in the rest of the city from working class South Boston, Dorchester, and Charlestown to more affluent West Roxbury and Hyde Park. Racial isolation is so strong that in the early 1970s there were only 388 blacks among the 38,488 residents of South Boston, and only 76 among the 15,353 "Townies" of Charlestown. [157] By and large, the middle class lives outside of the city limits. [158]

The growth in the black community developed rather late in comparison to other major cities. As it occurred, so did anti-black sentiment. One indication of this was the rise in power of Louise Day Hicks, first elected to the School Committee with 38 percent of the vote in 1961. During her initial term, an inter-racial group known as Citizens for the Boston Schools, along with the local NAACP and CORE chapters, began to raise the issue of *de facto* segregation in the schools. Their efforts culminated with a school boycott on June 19, 1963. Hicks spoke out in defense of neighborhood schools and campaigned for reelection using the slogan, "You know where I stand." Her vote total jumped to 69 percent in that November's election. [159, 160] A study of those who voted for Hicks in that election revealed that they held the strongest anti-black sentiments of all who voted. While 45 percent believed racial imbalance to be harmful and while 65 percent recognized that there was racial imbalance in the public schools of Boston, 87 percent opposed the busing of whites and 71 percent opposed the busing of blacks to alleviate that condition. Busing, they thought, would lead to the desegregation of their neighborhoods, something anathema to this group of citizens who chose to live among persons descendant from the same European country as they. [161]

Racial imbalance was a much discussed topic in the Commonwealth of Massachusetts at that point in time. Earlier in 1965, the State Board of Education released a report, "Because It is Right, Educationally," which indicated that forty-five schools in Boston, eight in Springfield, one in Cambridge, and one in Medford, had black enrollments in excess of 50 percent. In Boston, these schools educated three-quarters of the black elementary school children. [162] In response to the report, the Great and General Court (the state legislature) passed the Racial Imbalance Act, a measure that required local school systems to eliminate the racial imbalance in any school whose enrollment was more than 50 percent nonwhite, or lose state educational aid. The statute passed despite the solid opposition of Boston's legislators. It was a clear case of the traditional suburban and rural distrust of Boston's Irish politicians.

Resistance in the Boston School Committee proved to supporters of the Racial Imbalance Act that their distrust was warranted. It was not until March, 1967 that the School Committee submitted a desegregation plan that was approved by the State Board of Education. Despite a study prepared in 1966 by the Harvard-MIT Joint Center for Urban Studies indicating that busing was the only way to alleviate racial imbalance (since simple redistricting plans could not reach two-thirds of the black children), that plan did not call for busing. Neither did those submitted in 1968, 1969, and 1971. In the meantime, the number of racially imbalanced schools in Boston grew to seventy. [163] [164]

Court activity proceeded in both state and federal court. On June 25, 1973, the Massachusetts Supreme Judicial Court ordered the School Committee to eliminate the racial imbalance by September, 1974. [165] The federal court ruling came on June 21, 1974. [166] At that point in Boston's history, its once proud school system had deteriorated educationally. Reading test scores revealed that, beginning in the third grade, Boston's students fell below the national norms, so far below that by the ninth grade there was a seventeen month achievement gap. Students from white South Boston and black Roxbury fared even worse. [167] [168] Not only were achievement levels discouraging but so were the attitudes of the teachers toward their students, particularly the black students. [169] When federal Judge W. Arthur Garrity issued his 150 page opinion, the proportion of blacks in the city's schools (33 percent) was double their proportion of residence due to high parochial school enrollments which drew approximately one-third of the school-aged children. [170] (Despite this, only about five percent of the permanent teachers and even fewer among the principals were black.) [171] Over 80 percent of the white students were in schools that were more than four-fifths white, and nearly two-thirds of the black pupils were in schools that were in excess of 70 percent black.

Judge Garrity's review of the actions taken by the Boston School Committee in the preceding years led him to find that the open enrollment policy and the neighborhood school policy had been used to promote segregation. For instance, South Boston High was over-enrolled by 676 students, while Girls High, a predominantly black school, had 532 vacant seats; no transfers had been mandated to relieve the overcrowding at "Southie" High. In essence, a racially dual school system existed, with majority black schools structured on a kindergarten through grade five elementary school, grade six through grade eight middle school, and grade nine through grade twelve high school basis; the majority white schools were structured on a six-three-three basis. He concluded that the School Committee "knowingly carried out a systematic program of segregation affecting all of the city's students, teachers and school facilities." He mandated that "every form of racial segregation in the public schools of Boston" be eliminated. The School Committee was to submit a plan by December 16, 1974, to be implemented in September, 1975. In the interim, he ordered a Phase I busing plan involving South Boston and Roxbury to be put into effect in September, 1974.

Boston had only a few months to prepare for desegregation. Some 30,000 students, approximately one-third of Boston's students, rode the buses prior to Garrity's order. Only 21,000 to 24,000 would need to be bused to fulfill his mandate. However, for many children the destination of their bus was to be different, and white Bostonians were not happy about that.[172] In an effort to stem any white flight, Humberto Cardinal Medeiros told the city's Catholics that their children would not be admitted to the parochial schools in order to help them avoid busing.[173] Sports figures and local celebrities went on television to urge that the opening of schools be orderly. However, that was not to be the case.

Louise Day Hicks, then a member of the City Council (having served a term in Congress and having been defeated on several occasions in bids for the mayor's seat), coordinated an antibusing group known as ROAR, Restore Our Alienated Rights. Tacit support from her and from South Boston's other politicians fueled the anger of "Southie" residents, 15 percent of whom were unemployed and feeling angry about that as well.[174]

When schools opened in September, they did so without 30 percent of the expected students, many of whom were engaging in a boycott that was to last for two weeks.[175] Blacks were beaten in the subways and streetcars near South Boston. One was pushed in front of an on-coming subway train and was nearly killed. Snipers shot at buildings in the mostly-minority Columbia Point housing project located near South Boston. Bus loads of black children were sprayed with broken glass as windows were shattered with barrages of rocks hurled by South Boston's adult population. Many in the crowds tauntingly waved hockey sticks as they chanted, "Here we go, Southie. Here we go."

The police, the majority of whom had strong ties to South Boston either through residence or family, did little about the initial violence.[176] However, in October, things got out of hand when an antibusing crowd near the Gavin Middle School in South Boston dragged a black maintenance man from his car which was stopped at a red light. The man was nearly beaten to death. A police officer was forced to fire his gun in order to halt the zealous attackers. Not satisfied, the crowd turned its attention to the yellow buses departing from Gavin. The police, attempting to hold back the mob, then became its target. Luckily, the buses that served as the focus of the assault had no children on them. As the decoys drove in the direction of the crowd, another set with the children departed from the back of the school and sped off in the opposite direction.[177]

Mayor Kevin White, believing that it was impossible to maintain safety, asked Judge Garrity to deploy 125 federal marshalls.[178] Six were eventually sent. The Tactical Police Force, Boston's version of SWAT officers, frustrated that they had been receiving the abuse of the crowds, responded the following evening by attacking an antibusing group in the Rabbit Inn, a South Boston barroom. It appeared as if total order was about to break down in that section of the city. The Boston *Globe* printed an editorial asking for swift federal action: "Calling in federal troops is strong medicine. But the costs of delay and prolonged unrest are higher." It noted that "Boston was supposed to be an enlightened city, the Athens of America." However, "brutal attacks on children in school buses and on innocent citizens about their business on our streets" had stunned the collective conscience of the city, said the *Globe*.[179] Taking a somewhat different tack, President Gerald Ford buoyed the spirits of the antibusing proponents in his press conference that day when he deplored the violence that had occurred in Boston but went on to say: "The court decision in that case, in my judgement, was not the best solution to quality education in Boston. I have consistently opposed forced busing to achieve racial balance as a solution to quality education." [180]

Trouble spread the following week to Hyde Park High School where a white student was stabbed. [181] Throughout the school year violence flared. Between September, 1974 and January, 1975, overtime charges for the Boston Police Department alone were $4.6 million. [182] The Metropolitan District Commission (MDC) Police, the State Police, federal marshalls, and the Massachusetts National Guard also supplied assistance during a 174 day school year that saw disturbances on 130 days. Twice as many students were suspended from school that year than the previous year. Thousands were disciplined and 459 students were arrested. [183] A review of the year indicates, however, that major problems were limited to only four schools. In most schools, desegregation was smoothly implemented. [184]

Not only were the students and their parents defiant, but so was the Boston School Committee. Three of its five members were found guilty of contempt of court by Judge Garrity in December, 1974 when they refused to vote to submit a Phase II plan to Garrity in conformance with his June, 1974, order. [185] Hearings conducted six months later by the United States Commission on Civil Rights identified such belligerence on the part of the School Committee that the Commission recommended that Garrity place the Boston schools in receivership so that he could insure that they were properly administered. [186]

Garrity was not yet ready to take that step. His attention was focused on the Phase II plan that would go into effect in September, 1975. Based on the work of four court-appointed Masters, the plan divided the city into a number of districts whose schools would be no more than 60 percent and no less than 40 percent of either race; East Boston was exempted due to its isolation from the rest of the city. [187] Further, there would be a city-wide magnet district whose schools were to be 40 percent to 60 percent white, 30 percent to 50 percent black, and 5 percent to 25 percent other minorities. (These schools were oversubscribed that September.) [188] In order to improve the quality of education in the schools, every school was paired with a participating local college, university, or major corporation that was to provide consultation and enrichment services to the school.[189]

The academic year opened in September with 1600 Boston Police, 200 MDC police, 500 State Troopers, six federal prosecuters, 100 federal marshalls, 50 FBI agents, and 600 National Guardsmen on alert.[190] Unfortunately, violence broke out at South Boston High School and Hyde Park High School again that year, and at Charlestown High School. South Boston High was so troubled that Garrity placed it in receivership on December 9, 1975. Under that order, the School Committee no longer had authority over the school; the Superintendent of Schools under Garrity's direction was to have that authority.[191] It was not until November 28, 1977 that South Boston High opened without a contingent of armed State Police in the building.[192] However, the school was not done with its violent episodes as serious racial fighting broke out there and throughout the city two years later in the aftermath of the sniper shooting of a black football player who was standing in a huddle during a game.[193] Often closed due to violent outbursts in the earlier periods of Phase I and II, Southie High was shut down for the first time since 1976 as a result of the tension that followed that fighting.[194]

Busing in Boston brought out the worst in too many people. Thomas Cottle, a Harvard sociologist, interviewed a number of Bostonians concerning their feelings about busing. He found great resentment among the white working class to what they felt was special treatment to undeserving blacks. Said one woman, "[blacks] want to claim [they] got something coming 'cause [their] great-great-grandparents had it bad. That's fine, but you better the hell make sure that everybody whose great-great-grandparents had it bad has it good now."[195] A white insurance salesman was ruled by stereotype: "You don't live that way over there [in the black community] with your drugs and your booze and those divorces, and all that rioting, and then send your kids out here to these schools."[196]

Harvard law professor Derrick Bell believes that the violent response among white Bostonians was predictable given attitudes such as those and given their knowledge that the more affluent suburbs were not to be included in the busing order.[197] Others have pointed to the fact that most of those bused, white and black, were from working-class families, and that greater success might be gained by busing such children to middle-class neighborhoods rather than to neighborhoods where economic competition in and of itself breeds hostility.[198, 199, 200] Perhaps even more basic to the white reaction in Boston than stereotypes or economic competition was the fear that their ethnic neighborhood would give way to people who were different, that their way of life was threatened. Those in South Boston, Charlestown, and, to a lesser extent, East Boston are people who do not have the means to move to the suburbs. They have bought homes in their communities and have made an investment in their city at a time when others have left its problems behind. They do not want anyone who might bring a new order to come to their neighborhoods, and they fear that such a challenge will follow busing.

Such motives do not seem to be on the minds of Boston's blacks. Even during the most violent moments, there was no organized effort on the part of Boston's blacks to resist the busing.[201] Their concern was for improved educational opportunities. Said one black, "Busing is more than a political or legal decision, it's more than anything you read about in the papers. It's peoples lives . . . You can survive eating the worst food, but you won't grow from it. You can only grow from eating the best foods. Busing's a way to get some of us closer to the best foods."[202]

Cottle, lying on the floor of the bus with a black child who was trying to avoid the shattering glass for the eleventh time, asked the child if he would be on the bus the next morning. "Sure," said the boy, a definitive indication that his education was important to him.[203]

Happily, as has been the case in city after city, the young children have been able to get along well despite the fury around them. The South Boston child who was bused to Roxbury said, "It ain't so bad like I thought it would be."[204] Hopefully, he will rule the day.

THE CHALLENGE AHEAD

As Abrams has noted, the problems that accompanied Judge Garrity's order indicate not that desegregation ought not to occur, but that it must.[205] And occur it will. Court actions or impending court actions are in progress in Buffalo, Chicago, Cleveland, Indianapolis, Los Angeles, New York City, and St. Louis, among others.[206] [212] Such activity may not be far behind in New Jersey, which, according to a 1979 HEW study, had five cities listed among the hundred most segregated school districts in the nation.[213]

The history of school desegregation since *Brown* has not been pleasant. Crain's 1968 study indicates that liberal school boards attempted to integrate but conservative ones did not.[214] Many have attempted to shift on to the courts the entire responsibility for compliance to the Constitution, and the courts have accepted that burden.[215] [216] Change, then, has been slow, generally on a case by case basis. Once desegregation plans have been put into action, they have often been accompanied by white resistance. Bullock and Rogers have found the strength of resistance to be positively related to the size of the black community, and negatively related to mean family income in the school district.[217] However, as has been stated, violent resistance is usually short-lived; Boston is the clear exception. No matter how intense the feelings of the resistors, they have come to realize in city after city that the school bus will not disappear as an integration tool.

Nevertheless, there remain millions of black children in racial isolation in many of our nation's largest school systems. In such cities as Detroit, Atlanta, and the District of Columbia (with black populations in the overwhelming majority) meaningful desegregation awaits the ability for metropolitan solutions. In many other cities, the key to desegregated schools is desegregated neighborhoods. Perhaps the ultimate solution to the continuing problem of separate schools in those cities is for the courts to begin issuing desegregation orders that jointly affect the schools and the neighborhoods. But, if school desegregation thus far has been characterized by too much deliberation and not enough speed, desegregation of the neighborhoods will be even slower.

REFERENCES

1. Cahn, E.: Jurisprudence. *New York University Law Review, 30:*157–158, 1955.
2. Clark, K.: Social science, constitutional rights and the courts. In Rist, R. and Anson, R. (Eds.): *Education, Social Science and the Judicial Process.* New York, Teachers College Press, 1977, p. 2.

3. Irion, H.: The constitutional clock: A horological inquiry. In Humphrey, H. (Ed.): *School Desegregation: Documents and Commentaries.* New York, Thomas Y. Crowell Company, 1964, p. 53.

4. Carmichael, P.: *The South and Segregation.* Washington, Public Affairs Press, 1965, p. 6.

5. Cook, E. and Potter, W.: The school desegregation cases: Opposing the opinion of the Supreme Court. In Humphrey, H. (Ed.): *School Desegregation: Documents and Commentaries.* New York, Thomas Y. Crowell Company, 1964, p. 43.

6. Wilkinson, J.: *From Brown to Bakke: The Supreme Court and School Integration: 1954-1978.* New York, Oxford University Press, 1979, p. 69.

7. Workman, W., Jr.: The deep south — segregation holds firm. In Shoemaker, D. (Ed.): *With All Deliberate Speed, Segregation-Desegregation in Southern Schools.* New York, Harper & Brothers, 1957, p. 98.

8. Bullock, H.: *A History of Negro Education in the South From 1619 to the Present.* Cambridge, Harvard University Press, 1967, p. 260.

9. Franklin, V.: American values, social goals, and the desegregated school: A historical perspective. In Franklin, V. and Anderson, J. (Eds.): *New Perspectives on Black Educational History.* Boston, G. K. Hall and Company, 1978, p. 201.

10. A Joint Resolution of the State of South Carolina. In Zeigler, B. (Ed.): *Desegregation and the Supreme Court.* Boston, D. C. Heath and Co., 1958, p. 102.

11. Blaustein, A. and Ferguson, C.: *Desegregation and the Law: The Meaning and Effect of the School Desegregation Cases.* New Brunswick, N.J., Rutgers University Press, 1957, p. 245.

12. Virginia Commission on Constitutional Government: *Did the Court Interpret or Amend? The Meaning of the Fourteenth Amendment, in Terms of a State's Power to Operate Racially Separate Public Schools, as Defined by the Courts.* Richmond, Virginia Commission on Constitutional Government, 1960, p. 43.

13. Muse, B.: *Ten Years of Prelude, The Story of Integration Since the Supreme Court's 1954 Decision.* New York, Viking Press, 1964, p. 63. A

14. Ervin, S.: Declaration of Constitutional Principles. In Zeigler, B. (Ed.): *Desegregation and the Supreme Court.* Boston, D.C. Heath and Co., 1958, p. 103.

15. Ervin, S.: The southern manifesto: declaration of constitutional principles. In Humphrey, H. (Ed.): *School Desegregation: Documents and Commentaries.* New York, Thomas Y. Crowell Company, 1964, pp. 32, 34.

16. Westfeldt, W.: Communities in strife — Where there was violence. In Shoemaker, D. (Ed.): *With All Deliberate Speed, Segregation-Desegregation in Southern Schools.* New York, Harper & Brothers, 1957, p. 38.

17. James, W.: The South's own Civil War — Battle for the schools. In Shoemaker, D. (Ed.): *With All Deliberate Speed, Segregation-Desegregation in Southern Schools.* New York, Harper & Brothers, 1957, pp. 17-18.

18. Peltason, J.: *Fifty-Eight Lonely Men, Southern Federal Judges and School Desegregation.* New York, Harcourt, Brace and World, 1961, p. 36.

19. Muse (A), op cit., p. 174.

20. Cohen, D. and Weiss, J.: Social science and social policy: Schools and race. In Rist, R. and Anson, R. (Eds.): *Education, Social Science and the Judicial Process.* New York, Teachers College Press, 1977, p. 78.
21. Peltason, op cit., pp. 7–8.
22. Vander Zanden, J.: Desegregation: The future? In Humphrey, H. (Ed.): *School Desegregation: Documents and Commentaries.* New York, Thomas Y. Crowell Company, 1964, p. 126.
23. Bullock, op cit., p. 235.
24. Blaustein and Ferguson, op cit., pp. 210, 217.
25. Lasch, R.: Along the border — Desegregation at the fringes. In Shoemaker, D. (Ed.): *With All Deliberate Speed, Segregation-Desegregation in Southern Schools.* New York, Harper & Brothers, 1957, p. 56.
26. Muse (A), op cit., p. 39.
27. Tumin, M.: Readiness and resistance to desegregation: A social protest of the hard core. In Humphrey, H. (Ed.): *School Desegregation: Documents and Commentaries.* New York, Thomas Y. Crowell Company, 1964, p. 120.
28. Muse (A), op cit., pp. 96–103.
29. *Cooper v Aaron*, 358 U.S. 1 (1958).
30. Blossom, V.: *It Has Happened Here.* New York, Harper and Brothers, 1959, p. 20.
31. Ibid., p. 41.
32. Jackson, N. and Rydingsword, C.: Little Rock, Arkansas: The land of opportunity. In Harris, N., Jackson, N., and Rydingsword, C. (Eds.): *The Integration of American Schools: Problems, Experiences, Solutions.* Boston, Allyn and Bacon, Inc., 1975, pp. 53–54.
33. Muse (A), op cit., pp. 132–133.
34. Peltason, op cit., p. 38.
35. Muse (A), op cit., p. 136.
36. Eisenhower, D.: Executive order providing assistance for the removal of an obstruction of justice within the state of Arkansas. In Ervin, S. (Ed.): *Desegregation and the Supreme Court.* Boston, D.C. Heath and Co., 1958, pp. 113–114.
37. Blossom, op cit., p. 126.
38. Ibid., p. 185.
39. Muse (A), op cit., p. 196.
40. Peltason, op cit., p. 52.
41. Muse (A), op cit., p. 29.
42. Muse, B.: *Virginia's Massive Resistance.* Bloomington, Indiana University Press, 1961, p. 31. B
43. Dillard, H.: Freedom of choice and democratic values. In Humphrey, H. (Ed.): *School Desegregation: Documents and Commentaries.* New York, Thomas Y. Crowell Company, 1964, pp. 286, 294.
44. Muse (B), op cit., pp. 44, 68, 74.
45. Ibid., pp. 123, 125.

46. Ibid., p. 135.
47. Wilkinson, op cit., p. 99.
48. *Griffin v. County School Board*, 377 U.S. 218 (1964).
49. Wasby, S., D'Amato, A., and Metrailer, R.: *Desegregation from Brown to Alexander, An Exploration of Supreme Court Strategies*. Carbondale, Southern Illinois University Press, 1977, p. 206.
50. Leflar, R.: Law of the land—The courts and the schools. In Shoemaker, D. (Ed.): *With All Deliberate Speed, Segregation-Desegregation in Southern Schools*. New York, Harper & Brothers, 1957, p. 10.
51. Humphrey, H. (Ed.): *School Desegregation: Documents and Commentaries*. New York, Thomas Y. Crowell Company. 1964, pp. 2, 6.
52. Carter, H.: Desegregation does not mean integration. In Humphrey, H. (Ed.): *School Desegregation: Documents and Commentaries*. New York, Thomas Y. Crowell Company, 1964, p. 139.
53. Parham, J.: Halls of ivy—Southern exposure. In Shoemaker, D. (Ed.): *With All Deliberate Speed, Segregation-Desegregation in Southern Schools*. New York, Harper & Brothers, 1957, p. 164.
54. Johnson, G.: Freedom, equality, and segregation. In Humphrey, H. (Ed.): *School Desegregation: Documents and Commentaries*. New York, Thomas Y. Crowell Company, 1964, p. 105.
55. Muse (B), op cit., pp. 53–54, 268.
56. Read, F.: Judicial evolution of the law of school integration since *Brown v. Board of Education*. In Levin, B. and Hawley, W. (Eds.): *The Courts, Social Science and School Desegregation*. New Brunswick, N.J., Transaction Books, 1977, p. 15.
57. Muse (B), op cit., pp. 250–253.
58. Orfield, G.: *The Reconstruction of Southern Education, The Schools and the 1964 Civil Rights Act*. New York, John Wiley and Sons, 1969, p. 265. A
59. Kearns, D.: *Lyndon Johnson and the American Dream*. New York, Harper and Row, 1976, pp. 190–192.
60. Civil Rights Act of 1964, Public Law 88–352, Section 407.
61. Kluger, R.: *Simple Justice, The History of Brown v. Board of Education and Black America's Struggle for Equality*. New York, Alfred A. Knopf, Inc., 1975, p. 958.
62. Orfield, op cit., pp. 101, 209.
63. Wasby et al., op cit., p. 214.
64. *Bradley v. Richmond School Board*, 382 U.S. 103 (1965).
65. *Rogers v. Paul*, 382 U.S. 198 (1965).
66. *Green v. County School Board of New Kent County*, 391 U.S. 430 (1968).
67. Wasby et al., op cit., p. 385.
68. *Monroe v. Board of Commissioners*, 391 U.S. 450 (1968).
69. Read, op cit., pp. 30–31.
70. Bolner, J. and Shanley, R.: *Busing: The Political and Judicial Process*. New York, Praeger Publishers, 1974, p. 11.
71. *Alexander v. Holmes County Board of Education* 396 U.S. 19 (1969).
72. *Carter v. West Feliciana Parish School Board*, 396 U.S. 290 (1970).

73. Wilkinson, op cit., pp. 120–121.
74. *Swann v. Charlotte-Mecklenburg Board of Education*, 402 U.S. 1 (1971).
75. Buncher, J.: *The School Busing Controversy: 1970–1975*. New York, Facts on File, 1975, pp. 39, 45.
76. Vitullo-Martin, T.: Private schools and urban integration. In Friedman, M., Meltzer, R., and Miller, C. (Eds.): *New Perspectives on School Integration*. Philadelphia, Fortress Press, 1979, p. 66.
77. Nevin, D. and Bills, R.: *The Schools That Fear Built, Segregationist Academies in the South*. Washington, Acropolis Books, 1976, p. 11.
78. Ibid., p. 140.
79. Ibid., pp. 15–16.
80. Witte, A.: Subsidizing segregation. *The New Republic*, 179(26 & 27):12, 1977.
81. Witte, op cit., p. 13.
82. U.S. Commission on Civil Rights: *Reviewing a Decade of School Desegregation 1966–1975, Report of a National Survey of School Superintendents*. Washington, U.S. Commission on Civil Rights, 1977, p. 56. A
83. Farley, R.: Residential segregation and its implications for school integration. In Levin, B. and Hawley, W. (Eds.): *The Courts, Social Science and School Desegregation*. New Brunswick, N.J., Transaction Books, 1977, pp. 166, 180, 182.
84. Glazer, N.: Is Busing Necessary. In Mills, N. (Ed.): *The Great School Bus Controversy*. New York, Teachers College Press, 1973, p. 200.
85. U.S. Commission on Civil Rights: *A Long Day's Journey into Light, School Desegregation in Prince George's County*. Washington, D.C., U.S. Government Printing Office, 1976, pp. 60–61, 65. B
86. New York *Times*, April 14, 1978.
87. Orfield, G.: *Must We Bus? Segregated Schools and National Policy*. Washington: The Brookings Institution, 1978, p. 91. B
88. Rist, R.: School integration: Ideology, methodology and national policy. In Levinsohn, F. and Wright, B. (Eds.): *School Desegregation, Shadow and Substance*. Chicago, University of Chicago Press, 1976, p. 120.
89. Morgan, P.: The case for the white southerner. In Humphrey, H. (Ed.): *School Desegregation: Documents and Commentaries*. New York, Thomas Y. Crowell Company, 1964, p. 140.
90. Foster, Jr., G.: The North and West have problems, too. In Humphrey, H. (Ed.): *School Desegregation: Documents and Commentaries*. New York, Thomas Y. Crowell Company, 1964, p. 172.
91. Nash, S. et al.: New Haven, Connecticut: New Haven chose to desegregate. In Harris, N., Jackson, N., and Rydingsword, C. (Eds.): *The Integration of American Schools: Problems, Experiences, Solutions*. Boston, Allyn and Bacon, Inc., 1975, pp. 94, 96.
92. Maslow, W.: De facto public school segregation. In Humphrey, H. (Ed.): *School Desegregation: Documents and Commentaries*. New York, Thomas Y. Crowell Company, 1964, pp. 156–157.
93. Orfield (A), op cit., pp. 152–153.

94. Urofsky, M.: *Why Teachers Strike: Teachers' Rights and Community Control.* Garden City, N.Y., Anchor Books, 1970, p. 3.
95. Congress of Racial Equality: A proposal for community school districts. In Mills, N. (Ed.): *The Great School Bus Controversy.* New York, Teachers College Press, 1973, p. 312.
96. Urofsky, op cit., p. 8.
97. Ibid., p. 12.
98. Ibid., p. 15.
99. Levine, N.: *Ocean Hill — Brownsville: A Case History of Schools in Crisis.* New York, Popular Library, 1969, p. 132.
100. Jencks, C.: Busing — The Supreme Court Goes North. In Mills, N. (Ed.): *The Great School Bus Controversy.* New York, Teachers College Press, 1973, p. 15.
101. *Keyes v. School District Number 1, Denver, Colorado.* 413 U.S. 189 (1973).
102. Jencks, op cit., p. 17.
103. Rose. A.: School desegregation: A sociologist's view. In Hill, R. and Feeley, M. (Eds.): *Affirmative School Integration, Efforts to Overcome DeFacto Segregation in Urban Schools.* Beverly Hills, Cal., Sage Publications, 1968, p. 134.
104. Waldrip, D.: Alternative programs in Cincinnati or. 'What did you learn on the river today?' In Levine, D. and Havinghurst, R. (Eds.): *The Future of Big-City Schools, Desegregation Policies and Magnet Alternatives.* Berkeley, McCutchan Publishing Corporation, 1977, p. 102.
105. Felix, J. and Jacobs, J.: Issues in implementing and evaluating alternative programs in Cincinnati. In Levine, D. and Havinghurst, R. (Eds.): *The Future of Big City Schools, Desegregation Policies and Magnet Alternatives.* Berkeley, McCutchan Publishing Corporation, 1977, pp. 109–110.
106. McMillan, C.: *Magnet Schools: An Approach to Voluntary Desegregation.* Bloomington, Ind., Phi Delta Kappa, 1980, p. 18.
107. New York *Times*, June 13, 1978.
108. New York *Times*, January 3, 1978.
109. Philadelphia *Inquirer*, January 21, 1979.
110. Philadelphia *Inquirer*, April 13, 1980.
111. Mills, N.: Busing: Who's being taken for a ride? In Mills, N. (Ed.): *The Great School Bus Controversy.* New York, Teachers College Press, 1973, pp. 4, 6.
112. Foster, G.: Desegregating urban schools: A review of techniques. *Harvard Educational Review, 43(1)*:31, 1973.
113. U.S. Commission on Civil Rights (A), op cit., p. 5.
114. NAACP Legal Defense and Education Fund: It's Not the Distance, 'It's the Niggers.' In Mills, N. (Ed.): *The Great School Bus Controversy.* New York, Teachers College Press, 1973, p. 332.
115. Orfield (B), op cit., p. 109, 113.
116. Bolner and Shanley, op cit., p. 242.
117. Jordan, V.: We stand at one of those turning points in history. In Harris, N., Jackson, N., and Rydingsword, C. (Eds.): *The Integration of American Schools: Problems, Experiences, Solutions.* Boston, Allyn and Bacon, Inc., 1975, p. 297.
118. Orfield (B), op cit., p. 2.

119. Rubin, L.: *Busing and Backlash, White against White in a California School District*. Berkeley, University of California Press, 1972, pp. 195–196, 203.

120. Jordan, op cit., p. 296.

121. NAACP Legal Defense and Education Fund, op cit., p. 355.

122. Orfield, G.: How to make desegregation work: The adaptation of schools to their newly-integrated student bodies. In Levin, B. and Hawley, W. (Eds.): *The Courts, Social Science and School Desegregation*. New Brunswick, N.J., Transaction Books, 1977, p. 317.

123. U.S. Commission on Civil Rights: *School Desegregation in Ten Communities*. Washington, U.S. Government Printing Office, 1973, p. 17. C

124. U.S. Commission on Civil Rights: *Fulfilling the Letter and Spirit of the Law, Desegregation of the Nation's Public Schools*. Washington, U.S. Commission on Civil Rights, 1976, p. 125. D

125. U.S. Commission on Civil Rights (A), op cit., pp. 7, 91.

126. Barrows, F.: School busing: Charlotte, N.C. In Mills, N. (Ed.): *The Great School Bus Controversy*. New York, Teachers College Press, 1973, pp. 261–262.

127. Sullivan, N.: The buses reach their destination. In Mills, N. (Ed.): *The Great School Bus Controversy*. New York, Teachers College Press, 1973, pp. 274–275.

128. Hennessey, G.: The history of busing. *Educational Forum, 43(1):* 48–49, 1978.

129. Showell, B.: The courts, the legislature, the Presidency, and school desegregation policy. In Levinson, F. and Wright, B. (Eds.): *School Desegregation, Shadow and Substance*. Chicago, University of Chicago Press, 1976, pp. 99–100.

130. Bickel, A.: Untangling the busing snarl. In Mills, N. (Ed.): *The Great School Bus Controversy*. New York, Teachers College Press, 1973, p. 33.

131. Lenin, B. and Moise,.P.: School desegregation litigation in the seventies and the use of social science evidence: An annotated guide. In Levin, B. and Hawley, W. (Eds.): *The Courts, Social Science and School Desegregation*. New Brunswick, N.J., Transaction Books, 1977, p. 85.

132. U.S. Commission on Civil Rights (D), op cit., p. 13.

133. Bickel, op cit., p. 32.

134. Orfield, (B), op cit., p. 309.

135. Ibid., pp. 316–318, 358–359.

136. Pettigrew, T.: A sociological view of the post-*Milliken* era. In U.S. Commission on Civil Rights: *Milliken v. Bradley: The Implications for Metropolitan Desegregation*. Washington, D.C., U.S. Govt. Print. Office, 1974, p. 70.

137. Gittel, M.: The political implications of *Milliken v. Bradley*. In U.S. Commission on Civil Rights: *Milliken v. Bradley: The Implications for Metropolitan Desegregation*. Washington, D.C., U.S. Govt. Print. Office, 1974, p. 44.

138. Hain, E.: The Detroit case, Sealing off the city: School Desegregation in Detroit. In Kalodner, H. and Fishman, J. (Eds.): *Limits of Justice, The Courts' Role in School Desegregation*. Cambridge, Ballinger Publishing Company, 1978, p. 306.

139. Bell, D.: Defining *Brown's* integration remedy for urban school systems. In Friedman, M., Meltzer, R., and Miller, C. (Eds.): *New Perspectives on School Integration*. Philadelphia, Fortress Press, 1979, p. 25.

140. Ozmon, H. and Craver, S.: *Busing: A Moral Issue.* Bloomington, Ind., Phi Delta Kappa, 1972, p. 33.
141. Seldon, H.: METCO: A voluntary desegregation option. In Friedman, M., Meltzer, R., and Miller, C. (Eds.): *New Perspectives on School Integration.* Philadelphia, Fortress Press, 1979, pp. 149, 152.
142. Coleman, J.: Presentation to the Massachusetts legislature — March 30, 1976. In Friedman, M., Meltzer, R., and Miller, C. (Eds.): *New Perspectives on School Integration.* Philadelphia, Fortress Press, 1979, p. 116, 121.
143. *Milliken v. Bradley,* 418 U.S. 717 (1974).
144. Levine, I.: Pluralistic Education — Beyond Racial Balancing. In Friedman, M., Meltzer, R., and Miller, C. (Eds.): *New Perspectives on School Integration.* Philadelphia, Fortress Press, 1979, pp. 39–40.
145. *Newburg Area Council v. Jefferson County Board of Education,* 421 U.S. 931 (1974).
146. *Evans v. Buchanan,* 423 U.S. 963 (1975).
147. Philadelphia *Inquirer,* September 10, 1978; September 19, 1978.
148. New York *Times,* April 29, 1980.
149. New York *Times,* May 13, 1980.
150. New York *Times,* May 18, 1980.
151. Ozmon and Craver, op cit., p. 22.
152. Shrag, P.: *Village School Downtown, Politics and Education — A Boston Report.* Boston, Beacon Press, 1967, p. 31.
153. U.S. Commission on Civil Rights, *School Desegregation in Boston,* Washington: U.S. Govt. Print. Office, 1975, p. 38. E
154. Hillson, J.: *The Battle of Boston.* New York, Pathfinder Press, 1977, p. 199.
155. Orfield (B), op cit., p. 146.
156. U.S. Commission on Civil Rights (1975), op cit., p. 8, 15.
157. Ibid., p. 24.
158. Shrag, op cit., p. 8.
159. Bolner and Shanley, op cit., p. 189.
160. Levy, F.: *Northern Schools and Civil Rights, The Racial Imbalance Act of Massachusetts.* Chicago, Markham Publishing Company, 1971, pp. 37, 43, 45.
161. Bolner and Shanley, op cit., pp. 206–207.
162. Levy, op cit., p. 48, 79.
163. Smith, R.: The Boston case, Two centuries and twenty-four months: A chronicle of the struggle to desegregate the Boston Public schools. In Kalodner, H. and Fishman, J. (Eds.): *Limits of Justice, The Courts' Role in School Desegregation.* Cambridge, Ballinger Publishing Company, 1978, p. 39.
164. Bolner and Shanley, op cit., p. 188.
165. Smith, op cit., p. 42.
166. *Morgan v. Hennigan 379 F. Supp. 410.*
167. Shrag, op cit., p. 113.
168. U.S. Commission on Civil Rights (E), op cit., pp. 18–19, 31.

169. Kozol, J.: Death at an Early Age. The Destruction of the Hearts and Minds of Negro Children in the Boston Public Schools. Boston, Bantam Books, 1967, pp. 25, 48.
170. Smith, op cit., p. 32.
171. U.S. Commission on Civil Rights (E), op cit., p. 15.
172. Willie, C.: Racial balance or quality education? In Levinsohn, F. and Wright, B. (Eds.): *School Desegregation, Shadow and Substance.* Chicago, University of Chicago Press, 1976, p. 9.
173. Hornburger, J.: Deep are the roots: Busing in Boston. *Journal of Negro Education, 45(3):235,* 1976.
174. Hillson, op cit., p. 21.
175. Smith, op cit., p. 60.
176. Ibid., pp. 63–64.
177. Hillson, op cit., pp. 15–18.
178. U.S. Commission on Civil Rights (E), op cit., pp. 145–146.
179. Buncher, op cit., p. 253.
180. U.S. Commission on Civil Rights (E), op cit., p. 116.
181. Hillson, op cit., p. 69.
182. U.S. Commission on Civil Rights (E), op cit., p. 133.
183. Smith, op cit., pp. 67–70.
184. U.S. Commission on Civil Rights (D), op cit., p. 29.
185. Smith, op cit., p. 76.
186. U.S. Commission on Civil Rights (D), op cit., p. 31.
187. Smith, op cit., p. 95.
188. Willie, op cit., p. 10.
189. Dentler, R.: Educational Implications of desegregation in Boston. In Levine, D. and Havinghurst, R. (Eds.): *The Future of Big-City Schools, Desegregation Policies and Magnet Alternatives.* Berkeley, McCutchan Publishing Corporation, 1977, p. 182.
190. Case, C.: History of the desegregation plan in Boston. In Levine, D. and Havinghurst, R. (Eds.): *The Future of Big-City Schools, Desegregation Policies and Magnet Alternatives.* Berkeley, McCutchan Publishing Corporation, 1977, p. 171.
191. Hillson, op cit., pp. 176, 181, 195, 200.
192. New York *Times,* November 29, 1977.
193. New York *Times,* October 19, 1979.
194. Philadelphia *Inquirer,* November 11, 1979.
195. Cottle, T.: *Busing.* Boston, Beacon Press, 1976, p. 56.
196. Ibid., p. 87.
197. Bell, D.: Waiting on the promise of *Brown.* In Levin, B. and Hawley, W. (Eds.): *The Courts, Social Science and School Desegregation.* New Brunswick, N.J., Transaction Books, 1977, p. 372.

198. New York Times, October 22, 1979.
199. Orfield (B), op cit., p. 149.
200. Usdan, M.: School desegregation: An educator's view. In Hill, R. and Feeley, M. (Eds.): *Affirmative School Integration, Efforts to Overcome De Facto Segregation in Urban Schools*. Beverly Hills, Sage Publications, 1968, p. 118.
201. Poussaint, A. and Lewis, T.: School desegregation: A synonym for racial equality. In Levinsohn, F. and Wright, B. (Eds.): *School Desegregation, Shadow and Substance*. Chicago, University of Chicago Press, 1976, p. 27.
202. Cottle, op cit., p. 39.
203. Ibid., p. 126.
204. Ibid., p. 121.
205. Abrams, R.: Not one judge's opinion: *Morgan v. Hennigan* and the Boston schools. *Harvard Educational Review, 45(1):* 15, 1975.
206. New York *Times*, November 16, 1979 (Buffalo).
207. New York *Times*, April 22, 1980 (Chicago).
208. New York *Times*, March 25, 1980 (Cleveland).
209. New York *Times*, April 25, 1979 (Indianapolis).
210. New York *Times*, May 20, 1980 (Los Angeles).
211. New York *Times*, November 15, 1979 (New York).
212. New York *Times*, May 23, 1980 (St. Louis).
213. The *Trentonian*, December 12, 1979.
214. Crain, R.: *The Politics of School Desegregation*. Chicago, Aldine Publishing Company, 1968, p. 358.
215. Kalodner and Fishman, op cit., p. 3.
216. National Academy of Education: *Prejudice and Pride, The Brown Decision After Twenty-Five Years, May 17, 1954–May 17, 1979*. Washington, U.S. Department of Health, Education and Welfare, 1979, p. 31.
217. Bullock, C. and Rogers, H., Jr.: Coercion and southern school desegregation: implications for the north. *School Review, 83 (4):* 654, 1975.

PART II

COMPENSATORY EDUCATION
AND BEYOND

CHAPTER 4

TOWARD EQUALITY OF EDUCATIONAL OPPORTUNITY: HEAD START, TITLE I, THE COLEMAN REPORT

D uring the decade following the 1954 landmark *Brown* vs. *Board of Education* Supreme Court Decision, a growing number of American educators experimented with alternative means of educating poverty-stricken underachieving children. The social and educational issues publicized by the desegregation struggle seemed to be the impetus for much greater attention being given to the role of the schools, whether segregated or integrated, in promoting equality of educational opportunity and achievement. Throughout the late 1950s and early 1960s, school districts across the country initiated and expanded what was often labeled "compensatory education" programs for "culturally deprived" children. By the middle sixties the local initiatives had swelled to national commitments, manifested by Congress legislating Head Start for impoverished pre-schoolers in 1964, the Elementary and Secondary Education Act (Title I) for "educationally deprived children" in 1965 and ordering a massive study of educational inequalities (the Coleman Report) also in 1965. This chapter will review the rationale for compensatory education, describe the early implementation of these projects at the local and national levels, and review the startling conclusions of perhaps the most controversial and influential educational study in American history, James Coleman's *Equality of Educational Opportunity Survey*.

THE RATIONALE FOR COMPENSATORY EDUCATION TO 1965

In reviewing much of the social scientific and educational literature that was used to establish the wisdom of such programs as

Head Start, one can conclude that the following three fundamental assumptions constituted a broad rationale for compensatory education: (1) The environment had a profound influence on children's measured intelligence and school achievement, (2) schools constituted an important part of children's environment, and (3) schooling could compensate for the environmentally determined deficiencies in measured intelligence and pupil achievement. In the late 1950s and early 1960s, the process of schooling was often viewed as largely irrelevant for much of the nation's poor and "culturally deprived" school population. Among the black population, racism and poverty were typically seen as unusually dehumanizing and as stifling normal intellectual growth and academic progress. Moreover, the schools aided and abetted black underachievement by their adherence to white middle-class values, usually manifested by the employment of racially and culturally biased teachers, methods, and materials. Therefore, it seemed appropriate to design schooling experiences for millions of *culturally deprived* and educationally disadvantaged children that gave greater recognition to, and fit more comfortably within, the childrens' socio-cultural milieu. For black youth, desirable educational experiences often involved concentrated efforts to improve teacher-pupil rapport. Affective components such as these combined with individualized and novel techniques in the cognitive areas would compensate greatly for environmental inadequacies and thereby maximize the chances of accelerating cognition and achievement.

Cumulative Deficit

In the late 1950s and 1960s, the longer most poverty-stricken children attended school the greater was their need for accelerated learning to reach the average scholastic levels nationally. It had been reported that the I.Q.s of children from low income families typically declined throughout their years of schooling, and the term *cumulative deficit* emerged as a commonly employed label for this hypothesis.* On the various standardized reading and math

---

*Martin Deutsch popularized the use of the term *cumulative deficit* in his book *The Disadvantaged Child*, published in 1967 by Basic Books, in New York. For a concise review of the origin of the term, see A. Jensen, Cumulative deficit: A testable hypothesis? *Developmental Psychology*, 10(6):996–997, 1974.

tests, most poor school children would fall further and further behind the national average, a phenomenon that was not necessarily caused by any absolute decline in cognitive capacities but by the cumulative effects of different learning rates.

The cumulative deficit in achievement was perhaps most simply illustrated by David Hawkridge and Michael Wargo and their staff at the American Institute for Research (AIR), who published a series of reports from 1968–1972 for the United States Office of Education (OE) on exemplary compensatory education programs (see Figure 1).[1] [2] [3] According to these AIR researchers, if one used achievement per month of instruction as the measurement criteria, it would be discovered that the achievement rate of "badly disadvantaged" children, as measured by standardized reading and math tests, would be approximately two-thirds (2:3) that of average children who learned at a 1:1 rate.[4] At this growth rate in reading and math, one could expect the average "badly disadvantaged" child to have fallen approximately one year behind the national norm at the end of the third grade, two years behind at the end of the sixth grade, three years behind after the ninth and four years below grade level if the student graduated high school.

Since the AIR studies, there has been considerable criticism of using achievement per month of instruction and grade equivalencies as the longitudinal measurement criteria,† and a growing controversy over how much of the cumulative deficit can be explained by possible differences in social class-related learning rates over the summer (see Chapter 5). There has also been data that challenges the two-thirds achievement rate generalization for such a nebulous description as badly disadvantaged children. But whatever the technical flaws of the AIR analysis, the relevant data from the 1950s and 1960s were virtually unanimous in suggesting that children from low income families in general, and impoverished black children in particular, were typically slower in acquiring the basic skills than their middle-class counterparts and that the resulting deficit was indeed cumulative.

Consequently, in the late fifties and early sixties, a growing

---

†For a concise review of the problems associated with measuring achievement in grade equivalencies, see D. Horst, *What's Bad About Grade Equivalent Scores.* Mountain View, California, RMC Research Corporation, October, 1976.

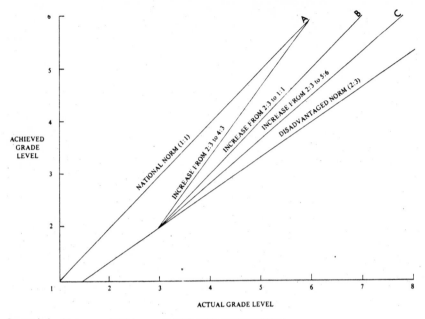

Legends for Marcus and Stickney — RACE AND EDUCATION
Figure 1. Learning rates children achieving at the national norm and the disadvantaged norm and three possible measures of program impact. Early compensatory educator evaluators tended to favor impact A in assessing program effectiveness. Figure adopted from M. Wargo, et al.: *Further Examination of Exemplary Programs for Educating Disadvantaged Children.* Arlington, VA, ERIC Document Reproduction Service, ED 055 128, 1971, p. 15.

number of educators became concerned with both preventing and reducing the scholastic retardation of culturally deprived children. At the preschool level, compensatory education programs often attempted to raise the IQs of lower-class children in order to improve their chances of normal achievement growth after entering elementary school. At the elementary and secondary school levels, compensatory programs concentrated more on accelerating the achievement of disadvantaged children than on raising the IQ. Therefore, one cognitive objective of the preschool programs was to prevent the cumulative *achievement* deficit from ever occurring, while the programs for older children proposed to reduce or even eliminate the progressive achievement gap. The early United States Office of Education AIR investigations noted that for disadvantaged children who had already fallen behind, the achievement deficit could only be eliminated if special programs raised the rate of gain of these children to a point that exceeded the national growth rate of a month of learning per month of instruction (1:1). "At a month-for-month rate, they will neither catch up nor fall farther behind but . . . rate of gain must be greater than month-for-month if disadvantaged children are ever to reach the point where they can perform at grade level (e.g., . . . increase from 2:3 to 4:3). Since this is the ultimate objective of compensatory education, an achievement rate of gain greater than month-for-month was established as the criterion for educational significance."[5]

According to AIR, "educational significance" meant program success and how successful compensatory education programs have been in significantly reducing the class related inequalities in academic achievement is an issue we will address in Chapter 5. For now, it is important to continue reviewing the rationale for the many enrichment programs by taking a closer look at the underlying assumptions regarding the relationship among the environment, the schools, and learning.

The Environment and Cognition

At the time large scale compensatory education efforts were legislated at the federal level, there existed a preponderance of opinion in the literature contending that the environment had considerable influence on measured intelligence and school achievement. Interpretations of the data by many social scientists expressed the interactionist position on the development of human intelligence, which assumed that a child's cognition was the product of complex encounters between his genetic endowment and the environment's unfolding of these innate abilities.

Two of the more influential reviews of the literature were published in book form as *Intelligence and Experience* by J. McVicker Hunt[6] and *Stability and Change in Human Characteristics* by Benjamin Bloom.[7] Between these two volumes, educators could address the nature–nurture question by drawing on studies of animals, twins, siblings, foster children, institutionalized children, and similar populations over time.

If one reads the studies reviewed by Hunt and Bloom with any objectivity, it is difficult to avoid emerging with the strong impression that heredity plays a major role in explaining the variation in measured intelligence among persons in a given population. There were simply too many cases of identical twins, who had been separated in early childhood, scoring strikingly similar on I.Q. tests when reunited as adults[8, 9] and of unrelated children reared together, having lower intelligence correlations than siblings reared apart.* One of the most frequently cited twin studies was conducted in the 1930s by Horatio Newman, Frank Freeman, and Karl Holzinger (the Chicago Group), all from the University of Chicago. These researchers collected longitudinal intelligence data on nineteen pairs† of identical twins separated in most cases before the age of two.[10] When tested in adulthood, the average IQ difference of thirteen pairs raised in rather similar environments was only 4.4 points, which is approximately the same as the 2 to 3 point average IQ difference of identical twins reared together.‡ In reviewing studies of two groups of siblings reared apart and five groups of unrelated children reared together, one finds more position intelligence test score correlations for the separated siblings (typically falling in the +0.30 to +0.50 range) than for the commonly reared unrelated children (averaging somewhere between +0.10 and +0.30).[11]

If the research data made a strong case for the influence of heredity on determining measured intelligence differences, how could advocates of compensatory education emerge from their reading of Hunt and Bloom with an environmentalist interpretation? The answer seemed to lie in the *degree* of the environmental differences. For example, if two identical twins were separated as toddlers and raised in *rather similar* environments, the IQ differences at adulthood rarely exceeded 7 points.§ When comparing

---

*See L. Erlenmeyer-Kimling and L. Jarvik, Genetics and intelligence: a review, *Science*, 142:1477–79, 1963, for a summary of many of the studies of Hunt and Bloom and a graphic analysis showing IQ variations of unrelated persons, foster parents and children, natural parents and children, siblings, and twins.

†The Chicago Group actually reported twenty pairs, but because number 20 did not include data on social and physical environmental advantages, it is excluded from analysis in this volume.

‡See a charting of the twins in the Chicago Group Study by A. Anastasi, in *Differential Psychology*, New York, MacMillan, 1958, p. 299.

§See a review of this research by A. Jensen: The heritability of intelligence. In H. Munsinger (Ed.): *Readings in Child Development*, 2nd ed. New York, Holt, Rinehart and Winston, 1975, pp. 131–135.

this figure to the roughly 12 point IQ difference between fraternal twins reared together and among siblings raised in the same home, and the 15 to 16 point difference found between genetically unrelated children reared together,[12] it would appear, at least from this analysis, that environmental differences within a given community account for a relatively small fraction of the average IQ differences that exist among persons of that community. However, if the environmental differences are *substantial*, there is evidence that persons with identical genetic endowment will differ considerably in measured intelligence. A closer look at the Chicago Group twin data will reveal that six of the twenty pairs reared in the most contrasting social environments averaged 12.5 IQ points difference, and the six differing greatest in education differed by an average of 15 IQ points.[13]

Both Hunt and Bloom use the correlations between the contrasting socioeducational environments and substantial I.Q. differences reported in the Chicago Group study as providing evidence to support the plasticity of intelligence.[14] They also refer to reports of children raised in institutions as making a strong case for environmental influence. One of the more prominent studies was conducted by Rene Spitz, who, in the middle 1940s, measured the effects of maternal deprivation and "hospitalism" on the psychomotor, affective, and cognitive behavior of children during their first year of life, reared in two contrasting Latin American institutions. Documenting behavior by films and by performances on the Hertzer-Wolf baby tests, Spitz concluded that the considerable maternal contact provided by one institution (a nursery attached to a reformatory for delinquent young women) was largely responsible for what appeared to be normal infant development while the relatively limited maternal and other adult contacts of a foundling home for children of economically destitute mothers explained the declining developmental quotient and increasing susceptibility to diseases of these poorly stimulated infants.[15] The Spitz observations gained some support from the work of Ruth Levy who, in 1947, reported on comparisons of orphans raised in boarding homes with similar children reared in nurseries. At the age of two and one-half years, the boarding children, who received the greater adult attention, were clearly superior to the nursery children on a "developmental quotient" index. [16]

By the mid-1960s, perhaps the most convincing evidence supporting the contention that intelligence is not "fixed" had come from the reports of Harold Skeels, who studied not only the effects of institutionalism in early childhood but also its longitudinal influence on behavior. In the original study, thirteen of twenty-five "mentally retarded" orphans residing in an "affectionless" institution were removed by the age of eighteen months to another orphanage where they had intimate contact with several mildly mentally retarded women. The remaining twelve children, constituting a contrast group, remained in the original orphanage. After periods ranging from several months to over two years (depending upon the time of removal and testing) the mean IQ of the experimental group improved dramatically (64.3 to 91.8) while the measured intelligence of the contrast group suffered considerable decline (86.7 to 60.5). [17]

Because of the low reliability of intelligence tests at such an early age, methodological flaws and controversy over statistical regression, the Skeels work (coauthored with H. M. Dye in 1939) was less than convincing until more recent reports in 1965 and 1966 revealed the results of follow-up interviews with all the subjects some twenty years later. Eleven of the thirteen children in the experimental group were adopted, and all were self-supporting leading normal productive lives, virtually indistinguishable from the general population. On the other hand, subjects in the contrast group either remained wards of institutions or were generally living marginal lives on the outside as unemployed dependents or unskilled laborers. [18] [19]

In comparing the educational attainments of the two groups, Skeels reported that "In the experimental group the median grade completed was the twelfth; in the contrast group, the third" and that one of four experimental group subjects attending college for one or more years received a B.A. degree. One of the adopted girls ("who initially had an I.Q. of 35 ...") and might "... have been sterilized in late adolescence or early adulthood" if she had been in the contrast group) had graduated high school, attended college for a term, and was married with two sons, who had IQs of 128 and 107. [20] Unfortunately, Skeels did not administer IQ tests in adulthood to any of the subjects.

By the mid-1960s, the large scale longitudinal studies of intelligence, which included IQ test data collected over a number of years, were in general agreement that the IQ of most persons varied very little after about four years of age. [21] [26] In his influential publication *Stability and Change in Human Characteristics*, Benjamin Bloom reviewed the major multi-year studies to date and concluded that ". . . intelligence develops in an exceedingly lawful way . . . ," which involves a ". . . rapid increase in the correlation between the criterion measure and measurements made in the early years and a less rapid increase after age four." [27] According to Bloom, the correlations between IQ at age seventeen and at age two is +0.41, at age four it is +0.71 and by age eleven is +0.92. [28] In other words, after the critical period of early childhood, measured intelligence becomes a relatively stable characteristic, at least until maturity. Bloom's analysis of an infant's susceptibility to environmental influence will be addressed later in this chapter.

Since most subjects in the major longitudinal studies were middle income and probably grew to maturity in environments that were rather stable, it may come as no surprise that the IQ scores varied little between the ages four and seventeen. (In reviewing the major longitudinal studies in *Intelligence and Experience*, Hunt cites two cases — one from the California guidance study and another from the Berkeley study — in which poor health and maternal overindulgence were thought responsible for respective increases and declines in IQ from 85 to 140 between ages two and ten and from 133 to 77 between two and eighteen.) [29] But what of studies of persons whose environment has undergone considerable changes over the years or reports of children reared in atypical surroundings? Bloom and Hunt both cite the research of Otto Klineberg, which concluded that the length of residence by blacks in New York City, who had migrated to that point from the South in the 1920s and early 1930s, correlated positively with the growth of measured intelligence. [30] They also included a study published by E. S. Lee in 1951, which reported a significant increase in the IQ of Southern black children after they moved to Philadelphia. [31]

Most research on poverty stricken and black children, however, reported a gradual decline in children's IQs as long as they resided in a culture of poverty. There was a study reporting a 20 point IQ decline (100 to 80) of Appalachian children between ages six and sixteen[32] and a number of studies showing a similar cognitive decline in samples of the black population. Therefore, it was the environmentalist position that the moderate correlation (commonly in the area of +0.25 to +0.50) between measured intelligence and social class could be largely attributed to the depressing effect of certain deprivations in the cultures of poverty.

But what was viewed as a culture of poverty and what were the environmental variables within it that may have contributed to the stifling of intellectual growth? Perhaps the most interesting and influential analysis of the phenomenon in the late 1950s and early to middle 1960s was made by anthropologist Oscar Lewis. Basing his generalizations on a number of cross-cultural observations (most extensively conducted in Mexico, Puerto Rico, and New York City), Lewis contended that a "sub-culture of poverty" existed in many places in the world, particularly in "class stratified, highly individuated, capitalistic" societies. Aware of middle-class values and cognizant of the difficulty of upward mobility, persons sharing Lewis' subculture of poverty had feelings of hopelessness, had negative self-images and suspicious attitudes toward such dominant culture-controlled institutions as the police and the schools. Such alienation, despair, and economic want existing aside relative affluence contributed a number of poverty culture characteristics, most prominent of which included matricentrism, present-time orientation, impulsiveness, irrationality, disorganization, and general authoritarianism. Since these cultural variables were self-perpetuating and therefore contributed to the maintenance of ignorance and destitution, Lewis concluded that " . . . the poverty of culture is one of the crucial aspects of the culture of poverty"[33] and that it would be best "transformed and eliminated."[34]

Despite Lewis' contention in 1965 that the culture of poverty had been largely eliminated in the United States (including only 6 to 10 million people) and a number of reports that took issue with Lewis on such suggested poverty-related variables as "feelings of hopelessness," the flavor of his writing typifies a number of other important manuscripts of this period such as *The Culturally Deprived*

Child by Frank Riessman (1961),[35] *Slums and Suburbs* by J. B. Conant (1959)[36] and *The Dark Ghetto* by Kenneth Clark (1965).[37] Theoretically, poverty was viewed as intricately interwoven with many attitudes and behavioral patterns that often severely impaired a child's chances to acquire those aptitudes and skills that permit one to succeed in school. Lewis' anthropological studies seemed to have given a certain credibility to this "deficit model" (which was often interpreted as putting the blame for poverty and poor school achievement on poor people themselves) and could be interpreted as providing a tidy explanation for such platitudes that the poor (particularly the black poor) were relatively deprived of motivation, of language, and/or learning stimuli.

In the affective area, the dehumanizing conditions permeating the black experience in the United States was typically viewed as contributing to low self-concept and aspirations.* Without strong egos, black children could not make maximum use of their intellectual abilities, and without a promising view of the future, black youth could hardly be expected to care much about occupational status or getting ahead someday. These feelings left black school children very poorly motivated, thus contributing to their underachievement.

As plausible as this argument may sound, the social scientific research did not necessarily support the contentions that blacks had weak egos or low aspirations. In 1963, Ausubel and Ausubel reviewed the research on ego development of black children and argued emphatically that the majority of segregated black children in American society, perceived themselves as "an object of derision and disparagement." The authors based their conclusion mainly on the perceptions of several observers and a handful of studies of children's color preferences.[38]

But the material they cite provides far from convincing evidence. For example, one of the most frequently mentioned series of studies were those conducted by Kenneth and Mamie Clark in the 1940s on the doll color preference of Northern and Southern Negro children (see Chapter 1). The Clark's work had unexpectedly

---

*See; for example, B. Bloom, A. Davis, and R. Hess's accounting of the subject in *Compensatory Education for Cultural Deprivation.* New York, Holt, Rinehart and Winston, Inc., 1965, pp. 30–31.

found that Northern Negroes were more likely to accept a "white" doll than their Southern counterparts. The Clarks had argued that the difference may have been caused by "... the fact that in this sample there are many more light colored children in the North than there are in the South."[39] However, it could have been just as easily argued that the Negro children in the more racially integrated Northern city (Springfield, Massachusetts) may have had greater interaction with white persons than the children in the Southern sample, which served to broaden the former group's frame of reference in terms of social status beyond the immediate black community. Although they may have been more integrated with whites, there was little question which race in Springfield in the 1940s enjoyed the greater social status. On the other hand, in a highly segregated Southern community, a black child's frame of social reference may have only included his immediate racial group, and his self-concept may have depended largely upon his relative position within that social entity. A study conducted in the early 1960s of black and white attendants in a mental hospital may serve to illustrate this point. On a self-esteem scale, it was reported that the black employees had even a higher self-image than the white workers. "In this middle Atlantic city, the job of attendant is a relatively good job for a Negro but a very poor position for a white. Self-esteem may be more a matter of one's position within one group than the rank of the group in relation to other groups."[40]

In short, by the middle 1960s there existed little, if any, solid evidence that black children had a lower general self-concept than white children, and even if they did, the research data showed only that self-concept correlated positively with cognitive achievement. It could be argued just as easily that higher achievement caused higher self-concept as it could that higher self-concept contributed to greater achievement.

There was also research to challenge the assumption that black children had lower aspirations[41, 42, 43] and indeed the Ausubels' review had concluded that pencil and paper measures often indicated very similar motivational levels of black and white children. In their commentary on social class findings, the Ausubels probably echoed the feelings of many social scientists when they dismissed the results as invalid because of the "unrealistic" defensiveness of poor children. While this analysis might have been plausible, it was at best speculative. Accordingly, compensatory education programs that used the findings of empirical inquiry as justification for their emphasizing the raising of self-concept and aspiration levels to improve motivation instead of prioritizing the actual teaching of reading were probably going well beyond the data.

Regarding the language of poverty, few could argue with the notion that a child whose native language or dialect was different from that used in the school usually faced a greater handicap than his counterpart who was reared speaking standard American English. Many educators went a step further, however, by suggesting that the speech of the impoverished actually inhibited cognition.* Probably the most frequently cited research was that conducted by British sociologist Basil Bernstein, who in 1962 labeled as "restrictive" the linguistic code of many working-class families and "elaborated" the dialect more often associated with middle-class families. According to Bernstein, characteristics of a restricted language include short or incomplete sentences, a repetitive use of conjunctions, and a limited use of subordinate clauses, modifiers, and the impersonal pronoun. Described as a language of implicit rather than explicit meaning, the restricted code may retard the ability to think abstractly. [44]

In this country, several prominent educators reached linguistic conclusions similar in tone to those of Bernstein. In 1964, David Ausubel viewed complex conceptualization as more difficult for typical lower-class children because of their constant shifting from concrete to abstract modes of thought and comprehension. [45] A year earlier, Vera John concluded that the language of middle-class black children was more adultlike than the language of lower-class black youth. Because of greater middle-class parent–child verbal interaction during childhood, John felt that "the middle class child had an advantage over lower class in tasks requiring precise

---

*Many have associated Siegfried Engelman with this position because of his insistance that disadvantaged children need language training programs that will effectively teach "language and reasoning skills." For an accounting of how to teach language and reasoning, see S. Engleman, How to construct effective language programs for the poverty child. In F. Williams (Ed.): *Language and Poverty.* Chicago, Markham Publishing Company, 1970, pp. 102–121.

and somewhat abstract language." [46]

Despite condemnation by many linguists and a later denial by Bernstein that his work had any relevance for compensatory education, many educators were convinced that poor children (particularly black poor children) needed some sort of systematic language training.† Martin Deutsch sounded a popular theme when he stated in 1964 that lower class pre-schoolers needed a "language training program where words are repeatedly placed in meaningful context ..." Drawing on Bernstein and his own research in Harlem, Deutsch noted that lower class children are not restricted in expressive language ability the way in which words are put together but in the level of "syntactical organization and subject continuity." It was his minimal contact with any systematic inputs from the home environment and the limited exposure to a variety of stimuli that affected the impoverished child's level of verbal usage. [47]

The notions that an environment deprived of a variety of visual and auditory stimuli affected cognition and that impoverished children were likely to be influenced by the deprivation of such stimuli constituted a popular explanation for the underachievement of millions of American children in the early 1960s. Prominent spokespersons for this position were Martin and Cynthia Deutsch, psychiatrists at New York Medical College, where Martin initiated much of his work on language development.

Fundamental to this argument was the belief that perception was largely dependent upon past experience, taking issue with the Gestalt belief that the internal configuration determined the internal order. The research on animals had indicated that the visual experience had a marked influence on the cognitive behavior of cats, chimpanzees, and rats, and studies of auditory and visually deprived humans suggested detrimental effects. Blindfolded college students kept in a soundproof room were observed to have developed an impaired reticular system (which rejected further audio-visual stimulation) and lethargic behavior after a day or two. [48] A study of persons blinded at birth by cataracts reported that the subject had an extraordinarily difficult time discriminat-

---

†For a more complete description of the rationale for and implementation of a language training program see C. Bereiter and S. Englemann's *Teaching Disadvantaged Children in the Preschool.* Englewood Cliffs, N.J., Prentice-Hall, 1966.

ing even the most simple figures (such as squares and triangles) after the removal of these impairments in adulthood. [49] Correlations were also found between figured sheets, complex crib stabiles and the early psychomotor development of infants. [50]

If it was likely that under certain conditions the presence or absence of certain environmental stimuli could either enhance or curtail an organism's cognitive behavior, what evidence existed by the mid-1960s that the condition of economic poverty deprived children of the necessary sensory input for normal intellectual functioning? Linking underachievement to a culture of poverty's stimulus deprivation was almost entirely speculative, but the widely publicized views of the Deutschs did have modest empirical support. Perhaps Martin's most important research on the subject was a study he conducted with Phyllis Katz (published in 1963) that attempted to assess the relationship between the perceptual and cognitive performances of black lower class boys in Harlem. Good and poor readers at the first, third, and fifth grade levels were given a variety of tests to measure perceptivity. The study's major finding was that "normal" readers were superior to "poor" readers in such areas as simple reaction time, shifting auditory and visual modalities, sustained attention, visual signal detection, and visual and auditory word discrimination. Although there was evidence in the study that could have been interpreted as suggesting that maturation, rather than environmental condition, may have affected the reported perceptual differences of good and poor readers (the differences generally decreased in the older children), the authors comment on the findings by stating that many poor children may require "specific intervention" to correct culturally determined, poor auditory and visual responses. [51]

According to Deutsch, the urban slum, with its overcrowded living conditions, contained apartments with " . . . few if any pictures on the wall" and household objects ("be they toys, furniture or utensils," which tended "to be sparse, repetitive and lacking in form and color variations"). He admitted that the paucity of data on the subject mitigated against drawing any conclusions about the effects of "sparsity of manipulative objects on visual perception." However, Deutsch considered it "an important area, as among the skills necessary for reading are form discrimination and visual spatial organization."[52]

Zeroing in on the modality of hearing, Cynthia Deutsch reported a significant correlation between social class and auditory discrimination skills among black and white first and fifth graders. She contended, however, that it was not the paucity of sounds that may restrict auditory discrimination in the slum child, but his saturation by sounds, his chaotic bombardment by "noise" which may have caused interference and a "turning out" of auditory stimuli ("learned inattention").[53]

Whatever the nature of cognition's interaction with visual and auditory stimuli, by the mid-1960s there was a belief in some educational circles that middle-class children did enjoy an advantage over lower-class children (particularly black children) because the impoverished youth lacked many of the sensory amenities characteristic of the social milieu of their more affluent counterparts. Without these stimulants, schooling for many lower-class children was thought to be a difficult and an increasingly unrewarding experience. Surely Martin Deutsch summed up the feelings of many educators in his introduction to his 1963 article on stimulus deprivation. "The thesis here is that the lower-class child enters the school situation so poorly prepared to produce what the school demands that initial failure is almost inevitable, and the school experience becomes negatively rather than positively reinforcing."[54] Deprived of the proper stimuli, restricted by an unappropriate language and dehumanized by a weak self-concept, the academic failure of millions of black children did seem almost inevitable in the early 1960s. In education, something needed to be done to arrest the tide, and preschool education, with its emphasis upon the building of adequate cognitive skills, was viewed as perhaps the best means to give black children not only initial school success but also long term cognitive benefits.

The Issue of Critical Periods

One of the most important of the many topics germaine to the effects of the environment on cognition in the early 1960s was the so-called critical periods hypothesis. Behavioral scientists and educators, such as Benjamin Bloom, J. McVicker Hunt, and Arthur

Jensen, seemed to believe that there are certain optimal periods in the development of an organism during which exposure to appropriate experiences or stimuli will bring about learning much more easily than in other periods. In *Stability and Change in Human Characteristics*, Bloom did not use the term *critical period* but argued nonetheless that it is during the early years, when the human organism is undergoing its greatest change, that the environment has greatest influence. "Variations in the environment have greatest quantitative effect on a characteristic at its most rapid period of change and least effect on a characteristic during the least rapid period of change."[55] Bloom argued that it is during childhood that at least half of human intelligence develops (perhaps 40% by age four; 80% by age eight), and that it would be difficult to make up at a later period whatever effects a "deprived" environment may have had during the critical early years.[56] "... we have assumed that the loss of development in one period cannot be fully recovered in another ... that is, deprivation in the first four years of life can have far greater consequences than deprivation in the ten years from age 8 through 17."[57] Bloom contended that in "extreme" environments an average of 2.5 IQ points a year may be lost the first four years of life.[58]

Hunt also implied that those in economic want may have permanent scars ("The difference between the culturally deprived and culturally privileged is, for children, analogous to the difference between cage-reared and pet-reared rats and dogs"[59]), but contended that retardation that occurs during the second and third year of life "may be reversed to a considerable degree" by proper preschool treatment along the lines of those proposed by Maria Montessori.[60]

Indeed, so accepted was the critical periods hypothesis in this period that Arthur Jensen, now strongly associated with the hereditarian camp, (see Chapter 6) suggested in 1963 that the early experiences of "children of impoverished culture" had a substantial influence on their cognitive retardation. "Our present knowledge of the development of learning abilities indicates that the pre-school years are the most important years of learning in the child's life. A tremendous amount of learning takes place during these years; and this learning is the foundation for all further learnings."[61]

But what was "the present knowledge of learning abilities" Jensen was referring to, i.e. longitudinal data that supported the contention that the environment had greatest quantitative influence during the first few years of life. Jensen, like many other critical period theorists, cited animal studies and offered the above analysis after reviewing the lasting chemical and behavioral changes produced by a "nursery school" for rats at the University of California.[62] In the case of humans, Benjamin Bloom, probably the most influential and widely quoted spokesperson for the critical periods hypothesis, based his argument in the cognitive area on the dubious findings of principally three studies.

In his review of the several large scale longitudinal studies of IQ, he uses Nancy Bayley's Berkeley Growth Study, the most complete and carefully conducted of the group, as providing the clearest evidence of the rapid growth of intelligence during early childhood (IQ correlations at ages seventeen and two is +0.41, at age four is +0.71, at age eleven is +0.92). While Bayley's work may tell us a good deal about the stability of measured intelligence after age four, it by no means gives us evidence that either precludes a hereditarian explanation for the phenomenon or shows that measured intelligence is a more or less fixed characteristic after childhood. Once again, it should be emphasized that there is a strong correlation between IQ at ages eleven and seventeen, perhaps because there is typically very little environmental change during this six-year period.

Bloom then zeroes in on the research of E. S. Lee who measured the IQ of several groups of black children who spent varying periods of time living in Philadelphia. According to Lee, the IQs of children who were born and raised in that city changed hardly at all between grades one and nine, but the IQ change during this period for black children who moved to Philadelphia (usually from the South) by age six was six points. Children arriving by age nine and eleven showed IQ gains by grade nine, of four and two points respectively.[63]

Since Lee only measured IQ change up to grade nine, was it appropriate to argue that the environments most profound effect occurs during the early years? The fact that childrens' IQs changed six points in nine years (grade one through nine), four points in five years (age nine or fourth grade through ninth grade) and two points in three years (age eleven or sixth grade through ninth grade) may only tell us that the longer the environmental exposure the greater the change. If those children who arrived at ages nine and eleven had been followed for nine years (to ages eighteen and twenty), Lee might have found greater than four and two point changes in their IQ. If he had followed all children for at least nine years and found the greatest changes in the youngest children, one could then, and only then, conclude that the data suggested the significance of early environmental exposure.

The third report Bloom cites he considered "to be crucial in establishing the pattern of change in relation to the environment." In this study James Kirk followed eighty-one three-to-six-year-old mentally retarded children (IQs 45 to 80) over a period covering three to five years. Both the experimental and contrast groups were composed of children who lived in a regular community and children who resided at institutions for the retarded. The experimental subjects attended a preschool either in the community or at an institution; the control subjects did not. Kirk found that the IQs of most experimental subjects increased during their preschool experience (while the IQs of the controls did not) and that these gains did not decline but were generally maintained after the treatment. But what Bloom does not include in his interpretation is that the IQs of most children in the community contrast group, upon entering first grade or a special class at age six, increased to a level "approaching the score of the experimental children who had attended preschool." Commenting on this unexpected finding, Kirk questions the significance of preschools for retarded children "If these results are corroborated by later studies, it could mean that pre-schools for mentally handicapped children are not necessary, since the children will accelerate their rate of development after entering school at the unusual age of six."[64]

Kirk does argue, however, for preschool for children from "psychosocially deprived" homes, after analyzing his finding that the subjects' siblings from such environments did not show the characteristic IQ gain in the first grade. But his research also suggests that, under certain conditions, IQ can be increased as easily in the first grade as it can in preschool, which not only challenges the "earlier the better" assumptions but questions the irreversibility of early childhood experience.[65]

If the three studies emphasized by Bloom offer less than convincing support for the critical periods hypothesis, was there relevant research that was not cited in *Stability and Change in Human Characteristics?* A 1952 review of the literature on maternal deprivation conducted by John Bowlby for the United Nations suggested that a severely deprived early environment may do irreparable damage affectively. The study offered very little longitudinal data indicating any sustained effect on intellect.[66] A 1962 study by Sally Province, reporting the physical, emotion, and cognitive retardation of institutionalized infants, also found them generally below the norms on the various measures when tested shortly after placement in foster homes. But Province commented that "we have been impressed by and filled with admiration for the adaptability, resiliency, and capacity for improvement we have witnessed in the children in the course of this research."[67]

An interesting 1960 analysis by Wayne Dennis of the long-term effects of infant crib confinement of Iranian orphans has remained virtually ignored. These orphans spent up to twenty-four hours a day for "many months" during their first year in the supine position. Needless to say, the children enjoyed very little stimulation (they were even fed by a bottle resting on a pillow). In this situation, and at age three only 15 percent could walk alone. At approximately three years of age, however, many of these children were moved to another institution that offered them substantially greater environmental enrichment. In the second institution, Dennis observed the behavior of children between the ages of six and sixteen who were only similarly confined and ". . . presumably as retarded at ages two or three" as were the children whose behavior was described above. However, Dennis found these children ". . . attending school, playing games, doing chores and being trained in different skills, such as the weaving of Persian rugs. There was nothing in their general behavior to suggest that any permanent consequences ensued from the extreme retardation in motor development during the early years."[68]

The study that may have offered the strongest evidence to support the significance of early childhood was conducted by William Goldfarb. Published in 1943, it was for some reason given very little attention by critical period theorists of the early 1960s (Hunt gives it only the briefest reference near the end of *Intelligence and Experience*; Bloom does not cite it at all in *Stability and Change in Human Characteristics*). In any event, Goldfarb reported highly significant differences at age twelve years in IQ and achievement between a group of fifteen foster children who had spent most of their first two years of life in institutions and another group of foster children, equated by number, age, sex, and foster maternal background, who had always lived with "real families." The fact that Goldfarb reported on such a small sample and his omission of any explanation of the subject selection process may have mitigated against his study enjoying greater publicity. [69]

In general, the critical periods theory of the early 1960s was more a statement of faith than a working hypothesis. The longitudinal studies such as Bayley's only gave us age level correlational data on intelligence; the Lee, Kirk, and Dennis reports suggested that IQs may increase significantly at age six and that psychomotor normality can emerge following infant confinement. The work of Kirk and Goldfarb does offer some evidence for the sustenance of early learning experience, but the extensive Bowlby review suggests that it may have a greater effect on affective change, rather than cognitive growth.

In short, by 1965 much of the research on cognition suggested that the environment could have a profound effect on measured intelligence and school achievement, but it was unclear what cultural variables may have contributed to academic retardation and whether there was any optimal time in human development for receptivity to learning. Heredity seemed to account for most of the variation in IQ among a homogenous population, but the environment took on a greater dimension in explaining the IQ differences between people reared in contrasting environments. In the early 1960s, it was fashionable to describe the contrasting environment of the poor as deprived of proper self-concept, appropriate language, and sensory stimuli and that variables such as these within a deprived culture could prevent the natural unfolding of one's genetic potential. Did, however, the subculture of poverty of many black Americans actually depress cognition or did it simply develop different cognitive processes that were inadequately measured on culturally biased intelligence tests?

The question of whether the black subculture is a deficient or only a different environment will be discussed in Chapter 9. For the moment, it is sufficient to conclude that the theories and correlational research findings suggested that the sociocultural milieu of black children mitigated against normal intellectual growth, at least as defined by the dominant American culture. Accordingly, if these inadequate environmental conditions that inhibited measured intelligence and school achievement could be somehow compensated for by exposing disadvantaged blacks to the cultural variables strongly associated with intelligence, it should be possible to significantly reduce the inequality in cognitive achievement that existed between the white and black American population. By the early 1960s, a significant segment of the American population had come to regard the schools as the institution that could successfully provide that compensation.

The Schools and Cognition

If the attitude that the environment has a profound influence on cognition has historically enjoyed varying degrees of acceptance, there is little question that the assumption that the schools constitute a very important part of the learning has long been a part of the American ethos. Horace Mann's famous labeling of education as "the great equalizer" in 1847,[70] the unprecedented growth of public education in this country during the nineteenth century, and the compulsory attendance laws in existance in most states by 1900 are indicative of the value placed on the school's ability to offer millions of people, often from diverse cultural backgrounds, greater equality of opportunity.

The relevant research also supports the significance of formal education. Many elementary schools in Holland were closed for a prolonged period during World War II, and a reported IQ decline of some Dutch children at that time has been attributed to the absence of public education.[71] In Prince Edward County and in New York City the schools were closed for varying periods during the sixties because of respective battles over desegregation and teacher contracts. In both situations, children's achievement was apparently significantly affected by the closings.[72]

With the advent of the Civil Rights Movement, the schools, primarily through desegregation and compensatory education, were seen as playing a crucial role in the struggle to further democratize American Society politically, socially, and economically. The rhetoric of the period on compensatory education may be summarized by drawing on the statements of influential behavioral scientists and educators attending two conferences on the problems of disadvantaged students: one sponsored by Teachers College, Columbia University in 1962 and another by the University of Chicago in 1964.

Under a grant from the Ford Foundation, the Columbia conference invited scholars from twenty-four cities to New York in July of 1962 "... to examine the many dimensions of education in depressed urban areas and to develop sound guiding principles for program planners in city school systems."[73] According to Columbia's A. Harry Passow, the conference coordinator, "over and over, participants stuck on the question of whether the school can make the necessary impact without society really equalizing opportunities in employment, in housing, in civic affairs."[74] But it was unmistakable that the school was viewed as capable of effectively compensating for much of the depressing effects of urban poverty. Mel Ravitz, an Associate Professor of sociology and anthropology from Wayne State University concluded: "Major stress is placed on the school to broaden the horizons of children because often parents do not care or are unable to do very much to enrich their children's experience . . . The key figure in the entire educational process is the teacher. Good teachers can work miracles with children coming from any background . . ."[75] Referring to the perpetuating effects of poverty on "the general academic inadequacy of the majority of disadvantaged pupils . . ." Miriam Golberg of Teachers College suggested: "At some point the circular negative reinforcement has to be attacked. Perhaps the most accessible place is the school itself. One of the major issues confronting education today is to discover the means by which the school can compensate for the lack of readiness for learning which lower class children, in general, and the Negro and other discriminated-against groups of children, in particular, bring to their school work."[76]

Martin Deutsch saw the school as being able to "... significantly reduce the attenuating influence of the socially marginal environment" and Kenneth Clark professed considerable faith in education as a viable agent of social change. "Education has been one of the most effective means for social mobility in the American society. This problem in the future may be different from the similar problems in the past only in that it will involve different and larger groups of previously disadvantaged individuals."[77]

The second conference (the "Research Conference on Education and Cultural Deprivation") was held at the University of Chicago in June, 1964 to review "... the problems of educational and cultural deprivation, to make recommendations to solve some of the problems, and to suggest problems for further research." Funded by the United States Office of Education, the conference solicited working papers from thirty-one scholars from a variety of disciplines. Among the conference participants were Basil Bernstein, Benjamin Bloom, Martin Deutsch, Erik Erickson, Arthur Jensen, Lawrence Kohlberg, and Thomas Pettigrew.[78] A summary of the conference findings, by Benjamin Bloom, Allison Davis, and Robert Hess, should serve to capture the flavor of the attitudes expressed in the many meetings and papers. After reflecting upon the wisdom and extraordinary difficulty of revolutionizing American education as a whole to adjust to an increasingly complex and rapidly changing world, the authors address the specific problems of the culturally deprived.

> But, there is a much more immediate problem. This is in some ways an easier problem to attack and it must be solved in the present. We cannot wait for a decade in which to gradually find solutions for this problem.
> In the present educational system in the U.S. (and elsewhere) we find a substantial group of students who do not make normal progress in their school learning.
> ... We will refer to this group as culturally disadvantaged or culturally deprived because we believe the roots of their problem may in large part be traced to their experiences in homes which do not transmit the cultural patterns necessary for the types of learning characteristic of the schools and the larger society.[79]

Following a description of the nature of cultural deprivation, the conference turned to the educational alternative. "What is needed to solve our current as well as future crisis in education is a system of compensatory education which can prevent or overcome earlier deficiencies in the development of each individual. Essentially, what this involves is the writing and filling of educational prescriptions for groups of children which will enable them to realize their fullest development."[80] If there was a prevailing feeling among educators that a system of compensatory education could prevent or overcome environmentally determined deficiencies, what specific educational prescriptions should be offered that traditional treatment had failed to cure. There was, of course, no consensus. There was a paucity of research on the subject and few successful models to follow. These factors combined with the general idealism of the early 1960s contributed to what was probably a period of unprecedented experimentation in American education. But many proponents of compensatory education felt they were not entirely shooting in darkness. There was some psychological and sociological understanding of the relationship between poverty and emergent from the interpretations of this literature was a myriad of suggestions for educational reform that were divergent, yet typically contained certain common denominators.

At the preschool level, a great emphasis was placed on the use of language. Whether one is reading the teacher-directed behavioral technique of Carl Bereiter and Sigfried Engelmann, the cognitive-discovery approaches of Merle Karnes, David Weikart, and Martin Deutsch, or the more traditional preschool curriculum of Kuno Beller or the Howard University Project, the importance of the child's verbal interaction with adults is stressed. The suggestions of Martin Deutsch in 1964 were typical of those advocating more academic, structured preschool programs: "A language training program would require the creation of a rich, individualized language environment, where words are repeatedly placed in a meaningful context, and where the child is allowed multiple opportunities for expressive language demonstrations as well as for receiving language stimuli under optimal conditions and being encouraged to make appropriate responses."[81]

According to Deutsch, an enrichment language program would improve significantly the pre-school child's preparation for academic success in the early elementary grades thereby reducing the chances of motivational problems stemming from frequent failure.[82]

At the elementary and secondary school level it was often suggested that the schools work directly to improve the child's self-image—"building in these children," according to Kenneth Clark, "a positive self-esteem to supplant the feeling of inferiority and sense of hopelessness which are supported by the all too-pervasive pattern of social realities."[83] Strategies for improving self-concepts included the use of textbooks and materials that reflected to a greater degree the life experiences of disadvantaged minority children, the employment of teachers familiar with the culture and ethnic background of their pupils and a generous use of positive reinforcement, often in terms of verbal praise.[84]

Reforms in the administration and curriculum of the public elementary and secondary schools were suggested in the "Great Cities School Improvement Studies," of the late 1950s, sponsored by the Ford Foundation.

> 1. An extended school day and school week (to include field trips to civic, recreational, industrial and other centers of interest, as well as reading clinics, opportunities for recreational reading in the school library, small academic coaching and small group guidance) to improve the basic skills, motivation and prevent attrition.
>
> 2. A flexible, non-graded grouping of children in the elementary school.
>
> 3. The organization of centers or classes to provide a special program for the culturally deprived child who is of high school age. . . .
>
> 4. Varying the sizes of classes within the school day (so that the particular talents of some teachers are brought to large groups of children, and at the same time other teachers, who may have talents for working with the culturally deprived in small groups or as individuals, are freed for work of this type. . . .
>
> 5. An organization in which the length of the periods in the school day is altered to give the culturally deprived child some short periods of instruction in small groups in skill areas and longer periods of integrated unit activity will improve reading and arithmetic skills, establish the close, stabilizing relationship with an adult. . . .
>
> 6. Greater use of paraprofessionals . . . for such purposes as vision and hearing screening, . . field trips, operating projectors . . . will release professional personnel for teaching purposes and improve the academic achievement of the culturally deprived. . . .[85]

Educational reforms called for by Patricia Sexton in her 1961 publication *Education and Income* included an elimination of "segregated groupings and curriculum," a "replacement of the highly

competitive system of marks, exams and comparisons of all sorts . . .
by other types of incentives to learning, the removal of irrelevant
'dead weight' from the curriculum such as 'meaningless dates and
data,' an expansion of work-study programs, more attractive accessible libraries, and greater 'attention' to an unexplainably neglected
skill concentration. . . . "[86]

Effective teachers for disadvantaged children were viewed by
Sexton as perhaps more likely to be male ("efforts should be made
to encourage more men, of the type boys can readily identify with,
to enter teaching"), enthusiastic, and well paid; by Miriam Goldberg
as respectful, familiar with the child's cultural experience, sensitive to the "self-fulfilling prophecy," capable of showmanship, and
by David Riessman *The Culturally Deprived Child* (1962) as consistent, straight-forward, down-to-earth, sometimes physical, and dedicated.[87]

The suggested changes just cited in administration, curriculum,
and teaching represents only a microscopic glance at the proposed
reforms in the schools to improve the cognitive achievement of
disadvantaged pupils. Nevertheless, they do give us a "feel" for the
ideal characteristics of many, if not most, of the proposed compensatory education programs of the 1960s. Drawing on the suggested
reforms listed in this section and in many additional discussions of
the subject, the following listing includes some of the more commonly recommended components of early compensatory education
programs:

1. Improving the motivation of pupils.
2. Improving the self-concepts of pupils.
3. Increasing per pupil expenditures.
4. Lowering the teacher-pupil ratio.
5. Individualizing instruction where appropriate.
6. Liberalizing the administration of the schools to facilitate
   appropriate changes in class periods, class size, and student
   and teacher mobility.
7. Ordering or creating instructional materials which are more
   consistent with the socio-cultural background of the pupils.
8. Emphasizing "language training" at the preschool level.
9. Employing enthusiastic and dedicated teachers who are
   familiar with the pupils' socio-cultural background, under-

stand the nature of a "disadvantaged" environment's effect
on cognitive achievement, and think positively about the
school's power to effectively compensate for environmental
inadequacies.
  10. Involving members of the community — particularly the
      pupil's parents — in the children's learning process.
  In the early 1960s, compensatory education may have been
defined, therefore, as a process whereby *educators attempted to
compensate for the academic inadequacies of economically and/or
socially disadvantaged children by giving particular attention to
the strengthening of basic cognitive skills, motivation and self-
concept in an atmosphere imbued with the promotion of individual
needs by employing positive reinforcement, cultural enrichment,
student-centered materials and humanistic teaching.*

EARLY ELEMENTARY AND SECONDARY PROGRAMS

  The first compensatory education program to gain national
prominence began in a Harlem junior high in 1956. [88] Entitled the
Demonstration Guidance Project, it sought to identify pupils with
promising standardized test credentials (above the 50th percentile)
and provide them with intensive counseling and individualized
teaching. [89] After impressive gains were reported in achievement,*
the program was expanded in 1959 to a large-scale project entitled
Higher Horizons that provided comprehensive compensatory services to thousands of disadvantaged low achievers in the Harlem
area. In 1967, the United States Commission on Civil Rights
described the project as the largest program of its kind in American history "... involving by 1962, 64,000 children from 52 elementary schools, 13 junior high schools and 2 senior high schools." [90]
  Higher Horizons was not only the largest compensatory education
program of the early 1960s but probably the most influential. In
1963, Passow described the project as "... perhaps the most widely
known enrichment program ... now being adopted in numerous
other communities," and, in 1969, White House aide Roger Freemen
contended that "during the early 1960s Higher Horizons was widely

---

*For 147 of 250 pupils, a 4.3 years reading gain after 2.6 years of the program. [95]

promised as a shining example and was copied in many cities."[91] [92] Indeed, it was used as a model for DHEW's shaping of proposals for Title I ESEA.[93]

According to the U.S. Commission on Civil Rights

Four major techniques were used on Higher Horizons. First, teachers were trained and encouraged to improve both their expectations of the students and their own ability to teach disadvantaged children. Second, counseling and guidance services were extended and increased to raise aspirations ... Third, an effort was made to broaden cultural backgrounds and horizons of students through visits to museums, libraries, colleges and concerts. Lastly special remedial teachers were provided to upgrade reading, writing and arithmetic skills.[94]

Another well-publicized general enrichment program was Project Bannecker in St. Louis, initiated in 1957 under the energetic, vocal leadership of Samuel Shepard. By 1965, the project had become one of the nation's largest compensatory programs, involving twenty-three predominately black elementary schools with more than 14,000 pupils.[96] The Bannecker project made few curriculum changes and placed great emphasis on such affective and community modifications as improving the motivation and self-concepts of pupils, bettering the attitudes of teachers (often by "re-education"), and increasing the involvement of parents. Inter-school academic competition was staged, pep rallies were held, and staff home visits were encouraged.[97]

In addition to the influential pioneering efforts in New York and St. Louis, scores of enrichment programs emerged in many other American cities and towns.† Among those receiving the greatest attention were sponsored by the Ford Foundation's Great Cities Improvement Project, a comprehensive educational enrichment project beginning in 1957 targeted at the urban poor in Milwaukee, Berkeley, Pittsburgh, St. Louis, Washington, D.C., Cleveland, and Detroit. Although the programs varied considerably from city to city, Dorsey Baynham, a free lance education writer, wrote in 1963 that three factors common to each site were

---

†An exact number of pre-ESEA compensatory programs is impossible to determine. A 1965 inventory by the University of Chicago's Urban Child Center listed several hundred programs.

1. A "willingness to experiment with a broad range of teaching materials . . . and . . . administrative approaches"

2. "Strenuous efforts to search out and use community help . . ." and

3. Preparation of teachers to meet the special affective and cognitive needs of disadvantaged children. [98]

Early Preschool Programs and Head Start

At the preschool level, the major impetus for compensatory education both theoretically and practically came not from the school systems or social agencies but from a few academicians from the universities and colleges. [99] In the early 1960s, compensatory preschool programs may not have exceeded two dozen, [100] and most of them were experimental research projects. Among those · that received the greatest publicity and employed the most sophisticated research designs were Martin Deutsch's New York based Initial Enrichment Program, (one of the earliest, beginning in 1958), Merle Karnes' Ameliorative Pre-School Program at the University of Illinois (a cognitive oriented whole child model), Susan Gray and Rupert Klaus's Early Training Project at George Peabody College in Nashville (another cognitive "whole child" program), David Weikart's Piagetian Ypsilanti Perry Pre-School Project in Michigan and Bereiter–Engelmann's behavioristic design at the University of Illinois. [101]

The public sector made a rather dramatic entry into the preschool business, however, when it began serving through Project Head Start 561,000 children in 2,400 centers in the summer of 1965. Project Head Start was initiated by the War on Poverty's Economic Opportunity Act of 1964. Community action agencies, school systems and various voluntary organizations were eligible for sponsorship. [102]

Early childhood educator Millie Almy has described Head Start as a project that from its inception "captured the imagination of many people" and had originally the "rather modest and realistic goal" of developing "pleasure, confidence and courage" in disadvantaged preschoolers. She observes that "The scope of the program grew, however, to include an educational program, health services . . . , social services, psychological services, nutrition and a parent participation program." Despite its modest beginning, the focus of assessments of Head Start effectiveness, as they were for the university preschool models, soon became cognitive growth (see Chapter 5).

Title I

Even more encompassing than Project Head Start is the Elementary and Secondary Education Act (ESEA), which was passed in 1965 after a lengthy congressional debate over the wisdom of federal aid to education. ESEA represented the first legislation that contained a large-scale commitment to use federal funds to improve the equality of American education,[103] and Title I of the act was specifically written to finance compensatory programs for an academically disadvantaged school age population. One may appreciate the relative size of the monies appropriated by recognizing that the 1.2 billion dollars provided by Congress under Title I the first year exceeded "the total Office of Education direct appropriations" for the entire year of 1964.[104]

Although ESEA's many Titles monetarily supported such educational components as libraries, innovative education projects and civil rights compliance, its success in compensating for environmentally caused academic retardation soon became a primary measure of ESEA effectiveness. For, in the words of one close observer, in addition to its being the first large federal education act, ESEA's " . . . second unique feature was . . . the evaluation requirement included in Title I," which marked " . . . the first time that federal legislation included an evaluation requirement within the law itself."[105] This requirement became the impetus for annual evaluations of Title I at the national, state, and local levels and eventually nationwide searches for exemplary programs for proof that ESEA Title I was working. What generally came to be meant by *working* was hard data showing that programs were producing average pupil reading or math achievement gains of at least a month of instruction (1:1), i.e. at the same growth rate or better than the national average.[106]

CRITIQUING THE RATIONALE

Despite the cautiously realistic goals of many Head Start founders and the reservations expressed about the powers of schooling by many academicians, there appeared to be widespread acceptance of the notion that improved schooling could indeed compensate for the environmentally determined deficiencies in measured intelligence and pupil achievement.

What factors could have contributed to such an idealistic criteria by which to assess the success of effectiveness of preschool, elementary schools, and secondary school compensatory programs? There were only a handful of studies showing significant pupil gains in compensatory situations, a promising first year evaluation of Higher Horizons, a Bloom analysis of the Chicago Group twin data suggesting that "educational" advantage had a greater influence on IQ than "environmental" advantages. [107] But a careful reading of the basis for Doctor Bloom's argument on education and twins, just as in his argument for critical periods, will raise questions about the validity of this suggestion.

If the research was less than convincing, the common rationale for compensatory education was also of questionable logic. If we list the assumptions summarizing the rationale offered at the beginning of this chapter as premises, the illogic becomes apparent.

MAJOR PREMISE:

> The environment has a profound influence on measured intelligence and school achievement.

MINOR PREMISE:

> The schools constitute an important part of the environment.

CONCLUSION:

> Schools can compensate for the environmentally determined deficiencies in measured intelligence and school achievement.

Assuming the validity of the major and minor premises, it is theoretically impossible for any part of the whole to equal the whole. The word *compensate* as defined by Merriam-Webster, means "to be equivalent to" or "to supply an equivalent."[108] Consequently, it would be logical to argue that the schools can have an important influence on measured intelligence and school achievement, but illogical to argue they can wholly compensate for environmentally determined deficiencies.

Logic aside, in their recognition of the significance of the environment's influence, compensatory educators of the early sixties recommended schooling that would expose children to much more than the so-called basics. Cultural enrichment activities such as trips to museums, zoos, and concerts were often recommended for disadvantaged children. It is questionable, however, whether formalizing these experiences a few hours a week through the schools could offer an adequate substitute for the totality of the child's socio-cultural milieu. If educationally significant gains in reading and mathematics were the primary goals of the early programs, it may have been better to have devoted greater attention to the specific teaching of these skills.

The fact that the so-called culturally deprived model was adopted by many early compensatory programs may have compounded the problem. Exposing children to the cognitive processes of a given culture to facilitate the comprehension of its dialect may be educationally sound practice, no matter how limited the immersion. Designing for children ego inflating experiences, language training activities, and multi-sensory stimulations, however, may be another matter. Not only was such an approach potentially dehumanizing, but it had very little scientific justification. In the case of blacks, there was no solid evidence that they had lower general self-concepts than whites, only speculation that they spoke a restricted tongue and no empirical data suggesting that their physical environment was deprived of intellect-building stimuli. The fact that the black subculture was different did not necessarily mean it was deprived. It may have ill prepared its members to score well on middle-class measures of intelligence, but may not have inhibited cognition in any absolute manner. Calling black children culturally deprived probably did little to enhance their self-esteem, and advocating for urban preschoolers language training (as if they had been reared in attics or in cribs) as a prerequisite for normal achievement in reading may have unappropriately taxed the time and energy of many early compensatory education programs.

COLEMAN ADDS TO THE CONTROVERSY

Whatever may have been the inherent quality of the black way of life in 1965, there is no question that the influences of slavery, segregation, prejudice, and poverty had ill-prepared millions of black children for equality of achievement opportunities. For many other minority and white children, prejudices and poverty had also taken its toll. Because of a growing concern about education's relation to income and ethnicity, the year 1965 not only encompassed the origin of Head Start, the passage of ESEA but the initiation of the massive *Equality of Education Opportunity Survey* (the Coleman Report), directed by James Coleman. [109] The Coleman Report was initiated in response to Section 402 of the Civil Rights Act of 1964 that ordered that the Commissioner of Education "... conduct a survey and make a report to the President and the Congress ... concerning the lack of availability of equal opportunities for individuals by reason of race, color, religion or national origin in public educational institutions at all levels in the United States. ..." [110]

Called by Mosteller and Moynihan "... the second largest social science research project in history" (Project Talent it seems was larger), [111] the survey tested some 570,000 pupils and 60,000 teachers. [112] Data from over 4,000 schools was collected and analyzed in extraordinary detail. [113] To Coleman and his staff, equality of educational opportunity apparently meant not only equalizing inputs (school facilities and per pupil expenditure) but school outputs (pupil achievement on standardized tests), for their report went well beyond attempts to document the limited school resources generally available to racial and ethnic minorities. [114]

The Coleman Report is notable not for what it found but for what it did not find. To the surprise of almost everyone, the survey did not report gross inequalities in educational resources in schools with differing minority enrollment and did not find evidence that school facilities and curriculum in themselves had much at all to do with pupil achievement. [115] Nationally, whites did enjoy a greater quantity of school resources which were thought to affect learning, but, when available facilities for the two races were analyzed regionally (focusing on the South, Midwest, etc.), remarkably little difference in educational services was reported. [116] The input variables of "teacher characteristics" and "student body characteristics" did correlate with measured pupil learning, but "Differences in school facilities and curriculum, which are the major variables by which attempts are made to improve schools, are so little related to differences in achievement levels of students that, with very few exceptions, their effects fail to appear in a survey of this magnitude." [117]

On the standardized tests used by Coleman, minority children (with the exception of "Oriental Americans") scored well below "majority" children at each grade level reported in the survey,* and there existed a cumulative deficit in achievement between each of the minorities and the majority. [118] The achievement test scores of black children were the lowest of any racial or ethnic group measured, falling about one standard deviation below the white average. Certain teacher characteristics (particularly teacher verbal facility and educational background) were shown as likely to have some effect on black (but not white) achievement, [119] and the student's expressed feeling of destiny control had a strong relationship to achievement† ("stronger . . . than do all the 'school' factors together," [120]). Generally speaking, the percentage of white pupils in a school improved the achievement of black pupils but only consistently when whites were more than half the school population. [121] Finally, as one might expect, the school factors affecting achievement usually had a greater influence on minority students than on majority pupils. [122]

But even factors such as racial integration and the teacher's verbal facility showed a relatively small correlation with achievement when compared to student environmental background, which usually accounted for between 10 to 25 percent of the variance in individual achievement. [123] Eight background factors were included

---

*Grades 1, 3, 6, 9, and 12.
†The attitude of "sense of control of the environment" was highly related to achievement, but this feeling was not found to be influenced much by any school characteristics.

in the survey dealing with family structure and size, parental economic and educational backgrounds, parental attitudes toward education, availability of reading materials and certain technical amenities, and length of residence in an urban area. Collectively, the pupil background characteristics had a slightly greater effect on the variance in achievement at the earlier grades than the later grades* and a somewhat greater effect on white achievement than on black achievement. [124] The significance of family background compared to the other variables and the importance of the Coleman Report itself may be summarized by quoting the concluding paragraph from the 106 page section on "Pupil Achievement and Motivation."

> Taking all these results together, one implication stands out above all: that schools bring little influence to bear on a child's achievement that is independent of his background and general social context; and that this very lack of an independent effect means that the inequalities imposed on children by their home, neighborhood, and peer environment are carred along to become the inequalities with which they confront adult life at the end of school. *For equality of educational opportunity through the schools must imply a strong effect of schools that is independent of the child's immediate social environment, and that strong independent effect is not present in American schools.* [125]

The "independent effect of school" that was so critical and was found by Coleman to be so inconspicuous in the America of 1965 would be made more visible, it was hoped, by federal appropriation throughout the nation for compensatory education programs. Indeed, by the time the Office of Education had released *Equality of Education Opportunity Survey*, over one billion dollars had already been spent under Title I of ESEA, essentially to permit the schools to effectively educate children independent of their home environment.†

The Coleman Report has had far reaching implications for desegregation policies, compensatory education and educational

---

*Only grades 6, 9 and 12 were included. Information on pupil background was obtained from the children themselves; it was believed difficult to question younger children on this topic. But it is interesting that variation in schooling had a greater effect in the higher grades than in the lower grades.

†See F. Mosteller and D. Moynihan (Eds.): *On Equality of Educational Opportunity.* New York, Random House, 1972. for a reanalysis generally supportive of Coleman's conclusions.

research (see Chapter 5). For the moment it is sufficient to say that various reanalyses have both generally supported[126] [127] and strongly taken issue with his conclusions, and that more recent smaller scale studies have found that variation in schooling does affect variation in learning.

Perhaps Coleman's greatest contribution to educational sociology is not, therefore, his conclusion that schools make little difference, but his generation of thought and research on just *how much* difference schooling can make. The evaluations reviewed in Chapter 5 and the nature-nurture discussion in Chapter 6 will hopefully give us a better insight into the answer to this question. We may find the data suggesting that schools can improve the achievement of disadvantaged children but not compensate for environmental determined deficiencies. If this is the case, greater attention could be given to the inherent illogic of compensatory education's rationale. On the other hand, we may find data suggesting that schools are capable of such compensation and that will then raise questions about the entire environmental hypothesis. Or perhaps in this society it is education, not socio-cultural background, that tells us most about pupil achievement, and the impact of schooling is potentially so powerful that appropriate instruction *can* overcome what little influence the out-of-school environment may have. Another possibility is that genetic endowment is the primary cause of the gross inequalities in educational achievement and if this is the case, we must ask what the schools can do, if anything, to neutralize the effects of heredity.

REFERENCES

1. Hawkridge, D. et al.: *A Study of Selected Exemplary Programs for the Education of Disadvantaged Children*, Part 1. Arlington, VA., ERIC Document Reproduction Service, ED 023 776, 1968.
2. Wargo, M. et al.: *Further Examination of Exemplary Programs for Educating Disadvantaged Children*. Arlington, VA., ERIC Document Reproduction Service, ED 055 128, 1971.
3. Wargo, M. et al.: ESEA Title I: *A Reanalysis and Synthesis of Evaluation Data from Fiscal Year 1965 to 1970*. Arlington, VA., ERIC Document Reproduction Service, ED 059 415, 1972.
4. Hawkridge, D. op cit., 1968, pp. 30–31.
5. Wargo, 1971, op cit., p. 5.

6. Hunt, J. McV.: *Intelligence and Experience.* New York, Ronald Press, 1961.

7. Bloom, B.: *Stability and Change in Human Characteristics.* New York, John Wiley and Sons, Inc., 1964.

8. Bloom, B. op cit., pp. 33–34.

9. McV. Hunt, J. op cit., pp. 18–21.

10. Newman, H., Freeman, F., and Holzinger, K.: *Twins, A Study of Heredity and Environment.* Chicago, The University of Chicago Press, 1937.

11. Erlenmeyer and Jarvik, op cit., pp. 1477–79.

12. Jensen, A.: The heritability of intelligence. In Munsinger, H. (Ed.): *Readings in Child Development,* 2nd. ed. New York, Holt, Rinehart and Winston, 1975, pp. 131–135.

13. Anatasi, op cit., p. 299.

14. McV. Hunt, op cit., pp. 19–21.

15. Spitz, R.: Hospitalism, An inquiry into the genesis of psychiatric conditions in early childhood. *Psychoanalytic Study of the Child, 1:* 53–74, 1945.

16. Ibid.

17. Skeels, H. and Dye, H.: A study of the effects of differential stimulation on mentally retarded children. *Proceedings of the American Association of mental Deficiency, 44:*114–136, 1939.

18. Skeels, H.: Effects of adoption on children from institutions. *Children,* January–February, 1965, pp. 33–34.

19. Skeels, H.: "Adult Status of Children with Contrasting Early Life Experiences: A Follow-Up Study," *Child Development Monographs,* Serial No. 105, *31(3):* 1966.

20. Skeels (1965), op cit., p. 34.

21. Anderson, J.: The limitations of infant and pre-school tests in the measurement of intelligence. *Journal of Psychology, 8:* 851–79, 1939.

22. Bayley, N.: Consistency and variability in the growth of intelligence from birth to eighteen years. *Journal of Genetic Psychology, 75:* 165–96, 1949.

23. Ebert, E. and Simmons, K.: The Brush Foundation study of child growth and development, I. Psychometric tests. *Monographs of the Society for Research in Child Development, 8(21):* 1943..

24. Freeman, F. and Flory, C.: Growth in intellectual ability as measured by repeated tests. *Monographs of the Society for Research in Child Development, 2(2):* 1937.

25. Honzik, M., Macfarlane, J., and Allen, L.: The stability of mental test performance between two and eighteen years. *Journal of Experimental Education, 17:* 309–24, 1938.

26. Sontag, L., Baker, C., and Nelson, V.: Mental growth and personality: A longitudinal study. *Monographs of the Society for Research in Child Development, 23(2):* 1958.

27. Bloom, op cit., pp. 56–57.

28. Ibid., p. 57.

29. Hunt, op cit., pp. 24–25.

30. Klineberg, O.: *Negro Intelligence and Selective Migration.* New York, Columbia University Press, 1935.
31. Lee, E. Negro intelligence and selective migration: A Philadelphia test of the Klineberg hypothesis. *American Sociological Review, 16:* 227–33, 1951.
32. Wheeler, L.: A comparative study of the intelligence of East Tennessee Mountain children. *Journal of Educational Psychology, 33:* 321–34, 1942.
33. Lewis, O.: *La Vida. A Puerto Rican Family in the Culture of Poverty, San Juan and New York.* New York, Random House, 1965, p. ii.
34. Lewis, O.: *The Children of Sanchez: Autobiography of a Mexican Family.* New York, Random House, 1961, p. xxx.
35. Riessman, F.: *The Culturally Deprived Child.* New York, Harper, 1962.
36. Conant, J.: *Slums and Suburbs.* New York, McGraw-Hill, 1961.
37. Clark, K.: *Dark Ghetto.* New York, Harper & Row, 1965.
38. Ausubel, D. and Ausubel, P.: Ego development among segregated negro children. In Passow, A. H. (Ed.): *Education in Depressed Areas.* New York, Teachers College Press, Columbia University, 1963.
39. Ibid., p. 174.
40. Rosenberg, M.: *Society and the Adolescent Self Image.* Princeton, New Jersey, Princeton University Press, 1965, p. 65.
41. Boyd, F. The levels of aspirations of white and negro children in a non-segregated elementary school. *Journal of Social Psychology, 36:* 191–196, 1952.
42. Sears, R.: *Patterns of Child Rearing.* Evanston, Row and Peterson, 1952.
43. Weinger, M. and Murray, W.: Another look at the culturally deprived and their levels of aspiration. *Journal of Educational Sociology, 36:* 319–21, 1963.
44. Bernstein, B.: Linguistic codes, hesitation, phenomena and intelligence. *Language and Speech, 5(1):* 31–46, 1962.
45. Augusbel, D.: How reversible are the cognitive and motivational effects of cultural deprivation? Implications for teaching the culturally deprived child. *Urban Education, 1:* 16–38, 1964.
46. John, V.: Intellectual development of slum children: Some preliminary findings. *American Journal of Orthopsychiatry, 33:* 813–22, 1963.
47. Deutsch, M.: Facilitating development in the pre-school child: Social and psychological perspectives. *Merrill-Palmer Quarterly, 10:* 249–63, 1964.
48. Hebb, D.: The motivating effects of extrareceptive stimulation. *American Psychologist, 13:* 109, 1958.
49. Von Senden, M.: *Raum und Gestaltauffassung bei operierten Blindgeborener von und nach der Operation Leipzig:* Barth, 1932, cited by Cynthia P. Deutsch in
50. White, B.: *Informational Education during the first Months of Life.* Paper presented at the Social Science Research Council Conference on Pre-School Education, February 8, 1966.
51. Deutsch, M. and Katz, P.: The disadvantaged child and the learning process. Passow, A. H. (Ed.): *Education in Depressed Areas.* New York, Teachers College Press, Columbia University, 1963, pp. 163–79.
52. Ibid., pp. 170–171.

53. Deutsch, C.: Auditory discrimination and learning: Social factors. *Merrill-Palmer Quarterly*, *10*: 277–95, 1964.
54. Deutsch and Katz, op cit., p. 163.
55. Bloom, op cit., p. vii.
56. Ibid., p. 72.
57. Ibid.
58. Ibid.
59. Hunt, J. McV.: Environment, Development and Scholastic Achievement. In Deutsch, M., Katz, I., and Jensen, A. (Eds.): *Social Class, Race and Psychological Development*. New York, Holt, Rinehart and Winston, 1968, pp. 293–296.
60. Ibid.
61. Jensen, A.: Learning in the pre-school years. *The Journal of Nursery Education*, *18*(2): 133, 1963.
62. Ibid., pp. 133–139.
63. Lee, op cit., pp. 227–233.
64. Kirk, J.: *Early Education of the Mentally Retarded*. Urbana, Illinois, University of Illinois Press, 1958, p. 209.
65. Ibid., pp. 209–211.
66. Bowlby, J.: *Maternal Care and Mental Health*. Geneva, World Health Organization, 1952.
67. Province, S. and Lipton, R.: *Infants in Institutions*. New York, International Universities Press, 1962, p. 144.
68. Dennis, W.: Causes of retardation among institutional children: Iran. *The Journal of Genetic Psychology*, *96*(*1*): 56–57, 1960.
69. Goldfarb, W.: The effects of early institutional care on adolescent personality. *The Journal of Experimental Education*, *12*: 143(A),
70. Mann, H.: The 12th Annual Report to the Massachusetts Board of Education, 1848, In Noll, J. W. and Kelly, S. P. (Eds.): *Foundations of Education in America*, New York, Harper and Row, 1970, pp. 120–15.
71. Jencks, C. et al.: *Inequality*, New York: Harper and Row, 1972, p. 87.
72. Ibid.
73. Passow, A. (Ed.): *Education in Depressed Areas*. New York, Teachers College Press, Columbia University, 1963, p. vii.
74. Ibid., p. 351.
75. Ibid., p. 18.
76. Ibid., p. 89.
77. Ibid., pp. 144–145.
78. Bloom, B., Davis, A., and Hess, R.: *Compensatory Education for Cultural Deprivation*. New York, Holt, Rinehart and Winston, 1965.
79. Ibid., p. 4.
80. Ibid., p. 6.
81. Deutsch, op cit., 1964, p. 260.
82. Ibid., pp. 249–263.

83. Clark, K.: Educational stimulation of racially disadvantaged children. Passow, A. H. (Ed.): *Education in Depressed Areas.* New York, Teachers College Press, Columbia University, 1963, p. 157.
84. Ibid.
85. Great Cities School Improvement Studies, Ford Foundation Project, mimeographed, 1960, reprinted in *The Culturally Deprived Child* by F. Riessman, New York: Harper and Row, 1962, pp. 125–6.
86. Sexton, P.: *Education and Income.* New York, Viking, 1961.
87. Reissman, op cit.
88. Freeman, R.: The alchemists in our public schools. Quoted by J. Ashbrook in the House of Representatives, *Congressional Record,* April 24, 1969, pp. 10325–26.
89. Ibid.
90. United States Commission on Civil Rights, 1967, *Racial Isolation in the Public Schools,* V 1, U.S. Government Printing Office, Washington, D.C., February, 1967.
91. Passow, op cit., p. 343;
92. Freeman, op cit., p. 10326.
93. Ibid.
94. U.S. Commission on Civil Rights, op cit., pp. 124–125.
95. Ibid., p. 123.
96. Ibid.
97. Gordon, E. and Wilkerson, D.: *Compensatory Education for the Disadvantaged.* New York, College Entrance Examination Board, 1966, p. 250.
98. Baynham, 1963, quoted in B. Stickney, *Compensatory Education and Pupil Achievement,* Unpublished Doctoral Dissertation, University of Massachusetts, Amherst, 1976, p. 110.
99. Almy, M.: *The Early Childhood Educator at Work.* New York, McGraw-Hill, Inc., 1975, p. 84.
100. Stickney, B.: Compensatory Education and Pupil Achievement. Unpublished Doctoral dissertation, University of Massachusetts, Amherst, 1976, pp. 186, 193.
101. Ibid., pp. 188–190.
102. Almy, op cit., p. 88.
103. Hecht, K.: Title I federal evaluation: The first five years. *Teachers College Record,* 75(1): 67–78, 1973.
104. Ibid.
105. Ibid., p. 67.
106. Wargo, op cit., 1971, p. 5.
107. Anatasi, op cit., p. 299.
108. *Webster's New International Dictionary of the English Language,* Second Edition. Springfield, Massachusetts, Unabridged, G. & C. Merriam Company, Publishers, 1951, p. 545.

109. Coleman, J. et al.: *Equality of Educational Opportunity*, Washington, D.C., U.S. Department of Health, Education and Welfare, U.S. Government Printing Office, 1966.
110. Ibid., p. iii.
111. Mosteller, F. and Moynihan, D. (Eds.): *On Equality of Educational Opportunity*. New York, Random House, 1972.
112. Coleman, op cit.
113. Ibid.
114. Ibid.
115. Ibid., p. 122.
116. Ibid., p. 113.
117. Ibid., p. 274.
118. Ibid., pp. 317–318.
119. Ibid., p. 23.
120. Ibid., p. 32.
121. Ibid., p. 22.
122. Ibid., pp. 298–302.
123. Ibid., p. 300.
124. Ibid., p. 325.
125. Hecht, op cit.
126. Bowles, S. and Levin, H.: The determinants of scholastic achievement — An apprisal of some recent evidence. *The Journal of Human Resources*, 8: 3–24, 1968.
127. Hanushek, E. and Kain, J.: On the value of equality of educational opportunity as a guide to public policy. In Mosteller, F. and Moynihan, D. (Eds.): *On Equality of Educational Opportunity*. New York, Random House, 1972, pp. 116–145.

CHAPTER 5

THE EFFECTIVENESS OF COMPENSATORY EDUCATION: WHAT THE RESEARCH SHOWS

I f the period from 1945 to 1965 can be described as providing a rationale for integration and compensatory education policies and as contributing to the development of a consensus on what was appropriate educationally for black Americans, the years since 1965 may be logically referred to as a period of evaluation of these strategies and as cultivating considerable dissension among many reformist educators and academicians. By 1955, school desegregation had begun to be ordered, by 1965, Title I had been legislated, and by that mid-sixties summer a President from Texas was overseeing the enrollment of approximately 500,000 children in Head Start. But the release of the Coleman Report in 1966 and the onslaught of educational assessments that followed soon ignited continuous controversies surrounding the explosive issues of race and education. Indeed, by 1968, Head Start was judged by some observers to be ineffective, by 1969 a former proponent of compensatory education was offering a possible genetic explanation for the "apparent failure" of compensatory education, and, by 1975, Doctor Coleman, a man who formerly enjoyed impeccable liberal credentials, was under attack for yet another report on the alleged ineffectiveness of desegregation due to "white flight."

Coleman's first report, the massive *Equality of Educational Opportunity Survey* (EEOS), was perhaps not as inflammatory as his conclusions on busing, but was surely every bit as provocative. His finding that black achievement was related to the student body's racial composition generally furthered the interests of integration in general and busing in particular.[1] However, the fact that white pupil presence correlated only very modestly with black gains often contributed to a questioning of the necessity of racial balance in the schools. Coleman's data was gathered too early* to measure any effects of Title I, but his conclusions regarding the relative ineffectiveness of schooling in equalizing achievement triggered a number of reanalyses of his survey. In the fall of 1966, a Harvard hosted seminar entitled "On Equality of Educational Opportunity," was described by Daniel Patrick Moynihan as taking on "near conference proportions" and as instrumental in warranting the creation of an entire educational policy center at Harvard to begin a more sophisticated EEOS reexamination. [2]

In the field of compensatory education, a United States Commission on Civil Rights study of pre-Title I programs appeared in 1967 and a longitudinal study of Head Start was released in 1969. By far the greatest contributor to evaluation quantity, however, was that unique Title I feature that mandated objective assessments of the program's impact. In the five year period following ESEA passage, over one hundred of the myriad of Title I state and local evaluations found their way into the public records. In the late 1960s, extensive searches for exemplary compensatory education programs were conducted and their findings released and research to identify and publicize compensatory models continued generally unabated throughout the 1970s.

Collectively, the preschool and public school evaluations have reported mixing findings that have only served to foster moderate political and intense academic debate over how effective schools can be and how best they can be effective. During this period, early childhood programs have been judged effective, then ineffective, and finally successful; compensatory education in general has been seen as having failed and then having "worked;" and "back to the basics" proponents and "whole child" advocates have nearly come to blows on such topics as research design, the validity of standardized testing and the appropriate curriculum for increasing and sustaining pupil growth.

This chapter will summarize the relevant research by reviewing the major studies of compensatory education conducted at the

---

*The Fall of 1965

national and local levels from 1965 to 1975 and then from 1975 on when the findings became somewhat more encouraging. As contradictory and controversial as the findings have proven to be, it is proposed here that a review of the more scientifically promising evaluations of compensatory education can give us an insight into potential of schooling to redress the racial differences in achievement in America and what may be the most productive means of increasing the effectiveness of the public schools for underachieving black pupils.

NATIONAL EVALUATIONS TO 1975

Credit has been given to Senator Robert Kennedy, more than any other person, for the evaluation requirement being a part of Title I of the Elementary and Secondary Education Act (ESEA). Apparently Kennedy's interest in the evaluation component was based largely on his concern that poor people should be kept abreast of whether tax dollars were being spent wisely.[3] Accordingly, Kennedy proposed some sort of testing or reporting system as an accountability measure. Although Kennedy's enthusiasm for the bill was contingent upon it including an evaluation component (an enthusiasm that was thought critical to the Act's passage), the language of the evaluation section was much more general than the New York Senator had wanted.[4] According to the Rand Corporation's Milbrey McLaughlin "Kennedy's support was important to the passage of ESEA, but evaluation was also a traditional bugaboo of schoolmen. Thus to appease Senator Kennedy and not simultaneously anger educational interest groups, drafters resorted to additional political diplomacy. Kennedy's demand for an accountability measure was met as inconspicuously as possible, with a lonely worded evaluation mandate."[5]

One top Congressional liaison at the United States Office of Education (USOE) explained that when Kennedy's evaluation plan was put into Congressional language, "the guiding concern was that the [evaluation] amendment be broad and general, and open to multiple interpretations at the local level."[6] Consequently, the localities were told only that "... provisions for appropriate objective measures of education, will be adopted for evaluation, at least

annually on the effectiveness of the programs in meeting the
special educational needs of educationally deprived children."[7]

Because of the vague evaluation requirement of the Act and the
need to maintain considerable local autonomy, a loosely structured "three-tiered" Title I reporting system emerged.[8] Typically,
the Local Educational Agency (LEAs), which constituted the third
tier, would simply report its "objective" test results to the State
Educational Agency (SEAs) and a compilation of the various LEA
data by this second tier would be passed on to the Commissioner of
Education. Given this lowest to highest data collection system, the
evaluation inexperience of the USOE staff and the "severe time
restraints" facing first tier personnel in their writing and implementation of evaluation guidelines,[9] it should come as no surprise
that the earliest national reports on Title I effectiveness produced
data of little scientific value. The first year report was published
in 1966 and simply summarized state descriptions of their programs, most of which had only been in operation 3 or 4 months.[10]
A second annual report appeared in 1967 and once again contained
little more than a review of information submitted by the state.
(The state data found ". . . many Title I youngsters . . . improving,
sometimes gaining a full month for every month spent in the
classroom.") The document did mention, however, that reports
from the cities were "disheartening" with little evidence of significant pupil gains.[11]

It is McLaughlin's observation that the cumbersome three tier
data collection method and the suspected "faculty manipulation of
the limited data available" soon came under Congressional attack
for their contributing to empirical imprecision. According to
Kathryn Hecht, one of the USOE pioneers in the area of Title I
evaluation, it was primarily Congress, not USOE personnel, that
pressured the infant Title I evaluation staff to begin employing
achievement test scores as a principal criteria to assess Title I
effectiveness. "When it became obvious that aggravating locally
defined evaluations was not going to produce data to convince
Congress Title I was working, the emphasis on achievement tests
and aggregating more uniform test scores became an evaluation
emphasis."[12]

Hecht reminds us that the logic for original data gathering

process was "quite consistent with the language of the Act, in that local districts were to determine Title I needs and objectives and were to plan their evaluations relevant to those objectives." In keeping with empirical methodology but hardly with the democratization process, "Congress mandated using reading and math scores as effectiveness criteria regardless of their relationship to the program content."[13]

Accordingly, in 1967, Congress ordered that more sophisticated reports be made by the Commissioner each year on the achievement of Title I pupils. The 1968 survey sampled 465 of 10,544 districts receiving Title I funds. In order to facilitate the collection and analysis of the data, only grades 2, 4, and 6 were included in the study. USOE's interest in obtaining accurate information was indicated by its elimination of all reading achievement data that did not include such components as standardized pre– and posttests. Consequently, only the reading scores of 11,490 pupils were analyzed.

The survey concluded that "Pupils taking part in compensatory education reading programs were not progressing fast enough to allow them to catch up to nonparticipating pupils. A number of pupils among both participants and nonparticipants had reading achievement levels below national norms. For both participants and nonparticipants that 'deficit' grew progressively greater in each succeeding grade level samples."[14]

The survey also found evidence indicating that pupils with the greatest gains were among the *less* socially disadvantaged of the sample. "High gain pupils [came]...from families of higher income, their parents had more education, the occupations of the parents had greater skills, and they were predominately white."[15]

The 1968 survey found that compensatory reading programs at grades 2, 4, and 6 had virtually a random chance either of improving or worsening children's test scores when compared to similar children not recepients of Title I funding.[16]

Originally, the 1969 survey, which used essentially the same research design as the 1968 evaluation, "...was intended to replicate the 1968 effort" and thereby provide further evidence of compensatory education effectiveness. But following the disappointing findings of that study, it came as little surprise to USOE that a similarly designed study would yield an equally discouraging conclusion. [17] McLaughlin suggests some sort of cover up by USOE contending that the education office chose not to release the manuscript, after Gene Glass, the director of the survey, officially informed it of his negative findings.

> Although compiled and printed, it was not 'available' in the summer of 1970 even to qualified researchers under contract to DHEW's Title I Task Force. Gene Glass himself was not, at that time, able to distribute copies of the document, and the report now remains buried somewhere in USOE. Thus the report that was to provide 'definitive' information on the efficiency of implementation of Title I ESEA and the effectiveness of that program has never seen the light of administrative day, nor has it (officially) informed a single decision-maker. Since it failed to serve its main purpose for USOE—to provide positive data for a report to Congress—the report has been for all practical purposes, suppressed. [18]

By the end of the decade, the only nationally sampled study of the cognitive impact of compensatory pre-schools was an evaluation of Head Start undertaken by Ohio University and the Westinghouse Learning Corporation (Ohio-Westinghouse). Basing its analysis on a sample of 104 Head Start Centers, Ohio-Westinghouse's 1969 report found the summer Head Start programs to be only "marginally effective," but concluded that many well planned, structured full year programs were improving significantly the participants' aptitudes (children in more unstructured socialization programs were less likely). Indeed, many Head Start children who had begun the program well below advantaged children on IQ and reading readiness measures approached the national norms by grade one. Unlike the first annual Title I study, Ohio-Westinghouse reported greater gains for black children and for children in the Southeastern states and central cities. These encouraging reports were tempered considerably, however, by longitudinal data that indicated that the initial gains were not sustained. By the end of the second grade, most Head Start children who had made relative gains during the preschool years were little different on cognitive measures than similar children without preschool experience. [19]

The apparent failure of the Ohio-Westinghouse Study to produce sustained preschool gains contributed powerfully to the bewilderment felt in many educational circles at the end of the sixties. Tremendous faith had been placed in the powers of early enrichment, during the so-called magic years, but even the politically popular Head Start could not produce a significant lasting effect. To compound the problem, a new and more conservative Nixon administration in Washington could hardly be expected to dismiss the negative findings of the early national studies and to endorse enthusiastically a continuation of compensatory education. In a 1970 article, Roger Freeman, a White House education advisor, was quoted summarizing his impressions of the evaluations of Title I programs. "We now spend more than $1 billion a year for educational programs under Title I of the Elementary and Secondary Education Act. Most of these have stressed the teaching of reading, but before-and-after tests suggest that only 19% of the children in each program improve their reading, significantly; 13% appear to fall behind the two-thirds of the children remain unaffected—that is they continue to fall behind."[20]

The disappointing findings of the early national evaluations may have been distorted by what may be called a "canceling effect," a concept that may be best understood if we recognize that educational evaluators have typically used the figure 1.0 to describe the mean reading and math achievement gain in a single year. Since subjects in the national studies constituted a heterogeneous group exposed to an infinite variety of teachers employing a myriad of methods, what "works" for some children may not be effective for others. Consequently, students with appropriate instruction who are really benefiting from Title I (achieving above the norm at say 1.2) were averaged with children only achieving at 0.4, for whom compensatory education had been a meaningless or even negative experience. Since the large scale evaluations were unable to continue for what may have the relevant demographic variables and effectively isolate particular kinds of instruction, lumping together test scores such as these may have revealed that the overall academic growth was only 0.7 to 0.8 and that Title I was ineffective. The fact that some children in the early national samples did appear to be benefiting, at least initially, from compensatory education may lend credibility to this position. Furthermore, if the "canceling effect" hypothesis had validity, movement to smaller studies of individual programs, serving more homogeneous populations, should produce more encouraging results.

PROGRAM EVALUATIONS TO 1975

Given the many problems associated with conducting and interpreting studies with large national samples, a popular alternative strategy for assessing compensatory education effectiveness has been to search the nation for successful enrichment programs. Typically, through an extensive reading of published and in-house program evaluations, a research organization would gather information on several hundred programs. Researchers would then make site visits for further study to those programs reportedly making month-for-month or average achievement gains that appeared to be based on hard data. If the closer scrutiny confirmed that the programs were successful, the research organization would gather additional information on curriculum and methodology so these exemplary programs could serve as models for other educators constructing compensatory programs. [21] [22]

The disappointing findings of not only Coleman and the 1968 and 1969 Title I reports but of a U.S. Commission on Civil Rights Study of pre-ESEA compensatory education programs gave even greater meaning to the USOE sponsored searches. In its report, *Racial Isolation in the Public Schools*, the Commission reviewed evaluations of Higher Horizons and Project Bannecker, perhaps the two most publicized local precursors of Title I, and a number of programs funded by the Ford Foundation's Great Cities Improvement Project (See Chapter Four). According to the Commission, longitudinal test scores from Higher Horizons and Project Bannecker did not support earlier optimistic findings and the data from "...more than 20 other compensatory education programs in large cities...in most instances...did not show significant gains in achievement."[23] By the time the Commission's findings were published in 1967, the Office of Program Planning and Evaluation personnel were conceptualizing reviews of not twenty but more like 2,000 programs. It was hoped that a nationwide study of this many programs would be able to identify, in a relatively short period of time, a number of programs which were working.*[24, 25, 26]

The earliest, the most publicized, and eventually the most extensive search for exemplary programs was conducted by the American Institute for Research (AIR) of Palo Alto, California. Under contract to USOE, AIR identified thirty-one exemplary programs from pre-school to grade twelve in its first two reports which became the basis for the *It Works Series*, a thirty-one booklet package published by USOE providing detailed descriptions of each successful program.[27] Twenty-one of these programs were selected in the 1968 report after AIR reviewed written reports of over 1,000 compensatory programs in existence from 1963–68, chiefly by searching ERIC, libraries and collecting data from over 300 mail requests.[28] Using the same process eleven more programs were identified in the 1969 publication and another ten selected in a third report released in 1971.[29] In order to qualify for a site visit by AIR researchers, a program had to have some hard data indicating pupil achievement gains of at least a month's learning for a month of instruction. Programs that only matched but did not exceed the national achievement rate were labeled only "moderately successful." "Successful programs" were only those that produced gains greater than the 1.0 (average) growth rate since AIR took the position that disadvantaged children could only catch up to the national norm if they exceeded the achievement growth rate normally attained by advantaged children (1.0 Gains, See Chapter 4).

In a 1972 summary report, AIR explained that the forty-one exemplary programs identified by the three studies from 124 sites visited represented only 2.3 percent of the more than 3,000 documents initially reviewed.[30] In the 1971 publication, AIR lists the four primary reasons for program rejection as "(1) inadequate sample selection, (2) failure to employ reliable and valid instruments, and (3) failure to demonstrate statistically, any (4) educationally significant cognitive benefit."[31]

---

*In 1967, the American Institute for Research (AIR) was in the process of searching for exemplary programs, under contract with the U.S. Office of Education. In the first AIR search, over 1,000 projects were reviewed, a second search (published in 1969) extensively combed the literature (mailing letters of inquiry to 320 programs), and a third search (published in 1971) reviewed over 1,200 programs.

This study confirmed the conclusion of the earlier two studies in this series; namely, that very few compensatory education programs for disadvantaged children have clearly demonstrated success . . . It should be pointed out that most of the programs rejected during this study were not rejected because they were demonstrated failures, but rather because their evaluation methodology was so inadequate that a conclusion about success or failure could not be drawn. Clearly, improvement must be made in program evaluation before the effectiveness of compensatory programs can be *fairly* assessed. [32]

The problem involving inadequate data and program failure continued to plague even the thirty-one exemplary programs identified in the first two AIR reports, which had not only searched for new programs (begun after January, 1968), but included a follow-up study of the original thirty-one. According to the 1971 follow-up study publication, of the twenty-seven still in operation only nine provided new hard data indicating that they had remained successful.*[33]

At this point, it is appropriate to consider AIR's listing of features more characteristic of successful programs than unsuccessful programs.

Pre-School Programs
  • careful planning, including statement of objectives
  • teacher training in the method of the program
  • small groups and high degree of individualization
  • instruction and materials closely relevant to the objectives

Elementary School Programs
  • academic objectives clearly stated
  • active parental involvement, particularly as motivators
  • individual attention for pupils' learning problems
  • high intensity of treatment

Secondary School Programs
  • academic objectives clearly stated
  • individualization of instruction
  • directly relevant instruction.

The characteristics identified by AIR as "most common" to all forty-one successful programs at all levels were the following:

---

*Of these twenty-seven, one did not have any new data, five would not release their data, seven presented inadequate data, and five had adequate data that indicated the program was no longer successful.

"A. academic objectives clearly stated and/or careful planning
 B. teacher training in methods of the program
 C. small group or individualized instruction
 D. directly relevant instruction
 E. high treatment intensity
 F. active parental involvement "

The AIR exemplary program characteristics seemed to give general support to the findings of earlier studies of Project Head Start and Project Follow Through (a federally funded program for primary school age pupils), which suggested that well-planned, structured programs produced greater achievement gains. Further support for the importance of well-defined objectives and planning, as well as AIR's finding correlating achievement and parental involvement, came from the Center for Educational Policy Research (CEPR) at Harvard. The CEPR study reviewed some 750 Title I program evaluations at the elementary school level (grades one to three) focusing on two instructional strategies (structure and parental involvement) that earlier research had suggested were effective in increasing the achievement of disadvantaged pupils. Regarding parent involvement, the study reported some evidence that parent training programs, which helped the parents learn to be effective teachers in the home, can affect achievement gains." However, "more involvement in school affairs seems not to have this result.[35] The paper on structure concluded that most compensatory programs were not highly structured, but *all* that were reported encouraging achievement gains.

> We found that highly structured, prescriptive and teacher directed programs were extremely atypical of Title I programs and thus constitute a small sub-sample of project.† However, *every such program we located reported a minimum of a month gain on standard tests of verbal ability for every month of school.* Results of the more typical general enrichment programs, on the other hand, were highly variable. While a few such programs met the

---

† Of 672 programs sent to the Center by SEAs throughout the country as promising projects, only about 10 percent were described as structured. The Center appealed to the State Departments of Education to specifically identify additional structured programs and forty more were added to the sample.

minimum success standard of 1:1, most did not, even in this universe of
SEA nominated 'successful' programs. [36]

Of the evaluations reviewed by CEPR, 85 percent had data that
was so inadequate that these programs had to be eliminated from
consideration; consequently, the Center reviewed only thirty-four
structured programs. Nevertheless, it was encouraging that each
of these programs reported achievement gains of 1:1 or greater. [37]

The Center warned the reader, however, not to use its limited
data to reach any conclusions that Title I works or even that
structured programs represent a very small sample. In addition:

> Evaluations are done to satisfy several different groups of people—seldom
> is the researcher on the top of the list. Evaluations are often political
> documents, and must be read with that in mind.
>
> The most serious problem presented by the evaluations, however, stem
> from the lack of control, lack of randomization, and the concomitant
> possible confounding of treatment effects. Teacher differences, pupil char-
> acteristics or other programs/experiences in the school, not the treatment
> itself, may account for post-test gains. For example, most Title I evalua-
> tions do not make selection criteria clear. When—as is sometimes the
> case—children are chosen for their potential rather than degree of educa-
> tional disadvantage, the likelihood of impressive gain scores increases. [38]

CEPR feels that inflated pupil potential may have been the case at
one of the sites they visited in Robbindale, Minnesota, a Minneapolis "inner ring" suburb receiving Title I funds for the bottom 8
percent of underachievers in the Robbindale District. Only 750 of
30,000 Robbindale students came from welfare families and comparing underachievers in this district with low achievers in non-
affluent North Minneapolis may be like comparing "apples and
oranges." [39]

CEPR offered examples of typical "structured" and "general
enrichment" Title I programs that highlighted their philosophic
and methodological differences. The "structured" example zeroed
in on attacking reading retardation by diagnosing the child's reading problem and then building a "specific" "highly individualized" program to meet his needs. There was no room for a general
haphazard approach ("remedial instruction should be organized instruction"); teachers were expected to know a pupil's " . . . expected
sequence of word recognition skills," understand the student's

levels of comprehension" and "keep a good cumulative account of [the] child's progress." Emphasizing a diagnostic prescriptive methodology did not deny a teacher's expression of humanity. Indeed, the guidelines for teachers spelled out the necessity of considering the "child's personal worth" and the importance of offering a student ample encouragement. [40]

CEPR contended that a "general enrichment" program usually called for "multiple program objectives reflecting attention to the 'whole child'—e.g. cognitive, affective and physical objectives." The program content was seen as ". . . often based on a general inventory of student grade level needs, rather than individual diagnosis and prescription" and as ". . . often merely and extension of typical classroom methodologies." The report offered as typical a Title I program that gave attention not only to pupil's academics ("reading, writing, spelling, listening and talking") but to the children's health ("so that they may have the physical and emotional stamina to learn to live and like to learn") and self-acceptance. [41]

While it may be correct to state that programs designed specifically to teach reading have a better chance of meeting that objective than those constructed to develop the whole child, the fact that general enrichment programs did not emphasize the formal monitoring of pupil progress could have weighed heavily against their identification by CEPR as producing 1:1 or better pupil gains. Of the evaluations reviewed by CEPR, 85 percent had data so inadequate that their programs had to be eliminated from consideration. [42] Because the structured programs were more likely to give greater attention to keeping good records on achievement growth, it should come as no surprise that their success rate should far surpass the general enrichment projects.

Another important exemplary program search in the early 1970s was conducted by the RMC Research Corporation, but RMC reported no common characteristics of its selected programs. ". . . there is no single key to success in compensatory education. What characteristics make the selected project work while so many others fail can only be the subject of speculation at the present time." [43]

Under contract with USOE, RMC was asked to identify programs that were both successful (with "achievement gains at least one-third of a standard deviation greater than expectations based

on national norms or control group scores") and could be pack-
aged for possible dissemination nationwide. Originally, RMC
attempted to select for dissemination eight models identified as
exemplary by earlier researchers such as AIR but could find only
three that met the corporation's "rigorous established criteria."
Consequently, RMC had to scan over 2,000 projects before finding
six* that met their criteria for achievement, cost, and replication.

Despite RMC's contention that there was no "single key to
success in compensatory education," a reading of the project descriptions of the six models in OE's *Educational Programs that Work*
suggests that strong emphasis on basic skills acquisition, careful
planning and intensity of treatment are characteristics common to
all six programs. [44] Methodologically, all appear to prescribe
specific remediation, only after a careful diagnosis of pupil deficiencies. But assuming these denominators, RMC found that educationally disadvantaged students may enjoy educationally significant achievement gains through a structured programmed approach
employed by experienced teachers, through individualized tutori-
als by either teachers or peers or by integrating reading and math
curricula with games which simulate career interests. [45] (see
appendix A pp. 213–218).

1974 saw both the publication of the RMC models and the
creation by OE of the National Diffusion Network (NDN) as the
primary entity to disseminate information on exemplary programs. Discussion of such a dissemination network had been
going on for some time at OE. For nearly a decade, Title III of
ESEA had been sponsoring a variety of locally initiated "innovative" approaches to education and encouraging the formation of
"exemplary" programs for possible adoption. Once a program had
been identified, however, it became increasingly apparent that a
more systematic approach was necessary to disseminate information on its value. For example, the tidy *It Works Series* booklet,
which compiled descriptions of the AIR-selected projects, may
have been a useful political tool to champion compensatory
education's effectiveness but its contents remained virtually un-

---

*Intensive Reading Instructional Teams, Hartford, Connecticut; Programmed Tutorial
Reading, David County, Utah; Project R–3, San Jose, California; Project Catch Up of New
Port Beach, California; High Intensity Tutoring Center, Highland Park, Michigan; Project
Conquest of East St. Louis, Illinois.

known outside of Washington. [46]

Funding for innovative and/or exemplary programs under Title III was scheduled to terminate in 1974, this provided much of the impetus for NDN's emergence during Title III's waning days. Thirty-three exemplary programs, originating from the grass roots, had been identified by 1974, and the Title III staff wanted a mechanism to assure that these model projects would be used elsewhere. Consequently, the National Diffusion Network began by offering its thirty-three programs as "Developer Demonstration Projects." NDN also began funding a State Facilitator's Project in the various states to help spread the word. Part of the adoption costs of localities wishing to capitalize on the easy availability of a research tested program was financed by NDN. [47]

Most of the thirty-three Title III programs were compensatory in nature, but several of these locally created products were in such areas as environmental and physical education. [48] To assure the dissemination of Title I programs, OE's Office of Planning, Budgeting and Evaluation† soon plugged the six RMC Title I programs, which had been selected in part for their replicability, into NDN's delivery system.‡ Indeed, by 1976 OE had contracted with CEMREO, a research organization in St. Louis, to identify an additional six exemplary Title I (and four Bilingual) programs for dissemination. [49]

Beginning also in 1974 was the Joint Dissemination Review Panel (JDRP),* a consortium of twenty-two evaluators (half from OE, half from the National Institute for Education) that passes judgment on the authenticity and exportability of programs labeled *exemplary*. During the decade of the 1970s, approximately 250 programs, nominated by research organizations or state educators, passed the rigorous scholarly scrutiny of JDRP and roughly 150 have been funded as developer demonstration projects by NDN. [50] A scanning of the descriptions of these programs in *Educational*

---

†Now called the Office of Evaluation.

‡In 1975, the Stanford Research Institute, under contract with the Office of Planning, Budgeting and Evaluation, began a study of the infant NDN field test operations and by 1976 the data suggested that the Title III programs were being well implemented by NDN. At this point the relationship between Title I and NDN was cemented.

*Formally the Dissemination Review Panel (DRP), which originated at OE in 1972, before Congress credited the National Institute of Education. The thirty-three Title III programs passed reviewal by DRP in 1973–74.

Programs That Work will suggest that many are basic skills oriented.[51] Currently, twenty-two Title I programs have been validated
by JDRP.[52]

If the process of identifying programs was running smoothly by
the mid-1970s, the packaging and dissemination of the selected
models was undergoing growing pains. During the years 1974–76
RMC field tested each of its six exemplary programs in seventeen
different schools. The programs were distributed in what was
labeled Project-Information Packages (PIPs), plastic containers
designed to facilitate easy distribution and minimize cost, and
stuffed with adoption instructions and descriptions of the exemplary model. Although the results of the two year study found that
PIPs could be rather easily implemented elsewhere, the achievement gains of children at the adoption site did not parallel the
achievement growth of pupils at the original location. The Metropolitan Achievement Test (MAT) was given to participants in
the adopted program for both years of the study, and the authors
". . . found few gains meeting the criterion of the one-third standard deviation above the equal percentile growth expectation."[53]
However, the MAT was not used by any of the original programs
and there were questions raised about its ability to properly measure the reading areas covered by the PIPs. The researchers
recommended PIP's continuation and with the mixed findings in
hand OE initiated yet another search for exemplary programs for
PIPing in 1976.[54]

THE PROBLEM OF SUSTAINING EFFECTS

By the middle 1970s program evaluations of compensatory
education, particularly at the preschool level, had contributed to a
growing concern about the sustenance of measured gains. The
Ohio-Westinghouse national evaluation of Head Start had reported
a fading of the initial IQ gains of many Head Start children
following their exit from the enrichment experience. Now several
of the experimental compensatory preschool programs (See Chapter 4) were reporting a similar phenomenon. The description and
evaluation summaries of the following projects are among those
that received the greatest publicity (they were included in a 1974

OE review of pre-school compensatory education)[55] and employed the most sophisticated research design.

BEREITER–ENGELMANN. This behavioristic teacher-directed academic model originated at the University of Illinois and dramatically raised the IQs of participating disadvantaged children from the Champaign-Urbana community by nearly twenty points. The design has been copied throughout the country, but this highly structured program with a strongly emphasized verbal component, was unable to sustain the early gains, with fade out occurring shortly after entry into the first grade.[56] [57]

THE YPSILANTI PERRY PRESCHOOL PROJECT. This experimental program began in 1962 under the direction of David Weikart. It is a structured cognitive model relying heavily on Piagetian theory on the acquisition of intelligence. The program emphasized parental involvement with a project staff member visiting the home of each child once a week. The program successfully raised the IQs of participants well above the controls, but, by the third grade, these gains had nearly washed out.[58] [59]

EARLY TRAINING PROJECT, NASHVILLE, TENNESSEE. Begun by Susan Gray and Rupert Klaus of George Peabody College in 1961, this preschool program employed a rather structured, cognitive "whole child" approach for three summers before school entry. During the school year, staff members visited the home regularly to work with mothers in the areas of reinforcement and verbal communication. But like Bereiter-Engelmann and Weikart, the Gray-Klaus research found that promising early gains of experimental groups over controls had almost faded by the end of the fourth grade.[60]

THE HOWARD UNIVERSITY PRESCHOOL. This experimental program began at Howard University in 1963 to determine if disadvantaged children enrolled in a traditional nursery similar to middle class children could obtain normal IQs. This goal was accomplished during the preschool experience but by the end of the second grade the IQ differences between the experimental and control groups were no longer statistically significant.[61]

THE KARNES AMELIORATIVE PRESCHOOL PROGRAM, URBANA, ILLINOIS. Now housed in the same building as the defunct Bereiter-Engelmann preschool at the University of Illinois, the Merle Karnes preschool has since 1960 had behavioral objectives and structure within a cognitively oriented whole child academic model with a heavy emphasis on parental involvement. Karnes reported that the early IQ difference between experimental and control group children faded almost entirely by the end of the third grade.[62]

DEVELOPMENTAL RESEARCH LABORATORY, TEMPLE UNIVERSITY. E. Kuno Beller, the mastermind and director of this program, is one of the only well-known early childhood experimenters to measure longitudinally the effectiveness of a traditional preschool. Emphasizing the further development of the child's curiosity and creativity, Beller reported highly significant IQ differences remaining between experimental and control groups at the end of the third grade. No data was provided on academic achievement with the exception of school grades which reveal that experimental girls (but not boys) have a slight advantage over controls in grade four.[63]

LEARNING TO LEARN PROGRAM, JACKSONVILLE, FLORIDA. A structured cognitive preschool project, the Learning to Learn nursery school raised the IQs of participants on the average of twenty points (87.7 to 107.4), while control group children in a traditional preschool were unaffected (88.1 to 86.8). Highly significant differences have been reported between the two groups at the end of the first grade (107.0 to 91.1) and at the end of the second grade with another wave of children (103.6 to 86.3).[64] [65]

INITIAL ENRICHMENT PROGRAM, NEW YORK, NEW YORK. This program was initiated by Martin Deutsch in 1958 and became a comprehensive five year program from prekindergarten through the third grade with a heavy emphasis on language development, self-discipline, and individualized instruction. At the end of the third grade, one wave of experimental groups maintained a slight but significant advantage over control groups in IQ.[66]

If one judges preschool compensatory program effectiveness by its ability to demonstrate a sustenance of initial gains, by 1975, the Learning to Learn Program, the Developmental Research LAB, and the Initial Enrichment Program appeared to be the most successful. Under contract with OE to analyze the compensatory preschool data, Urie Bronfenbrenner did not comment on positive findings of Learning to Learn but did raise doubts about the validity of the Beller and Deutsch findings. Bronfenbrenner argued that "motivational effects" may have inflated the Beller results. "[There] . . . is the possibility of motivational bias in favor of the nursery families who were self-selected through their positive response to a written invitation sent out by the schools and against the children in the . . . comparison group, whose parents did not enter them in school until the first grade."[67] Regarding the Deutsch project—a five year intervention program that enrolled children at age three through the third grade—Bronfenbrenner remarks that in the case of at least one wave of children " . . . the means for the experimental group showed the characteristic hairpin turn while the children were still in the program." He stated that "at the final testing, after the children had been exposed to five years of the intervention, the I.Q. difference between the experimental and randomized control group was a non-significant four points."[68]

In 1975, Deutsch's study of his Initial Enrichment Program was one of the few published longitudinal reports that followed the same children in a post-kindergarten level compensatory education program. In 1971, the American Institute of Research published a follow-up study of its twenty exemplary programs of 1968 and 1969, but it offered no clues as to why only six of the twenty-seven still in existence were no longer labeled "effective."[69]

More Effective Schools

One of the original AIR programs, New York City's More Effective Schools (MES), released an evaluation in 1969 that may explain why AIR chose not to call it exemplary two years later. According to an evaluation of MES by the Psychological Corporation (PC), shortly after the program began in September, 1964, this general enrichment elementary school project, operating in seventeen schools, reported impressive achievement gains (well above 1:1) on the Metropolitan Achievement Test (MAT) in word knowledge and reading. The reported gains, however, were not sustained. According to the PC, the reading achievement scores on the MAT of children who entered the program in the second grade did not differ significantly at the beginning of grade two from the reading MAT scores of children in the control schools. By the end of the third grade, however, the average MES third grade was not only well ahead of the controls but surpassed the national norm in word knowledge and reading. In the 1968–69 school year the PC analyzed the MAT reading scores of only those MES and control group children who had taken the tests in the second and third grades, nearly four years after the original testing in the fall of 1964. At the end of the fifth grade "... differences between the means of the groups of paired MES and control schools in word knowledge and reading were not large enough to be statistically significant." The report explained that "the means of both groups fell below the national norm for this grade level (5.7) by three to eight months."[70]

HIGHER HORIZONS PROGRAM, NEW YORK, NEW YORK. One of the earliest and most influential compensatory education programs, Higher Horizons served as a model for Title I. A few weeks after ESEA was passed by Congress, New York City's Board of Education released an evaluation of Higher Horizons that found it to be ineffective. In 1965, the program was terminated.[71]

TABLE I

DIFFERENCES BETWEEN ACTUAL AND EXPECTED
MEAN GRADE SCORE FOR READING COMPREHENSION
OF PUPILS ON THE THREE TESTING DATES

	Nov.,	April,	May,
Actual grade score	2.73	3.46	4.21
Expected grade score	2.87	3.34	4.26
Difference	-0.14	+0.12	-0.05

From W. Wrightston et al.: *Evaluation of Higher Horizons Program for Underprivileged Children.* Bureau of Educational Research, Board of Education of the City of New York, 1964, p. 50.

The evaluation's longitudinal study on pupil reading achievement (see Table I) indicates a pattern similar to the early gain and fade out reported in the MES evaluation. The Board of Education Study of Higher Horizons included the Metropolitan Reading Test (MRT) scores of 855 third grade pupils who took the tests for the first time on November 4, 1959, less than a month after Higher Horizons was initiated. The mean grade scores for the 855 children at that sitting was 2.73, roughly a month and a half behind the expected grade score of 2.87 for this population. Approximately six months later, Higher Horizons children again took the MRT and the test scores of the same 855 pupils were obtained. During this period these third grade children had made a substantial gain in reading achievement. Their April grade score was 3.46, more than a month above the expected grade score of 3.34. At this point most Higher Horizon participants were exceeding a month's learning for month of instruction and closing the achievement gap. Roughly thirteen months later, on May 16, 1961, the MRT was given once again, and the test scores of the same 855 students, now concluding the fourth grade, were analyzed. This time the mean grade score was 4.26. In this thirteen month interval, most Higher Horizons children (while still enrolled in the program) had begun to fall behind.

The apparent fading of early gains that occurred in MES and Higher Horizons does not necessarily mean that the participants learned more during their first school year exposure to the program than they learned in subsequent school years. A review of multi-year state Title I evaluation reports published by the Stanford Research Institute (SRI) in early 1976 reported that "... the rate of gain for each grade [one to twelve] appears to be relatively constant."[72]

Because state evaluations of Title I have often been less than empirically sound, one should not place too much faith in their findings. Nevertheless, the SRI state data did show achievement gains averaging 1:1 during the school year, but in reviewing test scores of pupils from grades one through twelve suggested an average gain of no better than 0.7 SRI attributes part of this loss to the relative losses experienced by disadvantaged children over the summer.[73]

In GE scales, the achievement rate of the average student is defined to be one month-per-month during the nine month school year and one month over the summer [0.9 + 0.1 = 1.0 for a calendar year]. An aim of Title I has been to raise the achievement rate of disadvantaged students to this month-per-month level. . . .

Folk wisdom assumes that the disadvantage student's achievement follows the same pattern as that of the average student but at a slower rate. This rate is usually estimated at approximately 70% of that of the average student.

An extensive search of all the available empirical evidence, however, leads
us to conclude that the disadvantaged student does not gain 0.7 months
during the summer and therefore does not follow the pattern of the 50th-
percentile student. The disadvantaged student either makes no gain during
the summer or loses a month. [74]

Therefore, a month for month (1:1) school year learning rate for
disadvantaged pupils was not enough to prevent a cumulative
deficit in achievement. With no gains in the summer or perhaps a
month's loss during this period, disadvantaged pupils would have
to learn at greater than month for month during the school year to
keep from falling further and further behind. SRI suggested that
perhaps as much as one-half of the progressive achievement gap
between advantaged and disadvantaged students was caused by
relative losses the latter population suffered during the summer. [75]

If one-half of the deficit could be explained by differing summer
learning rates, what else contributed to maintenance of an achievement gap among Title I pupils achieving at 1:0 during the school
year? SRI zeroed in on the standardized test scores from three
states (California, Michigan, and New York) that had a uniform
testing system. If there were sustaining effects of Title I then in
states reporting Title I gains of 1:0 or greater at several grade
levels, "... we would expect to detect an upward shift in the state
test results for low income students." Since SRI found little evidence of any "upward shift" for economically disadvantaged students, it suggested that not only during the summer "... but over
the school years in which students returned to regular classes
instead of Title I." [76]

SRI concluded its report by finding it very encouraging that, for
the past several years, ESEA Title I must be judged a success by
the month-per-month pre– to posttest criteria, but warning that,
"... evidence presented in this report convinces us that the ultimate success cannot be assessed in this time period." [77]

The SRI findings raised the question whether compensatory
education can enjoy multi-year effectiveness without long term
plans and more careful longitudinal monitoring of pupil learning. Originally, Project Follow Through, begun in 1967, was
designed to sustain Head Start gains by providing compensatory
continuity in the primary grades, but limited funding appears to

have made it difficult for the Project and its evaluators to do more than implement and compare the effectiveness of various early childhood models.[78] Occassionally, a project site would report longitudinal data (test scores on children participating in both Head Start and Follow Through,)[79] but by 1975 the only studies of national significance were preoccupied with showing specificity of effects.*

The "discouraging" analysis concluding the SRI study was indicative of the prevailing mood of many people associated with compensatory education in 1975. Following the disappointing funding of the national evaluations and an almost frantic search for what works, compensatory policy makers began disseminating those few programs that had proven effective. But questions arose over whether exemplary program adopters could equalize the gains of the mother project and whether the gains of even the successful originals were only short term in nature. Most state evaluations were reporting impressive pupil gains, but the SEA reports were held suspect because of the serious technical flaws often associated with their data collection and analysis. The discouraging findings of compensatory education was not lost on the OE's evaluation staff. At a national research conference in 1977, Jerry Lynn Hendrickson of the Office for Planning and Evalua-

---

*A 1971 report by Joan Bissell evaluated several experimental programs by grouping them into three general categories designated as "pre-academic" (behavioral and highly structured), "cognitive-discovery" (a structured Piagetian strategy developed by David Weikart), and the "discovery" (Bank Street-whole child approaches). Bissell reported that the three approaches were roughly equally effective in raising measured intelligence and improving school readiness for at least one year with only a slight but statistically insignificant advantage for the more structured preacademic and cognitive discovery models.

"...differences *among* Planned Variation approaches in both Head Start and Follow
Through suggest a *specificity* of effects, such that in programs with specific objectives and well-formulated strategies to achieve these objectives somewhat more growth is found...than in whole child programs."

Another Follow Through evaluation was released in 1971 by SRI, which compared three approaches to early childhood education that roughly matched the categories of Bissell: (1) Highly structured-behaviorial, (2) cognitive discovery, and (3) open-"pragmatic." The trend suggesting a specificity of effects in the more structured models of the Bissell study reached statistical significance in the SRI report. SRI concluded that the sponsor groups whose approach is "most structured and concentrates most explicitly on developing academic and preacademic skills showed a consistently higher level and rate of achievement measured by the pupil achievement test battery.

tion offered the following summary of Title I reports released at
the midway point of the 1970s. "Up until 1975 reports on the
effectiveness of Title I as a whole were uniformly pessimistic.
Aggregation of data in the States' Annual Evaluation Reports . . .
always highlighted problems with the data and the finding that
Title I children were falling farther and farther behind their
peers, although they generally found month-for-month or better
gains were mentioned. National evaluations also showed, for the
most part, Title I children losing ground, while non-Title I children gained ground."[80]

1976 AND BEYOND

About the year 1976, there began what may be a new phase in
compensatory education evaluation. During the last half of the
1970s and early 1980s, we find not only the appearance of evaluations with more positive findings, but the emergence of a more
sophisticated and perhaps more realistic means of assessing Title I
effectiveness.

The New Reporting System

In 1976, USOE introduced to the states a new measurement tool
entitled Normal Curve Equivalents (NCEs), a statistical measure
that was scheduled to replace grade equivalents as the device to
assess Title I pupil gains.[81] Although grade equivalents are an
easily understood unit of measurement, they often give a gross
inaccurate estimate of a child's achievement. According to the
RMC Research Corporation (primary developer of not only Title
I PIPs but Title I's revamped evaluation system), "Errors of several months are not uncommon and are large enough to make an
unsuccessful project appear successful or a successful project appear
unsuccessful."[82] One of the major problems appears to lie with test
publishers who often base their grade equivalent scores (i.e. the
raw score 78 equals a GES of 5.8) on "an estimate [of] testing done
in some other month . . . [and] may not have actually tested any
norm-group students in the eighth month of the fifth grade."[83]
Another is with children who score either significantly below or

above grade level and in figuring out what skills they actually
have relative to their peers.[84] In a 1976 technical paper prepared
specifically for the LEAs, the RMC Research Corporation explained
the phenomenon.

> ... consider the meaning of a *below-grade-level* score; let us say an eighth
> grader receiving a score of 5.8 in math. This is an even more complicated
> situation. Can we say that this student has the math skills of an average fifth
> grader, whatever those may be? Are all of the sixth-, seventh-, and eighth-
> grade skills missing? We simply do not know.
>
> Eighth graders normally take a higher level of a test, and the older but
> slower student may have answered some of the higher level items correctly,
> items that the fifth grader had never studied and were not even on the
> fifth-grade test. At the same time, the eighth grader probably missed many
> fifth-grade level items that an average fifth grader would get correct. Thus,
> while, a GES of 5.8 for a fifth grader means average performance of
> fifth-grade skills, a GES of 5.8 for an eighth grader may mean a lower level
> of skill over a wider range of subject matter. In any case, the eighth grader
> cannot be compared to an average fifth grader.
>
> A comparable problem occurs in understanding scores of *above-grade level*
> students. For example, on one widely used standardized test, a first grader
> who got a perfect score on the math subtest would receive a GES of 5.1. The
> test manual points out that this does not mean the first grader can do
> fifth-grade math. It means that the median fifth grader would get a perfect
> score on the first-grade test if any fifth graders took the first-grade test.[85]

NCEs have been billed as a vast improvement over grade equivalents. They are placed at equal intervals along a normal curve,
and thus "a gain of five NCEs represents exactly the same amount
of improvement for pupils at the extreme low end of the achievement distribution as it does for average achievers."[86] NCEs are
similar to percentiles in that both an NCE and percentile of 50 are
average and the numbers 1 and 99 represent the extreme low and
high. Percentiles, however, are not uniformly intervaled and thus
mean different things at various points in the distribution. For
example, a three percentile point gain is much greater at the
extreme ends of the normal curve than it is in the center[87] (see
Figure 2).

Technical language aside, perhaps the most valuable feature of
NCE reporting is that it rids the Title I evaluator of having to
compare Title I pupil growth with the gains of average children.

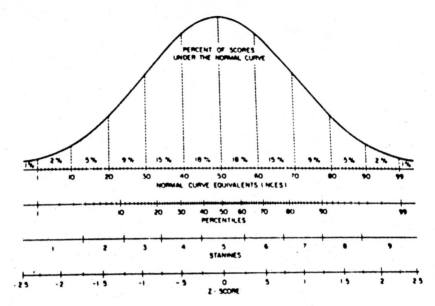

Figure 2. From G. Tallmadge: *Interpreting NCEs.* Mountain view. California, RMC Research Corporation, October, 1976, p. 3.

No longer is program success contingent upon 1:1 or better gains but simply on NCE gain greater than zero. Thus a NCE increase of one or better would mean the program had a better than expected impact. Since NCE gains take on different meanings at different grade levels and since converting such increases into grade equivalent improvement is of questionable value anyway, reporting in NCEs makes it more difficult to determine whether compensatory education is either producing gains that parallel or exceed the growth rate of the average child. In a second 1976 "Technical Paper" designed for LEA consumption, RMC made success sound easy to attain and comprehend and advises against establishing any absolute criteria for selecting a model program.

ALL NCE gains greater than zero are good!

Whenever the evaluation shows an NCE gain greater than zero, it means that the Title I pupils profitted from participating in the project. In general, the larger the NCE gain, the more effective the project. It is not possible, however, to designate any specific NCE gain as the criterion for exemplary or outstanding projects. A cost-effectiveness criterion seems more appropriate. Assuming that the same number of dollars were spent, for example, a 4-NCE gain produced in a treatment group of 200 pupils might be considered as good as an 8-NCE gain produced in a treatment group of 100 pupils.[88]

Although one can find little evidence in the public record to support this assumption, it is suggested here that one factor contributing to the OE decision to substitute NCEs for grade equivalents in Title I reporting was the realization that compensatory education was unlikely to have true compensatory impact (fully substituting for out-of-school influences) and that the NCE system permitted a more sensitive measure of what little impact Title I was likely to have. If future research showed compensatory education eliminating the progressive achievement gap, it would be all well and good. In the meantime, however, programs producing better than expected gains needed recognition as "good" ones and an improvement of one or two hundreths using NCEs would be easier to attain than one or two tenths (say from 0.7 to 0.8 or 0.9) using grade equivalents. Evidence in support of at least a discussion of improving the measurement of more modest expected gains is provided in a "working paper" by G. Kusten Tallmadge and Barbara Fagan of RMC. The manuscript was circulated at the highest administrative levels in the Office of Planning, Budgeting, and Evaluation (OPOE).* Entitled "Cognitive Growth and Growth Expectations in Reading and Mathematics" the paper discusses the ". . . frequently encountered, high expectations for compensatory, remedial, and other special instructional programs." Referring to the "'normal' growth patterns of children at different achievement levels" Tallmadge and Fagan make the following observation:

> . . . bringing underachieving groups up to grade level, or raising their performance by a quartile (or even by a stanine), would require instructional efforts two, three, or even five times as effective as the combination of maturation, regular school programs, and all out-of-school learning experiences. Such expectations appear generally unrealistic, and are more so when encountered in conjunction with projects or programs that provide only 15 to 30 minutes of instruction per day.

---

*The authors learned of the RMC "working paper" during a telephone conversation (June 19, 1980) with OE's Janice Anderson, an Evaluation Specialist, who has been closely affiliated with Title I evaluation. After learning of our interest in the new Title I reporting system, Ms. Anderson graciously mailed us a copy of the paper.

Unrealistically high expectations will usually go unmet, thus providing a
source of discouragement to educators and educational administrators alike.
A more serious problem, however, stems from the fact that the expectation
of large treatment effects is likely to lead to evaluation designs that are
insensitive to whatever real impact the special instruction may have. For
these two reasons, it seems important to analyze the kind of growth that *can*
be expected under normal conditions and to use the resulting information
as a framework against which to set objectives for educational interventions
and to evaluate their effectiveness. [89]

Recent Major Evaluations

At this point it would be convenient to conclude the review of
the research on Title I by discussing several recent empirically
sound national studies that reported only modest NCE's achievement gains for Title I pupils. One could then summarize the
findings as suggesting that our largest compensatory education
program is indeed improving pupil achievement but that it may
have been naive (an "unrealistically high expectation") to assume
that the schools could completely compensate for "all out-of-
school learning experiences." Unfortunately, the muddled world
of educational research has never permitted simplistic conclusions about schooling effectiveness, and the findings of the three
major studies of Title I since 1975 allow no exceptions to this
dictum in the field of compensatory education. However, the
Compensatory Reading Study, the *Compensatory Education Study and
the Sustaining Effects Study* may provide the strongest evidence to
date that Title I working and at least one of the reports may give
us some idea of how well and for how long.

Released in 1976, the *Compensatory Reading Study* tested over
50,000 compensatory education (CE) and noncompensatory education (NCE) students in grades two, four, and six during the 1972–73
school year, "a sample that is close to being truly nationally representative . . ." for that age group. Generally speaking, achievement gains in reading of CE students compared favorably with
NCE pupils. According to the Technical Summary, "The nature of
the results tended to vary somewhat depending upon the subtest
and grade level being examined and upon the analytic technique
employed. All of the analyses supported the assertion that com-

pensatory students tend not to fall further behind noncompensatory students during the academic year (the main exception was for a scale called word knowledge)."[90] Several serious questions concerning the study's assessment measures, however, marred the positive findings. According to George Mayeske, OE sponsor of the study, there were many significant technical problems, among the most serious being "lack of proper control for statistical regression."[91] Conducted before the NCE reporting system became fashionable, the Compensatory Reading Study reported pupil achievement gains by listing the average fall and spring Metropolitan Achievement Test raw score totals for each grade tested.[92]

In 1977, the National Institute of Education released the first of two reports on the effects of Title I services on pupil achievement. The Instructional Dimensions Study (conducted as part of the *Compensatory Education Study*) provided test data on pupils enrolled in fourteen projects scattered throughout the nation; each project had been nominated by various localities and state education department for their merit. In the 1977 report, NIE found impressive academic year gains in the first and third grade Title I reading and math pupils participating in the study.[93] "In general, the results were encouraging about the effectiveness of compensatory education. First graders made average gains of 12 months or 12 percentile points in reading and 11 or 14 percentile in mathematics. Third graders made average gains of 7 months or 9 percentile points in reading and 12 months or 17 percentile points in mathematics."[94]

Perhaps even more encouraging were the results of NIE's Instructional Dimensions Follow-Up Study, housed as a chapter within a final report the Institute made to Congress in 1978 on the *Compensatory Education Study*. In the follow-up study a representative subsample of CE pupils in seven of the fourteen original districts were retested the following fall and their scores compared with those of a sample of non-CE pupils (scoring at the 50 percentile or above). Contrary to the findings of other similar assessments of summer learning, the Instructional Dimensions Follow-Up Study reported ". . . that compensatory education students can maintain impressive gains over the calendar year" (fall to fall) which "raise questions about the generality of summer loss for compensatory education students." The second study found no "loss in absolute terms" (achievement decline) over the summer and no "consistent or substantial relative loss" (learning inferior to non-CE pupils) during this period"[95] (see Table II). According to the report, "The data indicate that low achievers do lose some ground to higher achievers over the summer period. However, the size of the differences varies considerably by grade level and subject matter, and only for first grade reading is the difference statistically significant."[96] The study also measured the summer growth of a small percentage of the original CE sample that attended summer school and did not find summer school participants gaining greater than nonparticipants between the spring and fall testing.[97]

One finding of some concern, however, would appear to be the fall gains of third grade CE pupils in reading. Their modest fall to spring gains combined with their spring to fall gains gave them a twelve month increase of only 0.8. This compares with a 1:6 gain of their non-CE counterparts during the calendar year (see Table II).

The third major report on compensatory education to appear since 1975 is the *Sustaining Effects Study.* Because of the growing concern about the durability of gains, the *Sustaining Effects Study* promises to be one of the most important research projects ever conducted in the field of compensatory education. The contract for the study was awarded by OE to the System Development Corporation in 1975. Reading and math achievement test scores were collected from national samples of elementary (grades one to six) CE and non-CE pupils for three consecutive years beginning in 1976.[98] Unfortunately, at press time, only test scores for the first calendar year have been analyzed, but the limited data have already yielded some interesting information. During the academic year, CE students (Title I pupils and participants in locally funded compensatory education programs) do not equal the gains of the average student but usually exceed the growth rate of pupil samples in need of, but not receiving, compensatory education.[99] In the various papers reviewing the preliminary findings, grade equivalent scores are not employed to demonstrate gains (and for some reason nor are NCE's) but comparisons are made by verticle scale scores, a graphic technique that can demonstrate the growth

TABLE II

MEAN ACHIEVEMENT GAIN SCORES OF NON-CE STUDENTS
WHOSE PRETEST SCORES WERE AT OR ABOVE NATIONAL NORMS
AND OF CE STUDENTS WHOSE PRETEST SCORES
WERE BELOW NATIONAL NORM

Study Group	Relationship to National Norm	n	Fall-to-Spring Gain	Spring-to-Fall Gain	Fall-to-Fall Gain
Grade 1 reading	At or above (non-CE)	269	56* 0.5**	10*** 0.1	66 0.6
	Below (CE)	344	69 1.2	0*** 0.0	69 1.2
Grade 1 math	At or above (non-CE)	435	39 0.5	6 0.1	45 0.6
	Below (CE)	97	43 1.1	2 0.1	45 1.2
Grade 3 reading	At or above (non-CE)	305	36 1.0	21 0.6	57 1.6
	Below (CE)	512	44 0.5	8 0.3	52 0.8
Grade 3 math	At or above (non-CE)	178	62 1.6	7 0.2	69 1.8
	Below (CE)	306	64 1.2	-1 -0.1	63 1.1

*Expanded Standard Scores
**Grade-equivalent scores
***Difference in gain significant (P .01)

From *Compensatory Education Study*. Final Report to Congress from the National Institute of Education, September, 1978, The National Institute of Education, U.S. Department of Health, Education, and Welfare, Washington, D.C., p. 86.

rate of various samples. Growth patterns are also recorded in percentiles. A glance at Figure 3 reveals that pupils in need of, but not enrolled in, CE had virtually a random chance of increasing or decreasing their Fall percentile score during the academic year. On the other hand, Title I students demonstrate an upward trend at every grade level. One problem area, however, appears to be the reading achievement growth rate of CE pupils in grades four to six. Although these students made modest percentile gains (Fig. 3), they appeared to be doing no better than their non-CE comparisons. Similar to the NIE follow-up study, the *Sustaining Effects Study* found no absolute loss for either regular or CE students between Spring and Fall but "a small loss over the Summer for CE relative to non-CE students." Once again, summer school was found to have little or no effect on reading and math achievement scores. [100]

In the area of preschool compensatory education, the remarkable

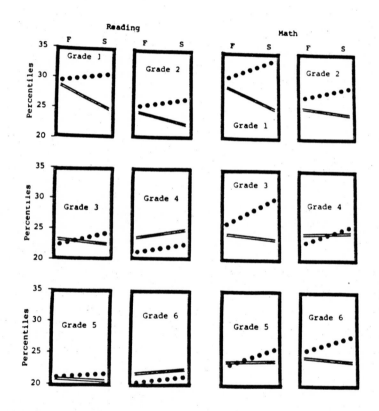

Figure 3. Reading and Math Gains, Fall-to-Spring in Percentiles, For Title I Selectees (••••••) and Non-CE Selectees at Non-CE Schools Judged by Their Teachers to be in Need of CE ══). From Ming-mei Wang: *Evaluating the Effectiveness of Compensatory Education.* Paper presented at the annual meeting of the American Educational Research Corporation, Boston, Massachusetts, April 7–11, 1980.

perserverance of many of the originators of the experimental programs of the early sixties has finally begun to pay robust dividends. Following the disappointing evaluations generally showing a near washout of the initial preschool IQ gains by the middle elementary grades, twelve of the pioneer early childhood investigators formed the Consortium for Longitudinal Studies. According to Richard Darlington and other coordinators* of the follow-up work, the consortium "pooled their original data and conducted a common follow-up study in 1976–77 of the original participants and control groups." (Additional pooling and follow-up analyses by consortium members have continued unabated into the early 1980s.) Darlington et al. inform us that although preschool experiences have apparently had no sustaining effects in measured intelligence (reporting an IQ "... tapering down to smaller but statistically significant effects three or four years after pre-school and vanishing thereafter"†), it did appear to have a profound influence on "whether a child had been retained in grade (held back) or assigned to special education classes at any time during his or her school career." Of the roughly 2,700 children in the eleven original consortium projects, 1,599 were available for the 1976–77 follow-up, and appropriate data existed on 802 subjects in seven projects. The data shows that experimental subjects were nearly twice as likely as controls (44.7 vs. 24.1) either to repeat a grade or to be recommended for special education. Apparently the pre-school compensatory experience can provide the foundation for environmental change which affects behavior many years later.

Despite the failure of the preschool programs to modify measured intelligence permanently, one cannot dismiss the multiyear influences of early childhood education as being exclusively affective in nature. In most cases the IQs of compensatory preschool participants were significantly higher than nonparticipants three or four years later, and an advantage in math achievement for the

---

*Darlington and Irvin Lazar of Cornell University, who did not conduct preschool programs, have been the principal coordinators. Jacqueline Royce, Ann Sniper, and Harry Murray, also of Cornell, have assisted Darlington in preparing at least one written summary of the consortium's major activities and findings.

†The consortium has not recently reported longitudinal IQ data for Gordon's research which included the once promising Learning to Learn Program.

experimental subjects has been reported lasting throughout most of elementary schooling (0.5 grade equivalents favoring preschool children in the fourth grade.) [101] [102] [103] According to Darlington et al., " . . . if one year of enrichment still has effects three or four years later, then twelve years of enriched schooling might have lifelong effects."

The Consortium for Longitudinal Studies and the *Sustaining Effects Study* have not been the only attempts since 1975 to measure compensatory education longitudinally. At least two state departments of education have monitored the achievement of the same Title I pupils for two consecutive years and both suggest a decreased growth rate during the second year.

A 1979 report from Rhode Island measured the two year growth of Title I children who were in the second and fourth grades at the initial testing. Pupils who remained in Title I for the two year duration of the study comprised the two-year group; students who for some reason left Title I after the first year of testing constituted the one-year group (see Table III). The achievement data on the one-year group should be of particular interest, for it represents perhaps the first reported assessment of what may happen scholastically to Title I children after exiting the program. Apparently most children in the one-year group graduated to the mainstream because of the success they attained in Title I. According to the Rhode Island study, "While there were generally small insignificant differences [between groups one and two] in reading achievement at pre-test time, by the end of the 1974–75 school year [the first year of the study] the one-year group scored significantly higher than the two-year group on most measures."

Table III includes the NCE scores for the two groups of second and fourth graders for two academic years. It is evident that both groups at both grade levels made larger gains the first year and that there was actually a NCE decline during year two. The greatest losses were suffered by group one during the year after their termination from the program. Despite the second year decline, however, growth " . . . across a two year period [still] . . . exceeded what would have been expected if students had not received compensatory education instruction." The study's authors suggested that the second year decline was caused in part by the

TABLE III
MEAN NCEs AT PRETEST,
FIRST AND FOLLOW-UP POSTTEST
FOR GRADES 2 AND 4 COMPOSITE READING

GRADE	GROUPS	PRETEST	FIRST POSTTEST	FOLLOW-UP POSTTEST
2	Two Year	28.2	43.0	37.7
	One Year	28.2	48.9	40.7
4	Two Year	21.8	35.8	30.3
	One Year	24.7	43.0	30.7

From P. De Vito and S. Rubenstein: *A Follow-Up Study of Title I Participants in Rhode Island.* Paper presented at the annual meeting of the American Educational Research Association, San Francisco, California, April 8-13, 1979, p. 7.

often reported "dramatic" drops in achievement of disadvantaged children during the summer months. This suggestion was highly speculative because the absence of a fall testing in the second year precluded measurement of summer losses.

A similar study was conducted by the Tucson Unified School District. Released in 1980, this report summarized a two year investigation of Title I's sustaining effects on junior high school pupils between the fall of 1977 and the spring of 1979. Table IV gives the grade equivalent, NCE, and expanded standard score gains for seventh, eighth, and ninth grade pupils at four testing times (fall and spring for two years) and does not show dramatic summer losses. The Title I sample may have lost ground in the summer relative to the average child but at least, in terms of grade equivalents, suffered no absolute losses. (Converted to NCEs, small absolute losses are evident for the eighth and ninth grade sample during the summer, suggesting the greater sensitivity of NCE reporting to achievement differences.) At each grade level, declines in achievement growth took place during the second year of the testing. The Tucson study's author, Stephen Powers, made the following commentary: "One might hypothesize that a regression effect caused the gains the first year. However, students were selected for Title I based on scores on a standardized test administered two years before the fall of 1977. These results suggest weaknesses in evaluation practices when a group of students is tested fall to spring without any follow-up study. Although students display an initial surge of achievement the first year, that rate of achievement may not be sustained the following year."[104]

TABLE IV

COMPARISON OF GAINS OF THE FIRST AND SECOND YEARS*
AND MEASURED IN GEs,NCEs, AND EXPANDED STANDARD SCORES

Grade	1977-78 Scale	Fall	1978-79 Spring	Diff	Fall	Spring	Diff
7	GE	3.4	4.3	.9	4.7	5.2	.5
	NCE	21.6	27.2	5.6	28.0	29.3	1.3
	SS	365.9	405.4	39.5	419.9	439.6	19.7
8	GE	3.9	4.9	1.0	4.9	5.3	.4
	NCE	22.0	26.8	4.6	25.6	25.7	3.5
	SS	390.2	428.6	38.4	427.0	442.9	15.9
9	GE	4.3	5.3	1.0	5.4	6.1	.7
	NCE	21.2	25.4	4.2	23.7	23.5	-.2
	SS	407.1	441.9	34.8	445.6	471.8	26.2

*Seventh Grade N = 138
Eighth Grade N = 106
Ninth Grade N = 65

From Stephen Powers: *A Comparison of Cognitive Gains of Seventh, Eighth and Ninth Grade Students*. Paper presented at the annual meeting of the American Educational Research Association, Boston, Massachusetts, April 7-11, 1980, p. 6.

Unlike the Rhode Island children, however, Tucson subjects lost little ground the second year. The NCE gains for first year seventh and eighth graders were respectively strengthened and generally maintained at the end of the second year. The small NCE loss of the eighth graders and modest loss of the ninth graders were caused largely by slight NCE declines during the summer. It should be also encouraging that, despite the second year decline, the seventh and ninth grade participants still gained eighteen months over the eighteen month testing period. At the ninth grade level the participants exceeded 1:1 for two consecutive academic years. And thanks to the new reporting system less than 1:0 grade equivalent gain rates for second year eighth and seventh graders became transferred as infinitestimal to modest NCE gains.

With the exception of the concerns over the sustaining effects of compensatory education at the elementary and secondary level, the research findings should place compensatory education in a more favorable light in the early 1980s than it enjoyed in the mid-1970s. The period since 1975 has also witnessed the growth of the National Diffusion Network. Many local evaluations suggest a number of compensatory programs are being successfully adopted. [105] In JDRP terms, success now does not necessarily mean solid evidence of 1:1 or better gains, but empirically sound research suggesting "better than expected" achievement gains.[106]

Other relevant post-1975 educational research reports, not strictly compensatory in nature, have challenged what the *Education Times* calls the "prevailing pessimism about the possibilities of education."[107] In 1977, the National Assessment of Educational Progress (NAPE) released the results of two national surveys of reading achievement, which compared the reading achievement of seventeen year olds, drawn from similar samples in 1971 and 1975. On NAPE administered reading achievement tests, seventeen year olds from low income urban areas gained five percentage points while middle-class children showed no gains. Broken down racially, black children out gained white children five percentage points to two.[108] A 1979 study from England entitled *15,000 Hours* attributed the schools ethos (i.e. high expectations, student feeling of willingness to consult with teachers, consistency of values) to much of the variation in achievement among London inner city secondary schools. In this country, the research of Ronald Edmonds in Detroit has led to the identification of several differences between relatively high achieving and low achieving schools with predominately black, low income student bodies. According to Edmonds,

> . . . (a) They have strong administrative leadership without which the disparate elements of good schooling can neither be brought together nor kept together; (b) Schools that are instructionally effective for poor children have a climate of expectation in which no children are permitted to fall below minimum but efficacious levels of achievement; (c) The school's atmosphere is orderly without being rigid, quiet without being oppressive,

and generally conducive to the instructional business at hand; (d) Effective schools get that way partly by making it clear that pupil acquisition of basic school skills takes precedence over all other school activities; (e) When necessary, school energy and resources can be diverted from other business in furtherance of the fundamental objectives; and (f) There must be some means by which pupil progress can be frequently monitored.[109]

As the newly appointed Assistant Chancellor for New York City Schools, Edmonds is currently both testing many of his Detroit findings and attempting to initiate more effective educational practices in New York.

In light of the more optimistic findings since 1975, is it possible to say that compensatory education is now working, i.e. that twenty odd years of research in this field has contributed to instructional behaviors that are finally yielding results? Unfortunately, one cannot make that claim with any certainty, for more sophisticated measurement, rather than improved practices, may account for greater measured impact of programs such as Title I. Differences in research design can apparently cause significant differences in the findings. For example, when George Mayeske, Supervisor of Evaluation Specialists, at OE, was asked why the *Sustaining Effects Study* did not show as much program impact at the *Compensatory Reading Study*, he said the former investigation "collected better data." He continued that "the *Sustaining Effects Study* used better comparison groups to rule out certain regression effects." According to Mayeske, it is the test themselves, rather than the ineffectiveness of compensatory education, that has contributed to much of the disappointments associated with Title I evaluations: "We will never get any effect with the tests we use. Essentially they are the same off-the-shelf stuff we've been using for fifty years as a sorting device. Our tests should be tied to a psycho-linguistic framework involving a hierarchy of skills. We can then relate assessment devices to points in that hierarchy."[110] Instead of data suggesting compensatory education is equalling the national growth rate (in the case of the *Compensatory Education Study*), apparently we now have more refined empirical inquiries (such as the *Sustaining Effects Study*) producing data suggesting more modest program effects or perhaps compensatory education was working all along, and the successes simply were not recognized. Furthermore, it may be that additional research will show compensatory education making far more than marginal impact and thus reveal it as having true compensatory powers.

Despite the flaws in research methodology and the standardized measures, which mitigate against making any "conclusions" about compensatory education's effectiveness, we summarize the findings by listing the following hypotheses, emergent from more than two decades of research on compensatory education:

(1) *Title I and associated programs are contributing positively to at least short term pupil gains in reading and math.* Whereas the early studies yielded disappointing results, the major research since 1975 has been virtually unanimous in suggesting compensatory education is making a difference during the pre– and posttesting period. The *Sustaining Effects Study* suggests this may be particularly true in math.

(2) *Longitudinal evaluations of compensatory education may raise serious questions about a program's ability to substitute entirely over a sustained period for out-of-school determinants of substandard achievement.* In the Tucson study, for example, children in grades seven and nine averaged month-for-month learning for a two academic year eighteen-month period (Fall of 1977 to Spring 1979) but the significant growth declines during the second academic year (Fall 1978 to Spring 1979) of the study must raise the question of whether following the same children for an additional eighteen months would find them maintaining the average growth rate of the eighteen month testing period. In discussing his findings, Stephen Powers, the author of the Tucson Study, makes the following commentary: "These results suggest weaknesses in evaluation practices when a group of students is tested fall to spring without any follow-up study. Although students display an initial surge of achievement the first year, that rate of achievement may not be sustained the following year."[111] What may be advisable as well are Title I assessments that follow the same children for longer than a two year period.

(3) *Relative losses during the summer account for part of the cumulative deficit in achievement.* Although there is contradictory data on how much decline in the achievement growth takes place during the summer, the research strongly suggests that most disadvantaged pupils experience a greater decrease in the achievement rate

between spring and fall than average achieving children.

(4) *Highly structured, prescriptive programs are more likely to produce greater short term gains than "whole child" general enrichment programs.* Much of the research on compensatory education programs has suggested that such variables as careful planning and specificity of objectives correlates with greater pupil learning. This data would appear to be in keeping with Barak Rosenshine's research on teaching which, has reported that "direct instruction" and "...high levels of student engagement within teacher-directed classrooms using sequenced, structured materials" is a more effective teaching strategy than less structured approaches.[112] The compensatory education research also seems to be consistent with the findings of the evaluations of "mastery learning" or Learning for Mastery (LFM), a structured instructional sequence originated by Benjamin Bloom in the late 1960s.[113] LFM advocates that an instructional package that includes behavioral (measurable) instructional objectives, direct attention to the defined behavior, small "bite size" steps and immediate positive feedback will maximize the chances for greater pupil learning.[114] A recent analysis of the research on "mastery learning" has concluded that the "mastery" method is much superior to the conventional techniques.[115]

One must interpret the results of the instructional effective studies with caution, however. It must be remembered that most educational research is not longitudinal in nature, and it is conceivable that multi-year reports on achievement may yield greater effects for the general enrichment approach. The long-term superiority of Progressive Education over traditional was evidenced in the 1930s when the Eight Year Study found that children who had attended more progressive high schools exceeded, in college grade point average, their matched comparison counterparts in every subject but foreign language.[116] Of course, the participants in the Eight Year Study were for more advantaged than the average Title I sample and different educational methods may have different effects on different populations. When the desired academic skills are not strongly associated with the children's socio-cultural milieux (such as a foreign language for advantaged college students), they may require more formal instructional strategies to successfully acquire these skills.

(5) *Preschool compensatory education has had little or no permanent effect on cognitive and achievement but may have had a robust influence on affective behavior.* With the exception of a slight advantage preschool participants enjoy over nonparticipants in math (at least through grade four), there seems to be no permanent cognitive effects of early childhood compensatory programs. Yet the recent findings of the Consortium for Longitudinal Studies should offer considerable hope to preschool educators. The degree of social and educational adjustment disadvantaged children attain may be strongly related to educational intervention during the preschool years. There appears to be a growing recognition in some educational circles that if compensatory education is to maximize its chances of being effective it should be more than a half hour to an hour pullout program to supplement regular school activities. In the domain of the basic skills, disadvantaged children may benefit a good deal more by educators presenting a united front. Currently, the national Title I office is emphasizing "coordination of efforts," which will hopefully lead to the program becoming intricately interwoven with the "regular" school curriculum. [117] If the research suggests that specificity of objectives and careful planning reap greater benefits within a single classroom, one may assume that a structured comprehensive commitment to basic skills acquisition within a given school will produce greater equality of education achievement.

Recognizing the possible potential of such a coordinated approach, Pueblo, Colorado, a city with a large minority school age population, is integrating its Title I program with the district wide Maintenance and Improvement Plan for Instruction (MIP), the latter described as a "strong, well organized instructional process" ... which "... provides teachers with assistance with the important classroom management tasks of setting instructional priorities ... identifying basic skills needs ... and aiding in instructing, monitoring, evaluating and reporting a student's progress." [118] Under the MIP, the Pueblo Central Administration assists school building professionals in establishing specific school wide goals to improve reading and math instruction. Typically, the selected pupil competencies professionals chose to cultivate are skills measured by the California Achievement Test, the district's major standardized assessment instrument. The city's Title I program plays an important role in the MIP's implementation by fostering close communication with principals and regular classroom teachers.[119] The Title I teachers develop and incorporate their "Title I Plan" within a prescriptive "Building Plan" which according to Peggy Seavy, Title I Director, "promotes a constant circle of implementation" and a "continual exchange of information concerning the development of each individual child."[120] Since the implementation of the Maintenance and Improvement Plan three years ago, Pueblo has reported significant district wide achievement gains. The coordinated efforts seem to be particularly successful in the predominately Chicano Title I elementary schools where pupils have equaled or surpassed the national average on the California Achievement Test for two consecutive years.[121] Chuck Sekera, Director of the Pueblo's Maintenance and Improvement Plan, attributes its success to a "much greater focus of the entire instructional program on basic skills." Continues Sekera, "We found that the competencies assessed by standardized tests were sufficient to constitute a core for our basic skills program. We then wrote the appropriate objectives, embraced them and found that when instruction is focused toward those objectives, measurable performance increased. Regarding Title I, the clarification of regular program goals makes it possible for Title I and other support programs to be much more effective in their efforts to compliment the established program."[122]

The fact that a federally funded program such as Title I can enjoy such harmony with a local school district may be indicative of a new spirit of cooperation among educators amidst a growing optimism about the effects of education. Indeed, Robert Kennedy's insistence on an evaluation requirement for Title I may have been instrumental in promoting professional partnerships and renewed hope, for Title I required to take a close look at itself, to come to grips with what works and to broadly disseminate this information. Hopefully, Title I evaluation processes and the findings of many Title I evaluations have not only been a valuable informational exchange for compensatory educators but has influenced other educators by demonstrating the significance of empirical inquiry, by identifying effective strategies and by promoting the sharing of such knowledge. Larry Bussey, a major participant in the implementation of the National Diffusion Network, stated it succinctly when he was asked to reflect on the value of NDN. "It's really too bad we didn't have NDN in 1968. If it had existed, the mechanisms for determining effectiveness could have been extended to other programs much earlier. The question of 'is it making a difference' is very important. The process forces us to ask questions about what it is that is making a difference or no difference. The information can then be shared with others."[123]

In conclusion, compensatory education has gone from a period of idealistic promise, to an era of indignation and pessimism, to a time of perhaps more realistic assessment and expectations more encouraging findings and renewed optimism. The research has identified methods and programs that make a difference, but we are still uncertain how much impact schooling can have and for how long its effect can be measured. We must also be cautious about generalizing the effects of compensatory education on educationally disadvantaged children in general to black participants in particular because the major evaluations rarely assess pupil progress by race or ethnicity. In 1980, blacks constituted only 26 percent of Title I enrollment nationwide.[124] From the data we have reviewed one would assume that Title I and associated programs are benefiting blacks and other underachievers academically, but more confident statements on compensatory education's ethnic and racial influences await the findings of future research.

APPENDIX

Examples of Exemplary Compensatory Programs

In terms of longevity, the programs described below may be the three most successful compensatory education programs in American history. Each one was identified as exemplary by AIR in its first report in 1968, by AIR in a follow-up study published in 1971, and by RMC in 1974. In June, 1980, these programs were still listed in *Educational Programs That Work*, an OE publication listing all programs approved as successful by researchers from the Office of Education and the National Institute for Education.

PROJECT: IRIT: Intensive Reading Instructional Terms

TARGET AUDIENCE: Pupils in grades 3–4 who are deficient in the basic skills of reading and language. Pupils receive this intensive instruction three hours daily for one ten-week cycle. IRIT was originally approved by JDPR as a grade 3–4 program. However, the program has been used with grades 5–6 with excellent success.

DESCRIPTION: *A laboratory project for third– and fourth-grade students with difficulty in reading.*

IRIT features a carefully individualized diagnostic approach made possible by low student-teacher ratios and the use of a wide variety of materials and equipment. The unique features of IRIT are high-intensity and team teaching directed toward reading disabilities. Forty-five students per team of teachers are selected for each of the three ten-week cycles. The teachers have classes of approximately 15 pupils each and all pupils see each teacher daily. The program design includes three areas of concentration: (1) decoding, (2) individualized reading, and (3) vocabulary and comprehension. Students move from one area to the next at approximately one-hour intervals and spend the entire morning in these language arts areas. Pupils return to their sending schools in the afternoon for instruction in other basic subjects. A balanced approach to reading is provided through the three areas of instruction. The instructional design provides this content: (1) the individualized reading area provides a wide variety of reading materials and offers assignments to enrich the student's background, promote written and oral language skills, and instill pleasure in reading; (2) the vocabulary and comprehension area puts emphasis on the various sub-skills of comprehension (meaningful experiences are provided in order to promote concept development); (3) decoding, the core subject, uses an individualized approach to assist the student in his/her ability to attack new words. The specific skills-needs in phonics are taught so as to develop independent methods of word analysis. The three areas are coordinated and reinforce and supplement each other, providing a balanced reading program. The IRIT teachers work with students for the entire morning and then spend the afternoons: (1) preparing the individualized lessons, collaborating on the skills of each student, and updating the records for each of the 45 students; (2) developing new instructions materials based on student needs; (3) meeting with teachers and parents from the sending schools; (4) participating in professional development and training sessions; and (5) providing inservice sessions for other classroom teachers. This program design prepares teachers who are very skilled in reading instruction. In addition, each IRIT Center has a team leader who is a certified reading specialist.

ASSURANCES/CLAIMS: The California Achievement Test (pre– and posttest) and the Botel Phonics Inventory are some of the tests used for evaluation. These tests are administered at the beginning and at the end of each cycle. Mean total reading scores for 1974–75 were raised from 2.6 to 3.7, a gain of one year and one month in 10 weeks. Additional test results from other years are available.

IMPLEMENTATION REQUIREMENTS: One reading specialist, the team leader, and two other teachers who have strengths in the teaching of reading. One IRIT Center requires three separate classrooms and office space for a part-time secretary and a part-time project director. Staff will need training in diagnosis and in the evaluation of test results. A school system might want to begin with one center, but a project director can easily supervise an additional center.

FINANCIAL REQUIREMENTS: Budget for one IRIT team is $59,072, serving 135 pupils in one year (approximately $400 per pupil). Start-up costs average an additional $25-$50 per pupil, depending on the specific equipment ordered.

SERVICES AVAILABLE: An NON-funded DeveloperDemonstrator project.

Awareness materials are available. Visitors are welcome by appointment. Training may be conducted on-site and out-of-state at no cost to the adopter, paid for by the Dissemination/Diffusion Grant. Project staff is available on a limited basis to assist with training at the adopter site, also at no cost.

PROJECT: PROGRAMMED TUTORIAL READING

TARGET AUDIENCE: First graders in the bottom quartile who need help learning to read are tutored on a one-to-one basis. Originally approved by the JDRP as a first grade program, this program now operates as a first and second grade program.

DESCRIPTION: An individualized tutoring program for first graders having difficulty learning to read.

Programmed Tutorial Reading (PTR) supplements, rather than supplants, conventional classroom teaching. The teaching strategy employs many elements of programmed instruction: frequent and immediate feedback, specified format, and individualized pace. However, whereas programmed instruction has often sought errorless or near-errorless learning with many cues at first, followed by a fading of cues, the tutorial program proceeds in the opposite manner with minimal cueing at first, followed by increased prompting until the child can eventually make the correct responses. The 15-minute tutoring sessions are highly structured. During their sessions, children read from their regular classroom basal readers while the tutor follows exactly one of 11 tutoring programs presented in the tutoring kits. The programs in the kit specify in detail *what* and *how* to teach. They are designed so that any decision made by a tutor about a child's reading is limited to judging the correctness or appropriateness of answers. Reinforcement and praise for success are essential parts of the instructional strategy.

ASSURANCES/CLAIMS: The original evaluation of program impact was a comparison of matched pairs of students, using the Gates-MacGinitie Reading Test, Primary A, form 1. Tutored children scored at 1.9 grade equivalent at the end of first grade, while non-tutored children scored at 1.5. Later evaluations, using the same test, have produced similar results using a treatment-control group design instead of matched pairs. The area in which the program is being used is middle-income suburban.

IMPLEMENTATION REQUIREMENTS: Implementation of the project requires a staff consisting of a part-time director, tutorial supervisors, tutors, and secretarial help. Facility requirements are limited to a quiet place and a side-by-side seating arrangement at a desk or table for the tutor and the child. Basal reading materials, a tutoring kit for each tutor, supplementary reading materials, and miscellaneous materials are also required. Training requirements include extensive training of tutorial supervisors and approximately 15 hours of training for tutors.

FINANCIAL REQUIREMENTS: The annual per-pupil cost ranges from \$150–\$250, depending upon rates of pay of tutors and supervisors. Personnel costs, which include all administrative and clerical assistance, account for approximately 98% of total budget.

SERVICES AVAILABLE: An NON-funded DeveloperDemonstrator project.

Initial and secondary awareness materials as well as a Project Information Package (PIP) are available. Project staff is available to conduct awareness and pre-adoption sessions out-of-state. Visitors to the project site are welcome by appointment. Implementation-phase training is available to a limited number of adopters.

PROJECT: PROJECT R-3, READINESS, RELEVANCY AND REINFORCEMENT

TARGET AUDIENCE: Students of all abilities, grades 7–9.

DESCRIPTION: A motivational basic-skill program that interrelates the reading and mathematics curricula through gaming simulation activities involving career awareness.

Project R-3 was jointly designed in 1967 by the San Jose Unified School District and the Education Systems Organization of Lockheed Missiles and Space Company, with the help of consultants from San Jose State University. It includes a curriculum that interrelates reading and mathematics with reinforcement through gaming/simulating intensive involvement (a three-day study trip), parental involvement, and an in-service training program for staff development. The main objective of Project R-3 is the upgrading of essential reading and mathematics skills. By deeply involving the students in classroom games and simulations, the program seeks to motivate them to achieve in learning experiences; to make them *ready* to learn, to make learning *relevant*, and to *reinforce* positive attitudes and behavior.

The project utilizes the diagnostic/prescriptive individualized approach in reading and math. Reinforcement of skill areas is provided through gaming/simulation activities that involve team learning, the decision-making process, and developing career awareness.

ASSURANCES/CLAIMS: The CTBS (Comprehensive Test of Basic Skills, Forms S2 and S3) shows that participants in the mathematics component (1976–77) made 2.4 months' gain for every month of instruction. For the reading component, 1.8 months' gain for every month of instruction was achieved. An outside evaluator is contracted for both product and process evaluation.

IMPLEMENTATION REQUIREMENTS: Reading and mathematics teachers should have a knowledge of the diagnostic/prescriptive approach to individualized instruction. Teachers must be receptive to team planning. All staff should develop expertise in gaming/simulation. Approximately 50 hours of inservice work is accomplished by each staff member in a given year.

FINANCIAL REQUIREMENTS: The basic materials of a reading program at the secondary level can be utilized. Special prepared math contracts cost approximately $150 for a complete set of masters to be duplicated. Other costs relate to gaming/simulation activities, contracts, and the cost of secondary instructional aides.

SERVICES   AVAILABLE: An   NON-funded   Developer/Demonstrator Project.

Awareness materials are available at no charge. Visitors are welcome by appointment, at both project and demonstration sites. Training is conducted at the project site (adopter pays only own costs). Training may be conducted out-of-state (exemplary project staff costs may be paid for). Project staff may be able to attend out-of-state conferences (costs to be arranged).

These three programs were reprinted from *Educational Programs That Work.* San Francisco, California, Far West Laboratory, Fall, 1980, pp. 9–35, 9– 52, 9–54. 52, 9–54.

REFERENCES

1. Coleman, J. et al.: *Equality of Educational Opportunity.* Washington, D.C., U.S. Government Printing Office, 1961, p. 22.
2. Moynihan, D. and Mosteller's, F.: *On Equality of Educational Opportunity Survey.* New York, Vintage Books, 1972, Introduction.
3. McLaughlin, M.: *Evaluation and Reform: The Elementary and Secondary Education Act of 1965, Title I.* San Monica, California, The Rand Corporation, 1974, p. 3.
4. Ibid., p. 16.
5. Ibid.
6. Ibid., p. 16.
7. Ibid., p. 17.
8. Ibid.
9. Ibid.
10. *The States Report — The First Year of Title I, Elementary and Secondary Education Act of 1965.* Arlington, VA., ERIC Document Reproduction Service, ED 021 946, 1967.
11. *The Second Annual Report of Title I of the Elementary and Secondary Education Act of 1965, School Year, 1966-67.* Arlington, VA., ERIC Document Reproduction Service, ED 021 946, 1967.
12. From a personal interview with Kathryn Hecht in Denver, Colorado, June 5, 1980.
13. Ibid.
14. *Education of the Disadvantaged: An Evaluative Report on Title I, Elementary and Secondary Education Act of 1965, Fiscal Year 1968.* Arlington, VA., ERIC Document Reproduction Service, ED 047 033, 1970.
15. Ibid.
16. Ibid., pp. 97, 375.
17. M. McLaughlin, op cit., p. 57.
18. Ibid., p. 59.
19. *The Impact of Head Start: An Evaluation of the Effects of Head Start on Children's Cognitive and Affective Development.* Arlington, VA., ERIC Document Reproduction Service, ED 036 321, 1969.
20. Beckler, J.: Congress and the Administration scrutinize the results of Title I. *School Management, 14(9):6, 1970.*
21. Hawkridge, D. et al.: *A Study of Exemplary Programs for the Education of Disadvantaged Children,* Part I. Arlington, VA., ERIC Document Reproduction Service, ED 023 776, 1968, pp. 1-2.
22. Tallmadge, K.: *The Development of Project Information Package for Effective Approaches in Compensatory Education, Final Report.* Arlington, VA., ERIC Document Reproduction Service, ED 099 457, 1974, pp. ii, v, vi.
23. United States Commission Civil Rights, 1967: *Racial Isolation in the Public Schools,* Vol. I. Washington, D.C., U.S. Government Printing Office, February, 1967, pp. 121, 125, 127.
24. Hawkridge et al. (1968), op cit., p. 1.

25. D. Hawkridge, et al., *A Study of Further Exemplary Programs for the Education of Disadvantaged Children*, Part II. Arlington, VA., ERIC Document Reproduction Service, ED 036 668, 1969, p. 6.

26. Wargo, M. et al.: *Further Examination of Exemplary Programs for Educating Disadvantaged Children*. Arlington, VA., ERIC Document Reproduction Service, ED 055 128, 1971.

27. *It Works Series: Summaries of Selected Compensatory Education Projects*, Washington, D.C.: U.S. Government Printing Office, 1970.

28. Hawkridge, et al., op cit., 1968, p. 1.

29. Hawkridge, et al., op cit., 1969, p. 6.

30. Wargo, M. et al.: *ESEA Title I: A Reanalysis and Synthesis of Evaluation Data from Fiscal Year 1965 to 1970*. Arlington, VA., ERIC Document Reproduction Service, ED 059 415, 1972, p. 180.

31. Wargo, op cit., p. iii.

32. Ibid., pp. iii–iv.

33. Wargo, 1971, op cit., p. 44.

34. Ibid., pp. 185–186.

35. McLaughlin, M. et al.: *The Effects of Title I ESEA: An Exploratory Study*. Arlington, VA., ERIC Document Reproduction Service, ED 073 216, 1971, p. 4.

36. Ibid., p. 2.

37. Ibid., pp. 1–8 and 13.

38. Ibid., p. 17.

39. Ibid., p. 18.

40. Ibid., pp. 13–14.

41. Ibid., p. 16.

42. Ibid., p. 13.

43. Foat, C.: *Selecting Exemplary Compensatory Education Programs for Dissemination Via Project Information Package*. Arlington, VA., ERIC Document Reproduction Service, ED 099 456, 1964, p. 14.

44. Ibid., pp. 14, 31–52.

45. Ibid., pp. 31–52.

46. From a telephone interview with Ann Weinheimer, Evaluation Specialist in the Office of Evaluation, Department of Education, June 19, 1980.

47. Ibid.

48. Ibid.

49. Ibid.

50. Ibid.

51. *Educational Programs that Work*. San Francisco, California, Far West Laboratory, Fall, 1980.

52. Ibid.

53. Stearns, M. et al.: *Evaluation of the Field Test of Project Information Packages*, Volume I. Arlington, VA., ERIC Document Reproduction Service, ED 142 567, 1977, p. 36.

54. Weinheimer, op cit.

55. Ryan, S. (Ed.): *A Report on Longitudinal Evaluations of Pre-School Programs, Vol. 1: Longitudinal Evaluations.* Arlington, VA., ERIC Document Reproduction Service, ED 093 500, 1974.

56. Bereiter, C. and Engelmann, S.: *Teaching Disadvantaged Children in the Pre-school.* Englewood Cliffs, New Jersey: Prentice-Hall, 1966.

57. Weikart, D.: Relationship of curriculum, teaching and learning in pre-school evaluation. Stanley, J. C. (Ed.): Preschool Programs for the Disadvantaged. Baltimore, Maryland, The Johns Hopkins University Press, 1972, pp. 22–66.

58. D. Weikart, et al., *Longitudinal Results of the Ypsilanti Perry Preschool Project, Final Report.* Arlington, VA., ERIC Document Reproduction Service, ED 044 536, 1970.

59. Weikart, 1972, op cit., pp. 22–26.

60. Gray, S. and Klaus, R.: The early training project: A seventh-year report. *Child Development, 41:*909-24, 1970.

61. Herzog, E., Newcomb, C., and Cisin, I.: Double deprivation: The less they have, the less they learn. In Ryan, S.: *A Report on the Evaluations of Preschool Programs, Vol. I: Longitudinal Evaluations.* Arlington, VA., ERIC Document Reproduction Service, ED 093 500, pp. 53–69. .

62. Karnes, M. et al.: The Karnes pre-school program: Rationale, curricular offerings and follow up. In Ryan, S.: *A Report on the Evaluations of Preschool Programs, Vol. I.: Longitudinal Evaluations.* Arlington, VA., ERIC Document Reproduction Service, ED 093 500, 1974, pp. 95–108.

63. Beller, E.: The impact of early education on disadvantaged children. In Ryan, S.: *A Report on the Evaluations of Preschool Programs, Vol. I.: Longitudinal Evaluations.* Arlington, VA., ERIC Document Reproduction Service, ED 093 500, 1974, pp. 15–48.

64. V. Van De Riet and M. Resnick: *Developmental and Educational Implications of a Successful Model of Compensatory Education, The Learning to Learn Program.* Arlington, VA., ERIC Document Reproduction Service, ED 082 852, 1973.

65. Springle, H.: Learning to learn program. In Ryan, S.: *A Report on the Evaluations of Preschool Programs, Vol. I.: Longitudinal Evaluations.* Arlington, VA., ERIC Document Reproduction Service, ED 093 500, 1974, pp. 109–124.

66. Deutsch, M. et al.: Brief synopsis of an initial enrichment program in early childhood. In Ryan, S.: *A Report on the Evaluations of Preschool Programs, Vol. I: Longitudinal Evaluations.* Arlington, VA., ERIC Document Reproduction Service, ED 093 500, 1974, pp. 49–60.

67. Ibid., p. 15.

68. Ibid.

69. Wargo, op cit., p. 44.

70. North, R. et al.: *Evaluation Report for the Project 'More Effective Schools Program' in Poverty Area Schools,* 1968–69. Arlington, VA., ERIC Document Reproduction Service, ED 041 998, 1969, pp. 109–110.

71. Freeman, R.: The alchemists in our public schools. Quoted by J. Ashbrook in the House of Representatives, *Congressional Record*, April 24, 1969, p. 10326.
72. Thomas, T. and Delavin, S.: *Patterns in ESEA Reading Achievement.* Arlington, VA., ERIC Document Reproduction Service, ED 120 087, March, p. 39.
73. Ibid., pp. 38–41.
74. Ibid., pp. 37–38.
75. Ibid., pp. 40–41.
76. Ibid., pp. 42–43.
77. Ibid., p. 43.
78. Stebbins, L. et al.: *Education As Experimentation: A Planned Variation Model, Volume IV-A, An Evaluation of Follow Through.* Cambridge, Massachusetts, Abt Associates Inc.
79. Abelson, W. and Zigler, E.: Effects of a four-year follow-through program on economically disadvantaged children. *Journal of Educational Psychology*, 66(5): 756–771, 1974.
80. Hendrickson, G.: *Review of Title I Evaluation Studies.* Paper presented at the annual meeting of the American Educational Research Association, New York, New York, April 10–15, 1977, p. 38.
81. Weinheimer, op cit.
82. Tallmadge, G.: *Interpreting NCEs.* Mountain View, California, RMC Research Corporation, October, 1976, p. 1.
83. Horst, D.: *What's Bad about Grade Equivalent Scores.* Mountain View, California, RMC Research Corporation, October, 1976, p. 2.
84. Ibid., pp. 2–4.
85. Ibid., p. 3.
86. Tallmadge, op cit., p. 3.
87. Ibid., pp. 2–4.
88. Ibid., p. 6.
89. Tallmadge, G. and Fagan, B.: *Cognitive Growth and Growth Expectations in Reading and Mathematics.* Mountain View, California, RMC Research Corporation, prepared for U.S. DHEW's OPOE, November 1977, p. 4.
90. Mayeske, G.: *A Study of Compensatory Reading Programs: Technical Summary,* Washington, D.C., USOE, OPBE, Elementary and Secondary Programs Division, September, 1976, p. 61, quoted in Rossi, Robert et al.: *Summaries of Major Title I Evaluations.* Arlington, VA., ERIC Document Reproduction Service, ED 145 012, p. 128.
91. From a telephone conversation with George Mayeske, June 25, 1980.
92. Ibid.
93. Hill, P. and Rotberg, I.: *The Effects of Services on Student Development.* Washington, D.C., U.S. Government Printing Office, September 30, 1977.
94. Ibid., pp. 19–20.
95. *Compensatory Education Study.* Washington, D.C., U.S. Government Printing Office, September, 1978, p. 83.
96. Ibid., p. 84.
97. Ibid., pp. 84, 87.

98. Wang, M.: *Evaluating the Effectiveness of Compensatory Education.* Paper presented at the annual meeting of the American Educational Research Corporation, Boston, Massachusetts, April 10, 1980.

99. Ibid.

100. Carter, L. *The Sustaining Effects Study: Evaluating the Effectiveness of Compensatory Education.* A presentation at the Second Colorado Title I Conference, Colorado Springs, Colorado, January 4, 1980.

101. Darlington, R. et al.: Preschool programs and later school competencies. *Science, 208(4440):*202–204, 1980.

102. DeVito, P. and Rubenstein, J.: *A Follow-Up Study of Title I Participants in Rhode Island.* Paper presented at the annual meeting of the American Educational Research Association, San Francisco, California, April 8–13, 1979, p. 5.

103. Ibid., p. 8.

104. Powers, S.: *A Comparison of Cognitive Gains of Seventh, Eighth and Ninth Grade Students Across Two Years of Title I.* Paper presented at the annual meeting of the American Educational Research Association, Boston, Massachusetts, April 7–11, 1980, p. 14.

105. Weinheimer, op cit.

106. Ibid.

107. British researchers look at urban secondary schools and their effects on disadvantaged children. *Education Times,* Monday, January 28, 1980, p. 2.

108. From a telephone interview with Ida Brooks of the National Association for Educational Progress, June 26, 1980.

109. Edmunds, R.: Effective schools for the urban poor. *Educational Leadership, 37(1):*22, 1979.

110. Mayeske, op cit.

111. Powers, op cit., p. 14.

112. Rosenshine, B.: Academic engaged time, content covered, and direct instruction. *Journal of Education, 160(3):*46, 1978.

113. Burns, R.: Mastery learning: Does it work. *Educational Leadership, 37(2):*110–113, 1979.

114. Ibid.

115. Ibid.

116. Aikin, W.: *The Story of the Eight Year Study.* New York, Harper & Brothers, 1942.

117. Perry, P.: *Characteristics of Successful Title I Programs.* From a presentation at the Second Colorado Title I Conference, Colorado Springs, Colorado, January 4, 1980.

118. From a telephone interview with Chuck Sekera, June 27, 1980.

119. Ibid.

120. From a telephone interview with Peggy Seavy, June 27, 1980.

121. Ibid.

122. Sekera, op cit.

123. From an interview with Larry Bussey, June 16, 1980.

124. From a telephone interview with OPOE's Janice Anderson, September, 1980.

CHAPTER 6

DESEGREGATION, HEREDITY AND BEYOND

I f compensatory education in America has been less than a panacea for underachieving blacks, what contribution has school desegregation made to improving the academic performance and social stature of blacks? And if compensatory schooling and desegregated education strategies have not dramatically altered the racial inequalities in measured intelligence and school achievement, what has gone wrong? Can the persistence of measured racial differences in various aptitude and scholastic tests be largely or partly attributed to hereditarian influences, to the continuation of differences in backgrounds between blacks and whites or to the incompetence of the educational system? This chapter will address these questions by summarizing research reviews of the effects of desegregation, discussing the racial implications of the nature–nurture controversy and describing some of the alternatives to both the present educational and political system.

The Effects of Desegregation

The educational literature abounds with studies attempting to measure the relationship between school desegregation and pupil achievement. Perhaps the two most important reviews of this information were compiled by Meyer Weinberg and Nancy St. John, both of whom published their findings in 1975. Both authors contend that desegregation seldom has any negative effect on black pupil achievement and in many cases has a positive impact. The relevant studies are virtually unanimous in suggesting that white pupils do not suffer academically because they attend school with blacks.[1] Regarding black attainment, Weinberg concludes that "... overall, desegregation does indeed have a positive effect on minority achievement"* whereas St. John appears a bit more cautious by her stating that "There is no indication . . . that we need to revise the basic hypothesis that in the long run integration benefits children."[2] In a discussion of the Weinberg and St. John books, Caroline Persell concisely lists under what circumstances desegregation appears to be most related to achievement.[3] According to Weinberg, attending school with whites seems to reap greatest academic benefits for racial minorities under the following conditions:

1. There is relatively little racial hostility among students.
2. Teachers and administrators understand and accept minority students, and these characteristics are encouraged by effective inservice training programs if necessary.
3. The majority of students in any given class are from middle or upper socioeconomic classes.
4. Desegregation occurs within the classroom, not just at the schoolwide level.
5. Rigid ability grouping and tracking do not occur.
6. The community is not inflamed by racial conflict.

St. John reached the following conclusions concerning school desegregation:

1. Younger children (especially those of kindergarten age) seem to benefit more than older children.
2. City size or region is unrelated.
3. The length of exposure to desegregation has not proved to be an important variable so far, perhaps because so many experiences are of such short duration.
4. Findings do not seem to depend upon the definition of desegregation (that is, what proportion of different races constitutes desegregation).
5. The method used by a community to achieve desegregation (whether bussing, demographic changes in neighborhoods, schoolboard rezoning of districts, voluntary transfer of selected pupils, or districtwide desegregation) does not determine whether academic gains result.

A more recent review of the achievement-desegregation literature by Robert Crain and Rita Mahard of the Rand Corporation concludes by stating that desegregated schooling " . . . sometimes . . . works, sometimes it doesn't. But that is true of any intervention." It is important to recognize " . . . that desegregation is not a laboratory-controlled experiment that is identical in Jackson-

---

*The vast majority of studies reviewed by Weinberg focused on blacks as the minority.

ville, Florida and Berkeley, California. Every case is different and different results should be expected."[4] Nevertheless their review found the weight of the evidence supporting the likelihood of positive achievement gains in desegregated situations. In an analysis of thirty-nine desegregation studies involving "mandatory assignment of black pupils," positive achievement affects were reported in the greater majority of the evaluations (exceeding negative effects by a four-to-one ratio). Several of the studies in the Rand review reported gains of one-half grade level or greater in the first one or two years following desegregation.[5]

Not unexpectedly, the school desegregation research has not found multi-racial school attendance having profound affects on black scholastic performance. It may have been pompous of whites to believe that school desegregation in itself would ever assume such powers. Perhaps fairer, more realistic assessments of desegregation's impact can be made if one looks at its effect on nurturing a more integrated society, at least to the degree in which it has afforded blacks greater access to economic and political amenities of American society. Before looking at desegregation from this egalitarian perspective, however, one must deal with the attacks on busing levied by James Coleman who recently contended that this means of desegregating schools is contributing to, rather than reducing, racial segregation.

Just as his *Equality of Educational Opportunity* had planted the seeds of controversy a decade earlier, Coleman's conclusion from his research on busing has fueled an already heated national debate. In a study of demographic changes in major urban school districts, Coleman and his colleagues argued that desegregation in the twenty largest central city districts has hastened the exodus of whites.[6] In a 1975 article, Coleman concluded that "Ironically, desegregation may be increasing segregation ... Eliminating central city segregation does not help if it increases greatly the segregation between districts through accelerated white loss."[7] Forced desegregation, principally via busing, was, in Coleman's mind, perhaps, the major culprit causing the phenomenon that has come to be widely labeled "white flight."

Coleman expounded his views throughout much of 1975 in public testimony in such places as racially troubled Boston and before the Senate Judiciary Committee. Needless to say, as a former champion of integration, his apparent about face received wide-spread media coverage.[8] Numerous rebuttals to his arguments also appeared in the professional press. They generally accused Coleman of going well beyond his data in forming his conclusions. For example, in the *Harvard Education Review* Thomas Pettigrew and Robert Green pointed out that his "twenty largest districts" were really nineteen in number and were "*not* the largest urban school districts in the United States."[9] According to Pettigrew and Green:

> Omitted and never mentioned in any of the four versions of Coleman's paper are Miami-Dade, Jacksonville-Duval, and Fort Lauderdale-Broward, all county-wide urban systems in Florida. Yet Tampa-Hillsborough, also a Florida metropolitan school district, was included, although it is smaller than the three omitted districts. Miami and Jacksonville, like Tampa, experienced widespread court-ordered school desegregation without a significant decline in white enrollment, while Fort Lauderdale's white enrollment *increased* by 39.2 percent from 1968 to 1972 during an extensive school desegregation program. Thus, Coleman's unexplained exclusion of these three huge districts may have contributed to his findings."[10]

Pettigrew and Green argued further that of the cities Coleman studied, only in Atlanta and Memphis could white decreases be scientifically associated with desegregation.

In another critique by Stanley Brown and James Bosco, Coleman is accused of inaccurately attributing the continuation of a long established demographic trend to court ordered school desegregation. They contend that "Since well before 1968, demographers have noted that the proportion of blacks in cities was growing because whites were leaving . . ." and that Coleman is unable to show any solid evidence ". . . to link this white movement to the introduction of desegregation law and policy. . . ."[11]

Whatever the merits of Coleman's conclusions may be, two things seem to be certainties: *de facto* school segregation is still widespread in many major urban areas throughout the country, and desegregation efforts have done little to alter this situation.

When desegregation does occur, however, it appears that it often has positive long-term affects on the equalization of the social order. Perhaps the most comprehensive research on the longitudinal effects on school desegregation has been conducted at the

Center for Social Organization of Schools at Johns Hopkins University. The center's co-director, James McPartland, has investigated the relationship between desegregated schooling and such later life stations as higher education attendance and occupational attainment. In a 1978 review of the longitudinal data, McPartland found that most of the relevant desegregation-higher education research appears to support the positive effects of desegregation. After controlling for region and family background, it was reported that blacks attending desegregated schools, during a period from the 1930s to early 1960s, were more likely to have completed both elementary and high school and to have entered and completed a university or college than blacks who went to segregated public schools. McPartland cites additional evaluations of Boston's METCO program, in which black students were voluntarily bused to predominately white metropolitan schools, and of New York City's highly selective ABC ("A Better Chance") program, an educational adventure which awarded scholarships to blacks permitting them to enroll in prestigious secondary schools. The longitudinal research reported that METCO students were more likely to enter and remain in high quality colleges than the control pupils (two years after high school graduation there was no difference between METCO and control pupils in college attendance at lower quality and/or two year colleges). ABC pupils—many of whom attended predominately white boarding schools—were twice as likely as the control students to enter college and tended to be enrolled in higher quality colleges. A much larger scale study entitled the National Longitudinal Study (NLS) of the High School Graduating Class of 1972 includes data suggesting that desegregated secondary schooling has a nonsignificant negative effect on black college enrollment in the South and a positive influence on black higher education attendance in the North. [12]

It would appear that the evidence to date in support of the positive long-term effects of school desegregation has been gathered by Jomills Braddock (also from Johns Hopkins) and McPartland in a further analysis of the NLS data. The researchers have analyzed the probability of Northern and Southern blacks enrolling in predominately white colleges based on the number of years (up to four) that they attended desegregated elementary and secondary schools, and have reported a definite trend associating desegregated elementary and secondary schooling in both regions with attendance at desegregated two and four year colleges. [13]

As far as the relationship between desegregation and occupation is concerned apparently the only data addressing this association was gathered by the United States Commission on Civil Rights in 1966. According to McPartland's accounting of the analysis, black men who had attended integrated high schools "... were more likely to hold nontraditional jobs in sales, crafts, and the professions (33%) than those who attended segregated schools (21%)." Educationally desegregated blacks also had slightly higher occupational prestige and income, although the income advantage was only $100.00 after controlling for environmental background. [14]

THE GENETIC CONTROVERSY

The controversies surrounding compensatory education and desegregation have typically been mild in comparison to the debate engendered by a few academicians who have suggested innate differences between the black and white populations in mental capacities. Among the more prominent spokespersons for the hereditarian position have been Harvard's Richard Hernstein and Stanford's William Shockley.

But it has been Arthur Jensen, the eminent educational psychologist from the University of California, Berkeley, who has provoked most of the discussion and ignited most of the furor, principally by his writing a lengthy article on the inheritability of intelligence, which appeared in the prestigious *Harvard Educational Review* (HER) in 1969. [15] Had a similar article been written by a less distinguished behavioral scientist or published in another journal or appeared at another time or been less scientific in tone, it may have gone relatively unnoticed. But the combination of author, publisher, year, and scholarship provided a chemistry for controversy that has made Doctor Jensen, if not a household word, then one of the best known, living psychologists in the world. With a single, perhaps daring, blow, Jensen struck out against what he saw as the established environmental order of academe. Since 1969, Jensen's pursuit of further substantiating his unconventional biologically deterministic conclusions has appeared to be so unrelenting that he has loomed as almost an arsenal unto himself in the battle against what he has labeled "environmentalist fantasies." Accordingly, in reviewing the hereditarian argument, we will give almost exclusive attention to Doctor Jensen's positions within that camp and include rebuttals to his views by several persons who interpret the data differently.

The 1969 Article

Entitled "How Much Can We Boost I.Q. and Scholastic Achievement," Jensen's article offered little new information on inheritability. Essentially, it provided a highly readable synthesis of the history of I.Q. testing, a carefully developed description of intelligence, an explanation of genetic processes, research reviews of cognitive growth and of compensatory education effectiveness, suggestions as to what may be done educationally and a discourse on the ethics of it all. This comprehensive analysis was preceded by the provocative opening sentence "Compensatory Education has been tried and has apparently failed." According to Jensen, here may be the reasons why.

1. *Intelligence can be measured and does not defy definition.* Jensen begins by tracing the history of mental testing and by exploring the difficulties involved in coming to grips with the nature of intelligence ("Intelligence, like electricity, is easier to measure than to define.") He explains that the "first really useful test of intelligence and the progenitor of nearly all present-day tests was . . . devised in 1905 by Binet and Simon . . . in Paris for the explicit purpose of identifying children who were likely to fail in school." Rather ironically, the first significant measure of intelligence was used to help decide who " . . . should be placed in special schools or classes before losing too much ground or receiving too much discouragement."[16] Jensen emphasizes the importance that must be attached to the Parisian origins of the intelligence tests, and the fact that their growth was nurtured implicitly by Euro-American educational traditions.

> The content and methods of instruction represented in this tradition . . . are a rather narrow and select sample of all the various forms of human

learning and of the ways of imparting knowledge and skills. The instructional methods of the traditional classroom were not invented all in one stroke, but evolved within an upperclass segment of the European population, and thus were naturally shaped by the capacities, culture, and needs of those children whom the schools were primarily intended to serve. At least implicit in the system as it originally developed was the expectation that not all children would succeed. [17]

Jensen pointed out that the methods of schooling have changed very little since the nineteenth century and that these educational strategies, originally designed for the upper crust, "... have actually worked quite well for the majority of children ... And the tests that were specifically devised to distinguish those children least apt to succeed in this system have also proved to do their job quite well." [18]

What are the cognitive processes one needs to succeed in the European and American educational system? Jensen discussed the labors of English psychologist Spearman that resulted in the discovery of a high correlation among tests involving complex mental activities ("as opposed to sheer sensoracity, reflex behavior, or the execution of established habits"), despite their apparent differences. The tests may be measures of word knowledge, verbal analogies, design copying, or spatial relationships, but there seemed to be a common, underlying factor that accounted for their intercorrelations. Spearman labeled it *general intelligence* or *g*. He went on to construct a means to measure this common denominator in the various mental tests through a process called factor analysis. Essentially, *g* is the cognitive aptitude necessary for complex problem solving, involving, according to Spearman, "the ability to educe relations and correlations" and in Jensen's words, "to see the difference between things which seem similar and to see the similarities between things which seem different." Jensen stated further that "These are essentially the processes of abstraction and conceptualization [and] tasks which call for problem solving requiring these processes are usually the best measures of *g*." Because we are a complex, technological society (if we were a hunting and gathering culture the definition of general intelligence may have been defined rather differently), occupations requiring the usage of *g* are, in the public mind, the top positions on the vocational prestige hierarchy. Like it or not "Even if all occupations paid alike and received equal respect and acclaim, some occupations would still be viewed as more desirable than others." Given the nature of our society, Jensen implied that jobs demanding relatively high general intelligence for satisfactory performance will always be the most desirable and probably most important.[19]

2. *Intelligence is largely inherited.* In building the case for biological determinism, Jensen drew on much of the IQ research on twins, foster parents vs. natural parents, institutional children, and population mental longevity. In analyzing these studies, he estimated that heredity accounts for roughly 80 percent of the IQ variance, at least in the Caucasian populations of North America and England where most of the research was conducted.[20] Given the evidence that identical twins raised apart are usually more alike in measured intelligence than unrelated children or even siblings reared together, and foster children are much more like their natural parents than their adopted parents, Jensen contributed little here to the conventional psychological wisdom (see Chapter 4). His 80 percent heredity estimate was a bit higher than is typically offered, but few people in the field dispute the powerful influence of heredity. What distinguishes Jensen's analysis from many other reviews was his contention that prenatal environmental influences account for much of the nongenetic variance, and his manner of interpreting three of the more critical studies. (A discussion of the differences in interpretation is included under the next subheading, for it is more related to the forthcoming Jensen argument.)

Regarding prenatal influences, Jensen noted that twins are, on the average, roughly 4 to 7 points lower in IQ than single children, and that monozygotic (identical—MZ) twins score slightly lower on intelligence tests and have a higher mortality rate than dizgotic (fraternal—DZ) twins. Furthermore, on the average, boy twins do not match girl twins in IQ, and twins with lower birth weights typically have lower IQs. Jensen explained that in twin pregnancy "nutrient supplies may be inadequate for proper body and brain development" . . . and that the unequal sharing of nutrients and space stunts one twin more than its mate."[21] Boys are more susceptible to prenatal impairment, thus, explaining, perhaps, their lesser weight and the lower IQ of MZ males. Concluded Jensen:

> Thus, much of the average difference between MZ twins, whether reared together or reared apart, seems to be due to prenatal environmental factors. The real importance of these findings, of course, lies in their implications for the possible role of prenatal environment in the development of all children. It is not unlikely that there are individual maternal differences in the adequacy of the prenatal environment. If intrauterine conditions can cause several points of IQ difference between twins, it is not hard to imagine that individual differences in prenatal environments could also cause IQ differences in single born children and might therefore account for a substantial proportion of the total environmental variance in IQ.[22]

3. *The environment as a threshold.* Jensen contended that the postnatal environment can have a profound affect on IQ but only "below a certain threshold of environmental adequacy." For example, living children in environments with extreme sensory and motor restrictions may score from 20 to 70 IQ points below their potential. By moving these children to "good average environmental circumstances," however, their genetic capacities can be accounted, and the measured changes in intelligence is often phenomenal." But above this threshold," he argued "environmental variations cause relatively small differences in intelligence."[23] Jensen explained, "The environment with respect to intelligence is thus analogous to nutrition with respect to stature. If there are great nutritional lacks, growth is stunted, by above a certain level of nutritional adequacy, including minimal daily requirements of minerals, vitamins, and proteins, even great variations in eating habits will have negligible effects on persons' stature, and under such conditions most of the differences in stature among individuals will be due to heredity."[24]

To Jensen, the "lack of middle class amenities" does not place one at "subthreshold environmental deprivation," thus placing most of the American economically and educationally underprivileged within an environment adequate for genetic fulfillment.[25]

But what about the substantial IQ point differences in the IQs of identical twins and groups of foster children reared in contrasting environments and the IQ depressions reported by Wheeler in his study of Tennessee mountain children? Were not the less abundant environments in these studies above the environmental threshold? Regarding twins, Doctor Jensen mentioned only the high correlations (0.77, 0.77, and 0.86) between separately reared MZ twins in the respective studies by Newman, Freeman, and Holzinger, Shields and Burt. He then discussed the extremely high correlations reported by Burt, which were the "most interesting" and "most important" because "... the separated twins were spread over the entire range of socioeconomic levels ..."[26] In the case of institutionalized children, Jensen contended that the extreme social isolation of Skeels and Dye orphanage children placed them at the subthreshold environmental level, and they "... gained in I.Q. from an average of 64 at 19 months of age to 96 at age 6 as a result of being given social stimulation and placement in more nurturant homes between 2 and 3 years of age."[27] Regarding the depression of IQ over time, Jensen apparently attributed the substantial IQ decline of two samples of Tennessee mountain children in the 1930s and 1940s to the "... phenomenon of children's gravitation toward the parental I.Q. with increasing age."[28] Jensen was referring here more to an IQ decline of a sample of black children in Chicago but attempted to explain the maturation phenomenon further by offering the following description and interpretation of the Wheeler research:

> It is far from certain or even likely that all such decline in I.Q. is due to environmental influences rather than to genetic factors involved in the growth rate of intelligence. Consistent with this interpretation is the fact that the hereditary of intelligence measures increases with age. We should expect just the opposite if environmental factors alone were responsible for the increasing I.Q. deficit of markedly below average groups. A study by Wheeler (1942) suggests that although I.Q. may raised at all age levels by improving the environment, such improvements do not counteract the decline in the I.Q. of certain below average groups. In 1940 Wheeler tested over 3000 Tennessee mountain children between the ages of 6 and 16 and compared their I.Q.s with children in the same age range who had been given the same tests in 1930, when the average I.Q. and standard of living in this area would characterize the majority of the inhabitants as 'culturally deprived.' During the intervening 10 years state and federal intervention in this area brought about great improvements in economic conditions, standards of health care, and educational and cultural opportunities, and during the same period the average I.Q. for the region increased 10 points, from 82 to 92. But the decline in I.Q. from age 6 to age 16 was about the same in 1940 (from 103* to 80) as in 1930 (from 95 to 74).[29]

*More accurately 95

Apparently, Jensen felt that although the mountain children initially had slightly higher IQs than the region as a whole, their genetic endowment (better measured at age sixteen than at age six) precluded their responding positively to governmental efforts to develop the area. Above the environmental threshold but hopelessly retarded, these children apparently approximated their parents' IQs with maturation.

4. *Racial differences*. It was Jensen's contention that all the differences in IQ between social classes and races cannot be fully explained by environmental circumstances and that one must look to possible genetic explanations. Regarding race *per se*, he explained (citing a study conducted in California showing a group of "professional and managerial" blacks having IQs 3.9 points lower than a sample of "lower-class" whites) that there are marked differences in IQ between blacks and whites even when one controls for socioeconomic factors. [30] The possibility of genetic differences in the mental capacities of races should come as no surprise, he contended, for "Any groups which have been geographically or socially isolated from one another for many generations are practically certain to differ in their gene pools..." Since races are "breeding populations" which mate more often within the group than outside the group and are "populations having different distributions of gene frequencies," it is axiomatic that they are going to have many physical differences. [31] According to Jensen, these differences probably involve the physiology of the intellectual processor as well.

> These genetic differences are manifested in virtually every anatomical, physiological and biochemical comparison one can make between representative samples of identifiable racial groups. . . . There is no reason to suppose that the brain should be exempt from this generalization. . . .
>
> The real questions, geneticists tell me, are not whether there are or are not genetic racial differences that affect behavior, because there undoubtedly are. The proper questions to ask, from a scientific standpoint are: What is the direction of the difference? What is the magnitude of the difference? And what is the significance of the difference — medically, socially, educationally, or from whatever standpoint that may be relevant to the characteristic in question? [32]

Jensen went on to suggest that the 15 point IQ point difference between the American black and white populations places blacks at a significant intellectual disadvantage. Statistically this fifteen point spread equals a standard deviation, which means that only 15 percent of the black population exceeds the IQ average of the white population. [33]

Jensen implied that four to six of the fifteen IQ points separating the races could be the workings of the postnatal environment but that the remaining nine to eleven points are genetically determined. [34] He explained that so-called culture fair tests fail to reduce the measured intellectual racial differences, and pointed out that blacks score lower on aptitude and achievement measures than American Indians, perhaps the most "environmentally disadvantaged" minority group in the United States. [35]

It was Jensen's contention that blacks do not perform relatively low in all intellectual functioning; they score about as well as whites on tests measuring associative ability (digit memory, serial rate learning, selective trial and error learning with feedback for correct responses, etc.). It is on measures of conceptual ability (g) that blacks do poorly. [36] Jensen labeled associative ability Level I intelligence and conceptual ability Level II. [37] One of the major problems with our educational system, he implied, is that the traditional methods of classroom instruction (which had their origins in nineteenth century Europe and North America) have not been changed. Since these traditional methods were discussed to serve "populations having a predominately middle-class pattern of abilities, they put great emphasis on cognitive learning rather than associative learning. [38]

Jensen concluded his article rather optimistically, suggesting that children with average Level I intelligence but who are weak in Level II ability can learn the basic skills adequately if the proper methods are employed. "I am reasonably convinced that all the basic scholastic skills can be learned by children with normal Level I learning ability, provided the instructional techniques do not make g (i.e. Level II) the *sine qua non* of being able to learn." [39] Unfortunately, Jensen, saying only that "Educational researchers must discover and devise teaching methods that capitalize on existing abilities for the acquisition of those basic skills which students will need in order to get good jobs when they leave school," suggested no specific instruction techniques for Level I mastery of the basics. To Jensen "... the ideal of equality of educational opportunity should not be interpreted as uniformity of facilities, instructional techniues, and educational aims for all children. Diversity rather than uniformity of approaches and aims would seem to be the key to making education rewarding for children with different patterns of ability. The reality of individual differences thus need not mean educational rewards for some children in frustration and defeat for others." [40]

The Critics Respond

Following the appearance of Jensen's article, the *Harvard Educational Review* featured critiques of Jensen's article in its next two issues. [41] So provacative and contrary were Jensen's views that before they were even published, *HER* solicited responses from six psychologists and a geneticist for its next edition. In its second issue following the publication of Jensen's article, the journal devoted the entire issue to responses to Jensen from an assortment of scholars plus a reply to the Spring edition critics by Jensen himself. Included also were a number of letters from readers, including a statement by the Black Student Union of Harvard's Graduate School of Education, chastising the *HER*'s editorial board for giving "... tacit support, whether intended or not, to the argument that Black Americans are inferior." [42] It was Jensen's suggestions regarding inherent racial differences in mental capacities that generated the greatest scholarly objection and emotional furor. But by no means were all the responses published by *HER* antagonistic in tone. In fact, most scholarly rebuttals expressed respect for Jensen's academic talents and a few letters applauded his "courage."

Regarding the nature of intelligence and its general inheritability in a given population, most critiques neglected to comment on the validity of Jensen's discussion of g and took little issue with his contention that heredity plays a dominant role in explaining IQ variation. Indeed, Carl Bereiter, one of the leading behavioristic preschool educators, acknowledged that "The heritability of intelligence is unquestionably high ..." [43] and J. McVicker Hunt, often erroneously associated with blinded environmentalism, agreed

" . . . that there is abundant evidence of genetic influences on behavior and that one can increase or decrease by selective breeding the measures of any phenotypic trait."[44] What appears to have most disturbed the critics is what Harvard's Jerome Kagan contended was the inherent illogic to Jensen's fundamental argument:

> Professor Jensen notes first that scores on a standard intelligence tests are more similar for people with similar genetic constitutions. The more closely related two people are, the more similar their I.Q. scores, suggesting that there is a genetic contribution to intelligence test performance. The second fact is that black children generally obtain lower I.Q. scores than whites. Unfortunately, Jensen combines the two facts to draw the logically faulted conclusion that there are genetic determinants behind the lower I.Q. scores of black children.[45]

Kagan drew an analogy using stature, reminding us that "Height is controlled by genetic factors [and that] the more closely related two people are, the more similar their height." But most Central and South American rural Indian children are significantly shorter than their Indian urban counterparts and Jensen's logic would necessitate attributing this difference to genetic endowment. According to Kagan, "However, the data indicate otherwise. The shorter heights of the rural children do not seem to be due to heredity but to disease and environmental malnutrition." During the past generation or so the stature of children throughout most of America and much of the world has increased markedly " . . . due to better nutrition and immunization against disease, not as a result of changes in genetic structure.[46] Yet height is still subject to genetic control. Kagan summarized the alleged fallacy: "The essential error in Jensen's argument is the conclusion that if a trait is under genetic control, differences between two populations on that trait must be due to genetic factors. This is the heart of Jensen's position, and it is not persuasive."[47]

Geneticist James Crow agreed "for the most part with Jensen's analysis" but expressed reservations similar to Kagan's when comparing populations occupying different environments.

> It is clear, I think, that a high heritability of intelligence in the white population would not, even if there were similar evidence in the black population, tell us that the differences between the groups are genetic. No matter how high the heritability . . . ., there is no assurance that a sufficiently

great environmental difference does not account for the difference in the two means, especially when one considers that the environmental factors may differ qualitatively in the two groups. So, I think, evidence regarding the importance of heredity in determining group mean differences must come from other kinds of studies. [48]

The studies Jensen cited in his 1969 article did not appear to cut the mustard in his building a strong case for the environment operating in a nonlinear fashion. It was Jensen's contention that the environment can affect IQ profoundly below a certain threshold level, but at some point (which he implied was exposure to an adult linguistic community) just above severe sensory or physical deprivation, the environment triggers the flowing of genetic capacities. But one cannot satisfactorily explain away the substantial IQ differences of twins reared in contrasting environments by crowded conditions in the womb. No doubt prenatal deprivations contribute to genetic impairment; however, prenatal inadequacies would be just as likely to afflict orphan twins eventually reared in adequate homes as those taken into less desirable environments. If the birth defect was profound, causing mental retardation, it could perhaps be argued that adults of lower social stature and education would be more likely to match up with mentally retarded children. In the MZ twin pairings, however, in the Newman, Freeman, and Holzinger study, the six reared in the poorest environments had average IQ differences in adulthood of 13 points, hardly low enough to influence the decision of a parent or guardian decision in selecting a toddler.

Regarding twins, Kagan cited I. I. Gottesman, a distinguished behavioral geneticist, who somewhat ironically was quoted from his opening chapter in his *Social Class, Race and Intelligence*, a book coedited by Jensen and published in 1968. Kagan's account of Gottesman on twins:

'even when gene pools are known to be matched, appreciable differences in mean I.Q. can be observed that could only have been associated with environmental differences.' In a study of 38 pairs of identical twins reared in different environments, the average difference in I.Q. for these identical twins was 14 points, and at least one quarter of the identical pairs of twins reared in different environments had differences in I.Q. score that were larger than 16 points. This difference is larger than the average difference between black and white populations. Gottesman concludes, 'The differ-

ences observed so far between whites and Negroes can hardly be accepted
as sufficient evidence that with respect to intelligence the Negro American
is genetically less endowed.' [49]

Hunt followed suit by taking issue with Jensen's description of
the Skeels and Dye studies. Doctor Jensen correctly noted the 32
point average increase of the experimental group following their
removal to a better institution and their eventual adoptions, but
did not mention the adult stature of the control group.

> Professor Jensen neglects to report the results of the follow-up study of the
> adult status of the Skeels-Dye children left in the orphanage (Skeels, 1966).
> Those who were removed from the orphanage before they were 30 months
> old and placed on a women's ward at a state institution for the mentally
> retarded, and then later adopted, were all self-supporting and none became
> a ward of any institution. Their median educational attainment was 12th
> grade. Four had one or more years of college work, one received a bache-
> lor's degree and went on to graduate school. On the other hand, of the 12
> children who remained in the orphanage, one died in adolescence following
> continued residence in a state institution for the mentally retarded, and
> four remained on the wards of such institutions. With one exception, those
> employed were marginally employed, and only two had married. It is true
> that the effects of early experience can be reversed; the point to be made
> here, however, is that the longer any species of organism remains under
> any given kind of circumstances, the harder it is to change the direction of
> the effects of adaptation to those circumstances. [50]

A question one should ask here is whether the twelve contrast
group children in the Skeels' study remained at subthreshold level
(in Jensen's words experiencing "extreme sensory and motor restrictions") throughout their childhood.

Originally, the experimental and contrast group children resided
in institutional nurseries and dormitories that shielded them from
visual stimulation, permitted virtually no interaction with adults
(they were even fed by propped bottles) and harbored few or no
toys. The experimental group was tested thrice in early childhood: at one year seven months of age its IQ was 64.3, while still in
the affectionless institution; at three years three months it stood at
91.8 after transfer to the Glennwood State School where the children experienced much improved conditions. At age six, following
their adoption, it rose to 95.9. Similarly, the contrast group's IQ
stood initially at 81.7 at a year four months, dropped to 60.5 at two
years seven months while still in the orphanage, and increased

slightly to 66.1 at age seven. Between the second and third testing, the contrast group children did not continue their same level of destitution. Six went to another less than desirable institution called Woodward (where "they received, in general, less individual attention and had fewer interactions with adults" than the experimental group), and, of the remaining six, two were placed in the Glennwood State School (which housed the experimental group), three remained in the original orphanage but under vastly improved conditions, and one was placed in his grandparents home. Generally, those who went to Woodward suffered IQ declines between ages 2.7 and 7 while the others experienced IQ gains. All but one child had IQs below 90 at age seven, the average, once again, being 66.1. Obviously, the contrast group children did not experience extreme sensory and motor restrictions, from roughly ages two and a half to seven years, and in the adult follow-up study Skeels suggested that most members of the group experienced no such confinement during the remainder of their childhood, most apparently had resided or worked for several years after age seven in institutions for the mentally retarded and had attended school. Yet the IQ evidence at age seven and their occupations (dishwasher, floater, institutional inmate, etc.) suggest a less than adequate unfolding of genetic potential. An average IQ of 66 for children experiencing limited adult verbal interaction and affection (but not extremely restricted sensorally or motorically) is about what one could expect. On the other hand, the corresponding scores of 92 and 96 for the experimental group children approximates expectations for children who at second testing were living with affectionate, verbal adults in an institution and at third testing in an adopted home. [51] [52]

Given the foregoing analysis, it would appear that the Skeels study lends little support to Jensen's "environment as a threshold" hypothesis, suggesting instead that a very socially disadvantaged group will have considerably lower measured intelligence than a group reared under more normal circumstances.

Further comparing populations, Stanford psychologist Lee Cronbach took issue with Jensen on his interpretation of the Wheeler Study, arguing that the Tennessee mountain children ". . . were dropping behind the norm group." [53] Jensen had attributed the drop to the inevitable IQ decline "of certain below average groups" as they approach the feeblemindedness of their parents in adolescence.[54] While not commenting on Wheeler *per se*, Kagan discussed his longitudinal research on lower-class and middle-class children, which suggests what the affects of different child rearing behaviors may be on IQ:

> These class differences with white populations occur as early as one to two years of age. Detailed observations of the mother-child interaction in the homes of these children indicate that the lower class children do not experience the quality of parent-child interaction that occurs in the middle class homes. Specifically, the lower class mothers spend less time in face to face mutual vocalization and smiling with their infants; they do not reward the child's maturational progress, and they do not enter into long periods of play with the child. Our theory of mental development suggests that specific absences of these experiences will retard mental growth and will lead to lower intelligence test scores. The most likely determinants of the black child's lower I.Q. score are his experiences during the first five years of life. These experiences lead the young black child to do poorly on I.Q. tests in part because he does not appreciate the nature of a problem.[55]

Responding specifically to Jensen's remarks on racial differences, Harvard's Richard Light and Paul Smith challenged his apparent acceptance of "one or another of the current indexes of socioeconomic status (SES) as being a comparable measure of the social conditions of blacks and whites." Although SES indices such as education, income, and occupation can be useful descriptions of environmental advantage, these ". . . measures do not work equally for both races."[56] Because of the caste-like status blacks endure in the United States, it may be fallacious to assess the level of destitution unique to American blacks in class related terms: "Black and white families with identical incomes do not have the same economic options open to them—housing discrimination is only the most obvious reason for assuming that a dollar is worth less to a black family than to a white one. Further, equal number of years of education do not imply equal education; nor do they imply equal access to further benefits, such as job or income levels."[57] Light and Smith conducted a computerized analysis of the disparity between the races using what they considered a more accurate estimate of the deprivations of the black experience. They concluded that the 15 point IQ difference can be easily explained nongenetically.[58]

Berkeley's Arthur Stinchcombe attacked what he saw as Jensen's failure to recognize the cumulative effects of environments. According to Stinchcombe, Jensen himself appeared to recognize that one can increase children's IQ by 5 to 8 points by removing the fear from the test-taking experience, that temporary preschool enrichment can easily increase black intelligence by five points (at least temporarily) and that there is evidence of a significant environmental variation within a white group explaining an approximate 6 point differential. If effects such as these are additive, the IQs would be equalized.[59]

Martin Deutsch's *HER* critique of Jensen's work was almost virulent in tone. Deutsch, a long time Jensen acquaintance,* raked Jensen over the coals for his "many erroneous statements, misinterpretations and misunderstandings" of the environment, genetics, and education, and for the inescapable conclusion "that the central theme of the Jensen piece is a wholly anti-democratic eugenic position."[60] It was Deutsch's contention that Jensen made at least seventeen errors† in his analysis, an incomprehensible fact given Jensen's nearly flawless previous writings, and the fact that all the mistakes were slanted toward maximizing black-white differences and toward minimizing environmental influence. An example of an omission of environmental data was Jensen's failure to include a wave of Deutsch's initial enrichment preschool children who sustained greater IQ gains than the control group; he drew only on a wave that failed to do so longitudinally.[61] Deutsch strongly reprimanded Jensen for mentioning only Spearman's theory of

---

*Along with Irwin Katz, Jensen and Deutsch had just edited the book *Social Class, Races and Psychological Development* which took an environmental position on measured racial intellectual differences.

†At the beginning of the critique, Deutsch gave four other examples of such errors. One was a Jensen citation suggesting an 80% heritability factor in EEG patterns, without mentioning that the subjects were identical twins. A second was Jensen's failure to mention that the advanced brain wave development of African new borns involved only eight subjects. Jensen did suggest, however, that this could provide evidence for black superiority. ("This finding especially merits further study, since there is evidence that brain waves have some relationship to I.Q.") The third was the charge that Jensen changes 68% to 86% on pp. 86–87 but a careful reading of these pages reveals no such error. The fourth was Jensen's citing data reported in *The Medical World News* and the *U.S. News and World Report*, less than scientific periodicals.

intelligence while basically ignoring the work of many others including Piaget.[62] Regarding interpretations of the twins data, Deutsch criticized Jensen for failing to include more information on Newman, Freeman, and Holzinger twins reared in contrasting environments and the IQ differences such environmental separation produced.[63] Deutsch also scolded Jensen for suggesting that diverse instructional methods for children with Level I mental capacities can somehow lead to anything less than second class citizenship. Jensen, he claimed, did not recognize that it is "the failure of the school system or the larger society," not the cognitive level of the children, that has produced massive underachievement in America.

> At an early age, children, often with considerable intuition and great intelligence, learn not to cope with school situation, not to attend, not to take it seriously. In other words, they find it intellectually non-stimulating, non-motivating, and in circumstances where children and teachers come from different social class and caste backgrounds, children are likely to find the interaction as well as the instruction threatening to their ego structures and personal identities. This is true for normative circumstances; it is most objective and descriptive of ghetto situations.[64]

Finally, Deutsch challenged Jensen to "...summon the social courage necessary to repudiate the positions which have been taken in his name." Such social courage would be a sign of inner conviction and an important recognition of the "punishment potential" that such a destructive monograph might have in a time of "serious social crisis." Therefore, Jensen should "...reexamine his thinking, reevaluate his sources of information, reassess his argument and retract his genetic conclusions in the light of data about and understanding of environmental factors with which he was apparently not familiar at the time he wrote the article." Such a repentance "would be a positive act" showing the respect social scientists can have for our "changing social structure," and how "gifted experimentalists like Jensen can play important roles in generating the interactions individuals have with it."[65]

Jensen Replies to his Critics

It is interesting to speculate what course Jensen would have taken if the published responses to his monograph had been fewer in number and more subdued in tone. In the two *HER* issues that followed his article, the journal dedicated some 300 pages to accommodate the replies of thirty-one persons. Although several of the letters supported Jensen, articles by scholars generally included more political overtones in the Summer issue than in the Spring issue. (This may have been attributed in part to the fact that in the Spring edition, the critics wrote their responses before *How Much Can We Boost I.Q. and Scholastic Achievement* was ever published in the Winter edition and before its provocative impact was felt.) By the summer of 1969, *Jensenism* was in many minds synonymous with racism and white supremacy. Thrashings, from people such as Deutsch, urging that he repudiate his elitist views in light of new evidence, could hardly be expected to mellow the determination of a scholar of Jensen's stature. Whatever the impetus might have been for steering the direction of his considerable energies, Jensen's behavior since 1969 had led observers to three unmistakable conclusions:

1. He has pursued with extraordinary vigor the research on the heritability of intelligence (much of it involving black/white differences as measured by IQ).
2. In so doing he has become one of the most prolific educational psychologists in America.
3. He is still the subject of considerable controversy, at least in academic circles.

Since that winter of 1969, Jensen has written more on race and intelligence, and has continued to be a figure of controversy. In his article entitled, "Reducing the Heredity–Environment Uncertainty: A Reply," Jensen answered the first onslaught of critics by first marveling at how much in agreement they really were. He vehemently defended himself on points on which he and his critics differed. Regarding the implications that he considers black genes inferior and, thus, is a white supremist:

> . . . I am advocating that we seek objective answers regarding genetic differences through appropriate scientific research. Again, the point I made in my article was that the present evidence on this topic is such that the hypothesis of genetic racial differences in intelligence is not an unreasonable one and should therefore be the subject of scientific investigation. Second, why does Cronbach put quotation marks around the word *inferior?* . . . let me note that I myself to not use this term and I object to it in this

general context . . . Cronback knows as well as I that it is nonsense to speak of different racial gene pools in general as *superior* or *inferior*. [66]

And later:

> . . . it may be of interest of some to note that on the basis of the evidence I have been able to review so far, if I were asked to hypothesize about race differences in what we call *g* or abstract reasoning ability, I would be inclined to rate Caucasians on the whole somewhat below Orientals, at least those in the United States. [67]

Jensen went on to argue that his position is not illogical, i.e. that he never concluded that blacks and whites are inherently different based on the premises of high heritability of intelligence in the white population and a 15 IQ point racial difference on intelligence tests. "Heritability coefficients by themselves cannot answer the question of genetic differences," he contended, "but when used along with additional information . . ." one could formulate a ". . . testable hypothesis that could reduce the heredity environment uncertainty concerning group differences." [68]

Jensen did defend his right to raise the genetic issue without spelling out the policies that should follow. "This is, of course, another job. I am not a social or educational philosopher and I am sure that neither I nor anyone else at present has thought through all the policy implications of my article. I do believe that educational policy decisions should be based on evidence and the results of continuing research—and not just evidence which is comfortable to some particular ideology position but *all* relevant evidence." [69] In the summer of 1969, there seemed to be little question as to who in the hereditarian camp was to have the dubious distinction of being at the forefront of gathering such evidence.

Since 1969

It would be unfair to Jensen to leave the impression that the Berkeley professor's zealous pursuit of evidence to reduce heredity –environment uncertainties was in large part caused by the magnitude of the assault on his positions. Following the 1969 article, other people in academic circles appeared to be just as interested in this topic as Jensen was. (Indeed, it is Jensen's contention that the *HER* had invited him to submit the 1969 article, knowing full well it would deal with the possible genetic base for individual differences.) Within the next two years he was invited to address many scientific symposia on possible differences in racial intelligence. Although Jensen probably could not resist the temptation of envisioning himself at times in Copernican grandeur, the acclaim for his research, particularly in Europe, has been no doubt, partly responsible for this preoccupation that has steered his career to the study of alleged racial differences. When publications such as the *Wall Street Journal* use the word *Jensenism* as synonymous with certain theoretical formulations on genetics and education, the founder of the movement has almost a responsibility to oversee its course.

Following the *HER* article, Jensen published *Educability and Group Differences* in 1973. On the first page of the preface, he was careful to stress to the reader the error of trying to "formally generalize from *within*-group heritability to *between*-group heritability." Yet, despite his own warning, Jensen stated that "My review of the evidence, with its impressive consistency, does, I believe, cast serious doubt on the currently popular explanations in terms of environment."[70] Thus, Jensen rather meticulously set an empirical tone, evident in much of his writing in the 1970s, that apparently escaped many readers of his 1969 article. Since 1969, his reviews of evidence on race and intelligence can be divided into the following two categories: "environment as a threshold" and "testing bias."

ENVIRONMENT AS A THRESHOLD

Jensen's "environment as a threshold" hypothesis seems to have changed somewhat over the years. In 1969, he suggested that below a certain level the environment can have a profound effect on depressing IQ but above that level it has little effect. Children in "extreme social isolation" would be below the threshold while, presumably, socialized children would be above it. In 1973, however, Jensen used the plural, "threshold effects," to describe ". . . environmental variations in one part of the total scale of environmental advantages hav[ing] quantitatively or qualitatively different effects on the development of the phenotype rather than variations in another part of the scale."[71] In 1969, he emphasized that a subthreshold (singular) existence does "not refer to a mere lack of middle-class amenities" but to "extreme social and motor restrictions." On the other hand, by 1973, he spoke of a "very poor environment" as subthreshold and then went on to give an example of one possible threshold effect as "going from a typical slum environment to an average middle-class environment would presumably have a larger effect on IQ than going from a middle-class to an upper-class environment."[72] Whereas, once there was a single threshold somewhat near the extremely deprived end of the continuum, there now became the possibility of different environmental effects at various points on the scale.

In order to test such a possibility, Jensen, hypothesizing significant effects of poverty on IQ, came up with mixed findings. In one analysis, he reviewed the meager research on the variations in measured intelligence in the black population, as measured by the IQ testing of MZ and DZ twins. It was Jensen's contention that, if a sizeable percentage of the black population is below the environmental threshold (preventing a full realization and their genetic potential), heritability should be lower among blacks than among whites. In other words, if most whites are above the threshold, the reaction range (how much IQ can vary) should be much higher in samples of blacks than in samples of whites. Zeroing in principally on Sandra Scarr Salapatek's* study of 1,521 socially diverse twin pairs (36% of whom were white and 64% black), Jensen found no appreciable difference in inheritability of measured intelligence between the races. Consequently, he suggested that the threshold hypothesis cannot account for most black-white IQ differences, and that the threshold, if it exists at all, ". . . is far down the environmental scale." However, it can be also argued that the caste-like condition experienced by blacks throughout most of their history in America has permitted less variation in the black environment than in the white. In other words, because blacks have been forced to live together, attend school together, worship together, etc., it is not unreasonable to assume that blacks have more in common culturally (particularly in terms of academic

---

*Now Sandra Scarr

self-image and political outlook) than do whites. Therefore, it could have been argued that higher heritability in blacks would support the environmentalist position.[73]

In two studies of black-white IQ differences conducted by Jensen, himself, the researcher did not address "environment as a threshold" by name but nevertheless managed to collect evidence on the validity of the hypothesis. If the environment of poverty stricken groups in general and disadvantaged blacks in particular contributes to a less than full realization of genetic potential, one would expect a gradual decline in the IQ of children reared in low socioeconomic conditions. This occurred, for example, in the Wheeler study of white Tennessee mountain children and Kennedy, Van de Riet, and White's study of Southern blacks. In the latter report, some 1800 black children between five to twelve years of age in five southeastern states were tested, and highly significant respective IQ differences of 86 and 75 were reported in the five and twelve year olds. However, Jensen has been critical of this study for its possible sampling bias (as was Kennedy himself). He cited a more refined study of a similar sample of blacks by Kennedy that showed no such decline.[74]

In exploring the cumulative deficit hypothesis further, Jensen first compared the IQs of siblings in Berkeley, California and then conducted a similar study in rural Georgia. Published in 1974, the results of the Berkeley study suggested a decline in verbal but not nonverbal IQ among blacks between grades K through 6. However, Jensen attributed the small progressive decrement (of about 7 IQ points) in verbal IQ to a decline in "reading skills per se, rather than the abilities essentially defined as intelligence," and unlikely to explain the one standard deviation difference in measured intelligence between the black and white samples.[75] Three years later, the Georgia study was published and reached very different conclusions. Noting a "significant and substantial" decline (between 14 and 16 points) in both the verbal and nonverbal IQs of blacks (but not whites) between ages six and sixteen, Jensen attributed the phenomenon to social condition: "... the present results on Georgia blacks, when viewed in connection with the contrasting results for California blacks, would seem to favor an environmental interpretation of the progressive I.Q. decrement."[76] Jensen

continued the discussion by suggesting that the greater environmental disadvantages of Georgia blacks explains why they suffer
IQ decline in both verbal and nonverbal abilities while California
blacks experienced a only modest decrease in verbal IQ. Thus,
when Jensen spoke of threshold effects being far down the environment scale, the results of his cummulative deficit research
suggested that one threshold may be somewhere between the destitution of rural Georgia and the urban plight of Northern
California.

In both studies, Jensen's findings, of course, are open to various
interpretations. For example, Princeton's Leon Kamin has argued
that the higher IQ of the younger siblings in the Georgia study
may have been caused by the improved social conditions in the
rural South over the ten year period spanned by the study. "These
were not years during which racial discrimination in Georgia
remained constant. The data might be telling us not that individual blacks' I.Q.s deteriorated, but that changed social conditions
are narrowing the measured I.Q. gap between the races."[77]

In the report on Berkeley blacks, Jensen himself appeared to
leave open the reasonable possibility of an environmentalist explanation. "The results of the present study . . . suggest that the
causes of the Negro I.Q. deficit, whatever they might be, are not
reflected in age decrements beyond 5 but appear largely to involve
factors whose influences are already established before school age."[78]

Jensen has also investigated the hypothesized threshold effects
by further analyzing the IQs of identical twins raised apart. In a
1970 article, he charted the IQ differences of 122 separately reared
twin pairs and found only a 5.4 IQ difference (after correcting for
measurement error). Jensen noted that in "only four cases does
the difference exceed the average difference of 17 I.Q. points" (the
average difference in the general population)" and in only 19 cases
(16%) do the differences exceed the average difference of 12 I.Q.
points between full siblings reared together . . . " After statistically
plotting the IQ differences on a probability scale, Jensen contended
that the disparities are distributed normally and that "There is no
evidence . . . of asymmetry or of threshold conditions for the effects
of environment on I.Q."[79]

In his analysis, however, Jensen did not report on the environments of those twins who differ substantially in IQ. He mentioned only that Cyril Burt's was the "one study which classified subjects in terms of SES, based on parents' or foster parents' occupation," which is true.[80] However, Newman et al. gave detailed descriptions of the environments, and if one looks closely at every twin pair differing in IQ by 12 points or more, the environment of the "less intelligent" twin was not only rather disadvantaged relative to the "brighter" twin but was considerably impoverished relative to American society. Moreover, since Jensen's twin analysis, Burt, the researcher Jensen cited most frequently and who has reported the highest separated twin correlations, has been exposed as a possible fraud, allegedly having fabricated much of his data. Today, Jensen maintains that the remaining twin research on identical twins reared separately (now sixty-nine pairs) still upholds his position, but he acknowledges his need to reanalyze the data without Burt's fifty-three pairs.[81]

TEST BIAS

One commonly held assumption about the cause of black underachievement that has received little attention thus far is that the IQ and scholastic measures typically employed are culturally biased. In his 1969 article, Jensen remarked that so-called culture fair tests fail to reduce the racial IQ differential but he did not elaborate on the subject. Moreover, most of his *HER* critics did not take up the issue of test bias. For more than a decade following the publication of his 1969 article, Jensen has devoted considerable attention to the alleged unfairness of mental testing, having just completed a rather lengthy and highly technical book on the subject. While it is Jensen's contention that his latest book has nothing whatsoever to do with the *causes* of differences in test scores between racial and social groups, there is little question that many observers interpret his research on test bias as a chipping away of the environmentalist position.

In an earlier work, *Educability and Group Differences*, Jensen dealt with the subject of "language deprivation." Blacks, he argued, should perform more poorly in the verbal portions of intelligence tests than on the nonverbal sections, if linguistic deprivation plays an important role in their lower measured cognition. He stated, however, that just the opposite is typically reported. Citing Coleman's data, Jensen pointed out that all other minority groups (Puerto Rican, Indian, Mexican, and Oriental) did better on the nonverbal than the verbal measures, which is what one would expect if dialect placed children at a disadvantage. [82] Accordingly, the implication is that so-called black English does little or nothing to impair black measured intelligence.

In Jensen's most recent book, *Bias in Mental Testing*, he reviews the high correlations among the various intelligence tests and contends that g can be measured in a variety of ways. For example, tests measuring one's ability to compare cubes, count blocks and copy a figure are about as g loaded as verbal analogies and vocabulary. [83] In attempting to determine how biased mental tests may be, Jensen reviews the research comparing black and white performance on mental tests with grade point average (elementary school through college) and concludes that the tests predict school achievement equally well for blacks and whites. [84] Ability tests commonly used to predict job performance in the armed forces and in civilian life were found also to serve their function without discriminating against blacks. [85] Indeed, Jensen argues that several studies actually conclude that tests in the job market actually "over predict" black performance, as assessed by the supervisor's rating scales. [86] One such report was the Educational Testing Service–United States Civil Service Commission six-year study, which had as its major aim the exploration of testing bias against minority groups. The ETS researchers were particularly sensitive to supervisory prejudice in job rating. After extensive analysis of the evidence, however, the study concluded that "There is little in the data to support the hypotheses of differential validity for the wide variety of tests studied for the ethnic groups included in this study." [87]

Jensen also reviews the research on the internal validity of mental tests for different populations, i.e. whether blacks and whites differ in performance on certain test items. Once again, however, the two races tend to perform relatively well and poorly on the same test questions. [88]

The principle reason Jensen has had so little scholarly criticism of his conclusions on mental testing is that many psychologists have long recognized that attempts to create "culture free" tests which reduce the average black–white IQ differences have been futile. For better or for worse, the various mental tests do a reasonable job in predicting pupil achievement, particularly in higher education. It is not unreasonable to assume as well that the cognitive processes that involve problem-solving abilities have long been more developed in the average white American than in the average black American. The issue is not which race posesses greater "general intelligence" but whether the white *g* advantage is caused principally by genetic endowment or environmental advantage.

Doctor Jensen's empirical inquiry and articulate communication of his findings has challenged many of the sacred cannons of environmentalism and in so doing has provoked considerable discussion of the nature of black–white differences in measured intelligence. Although Jensen is generally a very thorough and creative empiricist, there are still too many holes in his argument. Based on the data he has gathered to date, his hypothesized hereditarian position remains unconvincing. On the other hand, there exists little published evidence that convincingly refutes Jensen's argument, and the nature-nurture racial question is certain to remain an unresolved issue for many years.

Perhaps the strongest rebuttal to Jensenism can be made by drawing on the fascinating research of Yale psychologist Sandra Scarr, who has recently published the results of longitudinal studies of black and mixed race adopted children and the results of an inquiry into the relationship between the degree of Caucasian ancestry and measured intelligence within a "black population."

Along with Richard Weinberg, Scarr compiled IQ data on 130 black and interracial (with one black and one white natural parent) who were adopted by social advantaged whites in the late 1950s and during the 1960s. The children came from twelve states but were nearly all reared in Minnesota, a state which is only 0.9 percent black and has been at the forefront of interracial adoption. At the time the IQ tests were administered, the children ranged from age four on. The average IQ for the sixty-eight children with one black parent and twenty-nine children with two black parents was 109 and 96. 8 respectively. More importantly, both the interracial and black children were above the national norm of standardized reading and math tests. A genetic explanation could be offered for IQ advantage of the interracial children, but Scarr and Weinberg emphasize the facts that "children with two black parents were significantly older at adoption, had been in the adoptive homes a short time, and had experienced a greater number of placements."[89] These early childhood environmental factors could thus conceivably explain the IQ differential.

The Scarr and Weinberg study has several flaws: the black sample is small in number; little description is given of the natural parents (except that their mean education level was high school graduation); and no comparisons are made in the IQs of younger and older children. Nevertheless, the fact that the interracial group scored well above average in IQ and the black group approached normally in measured cognition (despite their late adoption) may give further clues as to the mutability of intelligence. Moreover, one would wager that if genetically similar children (i.e. the sampler's siblings) were reared in an urban slum they would be far behind their adopted brothers and sisters in school achievement.

Scarr's ancestrial research focused on a sampling of school age black and white monozygotic and dizygotic twins in Philadelphia. Published in 1977, the study estimated the degree of Caucasian ancestry in the black twins by a measurement of skin color rejectance and by drawing blood samples. (Apparently, blacks and whites differ in blood group loci in such markers as red cell antigens and serum proteins.) The 160 twin pairs were also given a variety of g loaded mental tests. After no relationship was found between ancestrial estimates and measured intelligence, the report concluded that "the test between degree of African ancestry ... and intellectual skills failed to provide evidence for genetic racial differences in intelligence."[90]

In a seemingly unending nature-nurture scenario, Jensen has criticized the Philadelphia study and Scarr's environmentalist conclusion in the adoption study (the fact that mixed race children score higher than blacks he feels suggests heredity); Scarr has replied to Jensen's Philadelphia reply; and, in 1978, she added to her black and multi-racial adoption findings by publishing yet another report on adoptive children drawn from an all white sample.[91] [92]

Scarr's research on white adoptives gave her the opportunity to assess the relationship among the IQs of the biological parents, the adoptive parents, and adopted children in varying occupational and economic settings, ranging from stable working class to highly educated professional class. But, in this study, Scarr concluded that very little of the adoptees' measured intellectual differences could be attributed to environmental factors. Scarr offers little explanation for the different conclusions in her adoption studies, but it would appear that her adoption work is in keeping with the findings of previous research.

As has been stated earlier, heredity appears to account for much of the variation within the larger American culture but environmental influences account for a significantly greater difference in intellectual variation, when one compares the mean IQ differences between samples from the larger culture and various subcultures. Environmental differences may not have affected the measured intelligence of working class reared and professionally reared white children because the fundamental cognitive processes of the larger society were common to both nurturing situations. The fact that black and multi-racial adoptees who were reared in white homes have either approached or exceeded the IQ norm for the white population suggests that any black–white intellectual difference (whatever the direction may be) has less to do with heredity and more to do with considerable white environmental advantage.

REFERENCES

1. Weinberg, M.: The relationship between school desegregation and academic achievement: A review of the research, *Law and Contemporary Problems,* Winter–Spring, *39(2):*1975.
2. St. John, N.: *School Desegregation, Outcomes for Children.* New York, Wiley, 1975, p. 119.
3. Persell, C.: *Education and Inequality A Theorectical and Empirical Synthesis.* New York, The Free Press, 1977, p. 145.
4. Crain, R. and Mahard, R.: Desegregation and black achievement: A review of the research," *Law and Contemporary Problems, 42(3):* 216,. 1978.

5. Ibid., p. 48.
6. Coleman, J., Kelly, S., and Moore, J.: *Recent Trends in School Integration*. Paper presented at the annual meeting of the American Educational Research Association, Washington, D.C., April 2, 1975.
7. Coleman, J.: Racial segregation in the schools: New research with policy implications. *Phi Delta Kappan*, October, *57(2)*:75–78, 1975. Quoted in Ribin, S. and Bosco, J.: Coleman's desegregation research and policy recommedations. *School Review, 84(3)*:354, 1976.
8. Pettigrew, T. and Green, R.: School desegregation in large cities: A critique of the Coleman 'White Flight' thesis. *Harvard Education Review, 46(1)*:1–53, 1976.
9. Ibid., p. 33.
10. Ibid., pp. 33–34.
11. Robin and Bosco, op cit., p. 355.
12. McPartland, J.: Desegregation and equity in higher education and employment, Is progress related to the desegregation of elementary and secondary schools? *Law and Contemporary Problems, 42(3)*:109–132, 1978.
13. Braddock, J. and McPartland, J.: Assessing school desegregation effects: New directions in research. Center for Social Organization of Schools at John Hopkins University, 1980.
14. McPartland, op cit., pp. 109–132.
15. Jensen, A.: How much can we boost IQ and scholastic achievement. *Harvard Education Review, 39(1):* 1969. A
16. Ibid., pp. 5–6.
17. Ibid., p. 7.
18. Ibid.
19. Ibid., pp. 9–15.
20. Ibid., pp. 28–59.
21. Ibid., p. 68.
22. Ibid.
23. Ibid., p. 60.
24. Ibid.
25. Ibid.
26. Ibid., p. 52.
27. Ibid., p. 60.
28. Ibid., p. 62.
29. Ibid., pp. 62–63.
30. Ibid., pp. 83–84.
31. Ibid., p. 80.
32. Ibid.
33. Ibid., p. 81.
34. Ibid.
35. Ibid., p. 81 & 85.
36. Ibid., p. 81 & 112.
37. Ibid., pp. 110–111.
38. Ibid., pp. 115–116.

39. Ibid., p. 117.
40. Ibid.
41. *Harvard Education Review*, *39(2-3):* 1969.
42. Black student union statement. Harvard Education Review, *39(3):*590-591, 1969.
43. Bereiter, C.: The future of individual differences. *Harvard Education Review*, *39(2):*310-318, 1969.
44. Hunt, J. McV.: Has compensatory education failed? Has it been attempted? *Harvard Education Review*, *39(2):*278-300, 1969.
45. Kagan, J.: Inadequate evidence and illogical conclusions. *Harvard Education Review*, *39(2):*274, 1969.
46. Ibid., p. 275.
47. Ibid.
48. Crow, J.: Genetic theories and influences: Comments on the value of diversity. *Harvard Education Review*, *39(2):*308, 1969.
49. Kagan, op cit., p. 275.
50. Hunt, op cit., p. 290.
51. Skeels, H. and Dye, H.: A study of the effects of differential stimulation on mentally retarded children. *Proceedings of the American Association of Mental Deficiency*, *44:*114-116, 1939.
52. Skeels, H.: Adult status of children with contrasting early life experiences: A follow-up study. *Child Development*, Serial Number 105, *31(3):*1966.
53. Crowbach, L.: Heredity environment and educational policy. *Harvard Education Review*, *39(2):*338-347, 1969.
54. Jensen, op cit., p. 62.
55. Kagan, op cit., pp. 275-276.
56. Light, R. and Smith, P.: Social allocation models of intelligence: A methodological inquiry. *Harvard Education Review*, *39(3):*484-510, 1969.
57. Ibid., p. 488.
58. Ibid., pp. 489-510.
59. Stinchcombe, A.: Environment: The cumulation of effects is yet to be understood. *Harvard Education Review*, *39(3):*511-522, 1969.
60. Deutsch, M.: Happenings on the way back to the forum: Social science, I.Q., and race differences revisited. *Harvard Education Review*, *39(3):*523-557, 1969.
61. Ibid., p. 531.
62. Ibid., pp. 542-543.
63. Ibid., pp. 549-551.
64. Ibid., p. 529.
65. Ibid., p. 552.
66. Jensen, A.: Reducing the heredity-environment uncertainty. *Harvard Education Review*, *39(3):*451-452, 1969. B
67. Ibid., p. 480.
68. Ibid., p. 460.
69. Ibid., p. 479.
70. Jensen, A.: *Educability and Group Differences*. New York, Harper and Row, 1973, p. 1.

71. Ibid., p. 175.
72. Ibid., pp. 175–178.
73. Ibid., pp. 182–188.
74. Kennedy, W.: A Follow-Up Normative Study of Negro Intelligence and Achievement," Tallahassee, Florida: Florida State University, Human Development Clinic, 1965. Cited in Jensen, A.: Cumulative deficit: A testable hypothesis? *Developmental Psychology, 10(6):*996–1019, 1974.
75. Ibid.
76. Jensen, A. Cumulative deficit in I.Q. of blacks in the rural south. *Developmental Psychology, 13(3):*195-196, 1977.
77. Kamin, Leon J.: A positive interpretation of apparent 'cumulative deficit.' *Developmental Psychology, 14(2):*195-196, 1978.
78. Jensen (1974), op cit., p. 1018.
79. Jensen, A.: I.Q.s of identical twins reared apart. *Behavior Genetics, 1(2):*133-148, 1970.
80. Jensen (1969A), op cit..
81. Interview with Arthur Jensen, July 1, 1980.
82. Jensen, A.: *Bias in Mental Testing.* New York, Free Press, 1980, pp. 480–482.
83. Ibid., p. 167.
84. Ibid., pp. 482–488.
85. Ibid., pp. 490–512.
86. Ibid., pp. 512–514.
87. Ibid., pp. 505–512.
88. Ibid., pp. 585–587.
89. Scarr, S. and Weinberg, R.: I.Q. test performance of black children adopted by white families. *American Psychologist, 31(10):* 726–739, 1976.
90. Scarr, S. et al.: Absence of a relationship between degree of white ancestry and intellectual skills within a black population. *Human Genetics, 39(1):* 69–86, 1977.
91. Scarr, S. and Weinberg, R.: Intellectual similarities within families of both adopted and biological children. *Intelligence, 1(2):*170-191, 1977.
92. Jensen, A.: Obstacles, problems and pitfalls in differential psychology. In Scarr, S. (Ed.): *Race, Social Class and Individual Differences in IQ.* Forthcoming 1981.

PART III

HIGHER EDUCATION

CHAPTER 7

ENTERING THE IVORY TOWER

E xcept for busing, no federal policy was as controversial in the 1970s as was affirmative action, and there is little to indicate that the debate will be any less intense in the 1980s. At the center of the storm is the question of whether it is right (and constitutional) to accord a group special treatment to compensate for the competitive disadvantage that confronts its members due to the effects of past discrimination against the group. The issue is such a difficult one that it took three cases over a six year period before the Supreme Court of the United States rendered a definitive decision on the policy. Most Court observers agree that none of the three decisions were easily reached by the Justices, and that there are still a number of legal questions the Court has left unanswered.

Affirmative action is a continuation of longstanding federal equal employment opportunity policies. Several factors, though, made these earlier programs less controversial. First was the fact that the American economy was still growing at the time when they were in effect; second was that there was little evidence that the government intended to enforce these policies.

Equal employment opportunity was first a Federal concern during the presidency of Franklin Delano Roosevelt. His use of the "executive order" resulted in the establishment of the Committee on Fair Employment Practices, during World War II, to hear complaints of discrimination in hiring and conditions of employment and union membership in industries with defense or war-related contracts. (An executive order is not a law; it is not passed by Congress, but is issued by the President as a basis for future policy decisions involving the various departments and their subunits within the Executive Branch.) In 1951, President

Truman sought to monitor the adherence to the antibias regulations of the Federal contracts through another executive order creating the Committee on Government Contract Compliance. It was during the Kennedy Administration that the term *affirmative action* was first used in an executive order intended to combat racial and religious discrimination; not only were holders of Federal contracts bound by nondiscriminatory clauses, but they were also required to *seek out* qualified minority applicants for available positions.

In September, 1965, President Lyndon B. Johnson issued Executive Order 11246, which was intended to require organizations holding government contracts in excess of $10,000 to take affirmative action in their practices with regard to race, creed, or national origin, in all aspects of their operation, not only those portions covered by the contract(s); three years later, the provision was extended, through Executive Order 11375, to include women under its protection. The Office of Federal Contract Compliance (OFCC) was established within the Department of Labor in 1966 to monitor the specifications of the Johnson order. In an attempt to provide for expert supervision in specialized areas, OFCC delegated its watchdog authority to nineteen other Federal agencies.

In January, 1969, the Department of Health, Education, and Welfare (HEW) initiated a review of affirmative action compliance at the City University of New York; that was the first interface between affirmative action and higher education.[1] In October, 1972, guidelines for higher education, based on OFCC's Revised Order #4, were issued by HEW.

Statutorily, equal employment opportunity was promoted through Title VII of the Civil Rights Act of 1964, which established the Equal Employment Opportunity Commission (EEOC) as the enforcer of the nondiscriminatory employment practices set forth in the legislation, and in the investigation of complaints resulting from alleged violation. Extension of this provision to women came through Title IX of the Education Amendments of 1972 (Higher Education Act). Title VII was then amended by the Equal Employment Opportunity Act of 1972, which extended the protection to most organizations with fifteen or more employees, whether public or private.

Title VII and Executive Order 11246 (as amended) were brought together by the EEOC in 1970 when it stated that a "violation of Title VII is a violation of Executive Order 11246 and vice versa."[2]

The Higher Education Guidelines Under Executive Order 11246

Guidelines for higher education were issued by J. Stanley Pottinger, Director of the Office for Civil Rights (OCR) in HEW, on October 1, 1972. In his memorandum of transmission of the *Higher Education Guidelines* (1972) to the college and university presidents across the country, Pottinger stated the government's expectation "that all affected colleges and universities will henceforth be in compliance with the Order and its implementing regulations."

Under the terms delineated in the *Guidelines*, institutions having $50,000 in Federal contracts and employing fifty or more persons were to develop written affirmative action plans that were to include the following:

1. a statement of commitment to nondiscriminatory employment practices and equal employment opportunity;

2. procedures for dissemination of the institution's policy to its own employees and to interested and appropriate groups in the institution's recruitment area;

3. the appointment of an Equal Employment Opportunity Officer to organize and monitor the affirmative action program, said officer to have the appropriate institutional support for completing the task;

4. the collection and analysis of data by organizational unit and job classification relating to the presence of women and minorities on the staff (as compared to their availability in the recruiting area) and their conditions of employment (as compared to those of majority males), said data allowable under the principle of Federal supremacy over any state

and local laws to the contrary, and to be kept in strict confidence;

5. the development of mechanisms to correct any deficiencies identified by that analysis; and

6. the development of a monitoring system for the program, and the submission of annual reports to OCR.

The government recognized that the "success of a university's affirmative action program may be dependent in a large part upon the willingness and ability of the faculty to assist in its development and implementation."[3] Thus, Pottinger recommended that faculty and supervisory officials—especially those with personnel responsibilities—be involved in the effort, and suggested the development of committees or task forces for that purpose (as had been successfully accomplished on a number of campuses).

Specifically, the Order called for the establishment of goals and timetables for the resolution of any employment areas within the institution found to have fewer women and minorities than might be expected by their availability. Resulting from the analysis by the institution of its deficiencies, goals were to be based on normal growth and expected turnover as well as the availability of qualified affirmative action personnel; they were intended as target figures to help an institution overcome its underutilization of women and minorities. While it would serve as an indication of compliance, attainment of goals would not be the only criteria upon which an institution's adherence to the *Guidelines* would be judged. Such factors as changes in the estimated number of vacancies, general economic conditions or availability of qualified affirmative action candidates were cited as acceptable reasons for failure to achieve the stated goals. So long as a university could show that it had attempted to fulfill its commitment, it would not be found noncompliant. Quotas were "neither required nor permitted by the Executive Order."[4] Further, while it demanded nondiscriminatory hiring and employment practices, the Order did not mandate the hiring or promotion of persons who were unqualified; "reverse discrimination" or "preferential treatment" that might result in a dilution of standards of excellence in order to accomplish goals was cited as being unnecessary.

In order to attract affirmative action candidates, institutions were to make active efforts beyond the normal recruitment method, known as the "old boy network," by which candidates were identified through a word of mouth approach. In the traditional hiring process, white male faculty would ask their white male colleagues at other colleges and universities to identify interested candidates. This generally resulted in the hiring of a white male. To change this, efforts such as advertising in media thought to reach significant numbers of women and minorities, referrals from professional associations, vacancy announcements in professional journals, and contact with other institutions (including those outside of higher education) employing or educating women and minorities, were all suggested as a means toward the development of broader applicant pools. While universities were required to note in all advertisements their status as an equal opportunity employer, they were forbidden from advertising solely for affirmative action candidates. Search committees, which, hopefully, would include women and minority staff as active participants, were suggested by Pottinger as the best method for making selections since, presumably, they would take a more active approach to recruiting and would reduce the level of discriminatory — though, perhaps, unintentionally so — assumptions concerning women and minority applicants.

As stated in the *Guidelines*, women and minority appointees were to receive the same rank and title as held by equally qualified white males. Also, they were to receive "equal pay for equal work," and were to be given the same benefits, including the possibility for promotion. In order to insure their access to promotional ladders, women and minorities were to receive adequate training and, in the case of faculty, opportunity to participate in research projects; these career development programs were intended to resolve any deficiencies in their individual records or abilities when compared to white males who may have had more opportunity for prior preparation.

A university's affirmative action plan was intended to be a

blueprint for the elimination of any current condition of discrimination, whether intended or not, that may be present in employment, and a safeguard against any future discrimination. Where necessary, corrective action was to be taken; for hiring situations, this meant the establishment of goals (but not quotas) for the addition of women and minorities over a specified period of time to positions where they were not present in proportions comparable to their proportion of those qualified and available. Unqualified persons regardless of race and sex were equally as unacceptable under the terms of the Order as they had been prior to its announcement. However, approaches to recruiting, beyond the reliance on the network of collegial contacts, were to be utilized in order to insure that qualified affirmative action candidates might be made aware of vacancies. As well as in hiring, nondiscrimination was mandated in all conditions of employment. Failure to comply with the *Guidelines* could result in awards of back pay to individuals who had suffered discrimination and in the termination, suspension, or removal of future eligibility for Federal contracts from those institutions found to be noncompliant with the nondiscrimination clauses of their contracts.

To determine whether or not such a policy was responsible, it is necessary to examine the existing condition of women and minorities in higher education at the time of the announcement of the *Guidelines*.

Women and Minorities in Higher Education to the Early 1970s

As early as 1958, it was reported that "discrimination on the basis of race appears to be nearly absolute. No major university in the United States has more than a token representation of Negroes on its faculty.... Women tend to be discriminated against in the academic professions not because they have low prestige but because they are outside of the prestige system entirely."[5]

For blacks, the problem has been entry into the prestigious universities, both as students and as faculty. The first black graduated from a white college in 1826; by 1890 only eighty blacks had received degrees from white colleges (fifty of whom were graduated from Oberlin); at the time of the famous *Brown* decision outlawing segregation in the schools, less than 1 percent of the freshmen in white colleges were black. Similarly, the first black faculty member in a white university was hired in 1941, although there were 330 black Ph.D.s by that time. In 1960, there were no more than 200 black faculty employed outside of the black colleges.[6] The number of living black doctorates grew to approximately 2000 by 1969 and to over 3000 five years later; over 50 percent received their degrees from ten prestigious universities outside of the South, yet more than 70 percent were employed in traditionally black institutions within the South—no white institutions were among the top ten colleges and universities employing the greatest number of blacks.[7] In fact, 100 black colleges employed more black Ph.D.s than did 2000 predominantly white institutions.[8]

As a group, blacks represented only about 1 percent of those holding doctorates; in 1968–69, they held 2.1 percent of the faculty positions, and, in 1972–73, 2.9 percent.[9] However, their distribution among the various disciplines is limited. Of the black doctorates, 52 percent are in education and the social sciences.[10] Not only is this a historical phenomenon, but, as late as 1973, 60 percent of the doctorates awarded that year to blacks were in education.[11]

As has been mentioned, the problem for women has been somewhat different. Supply has not been as great a problem as it has in the case of minorities. In the 1920s, women constituted 16 percent of all doctorates, but, by 1969–70, that proportion had slid to 13.3 percent.[12] Women made up at least 10 percent of the doctorates in most fields.[13] In the humanities, they were 18 percent of the pool, in the social sciences, 15 percent, in the biological sciences, 14 percent, and in the physical sciences, 5 percent. However, in the top twenty-five universities, they represented 8 percent, 8 percent, 8 percent, and 3 percent of the faculties in those respective areas.[14] Since women constituted 18 percent of the total higher education faculties, it is evident that they were most likely to be found in the less elite four year and two year colleges.[15, 16, 17]

Perhaps even more disturbing was that women were generally overrepresented at the lower ranks, either as assistant professors, or in nontenure track instructor or lecturer positions.[18] While 25 percent of the males surveyed nationally by Astin and Bayer held full professorships, the same was true for only 9 percent of the women; however, while only 16 percent of the men were in the instructor rank, 35 percent of the women were there. [19]

Marriage and the societal obligation of the woman's responsibility for raising children were viewed as one of the sources of these discrepancies. [20] Astin found, in a 1963 study, that while married women held lower ranks, single women reached the professional level at a higher proportion than men. There was a perception that a woman is a less permanent fixture at an institution, especially if she is married and might leave to have children or to follow her husband to employment elsewhere. This accusation, however, was found to be less accurate than many thought. Of the women Ph.D.s of 1957 and 1958, 91 percent were still in the labor force seven or eight years later; 81 percent were working full time. Most (79%) had never interrupted their careers, while those who did had a median leave of only fourteen months. [21] Thus, the charge that women were usually not active in the profession during the important first ten years of their careers was more a myth than a reality.

Antinepotism regulations were an important barrier to women. Over half of the institutions surveyed in 1960 by the American Association of University Women had regulations forbidding the employment of close relatives at the institution. A 1970 AAUP study found that 75 percent of the land grant universities still had such policies at that time. Antinepotism policies in higher education were often devastating to a career, especially when one realizes that two-thirds of the major state universities are located in areas with a population of less than 100,000, and more than two-thirds of the liberal arts colleges, including most of the prestigious ones, are located in small towns. [22] Often, faculty wives, although highly trained (many as well as their husbands), were forced to assume clerical positions if they wanted to stay with their husbands. [23] Others had to settle for elementary or secondary school teaching jobs, or positions at nearby, less elite colleges. For those who have been able to gain faculty positions at the same institution as their husbands, the position was often a dead-end, part-time, nontenure track one. Hopkins and Abramson have written in some detail of their own frustrations at enduring such a captive condition and, finally, at being terminated despite the existence of positive evaluations.

Guidelines Announced

Beginning in the late 1960s, the new minority undergraduate populations began to place pressure on their institutions to hire more minority faculty. Commissions on the status of women on most campuses began to initiate activity to improve local conditions for women faculty soon thereafter. Higher education was rather slow to respond. In 1970, the Women's Equity Action League, under the leadership of Doctor Bernice Sandler, filed with the federal government formal charges against the major colleges and universities receiving substantial federal monies; the charges were based on widespread exclusion and discriminatory treatment of women based solely on sex.[24] Finally, the federal government concluded that if higher education was not going to deal on a voluntary basis with the issue of its employment practices, then the government must act to fill the void.[25] Thus, in 1972, the *Higher Education Guidelines* were announced.

The Debate Over Affirmative Action

Needless to say, there was generally little disagreement that racial and sexual discrimination had occurred in the past in higher education, but there was a major outcry that federal intervention into the day-to-day operation of higher education was a violation of academic freedom. While opponents claimed that affirmative action was inapplicable to higher education, since its specifics were developed in relation to the defense and construction industries, proponents wondered why higher education should be the only national industry exempt from the policy.[26] Discussion, beyond the complaints about the additional bureaucratic efforts and financial expenditures necessary for compliance with the Order, has focused primarily around three topics: the appropriateness and legality of preferential treatment; the concern that numerical goals and time-tables are, in reality, quotas, and; the effect the policy might have on traditional standards of excellence in higher education.

Preferential Treatment

That there have, indeed, been injustices to women and minorities in American society raised the issue of whether or not society has an obligation to members of those groups to provide them with preferential treatment in areas of past discrimination. Many felt that the Order specifically legalized such treatment based on race and sex. [27] [30] Those who argue on philosophical grounds against such treatment believe the accordance of such treatment in the past to have been wrong, and wrong still if it were to be used in the future in a compensatory manner. While past discrimination was to entire groups, the effects were felt differently by different individuals. Compensation on a collective basis, then, would be open to serious challenge, and, thus, ought to be made in some fair manner on an individual basis. [31] Further, it should be accorded first to those with the strongest claims of past damage. [32]

It was argued that the only basis for hiring should be the qualifications of the individual, and that for race and sex in themselves to be qualifications was repugnant. Compliance to the Order would force academic departments to hire the best qualified women or the best qualified minority, not necessarily the best qualified person. Such treatment might ruin the careers of young, highly qualified, white male scholars, and ultimately, would set groups against each other. [33,34] Those consequences are all the more likely in a constricting economy that is causing major shrinkage in higher education. Affirmative action was seen not as a tool to provide remedial justice toward equality of opportunity so much as it was one which eliminated equal opportunity altogether. [35] It has been claimed that the policy has, indeed, led to documented instances of reverse discrimination. [36, 37, 38]

Despite the fact, however, that the Office for Civil Rights consistently said that preferential treatment was not necessary under the terms of the Order, many academics came to a philosophical defense of preference in hiring. It was argued that although preferential treatment would perpetuate the use of morally irrelevant characteristics, it is valid if it seeks to compensate for past injustices. The objective of such activity is not merely to end past discrimination, but also to overcome its cumulative effects. Thus, preferential treatment in hiring would make up for the past denial of opportunity in a particular set of jobs, but also would compensate for the condition of poverty that such denial caused. Since the unjust treatment of the past had been accorded to an entire group, it is only fair to compensate the entire group. Because there is, then, an obligation to the group, no specific individual has a right to individual compensation; but, since the group (minorities and/or women) is not formally organized (like a corporation, church, etc.) so as to receive a group reparation, the only way to provide it is by according it to individual members of the group. [39-43]

Since the qualifications of blacks have been criticized by whites so as to avoid the necessity of collegial contact and those of women have been criticized since that group is not felt by males to be serious scholars, those groups have suffered in higher education and, therefore, ought to be granted compensatory treatment. The effect may be to take away from the white male his equal chance for a job that he does not have; that is not something that the white male does in reparation, but something that the community takes from him in reparation. Certainly, it would be better if the costs could be shared by all, and not just the white males, but such a solution may not be possible. [44] Because educational institutions were created to serve both society and the individual, application of such a principle in that setting is bound to create conflicts. [45]

While it has been argued that preferential treatment is just, it has also been stated that it is not necessarily required by society and that it ought to be done on a voluntary basis. [46, 47] Equally as strong has been the contention that society must give opportunity to groups previously discriminated against, that there is a compelling national interest to do so. In any event, it was hoped that preferential treatment would be a temporary phenomenon, necessary only so long as the past disadvantage and its historical consequences still remained. [48]

Bringing the debate from the realm of its philosophical foundations and into its application to reality, Sandler argued that affirmative action was not aimed at creating preference, but at removing the preference that had always existed in higher education for white males. [49] Passive nondiscrimination did not produce the results that proponents of such a condition would have hoped;

therefore, affirmative action merely forced institutions to deal with that fact, and, thus, was seen as the logical extension of nondiscrimination policies.

Goals and Timetables versus Quotas

Discussion of preferential treatment leads directly to the consideration of the contention that goals and timetables mandated by the terms of the Executive Order represented a disguised attempt to institute proportional hiring and quotas. Some of affirmative action's proponents argued for proportional hiring; others felt that specific quotas for specific periods of time to accomplish specific predetermined goals would be appropriate. Even if such solutions were to be implemented, it was evident to some affirmative action proponents that quotas and proportional hiring would not be effective in rooting out the sources of injustice. Most proponents, though, pointed to the specific statements in the Order that said that such practices were prohibited, and viewed the requirement of demonstrated "good faith" as an appropriate balance between the interest of higher education and the public interest.

The basic intent of affirmative action often took a subordinate position in the national debate behind the furor raised by the spectre of quotas. Basically, the argument of opponents of affirmative action was that numerical hiring goals become quotas because they were intended by H.E.W. as the primary indicator of compliance to the Executive Order. Most held that the lack of women and minorities qualified for academic positions was the reason for their apparent exclusion, not discrimination. [50, 51] Glazer pointed to a "Catch-22" situation in which an employer must set goals and timetables, not based on a specific charge of discrimination, but on the condition of receiving federal monies, and then is not able to reach those goals due to the short supply of qualified affirmative action candidates; at the point the employer's "good faith" becomes suspect, and the federal contract may be in jeopardy. [52] Thus, opponents believe that the ability to achieve proportional hiring and still maintain quality is impossible.

Standards of Excellence

It was this concern for the potential effect that affirmative action might have on quality that caused many to speak out on the issue. Affirmative action opponents felt that the statistical approach to determining discrimination or nondiscrimination would undermine the integrity and scholarship functions of the university. When one considers that tenure usually involves a commitment of employment for thirty to thirty-five years, it is no wonder that academic departments attempt to plan for excellence. There is usually stiff competition for the best available scholars; such practices, opponents held, would be severely limited by affirmative action. This is further complicated by the fact that hiring is generally done on a specialty basis; a person is not hired to teach history or chemistry, for example, but to teach in a specifically defined area within the field requiring specific prior preparation in that area. Since hiring pools are so limited in the first place, they are even more limited when examined on a specialty basis.[53] The results of hiring under quotas in the long run would be disastrous to the concept of a meritocracy since academic standards would have to be lowered in order to accommodate affirmative action candidates. Publishers would be forced to accept poor quality articles, and the traditionally unqualified might very well end up with tenure. A great disservice would be done to graduate students, and superior undergraduates might not see any reason to contemplate academic careers.[54, 55, 56]

Persons holding those beliefs also contended that the merit system in higher education, which is based on professional judgment, is different than those systems used in factories. Although faculty all perform basically the same function, they are rewarded through rank and pay at different rates according to their contributions to the profession, as well as the forces of the market place. Thus, opponents held that the disproportionate absence of women and minorities from the higher ranks, and of women from the higher salary levels was not a function of discrimination so much as it was a function of their records of scholarly achievement, their relative newness to the profession, or their having specialized in the lower paying fields.[57, 58, 59]

The issue of quota hiring and standards was also approached from the perspective of the psychological outcome it would have for women and minorities. There was a fear raised that having been hired under affirmative action would cause them to be perceived as being less competent, and only able to gain employment through federal intervention, not quality. It was felt that they may suffer from the uncertainty of not knowing whether or not they were hired on their merits or as a means toward meeting a quota; thus, they would be forced into a position of always having to "measure up."[60-63]

Some proponents of affirmative action were worried about a possible negative impact on quality if institutions buckled under to a perceived federal pressure to meet goals under any circumstances for fear of losing federal contracts. Most, however, believed that the majority of the fears of a decline in quality resultant from affirmative action were not based on quantifiable data, and were, thus, unfounded, since it is the institution and not the federal government that determines the qualifications criteria. No hiring of unqualified persons was called for under the Order. If a white male is the best qualified for the position, then, it was agreed, the position should be awarded to him.

While the basic meritocratic intent of decision-making in higher education is upheld by affirmative action proponents, it is also challenged as having been biased toward favored groups and against others. By not having included women and minorities in the past, access to meritorious status could only be gained by 30 to 40 percent of the American population.[64] Further, there is no doubt that even under the merit system, mediocre and incompetent white males received preference over highly qualified (and less qualified) affirmative action candidates.[65] A reexamination of standards of excellence, which may serve to exclude women and minorities, was suggested since such criteria were often based on standards of behavior, manners, and life-styles modeled after the predominant group (white males). The ideal of meritocratic evaluation exists in theory but rarely in practice, proponents agreed, since the judgment of professional competence, whether in teaching or research, is subjective.[66, 67]

DeFunis, Bakke and Weber: The Issues Come Together

The issues raised in the affirmative action debate have reached the United States Supreme Court on three occasions. Two of the cases, the *DeFunis* and the *Bakke* cases, concerned minority admissions programs in graduate professional schools. The third case, that of the *United States Steel Workers v. Brian F. Weber et al*, involved a collective bargaining agreement provision that allowed black workers access to half of the slots in a Kaiser aluminum training program intended to provide for the upward mobility of unskilled workers. Taken together, these cases affirm the constitutionality of the principle of affirmative action, though the Court did not have an easy time reaching such a position. The Court has a history of holding off the decision on matters not easily resolved until the closing phase of its annual term. The affirmative action cases all fit that pattern. Further, it can be reasonably argued that it was not until the third case that the Court's position was clear.

The first of these three cases, that of *Marco DeFunis et al v. Charles Odegaard et al*, reached the Supreme Court in the fall of 1973. The matter began several years earlier when, in 1971, 1601 candidates, seventy-five to eighty of whom were minority, applied for admission to the University of Washington Law School. Based solely on predicted first year averages, most of the group was qualified for admission. However, only 150 spaces were to be filled. DeFunis, despite a high academic standing, was not selected for admission. Since thirty-six minority applicants with lower predicted averages than DeFunis were accepted, he sued on the basis of reverse discrimination.[68] The University admitted that it gave special treatment to blacks, Chicanos, American Indians, and Filipino-Americans, but claimed the practice to be justifiable as compensation for long-standing discrimination against those groups—only by making extra efforts on behalf of the members of those groups could the effects of past discrimination be overcome.[69] In the course of the litigation, the University was ordered to admit DeFunis pending final resolution of the case.

(It should be noted that, as a result of preference being given to minorities in law school admissions over the preceding decade, minority enrollment rose from 700 to 7600.)[70]

As might have been expected, interest in the case was so strong that seventy-one civil rights groups, law schools, academicians, and state agencies co-authored thirty briefs that were presented before the United States Supreme Court when the case was eventually heard. [71]

Those who were opposed to the Law School's actions argued that classification and preference by race are not permissable under the Constitution (based on the Supreme Court's findings in the *Brown* case some twenty years earlier, which decried the objectionable stigmatizing effect of segregation). To use a remedy that is based on the same premise as it was designed to cure is dangerous and continues the denial of equal protection under the laws. If compensation is to be provided for past injustices, then compensation based on race is, at the same time, under-inclusive (since there are countless whites who have suffered from a history of denial and poverty), and over-inclusive (since not all minorities have suffered). Thus, race is not a satisfactory basis, they argued, upon which compensatory decisions should be made. [72]

Further, since any classification based on race must pass exacting tests proving that there are no adverse consequences to anyone on the basis of race, preferential admissions policies fall short due to the element of "scarcity." Since there is only a small number of spaces to which law students may be admitted, to give preference to minority candidates would be to deny access to white candidates, and is, thus, illegal. Race is ill-suited for meritocratic purposes. [73, 74] The goal to be served by preferential admissions can only faintly be perceived as integration, and, therefore, must be justified solely on the grounds of a means toward increasing the supply of black lawyers. [75] However, if such practices are designed to promote positive role models for minority children, again they fall short, since they result in less qualified, less respected, less trusted minority professionals. [76]

Proponents of the Law School's policies were quick to point out that admissions have never been based exclusively on such objective data as standardized tests or predicted averages. Other more subjective criteria have also been used, namely, athletic ability, family relationships to alumni and faculty, geographic distribution, etc. The evidence of the underrepresentation of blacks in the legal profession at that time is clear: there was one white lawyer for every 630 Americans but only one black lawyer for every 6,000 blacks; not more than 2 percent of American attorneys were black.[77] When it is considered, for example, that in 1974 there were only seventeen black attorneys in Mississippi, and that white lawyers had been historically unwilling to accept black clients in cases against whites, it can be viewed as a socially positive goal to have more minority lawyers.[78]

Whenever there is an over-abundance of candidates, some principle of distribution must be employed; race is unjustifiable as an excluding characteristic, but, as a short-term expedient in an effort to bring about a greater condition of equality, it should be used as a characteristic toward the inclusion of minorities.[79] There is no doubt that had DeFunis been black, he would have been selected for admission, but if preferential treatment had not been accorded minorities at the time that he applied, the law school class would have been like all those that preceded it, and a socially positive goal would have continued to go unrealized.[80]

Traditionally, the Supreme Court decides a case on the narrowest possible ground. *DeFunis* was no exception. In the course of the oral arguments made before the Court during the winter and spring of 1974, the University made it clear that if the Court found in its favor, it would not dismiss DeFunis who, by that time, was approaching graduation. On April 23, 1974, the Court surprised nearly everyone who was following the case by dismissing it on grounds that it was moot. In a 5-4 vote, the majority of the Justices held that since DeFunis was about to be graduated, he no longer had a reason to sue the University. The four dissenting Justices argued that the majority was wrong in not settling the constitutional question once and for all. They held that the public interest was best served by avoiding the repetitious litigation that was certain to follow this nonresolution.[81]

More cases did work their way through the lower courts, and in February, 1977, the Supreme Court agreed to hear the case of the *Regents of the University of California v. Allen P. Bakke*. Bakke, who held a master's degree in engineering, was denied admission to the Medical School at the University of California at Davis in both 1973 and 1974. The University had reserved 16 of the 100 places in the entering class for minority students in each of those years. After his second rejection, Bakke sued the University, claiming that he was denied equal protection of the laws due to the existence of a two track admissions system that allowed minorities access to all 100 entering positions but which allowed whites access to only 84. The California district court, which tried the case, ruled against the University but did not order Bakke's admission because he had not proven that he had been rejected as a result of the existence of the special admissions program. The California Supreme Court did order his admission but that order was stayed by the United States Supreme Court when it agreed to accept the case. Thus, the Court did not have the option of declaring this case moot.

This time, the number of *amicus* briefs that were submitted doubled the number provided in *DeFunis* and set a Court record.[82] The thrust of the philosophical and legal arguments presented by the friends of the Court as well as by the two parties involved basically parallelled those presented in the earlier law school case. The University's side was bolstered by the facts that as late as 1948, twenty-six of the seventy-seven American medical schools were openly segregationist; that by 1970, blacks were approximately 12 percent of the American population but were only 2.2 percent of the doctors and 2.8 percent of the medical students; and that at the time the case was being deliberated, there was one white doctor for every 599 whites but only one black doctor for every 2,779 blacks— in some Southern states there was only one black doctor for every 15,000 to 20,000 blacks.[83] Bakke's position was that the only fair and constitutional method of selecting prospective students for the Medical School was one that based admission on individual merit rather than on race.

The Court's response came on June 28, 1978 and, again, seemed to beg the issue. Two separate majorities came together in a complicated decision that ruled that admissions programs that take race into account are acceptable, but that racial quotas are not constitutional. Three separate opinions, none of which held majority support, formed the basis for the decision. Justice Stevens, writing for Chief Justice Burger and Justices Stewart and Renquist, concluded that "The University, through its special admissions policy, excluded Bakke from participation in its program of medical education because of his race." This group did not address itself to any constitutional issues, however. Justice Brennan, on behalf of Justices White, Blackman, and Marshall, ruled that a race conscious admissions program is constitutionally acceptable if it meets three criteria: (1) if it is intended "to remove a disparate racial impact" which is "the product of past discrimination, whether its own or that of society at large"; (2) that racial admissions criteria must be "reasonably used in light of the program's objectives"; and, (3) such practices cannot be used in a manner which "stigmatizes any discrete group or individual." The Brennan group concluded that the U. C. Davis admissions program met all of these tests and was, thus, constitutionally acceptable. The third opinion, written by Justice Powell, provided support for elements of both of the other opinions. He agreed with the Brennan group that Title VI of the Civil Rights Act of 1964 and the Constitution both placed constraints on race-conscious admissions policies, though he did not accept the three-pronged test set forth by Brennan. He did, however, accept the principle of a university's use of race as one factor in an admissions decision but not as a factor that rules someone in or out of consideration for a specified number of the total available spaces. Thus, on a 5 to 4 vote, race-conscious admissions programs may be constitutionally acceptable. Powell agreed with the Stevens group that the Davis admissions policy had excluded nonminority applicants from consideration for a predetermined number of spaces reserved for minorities. He found this objectionable and sided with the Stevens group in a 5 to 4 vote that ruled quotas based on race to be illegal and ordered Bakke into the Medical School.[84]

Thus, after consideration of the issues in the *Bakke* case for a period of seventeen months, the Court was not able to develop a position that could draw the support of a majority of its members. Instead, it had produced two overlapping majorities that left considerable room for confusion concerning the boundary between race-consciousness and quotas.

As one observed put it, *Bakke* was a landmark case but not a landmark decision.[85] Groups on all sides of the issue saw their position verified by the Court and, thus, claimed victory. President Carter felt it necessary in the confusion that followed the decision to issue a statement to the heads of all federal departments and agencies directing them to "continue to develop, implement and enforce vigorously affirmative action programs."[86] Conferences were held across the country by a variety of groups to attempt to determine the impact of the ruling. The conclusion of one such session, conducted by the NAACP, bears mention: that the *Bakke* decision is an early decision that will continue to be defined by future cases.[87]

That perception proved to be an accurate one as the Court ruled one year later in favor of a voluntary affirmative action program put into effect in 1974 at the Kaiser Aluminum plant in Gramercy, Louisiana. Under a collective bargaining agreement with the United Steelworkers of America, minority workers were guaranteed half of the in-service training positions in a program intended to provide upward mobility to unskilled workers. Brian Weber, a white employee, sued the union and the company, claiming that the program discriminated against him by accepting blacks who had less seniority than he did. Weber's position was supported by the federal district and appelate courts which heard the case but was rejected by the United States Supreme Court in a 5 to 2 vote. Writing for the majority, Justice Brennan noted that, prior to the collective bargaining agreement establishing the program, only 1.83 percent of the skilled workers at the plant were black, while blacks made up 39 percent of the local work force. He went on to make the case that a voluntary program to correct such an obvious imbalance was not prohibited by the Civil Rights Act of 1964; that, indeed, a prohibition against such efforts would disserve the ends of that legislation since it was intended to provide blacks with opportunities previously denied them and to bring them into the mainstream of American society. Acknowledging that some affirmative action plans may not be acceptable, he stated that the Court "need not today define in detail the line of demarcation between permissible and impermissible affirmative action plans. It suffices to hold that the challenged . . . plan falls on the permissible side of the line." He held that "the plan does not unnecessarily trammel the interests of white employees" since it does not require their replacement with blacks nor does it absolutely exclude them from the training program, and, since it is intended to end as soon as the percentage of black skilled workers at the plant approximates the percentage in the local labor force. Brennan was careful in his opinion to note the narrowness of the decision to voluntary programs not involving state action.[88] Presumably, that is why a quota was not acceptable in *Bakke* but was in *Weber*.

Affirmative action programs, then, have weathered the legal storm and have remained fairly well intact. To the chagrin of affirmative action opponents, the Supreme Court has upheld the constitutionality of race-conscious decision-making, although it has allowed a degree of uncertainty to remain by not having outlined the criteria of an acceptable affirmative action plan. Further, it has declared state imposed quota systems unconstitutional, but has sanctioned voluntary quota plans in the private sector so long as they are temporary in duration.

Obviously, the controversy will not be silenced by the latest Court decision. The fact that approximately five of every six Americans (including a majority of women and minorities) believe that ability, not preferential treatment, should be the main criterion for jobs and admissions to college, is an indication that affirmative action will continue to be as important a topic in the 1980s as it was in the 1970s.[89] As is the case with other matters of national importance, the federal enforcement effort will continue to be a factor of the political and economic conditions operant in the country, as well as a factor of who is sitting in the White House. In any event, additional court challenges and the resulting definition of legal boundaries are a certainty.

REFERENCES

1. Willis, V.: *Affirmative Action: The Unrealized Goal*. Washington, The Potomac Institute, 1973, p. 118.
2. United States Equal Employment Opportunity Commission: *Fifth Annual Report*. Washington, U.S. Govt. Print. Office, 1971, p. 36.
3. United States Department of Health, Education and Welfare, Office for Civil Rights: *Higher Education Guidelines, Executive Order 11246*. Washington, U.S. Govt. Print. Office, 1972, p. 17.
4. Ibid., p. 4.
5. LaNoue, G. and Miller, M.: Professional societies and equal employment. *Society*, 13(2):52, 1976.

6. Ballard, A.: Academia's record of benign neglect. *Change,* 5(*2*): 27–28, 31–32, 1973.
7. Mommsen, K.: Black Ph.D.s in the academic marketplace. *Journal of Higher Education,* 45(*4*):256–258, 265, 1974.
8. Moore, W. and Wagstaff, L.: *Black Educators in White Colleges.* San Francisco, Jossey-Bass, 1975, p. 187.
9. Sowell, T.: Affirmative action reconsidered. *The Public Interest, 42*:57, 1976.
10. White, G.: Affirmative Action programs in small institutions. ERIC Document Reproduction Service, 1974, ED 489 564, p. 2.
11. Carnegie Council on Policy Studies in Higher Education: *Making Affirmative Action Work in Higher Education.* San Francisco, Jossey-Bass, 1975, p. 35.
12. Roby, P.: Institutional barriers to women students in higher education. In Rossi, A. and Calderwood, A. (Eds.): *Academic Women on the Move.* New York, Russell Sage Foundation, 1973, p. 37.
13. Astin, H.: Career profiles of women doctorates. In Rossi, A. and Calderwood, A. (Eds.): *Academic Women on the Move.* New York, Russell Sage Foundation, 1973, p. 160.
14. Sells, L.: Availibility (sic) pools as a basis for affirmative action. ERIC Document Reproduction Service, 1973, ED 477 461, p. 3.
15. Centra, J.: Women with doctorates. *Change, 7(1)*:49, 1975.
16. Abramson, J.: *The Invisible Woman.* San Francisco, Jossey-Bass, 1975, p. 84.
17. Carnegie Council, op cit., pp. 5, 28.
18. Sells, op cit., p. 4.
19. Astin, H, and Bayer, A.: Sex discrimination in academe. In Rossi, A. and Calderwood, A. (Eds.): *Academic Women on the Move.* New York, Russell Sage Foundation, 1973, p. 339.
20. Chait, R. and Ford, A.: Affirmative action, tenure and unionization: Can there be peaceful coexistence? ERIC Document Reproduction Service, 1973, ED 090 808, p. 3.
21. Astin, op cit., pp. 154, 156.
22. Martin, D.: The wives of academe. In the Editors of Change (Eds.): *Women on Campus.* New Rochelle, N.Y., *Change,* 1975, pp. 36–38.
23. Holden, C.: Women in Michigan: Parlaying rights into power. *Science, 178* (*4064*):963, 1972.
24. Sandler, B.: Statements of Dr. Bernice Sandler before the senate judiciary subcommittee on constitutional amendments. May 6, 1970, p. 2.
25. Pottinger, J.: The drive toward equality. *Change, 4(8)*:29, 1972.
26. Sandler, B.: The hand that rocked the cradle has learned to rock the boat. In Sells, L. (Ed.): *Toward Affirmative Action, New Directions for Institutional Research, 1(3)*:15, 1974.
27. Bunzel, J.: The politics of quotas. *Change, 4(8)*:31, 1972.
28. Seabury, P.: HEW and the universities. *Commentary, 53(* 2 *)*:42–43, 1972.
29. Lorch, B.: Reverse discrimination in hiring in sociology departments: A preliminary report. American Sociologist, *8(3)*:119, 1973.
30. Ornstein, A.: Quality, not quotas. *Society, 13(2)*:10, 1976.

31. Cowen, J.: Inverse discrimination. *Analysis, 33(1)*:11, 1972.
32. Simon, R.: Preferential hiring: A reply to Judith Jarvis Thompson. *Philosophy and Public Affairs, 3(3)*:316, 1974.
33. Seabury, op cit., p. 43.
34. Hook, S.: On discrimination: Part one. In Sells, L. (Ed.): *Toward Affirmative Action. New Directions for Institutional Research, 1(3)*:29, 1974.
35. Raab, E.: Quotas by any other name. *Commentary, 53(1)*:42–43, 1972.
36. Hook, op cit., p. 26.
37. Glazer, N.: *Affirmative Discrimination: Ethnic Inequality and Public Policy*, New York: Basic Books, 1975, pp. 60–61.
38. Hook, S. and Todorovich, M.: The Tyranny of Reverse Discrimination. *Change, 7(10)*:42–43, 1975–76.
39. Nickel, J.: Discrimination and morally relevant characteristics. *Analysis, 32(4)*:114, 1972.
40. Miller, S.: The case for positive discrimination. *Social Policy, 4(3)*:65, 1973.
41. Sher, G.: Justifying reverse discrimination in employment. *Philosophy and Public Affairs, 4(2)*:161, 1975.
42. Taylor, P.: Reverse discrimination and compensatory justice. *Analysis, 33(6)*:182, 1973.
43. Bayles, M.: Reparations to wronged groups. *Analysis, 33(6)*:183, 1973.
44. Thompson, J.: Preferential hiring. *Philosophy and Public Affairs, 2(4)*:365, 381–383, 1973.
45. Havighurst, R.: Individual and group rights in a democracy. *Society, 13(2)*: 26–27, 1976.
46. Nagel, T.: Equal treatment and compensatory discrimination. *Philosophy and Public Affairs, 2(4)*:348, 1973.
47. Silvestri, P.: The justification of inverse discrimination. *Analysis, 34(1)*:31, 1973.
48. Miller, op cit., p. 71.
49. Sandler (1974), op cit., p. 11.
50. Lester, R.: *Antibias Regulation of Universities*. New York, McGraw-Hill, 1974, p. 140.
51. Ornstein, op cit., p. 10.
52. Glazer, op cit., p. 58.
53. Lester, op cit., pp. 15–18, 70.
54. Seabury, op cit., p. 42.
55. Hook, op cit., p. 28.
56. Bunzel, op cit., p. 34.
57. Lester, R.: The equal pay boondoggle. *Change, 7(7)*:39–40, 1975.
58. Lester, op cit., 1974, p. 49, 58.
59. Sowell, op cit., p. 54.
60. Raab, op cit., p. 43.
61. Hook, op cit., p. 28.
62. Rustin, B. and Hill, H.: *Affirmative Action in an Economy of Scarcity*. New York, A. Philip Randolph Institute, 1974, p. 3.

63. Hernandez, J., Strauss, J., and Driver, E.: The misplaced emphasis on opportunity for minorities and women in sociology. *American Sociologist, 8(3)*:123, 1973.

64. Janeway, E.: Women on campus: The unfinished liberation. In Editors of *Change* (Eds.): *Women on Campus.* New Rochelle, N.Y., Change, 1975, p. 13.

65. Hill, H.: Preferential hiring: Correcting the demerit system. *Social Policy,* 4(1):97, 1973.

66. Ringer, B.: Affirmative action, quotas and meritocracy. *Society, 13(2)*:12, 22–25, 1976.

67. Lovell, C.: Three key issues in affirmative action. *Public Administration Review, 34(3):*236, 1974.

68. Wilson, J.: DeFunis — What now? *Journal of College and University Law, 2(1)*:84–85, 1974.

69. Weaver, W.: Discrimination in reverse? Now that Marco DeFunis has his law degree.... *Compact, 8(4)*:6, 1974.

70. Askin, F.: Eliminating racial inequality in a racist world. *The Civil Liberties Review, 2(2)*:100, 1975.

71. Kirp, D. and Yudof, M.: DeFunis and beyond. *Change, 6(9)*:24–26, 1974.

72. Cohen, C.: Honorable ends, unsavory means. *The Civil Liberties Review, 2(2)*:107–112, 1975.

73. Ibid., p. 111.

74. Fiss, O.: School desegregation: The uncertain path of the law. *Philosophy and Public Affairs, 4(1)*:10–11, 1974.

75. Ibid., p. 12.

76. Cohen, op cit., p. 113.

77. O'Neil, R.: *Discriminating Against Discrimination: Preferential Admissions and the DeFunis Case.* Bloomington, IN, Indiana University Press, 1975, p. 94.

78. Kirp and Yudof, op cit., pp. 24–26.

79. Askin, op cit., pp. 102–103.

80. Fineburg, S.: Must affirmative action be divisive? *The Crisis, 82(9)*:287, 1975.

81. O'Neil, op cit., pp. 52–53.

82. Weaver, W.: High court backs some affirmative action by colleges, but orders Bakke admitted. *New York Times,* June 29, 1978, pA22.

83. Wilkinson, J.: *From Brown to Bakke, The Supreme Court and School Integration: 1954–1978.* New York, Oxford University Press, 1979, pp. 275, 267, 283.

84. McCormack, W. (Ed.): *The Bakke Decision: Implications for Higher Education Admissions.* Washington, American Council on Education, 1978, pp. 8–16.

85. Holloway, C.: *The Bakke Decision: Retrospect and Prospect.* New York, College Entrance Examination Board, 1978, p. 22.

86. Carter, J.: Memorandum for the Heads of Executive Departments and Agencies. July 20, 1978.

87. NAACP Bakke symposium report. *Equal Opportunity Forum, 5(11)*:20, 1978.

88. *United Steelworkers of America v. Brian F. Weber et al.,* June 27, 1979.

89. Poll finds little support for affirmative action. *Memo to the President, 178)*:2, 1977.

CHAPTER 8

HIGHER EDUCATION FOR BLACKS:
AN END TO SEPARATE INSTITUTIONS?

One can readily deduce, both from the data provided concerning the educational deprivation of blacks in American history and from the controversy that has been swirling around the federally-mandated concept of affirmative action, that blacks have not been accorded their proportionate and fair share of admissions to undergraduate programs in this nation's colleges and universities. Most blacks, who have been graduated from college, have attended institutions that have been as separate as the elementary and secondary schools from whence they came.

Separate Colleges for Most Blacks

John B. Russworm became the first black American to earn a college degree when he was graduated from Bowdoin College in Maine in 1826.[1] He was followed by fourteen others over the next fourteen years, and by a total of only twenty-seven by the Civil War.[2] One explanation for so few having received college educations is the fact that the overwhelming proportion of blacks were held as slaves throughout that period. However, discrimination in the North must also be cited as an additional factor. The belief that blacks had special educational needs led to efforts, dating to the early 1800s, to establish colleges specifically for blacks. While some unsuccessful institutions may have escaped the sight of historians, the first of the traditionally black institutions (TBIs) still in existence today was Lincoln University (originally called the Ashman Institute), founded in 1854 by the Presbyterian Church thirty or so miles southwest of Philadelphia. Two years later near Dayton, Ohio, Wilberforce University was begun by the Cincinnati Conference of the Methodist Episcopal Church. During its first six years, it served to educate the children of white Southerners and their black slaves.[3]

Immediately after the Civil War, the Freedman's Bureau and the American Missionary Association contributed to the establishment of additional colleges for blacks. Howard University, named for General O. O. Howard, the Commissioner of the Bureau, was established in Washington. Atlanta University, Fisk, Hampton Institute, Talladega and Tougaloo were all opened in states of the former Confederacy.[4] It should not go unnoticed that of the $6 million spent on these colleges during their early years, $750,000 was contributed by blacks.[5] But, blacks did not control their colleges; the churches, the missionary societies, and, later, the industrial philanthropists not only served as benefactors but also ran the institutions. White boards of trustees and white presidents were the rule in the black colleges.

Public higher education was rare in the United States prior to the Morrill Land Grant Act of 1862, which provided federal grants to states to establish colleges for the training of farmers and technical personnel. In most instances, these colleges developed into the state university. Needless to say, the post-Civil War South did not rush to admit blacks to these colleges. Thus, in 1890, Congress passed the Second Morrill Act that provided grants to those states which chose to establish "separate but equal" public institutions for blacks. It required that funds be "equitably divided" between the black and white institutions. However, the black colleges never received their fair share.[6] In addition to receiving a disproportionately low share of state funds, the public TBIs, until very recently, received less than 1 percent of their annual income from private donations and grants. They had to rely primarily on tuition and thus were kept in a state of poverty.[7] As late as 1968, white land grant colleges in states with black land grant institutions received nine times the public funding despite having only five times as many students.[8]

From the conclusion of the Civil War to 1895, black colleges in nineteen states had graduated over 1100 students. During that same period, fewer than 200 blacks had graduated from white colleges in the North, and, of course, none received degrees from white Southern institutions.[9] This pattern continued until the 1960s when enrollment at the 102 TBIs was in excess of 120,000 students.[10] By that time, over a third of a million students had graduated from the black colleges. Since blacks had been virtually excluded from other collegiate institutions, most of the country's black professionals, including doctors, lawyers, professors, school teachers, military officers, and civil servants, received their undergraduate degrees from these colleges.[11] Patricia Roberts Harris, Secretary of the Department of Health and Human Services (formerly HEW) under President Carter, has credited these institutions, which account for only about 3 percent of the total number of American colleges and universities, with building America's black middle class.[12]

Because the TBIs were a product of segregated society, they did not, as a group, reach the same heights as the most prestigious white institutions. As early as 1917, attention was focused by the Phelps-Stokes Fund on the academic deficiencies of the black colleges. Its report, *Negro Education*, indicated that programs needed strengthening, but rather than recommend the bolstering of the liberal arts curriculum, it suggested that attention be focused on industrial and agricultural education and on teacher education. It did, however, call for improvement of the natural and social science programs.[13] Thus, Phelps-Stokes did not choose to use the same yardstick that it would have for a New England college.

The difficulties confronting the black college were, at times, compounded by the postures taken by the institution's president. At one extreme were racist presidents who believed blacks were limited in their professional competence and intellectual ability.[14] At the other extreme were accommodationist presidents who, as DuBois complained, did not take "an honest position with regard to the Southern situation."[15] To have done so, feared these presidents, might have placed their colleges in financial jeopardy.

Racism was certainly a factor in the development of the TBIs. Accreditation and the respectability that accompanies it were denied to them by the accrediting association for that part of the nation (the Southern Association of Colleges and Secondary Schools), not because all of the colleges were inadequate, but because the Association would not admit black colleges. Instead, a parallel

association was established for the TBIs; it remained operative
until 1962. As American society began to change, so did the practices of the Southern Association. By 1969, all but eight private
four-year TBIs and one public one had received full accreditation. [16] [17]

Several very critical appraisals of the TBIs appeared a decade or
so ago. In their classic work, *The Academic Revolution*, Christopher
Jencks and David Riesman concluded that the black college: "was
usually an ill-financed, ill-staffed caricature of white higher
education . . . or perhaps it would be more accurate to say that the
Negro colleges served as a boring reminder of how bad most white
colleges in an earlier era had been—and a few still are." They held
that when judged "by almost any standard" the black colleges were
"academic disaster areas." [18]

In a study undertaken on behalf of the Carnegie Commission on
Higher Education, Frank Bowles and Frank DeCosta found that
when public TBIs were compared to historically white public
colleges in the same state, the black colleges fell short in such
measures as the proportion of the faculty with doctoral degrees,
the number of library volumes, the size of state budget appropriation, and the number of doctorates subsequently earned by those
who received bachelor's degrees at the institution. They concluded
that the black colleges were caught between two worlds: they had
not fully entered the world of academic excellence set by white
higher education, and they had not totally left the world of Jim
Crow. [19]

While these two widely read volumes confirmed in the minds of
many that the black colleges were inferior, they did not tell the
entire story. As has been noted in the previous chapter, over 70
percent of the black doctorates, most of whom received their
degrees from ten very prestigious Northern universities, teach at
the TBIs. Until relatively recently, almost all black Ph.D.s who
taught did so at these colleges. Discrimination by the professional
associations in the various academic disciplines and by the scholarly journals kept all but the very best of these faculty from
gaining national reputations. However, a careful examination of
the black colleges reveals that they have had their share of talented faculty who have dedicated their lives to educating future

generations of blacks.[20] In many instances they did this quite successfully. For example, 10 percent of all graduates of Morehouse College in Atlanta have gone on to earn doctorates.[21] No other college in Georgia can boast such a high proportion among its graduates, nor can any comparably sized college in the country.[22] Further, 24 percent of the graduates of black colleges go on to graduate school, an enviable record for institutions of their size and resources.[23]

The Color Line is Broken

Integration has had an effect on the black colleges. Black faculty and students now have access, though in some cases token access, to historically white colleges and universities. Despite this, however, the 1976 enrollment figures reported by HEW's National Center for Education Statistics indicated that the forty-three public TBIs enrolled nearly 147,000 students and that the private black colleges enrolled nearly 66,000.[24] This represented half of the blacks enrolled in four-year colleges.[25] A year earlier, the public colleges in Pennsylvania awarded 1330 bachelor's degrees to blacks; over 40 percent came from the state's two black colleges, Lincoln University and Cheney State College.[26] Thus, black colleges still draw a large number of students despite the fact that other colleges are now open to them.

The color line in higher education in the Southern and Border states slowly gave way beginning with the admission of Donald Murray to the University of Maryland Law School in the last half of the 1930s. By the time *Brown* reached the Supreme Court, blacks had been admitted to twenty-two public and twenty-seven private colleges in thirteen Jim Crow states and the District of Columbia. In most, desegregation was only token. However, the University of Arkansas was an exception, enrolling 200 blacks in 1953. The states of Alabama, Georgia, Florida, Mississippi, and South Carolina maintained solid segregation in each of their public and private colleges.[27] A week after the *Brown* ruling, the Supreme Court held in *Hawkins v. Board of Education*, a case involving the University of Florida, that the *Brown* mandate applied to higher education. The number of desegregated colleges doubled within a year.[28] The incidents surrounding the entrance of Autherine Lucy, James Meredith, Carlayne Hunter, and other blacks into the major public universities of resistant states was an indication that desegregation did not always come easily to the enlightened world of higher education. By 1966, most Southern institutions (including all but one public college) had signed agreements with HEW assuring their compliance with the nondiscrimination provisions of the Civil Rights Act of 1964.[29]

Black enrollments in historically white colleges across the nation began to escalate once Title VI was in force. They increased by 172 percent from 1964 to 1970. Even so, the college going rate for whites remained twice the level as that for blacks.[30] In only one (Texas) of twelve Southern states had blacks reached parity with whites in higher education by the 1974–1975 academic year. The other states ranged from a few points below (Florida) to 13.3 percent below (South Carolina). If black college attendance were to be of the same proportion as occurred among whites, over a million additional black students would have needed to be admitted.[31] A Ford Foundation study published in 1971 identified six barriers to the attendance of blacks in college.[32] The related problems of low scores on standardized admissions tests and poor academic preparation were foremost. Subsequent studies have indicated a high correlation between family income and scores on the Scholastic Aptitude Test (SAT). For example, in 1973–1974, students who scored above 750 on the test (whose point range is 200 to 800) had a mean family income of $12,124, while those who scored under 250 had a mean family income of $8639.[33] In 1968, black families earned only 63 percent of that earned by whites; by 1977 the gap had grown by 3 percent.[34] [35] Thus, the third barrier, that of money, was imposing. Since, by 1971, most blacks were urban and since most low-cost public colleges were not located in the cities, distance provided another barrier. Finally, the fact that blacks did not have the tradition of college attendance nor had they received the encouragement to attend from their teachers, guidance counselors, parents, and friends, combined with the barrier of racism in the college admissions office, further limited black enrollment.

It was not until the 1968 assassination of Doctor Martin Luther

King that these barriers began to fall. Colleges initiated special admissions programs for blacks, programs that sought to make judgements about their academic potential by means other than prior achievement as indicated by performance on standardized tests such as the SAT. Rank in high school class, references, and in-depth interviews played an important part in the adapted criteria. Along with this new approach to admissions came increased federal, state, and institutional financial aid programs, as well as special academic support programs including remedial courses, tutoring, and counseling. Additionally, public campuses in the cities were opened or expanded. At the same time, the high school drop-out rate for blacks dropped from 35 percent the year before the King assassination to 24 percent a decade later.[36]

As a result, black enrollments more than doubled to over one million by 1977.[37] Still, blacks were underrepresented; while 27 percent of whites aged eighteen to twenty-four were attending college, only 21 percent of blacks of the same age were.[38] Enrollment across the various sectors of higher education still remains uneven. Blacks are underrepresented in the four-year institutions and overrepresented in the two-year colleges. The concentration is even greater when it is revealed that eighty-three community colleges (7% of all two-year institutions) enroll 41 percent of minority community college students. These colleges and the TBIs account for 41 percent of black enrollment, yet these institutions represent only about 7 percent of the nation's colleges and universities.[39] [40] The isolation of blacks in the community colleges has major ramifications, since students who begin their collegiate educations in these institutions have a lower rate of receiving bachelor's degrees than do students who as freshmen enter a four-year college, particularly one with residential facilities: while 17 percent of black freshmen complete four years of college, 30 percent of whites do.[41] Thus, access to better jobs and to graduate school is blocked.

Blacks on White Campuses

Institutional isolation aside, about one-third of the most recent black and white high school graduates have entered college. However, there is a higher drop-out rate among the black students according to United States Census Bureau figures.[42] While the poor elementary and secondary educations available to blacks surely place them at a handicap in college (though Boyd's 1973 study of 785 randomly selected black students at forty historically white institutions across the country indicated that 85% maintained an academic average of C or better), there are other factors that affect the black persistence rate, particularly on historically white campuses.[43]

In fact, nonacademic reasons for withdrawal outnumber academic reasons two to one at four-year colleges and four to one at two-year colleges.[44] Many of the colleges with the best intentions were not ready for the increased numbers of black students who arrived in the 1970s. A survey taken of nearly all of the black freshmen in historically white colleges in North Carolina in the spring of 1970 revealed that two-thirds of those in the four-year institutions made their choice because they felt that they would get a better education at a white college; over three-quarters felt that the white college would provide them a better chance to receive a good job. Their experience on campus in most cases led them toward an increased consciousness of their blackness, "toward an identity not with all people but with black people."[45] Such was most likely the case at colleges across the country since a study of 1168 historically white institutions reported a few years later that higher education was not responding to the needs of black students.[46] The result was, at times, one of conflict between black students and white students as well as between black students and white administrations.

A study of thirteen historically white four-year institutions in the North published recently by Peterson and Associates revealed that transitional trauma seemed to follow the arrival of the first groups of blacks on campus.[47] The colleges under study had black enrollments which ranged from four percent to more than 13 percent of total enrollment; they included liberal, conservative, urban and rural campuses.[48] In the early 1970s there were twenty-four instances of major conflict that occurred on these campuses. In ten instances, the black students argued for the establishment of academic programs in Black Studies; in five they demanded that the institution provide cultural programs of interest to blacks; in nine they asked for recognition and funding of black student organizations. Other demands included increased black enrollment (nine), more black faculty and staff (ten), and improved support services (five) and financial aid (two). However, the largest number of complaints (17) concerned inter-racial issues such as student housing, discrimination on campus, and specific racial incidents. [49]

When Peterson's interviewers visited the thirteen campuses, the open conflict had long since passed, but it was clear that there was little understanding between blacks and whites. Whites thought blacks to be "cliquish" and to have a different life-style. They often resented the fact that blacks received special support programs (a fact confirmed by other studies as well). Blacks did not believe that whites were willing to mix with them and thus they did not actively seek their company. [50] [51] This finding was confirmed by Rosenthal's survey of one of every five blacks at Old Dominion University; two-thirds agreed that campus life was too segregated. A similar number had also encountered instances of racism by faculty members in the classroom, and 40 percent stated that they had received such treatment by administrators. [52]

Anecdotal studies by Lemieux and by Middleton and Sievert also found conditions on white campuses to be less than optimal for blacks. The former reported widespread feelings among black students that their faculty had difficulties relating to them and that their social life was limited due to the presence of small numbers of blacks. [53] Middleton and Sievert, surveying two dozen predominantly white campuses, found a considerable degree of alienation, avoidance, and distrust between the races. While they found a few examples of overt racial conflict (for example, a Halloween sprint by hooded whites through Harvard dormitories, a cross-burning at the University of Alabama after a black was elected student body president, and a sexually-oriented smear campaign against a white woman and black man who ran as a ticket for president and vice president of the student government at Greenville Technical College in South Carolina), most manifestations have been of a more passive variety. Seating in the cafeterias is usually racially based, and certain tables become identified as "black tables." The anonymity of the toilet stall provides some racists with the opportunity to scribe their feelings on the walls. Frustrations also come out during intramural sports when all-black and all-white teams compete with each other. One aspect of life that is equally as controversial inside the ivory tower as outside is housing. Blacks and whites assigned to the same room in the dormitory usually go their separate ways as soon as university rules allow. Also, despite the fact that fraternities and sororities no longer officially permit discrimination, integrated houses are rare. One encouraging aspect of the Middleton and Sievert study was their conclusion that students, who in elementary and secondary school have experienced busing, get along better in college with students of the other race than do students who have not been in such schools. For them, the initial shock of interacting with persons who are different is a thing of the past, and a posture of accommodation is more possible. [54]

Black Colleges Still Fill a Void

Thus, though the historically white colleges and universities have been opened to blacks, many blacks find themselves more uncomfortable in such settings and prefer to opt for a traditionally black college. This is particularly true for those who graduate from black high schools; the majority choose black colleges. (Interestingly, over three-quarters of blacks who graduate from predominantly white high schools enroll in predominantly white colleges.) [55] The sense of security provided by these colleges is made evident by the fact that while they currently enroll less than a fifth of black college students, they award 37 percent of all bachelor's degrees earned by blacks. [56]

The black college has provided a major avenue of access to those students from the lower end of the economic ladder. Nearly half of their freshmen in 1976 came from families with incomes of less than $8000. By comparison, white students from the same income strata represented only seven percent of those enrolled in historically white colleges. [57] Even more striking is a comparison between the black colleges and those institutions classified as universities (generally, institutions that award the doctoral degree).

Over 60 percent of the student bodies at the former come from families with incomes less than $10,000 as compared to 13 percent in the latter. Universities enrolled less than 2 percent of their students from the lowest economic level, families with annual incomes of less than $3000 per year; black colleges enrolled 17 percent.[58] These figures are so dramatic that it is clear that without the black colleges, many black students, particularly those from poor families, would never have access to higher education.

Thus, in an era when the law requires desegregation, black colleges still provide an important function. A former member of the NAACP's Legal Defense Fund group of attorneys, Conrad Harper, believes that the TBIs are "legally defensible largely in instrumental terms" since they provide "an education to students who would not otherwise be aided."[59] Vivian Henderson, president of Clark College in Atlanta, has emphasized that colleges such as his "need not and should not apologize for serving a clientele unhappily burdened with poor preparation for college work but nonetheless having abilities and potential for success in higher education."[60] Not only do these schools provide access but they are more willing than white institutions to provide remedial programs often necessary to make up for the academic and motivational deficiencies that students with such backgrounds often have.[61]

Howard University professor, Kenneth Tollett, has voiced concern over the impression that black colleges only serve the educationally disadvantaged. He notes that it is demeaning to black students to claim that if they were academically well-prepared they would attend a white college. Black colleges serve an important psychocultural function for black students.[62] Morehouse president-emeritus, Benjamin Mays, agrees. He believes that while white institutions can provide excellent academic training, "they can never give the black student the feeling that he is part of a great race."[63] Indeed, over half of those surveyed in a 1977 study of students enrolled in institutions supported by the United Negro College Fund stated that they chose their institution because they wanted to attend a black college.[64]

Not only does the black student benefit from the institution's concern with black culture, but the larger black community does as well. It is one of the functions of American higher education to serve as a repository and to promote culture. However, the predominantly white institution has never been concerned with nurturing the black tradition, something that has been of major importance to the black college.[65]

Existence of Black Colleges Threatened

Thus, while times have changed, and segregation is no longer the *raison d'etre* for the TBIs, Bowles and DeCosta point out that "the basic situation which brought [them] into existence and supported their development has not changed."[66] Nevertheless, they are in danger of losing their identity as black institutions, due either to financial pressures on the private ones or integration pressures on the public ones. Only one of the private black colleges is well-endowed; that is, it has significant wealth, accrued over the years through donations, gifts, and investments, to provide enough income from interest to provide it an operating budget beyond that which tuition alone would allow. Five other private TBIs have endowments sufficient to support an enrollment of a thousand students.[67] The remaining fifty-seven must depend primarily on tuition receipts for their survival. When tuition raises to a level too high for the students to pay, enrollments drop, thus causing tuition to increase even further. Several TBIs have closed during the last few years as a result of this spiral.[68]

To assist these institutions and others that serve low income students, Congress dedicated Title III, "Strengthening Developing Institutions," of the Higher Education Act of 1965 to them. Still in existence, the program has provided funds to over 400 colleges in recent years; 46 percent of the money has gone to eighty-two TBIs. However, increasing numbers of historically white private institutions as well as public urban colleges that serve the poor are beginning to demand a greater share of this federal money.[69] An apparent change in HEW policy to accommodate these institutions led to a major protest by black college presidents in 1978. HEW Secretary Joseph Califano further raised their hackles by publicly stating that the issue at hand was whether it is healthy for the private TBIs to become dependent on the federal government. "Are they viable institutions?" he pondered.[70] The uproar was so great from the TBI presidents that President Carter held a three-day conference in the fall of 1978 to assure them that he was committed to their institutions.[71] In early 1979, he told the heads of federal departments and agencies to find ways of financially assisting the black colleges in order to facilitate their ability "to participate fully in the educational and social progress of our nation."[72] Despite this, however, a 1980 Office of Education report indicated that the share of federal funds received by the black colleges after Carter's directive actually decreased slightly.[73] Thus, the financial threat is still present.

Integration has brought a different sort of threat to the public black colleges. Title VI of the Civil Rights Act of 1964 precludes the exclusion of minorities from institutions and programs receiving federal funds. Thus, as historically white colleges began to increase their black enrollments, there was a diminuition in the pool from which the black colleges could hope to draw their students. Several states put added pressure on their black colleges by opening or expanding competing branches of more prestigious public white universities across town from the black campus. Branches of Auburn University and the University of Maryland were respectively established in Montgomery near Alabama State, and in Baltimore near Morgan State and Coppin State. Texas expanded its system by taking over the University of Houston, but it was kept separate from the state controlled Texas Southern University, a black institution located in that city. The University of Tennessee broadened its continuing education center in Nashville into a degree granting institution in competition with nearby Tennessee State. Three new campuses were established near Savannah State, Albany State, and Fort Valley State by the Georgia Board of Regents in the 1960s. In Virginia, William and Mary sought to elevate a two-year branch campus in Petersburg to four-year status despite the existence there of Virginia State. A rival campus was also planned in Jackson, Mississippi close to Jackson State.[74, 75, 76] Suits by blacks in Alabama and Tennessee were unsuccessful in attempting to stop the development of the white campus. However, in Virginia, a court did halt the expansion of William and

Mary.[77] [78]

Critics of such approaches argued that alternatively those states could have placed additional resources in the black colleges in those cities. New buildings, new academic programs, and a new importance within the state higher education system could have made the campuses more attractive to white students. Those TBIs could have grown in size and prestige and could have done so without decreasing their black student enrollment or their black ethos.

Loss of blackness became a major fear throughout the black institutions. By the early 1970s, West Virginia State and the other public TBI in West Virginia, Bluefield State, were majority white. (By the second half of the decade the proportion of blacks enrolled was about one-quarter and one-sixth, respectively.) Similarly, Lincoln University in Missouri enrolled more whites than blacks. In two other instances, the trend was in the direction of the white majority; Office for Civil Rights data released in 1978 indicated that nearly one-third of Delaware State's students were white as were two of every five students at Kentucky State.[79] [80] [81] John Peoples, president of Jackson State, recently postulated that the rapid increase in white enrollment at his institution will ultimately raise its proportion of white students to 40 percent.[82]

An institution's black milieu is not only a factor of its black enrollment but also of its control by blacks. The governance of Maryland State (now U. Maryland—Eastern Shore) was transferred to the University of Maryland, while that for Prairie View A & M went to Texas A & M.[83] Arkansas A, M & N became the Pine Bluffs campus of the University of Arkansas after a court battle initiated by segregationist group led the legislature to reconsider the status of the black controlled campus. As a compromise against the strong legislative sentiment to close the campus, it was merged into the University of Arkansas in 1972.[84]

Thus, the premonitions uttered in 1952 by Martin Jenkins, then president of Morgan State, appeared in the early 1970s to be on the verge of ringing true. He warned that for most of the public black colleges, integration would mean a reorganization of the state higher education system to the benefit of whites. He feared that programs designed for black students would be negatively impacted under the guise of equality.[85] Nearly three decades later, the National Advisory Committee on Black Higher Education and Black Colleges and Universities, a group functioning under the auspices of HEW, concluded that the loss of a "minority sensitive environment" would be a setback for equal educational opportunity.[86]

The Adams Case

Recall that HEW was responsible for overseeing the desegregation of that portion of higher education that receives federal funds. (Nearly all of our colleges and universities have and continue to receive some combination of federal research grants, student aid monies, and dormitory construction subsidy. They also qualify for tax exempt status and their students are eligible for Veterans Administration benefits.) In 1969, HEW's Office for Civil Rights reviewed desegregation progress in ten states with black colleges. It concluded that all ten — Arkansas, Florida, Georgia, Louisiana, Maryland, Mississippi, North Carolina, Oklahoma, Pennsylvania, and Virginia — were continuing to operate segregated systems of public higher education and it ordered each state to submit a remedial plan. After some pressure was brought, five states submitted plans, but all were inadequate and were rejected. HEW wanted to bring about voluntary compliance — after all, President Nixon's southern support was important to his 1968 election victory — thus it did not initiate action to stop the flow of federal dollars to colleges and universities in those states.

Attorneys for the NAACP's Legal Defense Fund (LDF) feared that this voluntary approach would serve to limit opportunities for blacks, and, thus, filed suit to force HEW to bring the ten states into compliance with Title VI.[87] Officially, the plaintiffs were twenty-two families who claimed to suffer from the practices of their states, and two other parties who argued that their federal tax monies were being illegally allocated to the ten states. The defendant was the Secretary of HEW, Elliot Richardson.[88]

Adams v. Richardson was not a suit against the ten states for continuing illegal practices, but against HEW for failing to end those practices. In its complaint, the LDF asserted "a variety of

willful defaults by HEW through continued assistance to public
schools and colleges once segregated by law and now continuing to
segregate and discriminate in practice in violation of the Fourteenth
Amendment." They cited ten instances of racially identifiable
public institutions in close proximity to each other. For example,
there were only two whites enrolled at Savannah State College and
only forty-four blacks at Albany State; Grambling College had ten
whites while Louisiana Polytechnic Institute had ninety-four blacks;
North Carolina A & T had two whites while UNC-Greensboro had
110 blacks. They argued that the black colleges were not funded as
well as their white counterparts, that the white institutions continued to maintain essentially all-white faculties and staffs, and
that blacks were not represented on the governing boards of the
white institutions. Despite this obvious segregation, the LDF
claimed that "HEW has continued its substantial federal aid pay-
ments to those institutions." Not only had HEW been lax with the
ten states with which it had been interacting, but it had not even
contacted other states with worse records.

Judge John H. Pratt of the Federal District Court for the District of Columbia agreed with the LDF that HEW had not been
successful in bringing about desegregation on a voluntary basis.
In his ruling on November 16, 1972, he ordered HEW to issue
rules and regulations that, if not followed, would lead to the
withholding of federal funds from offending colleges. Several months
later, Pratt issued an amended order stronger than the first. He
stated that HEW has "a duty to commence enforcement proceedings"
if it failed to achieve voluntary compliance. [89]

Needless to say, HEW appealed the decision. At that point, the
case took on an added dimension. For the first time in history, an
important group of black educators broke with the position taken
by the NAACP's Legal Defense Fund. [90] In a brief filed *amicus
curaie*, the National Association for Equal Opportunity in Higher
Education (NAFEO), an organization of the presidents of historically black colleges, argued that Pratt's decision should be overturned since it painted the TBIs with the same brush as it did the
white institutions without taking into consideration the different
historical roles played by each. They pointed out that the black
colleges had served as a bridge from "a crippling and debilitating

elementary and secondary educational system" and contended that "any activity by the federal or state government to undermine the supportive role which these institutions presently perform is of itself discriminatory."[91] They noted that black colleges had always been open to persons of all races and that they had served as a source of "sterling talent which has benefited this Republic beyond measure of calculation."[92] Thus, since it had always been their mission "to make educational opportunities a reality rather than an empty expectation, it is impertinent to charge them with violating the law with the promotion of racism."[93]

While the appellate court did not overturn Judge Pratt, it did make note of the importance of the black colleges when it ruled that HEW could allow states no more than 180 days to file an acceptable statewide desegregation plan "that takes into account the special problems of minority students and of black colleges."[94] Thus, desegregation could not result in a reduction in the overall number and proportion of black students enrolled in a state's higher education system, nor could it result in the disappearance of the public TBIs.

Thus, it was now up to HEW at once to desegregate the institutions and to preserve the identity of the black colleges, while simultaneously bringing black enrollment across each system up to a level of parity with white enrollment. At that time, in none of the ten *Adams* states did parity exist. In Arkansas, for example, blacks were nearly 18 percent of the state's eighteen to twenty-four year old population but were only 12 percent of the enrollment in all of the public institutions of higher education; they were less than 6 percent of the enrollment in the major state universities. In Georgia, they were 25 percent of the college-aged population but 12 percent of the overall enrollment and 5 percent of the enrollment in the flagship institutions. Similarly, in North Carolina, there was a 16 point gap between the proportion of blacks in the college-aged population and their enrollment in the historically white public colleges. Lack of parity was equally as distressing in the nine non-*Adams* states that had black colleges.[95] [96]

Black faculty were shown to be isolated on the black campuses according to a study by the Southern Education Foundation. In Georgia, Maryland, and North Carolina, blacks were less than 5 percent and in some cases less than 2 percent of the faculty at the white colleges. In Mississippi, all but 8 of the 413 black faculty were in the traditionally black institutions. Discrimination was also apparent in faculty salaries. For example, faculty at the University of Arkansas at Pine Bluff averaged $2000 less at the instructor level and $7000 less at the level of full professor than their colleagues at the University's Fayetteville campus. [97]

Since institutional boards of trustees determine a college's agenda, the absence of blacks was an indication that little would change without compelling reason. As the LDF understood, change would be facilitated by the appointment of blacks to those boards. When the appellate court ruled, at least three *Adams* states included no blacks on the boards of their state universities; two counted only one black. The University of North Carolina Board of Governors had the best black representation, six of thirty-two members. [98]

Unfortunately for black America, HEW's willingness to implement the *Adams* mandate was hampered by the Nixon Administration's involvement in the Watergate affair. In order to stave off impeachment, Nixon counted on key senators from the states involved in the court decision. Said one OCR compliance team member, "It should have been clear to everybody that whatever the states submitted . . . would be approved . . . unless it was in open and flagrant violation of the law."[99] In June, 1974, HEW accepted plans from eight of the ten states. One submitted by Mississippi was deemed inadequate. Louisiana chose to ignore the submission deadline. The Justice Department was asked by HEW to file suit against both states. While the other eight plans were congruent with the Nixon Administration's sense of Judge Pratt's order, the LDF felt otherwise and asked HEW to rescind its approval. Once in receipt of the negative response from the government, the LDF sought further relief from Judge Pratt.

The LDF brief showed that the states did not meet the criteria initially set by HEW. [100] The LDF noted that no efforts had been undertaken to equalize any new programs to give them a competitive edge. They pointed to a number of instances in which enrollment progress had been negative. In North Carolina, while black enrollment in white colleges increased slightly, there was a small overall decrease in black enrollment. In Georgia, black participation increased somewhat but there were decreases in two universities, one state college, and five community colleges. In Maryland, the largest campus of the state university and the largest state college saw decreases in the number of black students. The experience in the other states was similar to the three described.

It was nearly two years before Judge Pratt issued his ruling. The case was then known as *Adams v. Califano* (Joseph Califano was Secretary of HEW). The court made no finding concerning four states: judicial proceedings against Mississippi and Louisiana were in progress in other courts; Pennsylvania had been removed by both parties from the non-compliant list because it had agreed to develop a plan that would conform to HEW criteria; Maryland was removed because it had filed suit against HEW. (Thus, HEW was being sued both for being too aggressive and too lackadaisical.) Concerning the states of Arkansas, Florida, Georgia, North Carolina, Oklahoma, and Virginia, Pratt found that they "have not achieved desegregation or submitted acceptable and adequate desegregation plans." A review of the enrollments of those states indicated that 73 percent of their white colleges enrolled a student body that was at least 90 percent white, while 92 percent of the TBIs were over 90 percent black. [101] He gave HEW ninety days in which to submit new guidelines to the states and gave the states sixty days after receipt of the criteria to submit new plans.

HEW's criteria, issued in the summer of 1977, were comprehensive and proved to be rather controversial. Beyond including such measures as requiring affirmative action programs to increase the numbers of black faculty and staff on white campuses, and mandating that enrollment of black high school graduates be of the same proportion as white high school graduates, the guidelines also required that new, high demand programs be placed in the black colleges and that unnecessary program duplication be eliminated at white and black campuses located in the same area— that the black campuses be favored in the relocation of such programs. [102] Each state had until February 3, 1978 to submit an acceptable plan.

The State Plans

The day before the court-imposed deadline, HEW Secretary Califano announced that three states, Arkansas, Florida, and Oklahoma, had submitted acceptable plans but that those from Georgia and Virginia had been rejected in their entirety. North Carolina's plan was only acceptable as regarded its community colleges; the rest of the plan was rejected. [103]

Arkansas had been the first of the former Confederate states to admit a black to its state university. By 1950, the University of Arkansas conducted integrated classes on three campuses. Desegregation, however, was never large scale. [104] In response to Judge Pratt's order, a Desegregation Advisory Committee of twenty-one whites and nineteen blacks was established to assist in the development of the state's plan. [105] Its focus was the University's Pine Bluff campus, which would receive up to seven new master's degree programs in education, ten high demand bachelor's programs (including ones in fisheries and water resources, computer science, and communications), and six high demand associate's degree programs (including graphic arts and diesel mechanics). [106] In addition, the campus would receive at least one new building and others would be renovated. Its faculty and support programs would also be improved. [107] It was hoped that these measures would strengthen the campus and would make it more attractive to whites. The plan also called for each historically white four-year college to raise its black enrollments to 16 percent by 1982–83. [108]

Florida, despite its reputation as a liberal Southern state, was a state which had established a segregated community college system three years after the *Brown* decision. Its final all-black two-year college was phased out in 1966. [109] Given that history and the fact that there was only one four-year TBI in Florida, one might have expected the state's plan to propose the merger of Florida A & M University with nearby Florida State. To the contrary, new programs in pharmacy, architecture, and construction technology as well as a new master's program in business administration were to be added to FAMU. Agriculture, architecture, business, education, and nursing programs at FAMU, Florida State, the University of Florida at Gainesville, and Tallahassee Community College were to be reviewed for the purpose of eliminating unnecessary duplication. [110] It should be noted that one critic of Florida's approach, Harvard law professor Derrick Bell, cites the fact that more programs went from FAMU to Florida State than vice versa, and that the latter received the best of the exchange. [111]

Oklahoma's plan mandated the elimination by 1982 of the disparity in the proportion of whites and blacks earning bachelor's degrees, the disparity in award of master's degrees was to be eliminated the following year, and the disparity in doctorates eliminated by 1986. (This aspect of its plan exceeded HEW's requirements.) Langston University, the state's only public black institution, would not only receive new high demand programs, but would also receive a new mission.[112] The following August, HEW rejected Oklahoma's proposal to give Langston a new urban studies mission and to reduce its black enrollment from 74 percent to 54 percent by 1984.[113] A month later, Oklahoma came back with a new plan that would give Langston $1.5 million in enrichment funds, $2.5 million in capital improvements, and 100 full tuition scholarships for whites in each of the following five years. It also proposed new academic programs in urban studies, physical therapy, gerontology, nursing, personnel management, and corrections be established at the University.[114] HEW's approval of this approach was largely a factor of the five year funding commitment to bolster Langston.[115]

The three remaining *Adams* states, Georgia, Virginia, and North Carolina, proved to be somewhat more recalicitrant. Virginia Governor Mills Goodwin complained in late 1977 that HEW was attempting to lower the quality of education in the state's higher education system by forcing the state to accept racial quotas as part of its statewide plan being developed to fulfill Judge Pratt's mandate.[116] Similar rhetoric was repeated by his successor Governor John Dalton, who, upon HEW's rejection of the Virginia plan, asked the legislature to appropriate a quarter of a million dollars to finance a Supreme Court battle.[117] Such a challenge proved unnecessary as HEW and Virginia came to partial agreement in March, 1978 and to final agreement in January, 1979.[118] [119] The stumbling block was the elimination of program duplication between Old Dominion University and Norfolk State College. Under the terms of the plan, ODU would transfer its early childhood education program and several business programs to Norfolk State. The threat of the withholding of $89 million in federal funds prompted the resolution.

Georgia, home of President Carter, did not finally reach agreement with HEW until a year after Judge Pratt's original deadline. Its plan included measures to strengthen the three black institutions by adding new programs and by reducing the program duplication at the nearby white institutions.[120] One feature of the plan—that which consolidated Savannah State's teacher education programs with those at Armstrong State, a white institution, and consolidated Armstrong's business administration programs under those at Savannah, a black institution—proved to be controversial. A group of black parents, students, and alumni known as Citizens for the Survival of Savannah State College voiced opposition to that approach and, instead, proposed the merger of Armstrong under the leadership of Savannah.[121] They filed suit to that end in federal court in the fall of 1979.[122]

North Carolina's Challenge

When HEW was split into the Department of Education (ED) and the Department of Health and Human Services in 1980, ED assumed responsibility for the desegregation of higher education. To date, North Carolina has not reached agreement with ED. University of North Carolina President William Friday has consistently maintained that his state has been making steady progress in the area of desegregation and that "North Carolina now provides a college education for a greater percentage of blacks than most states."[123, 124] While it seemed for a while that HEW and North Carolina had settled the matter, agreement broke down over the question of the elimination of program duplication.[125, 126] Friday saw the issue as one of academic integrity. He held that institutional effectiveness would be impaired as a result of the removal of programs for reasons that had more to do with politics than with education. Concerning the ability of merged programs to draw students, he stated, "If you close the business administration program in the better school, for example, nobody qualified for the better school would go over to the lesser school."[127] His position is one that has the support of the presidents of North Carolina's five public TBIs who believe the program transfer concept to be naive.[128]

When HEW Secretary Califano rejected North Carolina's plan in March, 1979, he pointed out that only 4 percent of the students at the TBIs were white and only 6 percent of those at the white schools were black. He noted that there was duplication in fifty-eight nonessential programs on North Carolina's campuses and that he was willing to delay their elimination for five years if North Carolina agreed to spend $90 million to improve the black campuses during that period. Citing his state's inability to afford such a program, Friday had rejected the compromise. [129, 130]

Court action followed. On March 27, the LDF returned to Judge Pratt's court to ask that all federal funds be withheld from North Carolina's higher education system. [131] A month later, North Carolina filed suit in federal court to halt HEW's administrative proceedings against the state. However, Judge Franklin T. Dupree subsequently ruled that the proceedings could begin, although he restrained HEW from commencing any withholding of federal funds until the proceedings had run their course. [132, 133] The administrative hearing began in July, 1980. ED lawyers accused North Carolina of "perpetuating discrimination." That state's attorneys retorted that the federal government was attempting to force an educationally unsound "quick fix." [134] The matter may eventually reach the Supreme Court.

Maryland Drops Its Challenge

For a time, it appeared that the Supreme Court opinion on the constitutionality of the federal government's approach to the desegregation of higher education would come in the case of *Lee v. HEW*, the suit initiated by the state of Maryland after HEW had rejected that state's plan to remedy the problems that had evolved from its racially dual system. Maryland charged HEW with "maladministration of a law that affects all Americans" and with refusing to engage in good faith negotiations. [135] The federal district court was convinced by the evidence presented by the state's attorneys and issued a temporary order injunction against any cut-off of federal funds. [136] HEW appealed and presented its case before all seven judges of the Fourth Circuit Court of Appeals. Despite the fact that Maryland's case had the support of the Attorneys General of thirty-four other states, the court ruled in favor of the federal government by a four to three margin. [137] However, before the decision had been rendered, one of the affirmative judges died. Thus, Maryland asked the Circuit Court to withdraw its opinion; the Court chose to do so.[138] To bring the matter to final resolution, the state asked the Supreme Court to hear the case, a surprising move since the district court's decision concurring with Maryland was in force. On October 2, 1978, the Supreme Court refused to review the case and it was again in the hands of the district court judge to determine whether or not to make the temporary injunction a permanent one.[139] Maryland, wanting to bring the matter to a speedy conclusion and preferring to focus its resources on education rather than attorneys fees, decided to drop its legal battle and enter into negotiations with HEW.[140]

Merger in Tennessee

While the states not directly affected by the *Adams* decision have not been exempt from compliance activity, perhaps the most interesting occurrence has been in Tennessee.[141] On January 31, 1977, Federal Judge Frank Gray ordered the merger of the predominantly white University of Tennessee-Nashville campus under the leadership of the historically black Tennessee State University. In upholding the decision, the Sixth Circuit Court of Appeals said that when a racially neutral approach to desegregation "neither produced the desired . . . nor promises realistically to do so, something further is required."[142] On July 1, 1979, the two institutions became one. Approximately 2500 students eligible to return to the new campus that fall declined to do so. However, admissions applications for the fall, 1980 semester indicate that many of them have since chosen to reenroll. When the 1979–80 academic year closed, the institution had a black enrollment of 60 percent and a white enrollment of 34 percent. Blacks numbered 55 percent of the faculty, whites 35 percent. Nearly all of the UT–N faculty had accepted TSU appointments and it was their perception that merger has worked well.[143] [144]

An Uncertain Future

While the Tennessee merger may have been successful, the end to racially dual public higher education will not come easily. A recent survey of 121 presidents of four-year public institutions in the District of Columbia and nineteen states with public TBIs indicated that 70 percent thought that there will continue to be racially identifiable colleges in their states by the end of the decade. The heart of the *Adams* decision is the mandate that desegregation occur on both the black and white campuses and that it not occur at the expense of the black institutions. Only about one-third of the presidents thought that black colleges will be able to maintain their black identity once integration had taken hold. [145] Not surprisingly, only 32 percent of those from historically white institutions thought that the placement of high demand programs on the black campuses would be effective in attracting white students to those campuses. (One must wonder how much of their skepticism toward this approach was a factor of their vested interest in retaining programs that they view as valuable.)

Sadly, the respondents to the survey cited periods as long as fifty years before parity will be reached between the proportion of minority population in their state and the proportion of minorities attending and graduating from the state's public colleges and universities; the modal response was twenty years—the HEW desegregation criteria called for parity by 1982–83. The recently reported enrollment figures of five of the *Adams* states were not heartening. Black enrollment had decreased by 7.5 percent; the greatest losses were at the community colleges and the traditionally black colleges. Florida and Virginia reported slightly increased numbers of blacks in their historically white institutions.

The goal of the LDF in the *Adams* litigation, as it has been throughout all of its efforts to desegregate education, is to bring black Americans into this country's socioeconomic mainstream. Black educators, secure in the knowledge that the courts have acknowledged the importance of the black colleges, believe that the *Adams* guidelines represent a major step toward equity for blacks in higher education. However, many officials of state departments of higher education resent the federal mandates because they come at a time when higher education is growing smaller due to declines among the traditional college-age population, and at a time when state governments are less willing to approve new spending initiatives. [146] Even more important, perhaps, is the fact that the educational merits of the Court order are not as apparent as its political side is to this group of educators.

Thus, there is little reason to believe that *Adams* will be but one more energy boost to the vehicle that embarked on its trek toward integration "with all deliberate speed" over a quarter of a century ago. Assuming that the *Adams* decision holds, blacks will have greater access to historically white colleges. Additionally, there will continue to be colleges whose cultural and educational concerns will be grounded in the black tradition. Hopefully, blacks and whites will feel comfortable in both.

REFERENCES

1. Woodson, C.: *The Education of the Negro Prior to 1861*, New York, Arno Press, 1968, p. 265.
2. Branson, H.: Black Colleges of the North. In Willie, C. and Edmond, R. (Eds.): *Black Colleges in America: Challenge, Development, Survival*. New York, Teachers College Press, 1978, p. 149.
3. Woodson, op cit., pp. 271–273.
4. Meier, A. and Rudwick, E.: *From Plantation to Ghetto, An Interpretive History of American Negroes*, New York: Hill and Wang, 1966, p. 143.
5. Dubois, W.: *The Souls of Black Folk*. New York, Dodd, Mead and Company, 1961, p. 24.
6. Bowles, F. and DeCosta, F.: *Between Two Worlds, A Profile of Negro Higher Education*. New York, McGraw Hill, 1971, p. 32.
7. Public black universities and colleges: Throwing off a 'second class' image to provide 'first class' education. *W. K. Kellogg Foundation Profiles, 1(1):2*, 1978.
8. National Advisory Committee on Black Higher Education and Black Colleges and Universities: *Black Colleges and Universities: An Essential Component of a Diverse System of Higher Education*. Washington, U.S. Department of Health, Education and Welfare, 1979, p. 12.
9. Ibid., p. 12.
10. Bowles and DeCosta, op cit., p. 68.
11. Carnegie Commission on Higher Education: *From Isolation to Mainstream, Problems of the Colleges Founded for Negroes*. New York, McGraw Hill, 1971, p. 14.
12. Harris, P.: The negro college and its community. *Daedalus, 100(3):723*, 1971.
13. Drake, St. C.: The black university in the american social order. *Daedalus, 100(3):842*, 1971.
14. Hine, D.: The pursuit of professional equality: Meharry medical college, 1921–1938, A case study. In Franklin, V. and Anderson, J. (Eds.): *New Perspectives on Black Educational History*. Boston, G. K. Halland Company, 1978, p. 174.

15. DuBois, op cit., p. 49.
16. Wiggins, S.: *The Desegregation Era in Higher Education*. Berkeley, McCutchan Publishing Corporation, 1966A, pp. 10, 48.
17. Carnegie Commission on Higher Education, op cit., pp. 70–81.
18. Jencks, C. and Riesman, D.: *The Academic Revolution*. Garden City, N.Y., Doubleday and Company, 1969, pp. 425, 433.
19. Bowles and DeCosta, op cit., pp. 144, 213.
20. Marcus, L. and Smith, F.: Black faculty and survival systems. *Integrated Education, 17(3 & 4):* 1979.
21. Willie, C.: Racism, black education and the sociology of knowledge. In Willie, C. and Edmonds, R. (Eds.): *Black Colleges in America: Challenge, Development, Survival.* New York, Teachers College Press, 1978, p. 12.
22. Mays, B.: The black college in higher education. In Willie, C. and Edmonds, R. (Eds.): *Black Colleges in America: Challenge, Development, Survival.* New York Teachers College Press, 1978, p. 24.
23. Brown, L.: In defense of black colleges: A response to Kenneth Clark. *ISEP Monitor, 3(3):*7.
24. Turner, W. and Michael, J.: *Traditionally Black Institutions of Higher Education: Their Identification and Selected Characteristics*, Washington, U.S. Government Printing Office, 1978, p. 2.
25. Watson, B.: Through the academic gateway. *Change Magazine, 11(7):*25, 1979.
26. Branson, op cit., p. 150.
27. Wiggins, op cit., p. 5.
28. Ibid., pp. 16–17.
29. Wiggins, S.: *Higher Education in the South*. Berkeley, McCutchan Publishing Corporation, 1966B, p. 167.
30. Crossland, F.: *Minority Access to College*. New York, Schocken Books, 1971, p. 16, 38.
31. Burrows, R.: The impact of desegregation on black public colleges and blacks in public higher education: Some views of black public college administrators. *Negro Educational Review, 28(2):*69, 1977.
32. Crossland, op cit., pp. 53–54.
33. Watson, op cit., p. 28.
34. Carnegie Commission on Higher Education, op cit., p. 21.
35. Morris, L.: *Elusive Equality, The Status of Black Americans in Higher Education*, Washington, Howard University Press, 1979, p. 83.
36. *Chronicle of Higher Education*, March 12, 1979.
37. *Chronicle of Higher Education*, January 29, 1979.
38. National Advisory Committee on Black Higher Education and Black Colleges and Universities: *Higher Education Equity: The Crisis of Appearance Versus Reality*. Washington, US Department of Health, Education and Welfare, 1978, p. 11.
39. Ibid., p. 14.

40. Olivas, M.: *The Dilemma of Access: Minorities in Two Year Colleges*; Washington, Howard University Press, 1979, p. 26, 28.
41. Olivas, op cit., p. 41.
42. *Chronicle of Higher Education*, March 12, 1979.
43. Boyd, W.: *Desegregating America's Colleges, A Nationwide Survey of Black Students, 1972–73.* New York, Praeger Publishers, 1974, p. 2, 96.
44. Olivas, op cit., p. 46.
45. Davis, J. and Borders-Patterson, A.: *Black Students in Predominantly White North Carolina Colleges and Universities,* New York, College Entrance Examination Board, 1973, pp. 4–5, 7–8.
46. Janssen, P.: Higher education and the black American: Phase 2. *Chronicle of Higher Education,* May 30, 1972, p. 1.
47. Peterson, M. et al.: *Black Students on White Campuses: The Impacts of Increased Black Enrollments.* Ann Arbor, Mich., Institute for Social Research, 1978, pp. 301–302.
48. Ibid., pp. 51, 77, 89.
49. Ibid., pp. 148–149, 156, 197.
50. Ibid., pp. 198, 206.
51. Middleton, L. and Sievert, W.: The uneasy current. *Chronicle of Higher Education,* May 15, 1978.
52. Rosenthal, S.: *Race Relations Research in Virginia: Still a Hazardous Undertaking.* Paper presented at the Annual Meeting of the Eastern Sociological Society, New York City, 1979, p. 4.
53. Lemieux, M.: Black students on white campuses. *Black Collegian, 8(4):*16, 1978.
54. Middleton and Sievert, op cit., pp. 10–12, 14.
55. Morris, op cit., p. 187.
56. National Advisory Committee on Black Higher Education and Black Colleges and Universities (1979), op cit., p. 30.
57. Ibid., p. 31.
58. Morris, op cit., p. 116.
59. Harper, C. The legal status of the black college. *Daedalus, 100(3):*778, 1971.
60. Henderson, V.: Negro colleges face the future. *Daedalus, 100(3):*642, 1971.
61. Wiggins (1966A), op cit., p. 72.
62. Tollett, K.: Commentary, In Bowles, F. and DeCosta, F.: *Between Two Worlds, A Profile of Negro Higher Education.* New York, McGraw-Hill, 1971, pp. 256–257.
63. Dr. Benjamin E. Mays speaks on black colleges. *ISEP Monitor, 3(3):*5.
64. *Higher Education and National Affairs, 26(26):* 7, 1977.
65. Jones, S.: The cultural mission of the black college, *ISEP Monitor, 3(3):*4.
66. Bowles and DeCosta, op cit., p. 233.
67. Nabrit, S.: Reflections on the future of black colleges, *Daedalus, 100(3):*61, 1971.
68. National Advisory Committee on Black Higher Education and Black Colleges and Universities (1978), op cit., p. 70.
69. National Advisory Committee on Black Higher Education and Black Colleges and Universities (1979), op cit., p. 61.

70. Holsendolph, E.: Title III storm signals. *Change Magazine, 10(11)*:56, 1978–79.
71. *Chronicle of Higher Education,* November 13, 1978.
72. *Higher Education and National Affairs, 28(3):*1, 1979.
73. *Chronicle of Higher Education,* April 14, 1980.
74. Egerton, J.: Separate but not equal: The public black colleges in the south struggle against the white man's odds. *Chronicle of Higher Education,* May 30, 1972.
75. Holmes, R.: An analysis of the Georgia statewide desegregation plan. In Haynes, L., III (Ed.): *An Analysis of the Arkansas-Georgia Statewide Desegregation Plans.* Washington, Institute for Services to Education, 1979, p. 87.
76. Jencks and Riesman, op cit., p. 470.
77. State Planning and Desegregation in Higher Education: A Panel Discussion. *Proceedings,* Annual Meeting of the Southern Regional Education Board, 1977, pp. 88–89.
78. Southern Education Foundation, *Ending Discrimination in Higher Education: A Report from Ten States,* Atlanta: Southern Education Foundation, 1974, p. 5.
79. Carnegie Commission on Higher Education, op cit., p. 8.
80. *Chronicle of Higher Education,* March 20, 1978.
81. Turner and Michael, op cit., pp. 4–10.
82. Kellogg Foundation, op cit., p. 9.
83. Egerton, op cit., p. 3.
84. Jones, A.: Black colleges fighting for survival. *Boston Globe,* October 7, 1973, A–92.
85. Browning, J. and Williams, J.: "History and Goals of Black Institutions of Higher Learning. In Willie, C. and Edmonds, R. (Eds.): *Black Colleges in America: Challenge, Development, Survival.* New York, Teachers College Press, 1978. p. 85.
86. National Advisory Committee on Black Higher Education and Black Colleges and Universities (1979), op cit., p. 55.
87. Egerton, J.: *Adams v. Richardson:* Can separate be equal? *Change Magazine, 6(10):*31, 1974–75.
88. *Adams v. Richardson,* 351 F. Supp. 636 (1972).
89. *Adams v. Richardson,* 356 F. Supp. 92 (1973).
90. Haynes, L., III, (Ed.): *A Critical Examination of the Adams Case: A Source Book.* Washington, Institute for Services to Education, 1978, p. III–5.
91. Ibid., p. C–23, C–25.
92. Ibid., p. C–28.
93. Ibid., p. C–29.
94. *Adams v. Richardson,* 480 F. 2d. 1159 (1973).
95. Haynes (1978), op cit., p. IV–11.
96. Southern Education Foundation, op cit., p. 12.
97. Southern Education Foundation, op cit., p. 11.
98. Ibid., p. 16.
99. Egerton (1974–1975), op cit., p. 34.

100. *Adams v. Califano*, 430 F. Supp. 118 (1977).
101. *Chronicle of Higher Education*, March 20, 1978.
102. Haynes (1978), op cit., pp. L–13–L–19.
103. *HEW News*, February 2, 1978, pp. 1–2.
104. Cobb, H.: A plan for the desegregation of public higher education in Arkansas: An analysis. In Haynes, L., III (Ed.): *An Analysis of the Arkansas-Georgia Statewide Desegregation Plans.* Washington, Institute for Services to Education, 1979. p. 28.
105. Ibid., p. 46.
106. *Higher Education and National Affairs, 27(5):2,* 1978.
107. Cobb, op cit., p. 57.
108. Ibid., p. 59.
109. White, A.: The desegregation of Florida's public junior colleges, 1954–1977. *Integrated Education, 16(3):32,* 35, 1978.
110. *Higher Education and National Affairs, 27(5):2,* 1978.
111. Bell, D.: The politics of desegregation, *Change Magazine, 11(7):52,* 1979.
112. *Higher Education and National Affairs, 27(5):2,* 1978.
113. *Chronicle of Higher Education,* August 7, 1978.
114. *Higher Education and National Affairs, 27(38):8,* 1978.
115. *Equal Opportunity in Higher Education, 4(21):,* 1978.
116. Rosenthal, op cit., p. 3.
117. Higher Education and National Affairs, *27(6):4,* 1978.
118. *HEW News,* March 17, 1979, p. 1.
119. *Chronicle of Higher Education,* January 22, 1979.
120. *Chronicle of Higher Education,* February 20, 1979.
121. Berrian, A.: *Savannah and Armstrong State Colleges: Is Merger Feasible?* Paper presented at the Annual Conference of the American Association for Higher Education, Washington, 1980, p. 4.
122. *Chronicle of Higher Education,* October 1, 1979.
123. New York *Times,* January 6, 1978.
124. *Chronicle of Higher Education,* March 27, 1978.
125. *HEW News,* May 12, 1978, p. 1.
126. *Chronicle of Higher Education,* May 22, 1978; December 18, 1978.
127. New York *Times,* January 22, 1979.
128. New York *Times,* February 5, 1979.
129. *Higher Education and National Affairs, 28(13):6–7,* 1979.
130. *Chronicle of Higher Education,* April 2, 1979.
131. Verified Motion for Order Suspending and Placing in Escrow Higher Education Aid to North Carolina's Traditionally Four Year Institutions. Civil Action No. 3095–70, Filed March 27, 1979, in re: *Adams v. Califano.*
132. New York *Times,* April 24, 1979.
133. *Higher Education and National Affairs, 28(24):6,* 1979.
134. *Chronicle of Higher Education,* July 28, 1980.

135. *Lee v. HEW,* Petition for a Writ of Certiorari, U.S. Supreme Court Action No. 78–86, p. 6.
136. *Mandel v. HEW,* 411 F. Supp. 542 (1976).
137. *Mayor and City Council of Baltimore v. Matthews,* 562 F. 2d 914 (1977).
138. *Mayor and City Council of Baltimore v. Matthews,* 571 F. 2d 1273 (1978).
139. *Equal Opportunity in Higher Education, 4(21):3,* 1978.
140. Interview with George A. Nilson, Deputy Attorney General, State of Maryland.
141. *HEW News,* February 2, 1978, p. 7.
142. *Chronicle of Higher Education,* April 30, 1979.
143. Humphries, F.: *The Tennessee State University and University of Tennessee at Nashville Merger.* Paper presented at the Annual Conference of the American Association for Higher Education, Washington, 1980, pp. 1–8.
144. *Chronicle of Higher Education,* February 4, 1980.
145. Marcus, L.: The *Adams* case: Views of college and university presidents. *Sociological Abstracts,* Supp. 99, *28(1):7,* 1980.
146. Haynes (1979), op cit., p. 14.

CHAPTER 9

THE UNENDING CONTROVERSY

The conclusion reached by the National Advisory Commission on Civil Disorders in 1968, after it studied the cause of a series of urban riots that had occurred in twenty-three cities during the mid-1960s, provides a sound warning even today: "Our nation is moving toward two societies, one black, one white—separate and unequal. . . . This deepening racial division is not inevitable. The movement apart can be reversed."[1] While there is evidence that the black middle class is growing and becoming more productive, America should not be lured into complacency by the citation of black middle income and occupation information. It must be remembered that the pre-Castro Cuba had perhaps the largest middle class in Latin America, and that the sizable middle class in South Vietnam did little to deter the dissatisfactions of much of that nation's poor.[2] In America, a large black underclass has been denied the benefits that desegregated schooling, compensatory education, and affirmative action were intended to provide. Moreover, the various political and social reforms of the past several decades have yielded few, if any, changes in the economic opportunities available to the black poor.

Given that disturbing fact, it must be asked, can the schools make a difference? Can the schools bring America closer to being a truly equal society? We believe that both questions can be answered in the affirmative. However, one must realize that the problem has been one of the long term and that the solution, therefore, must be long range and comprehensive. Policies such as those discussed in the previous chapters can contribute, but their successes, limitations, and related problems must be understood, and appropriate adjustments must be made.

316

Slavery and the Desegregation Struggle

While it is true that slavery officially ended over a century ago and that segregation has been illegal for some years now, there is little reason to believe that black behavior today is any less influenced by the slave codes and Jim Crow legality of the old South than white behavior remains influenced by the Protestant Ethic and the frontier spirit. In comparing the histories of white and black America, it must be remembered that the great majority of white settlers came to this country as products of nearly 2,000 years of Western civilization. As James Conant has noted, most European immigrants "came from an impoverished but stable society with its own ancient mores." Despite their poverty, Conant has concluded that "pride of family and often strong church connections were social cement that kept the [immigrant] slums from being complete social jungles."[3] Moreover, it is apparent that most of those immigrants came to this country with high hopes for a better life, and believed that with hard work they could find a stable, accepted position in the dominant culture. While it was not easy for them, many lived to see their dreams realized, if not for themselves, then for their children or grandchildren.

Blacks, however, came here against their will. But, even if they had immigrated freely and their African culture had been maintained, they still may have found acculturation an exceedingly difficult problem, given the alien Western environment that dominated North America. Their dilemma, as we know, was compounded by slavery that not only stripped them of their cultural foundations but also denied them access to the main culture as well. It must be remembered that American slavery was, indeed, a "peculiar institution." In other societies, including those of western Africa, there were many historical instances of slaves being allowed to have recognized families and to have an opportunity, however small, to earn or purchase their freedom.[4] In fact, the Spanish and Portuguese colonies of Latin America followed laws and customs regarding slavery that had been fixed for centuries in the homeland; slavery did not present a significant moral problem.[5] Slaves were simply people consigned to do the labor, and although their position in the social structure was a lowly one, they enjoyed most of the benefits of family life and in most cases could even own property.[6, 7, 8] But to the English colonists who inhabited North America, slavery was a new phenomenon and may initially have presented a rather severe moral problem. Unable to reconcile the dilemma of how a nation could simultaneously advocate the ownership of some people and the extension of political rights to others, many Britains disavowed any thought of blacks as being human. As slaves under the British system, blacks were stripped of most of the fundamental rights of people: the right to a family, the right of personal ownership and even, perhaps, the right to view themselves as human beings.[9]

Following the Civil War and for a hundred years thereafter, most blacks continued to exist in a state of semi-slavery. Anything approaching true emancipation for blacks in the South did not really begin until the early 1960s. It was as recently as 1964 that blacks could legally be excluded from theaters and places of worship throughout America; they were prohibited from voting across much of the South, and were relegated to rigidly segregated communities and schools. No American immigrant group can tell such a dehumanizing story, nor does any have such a history of destitution while on these shores.

Yet, by 1969 — only five years after passage of the Civil Rights Act and only four years after enactment of both the Voting Rights Act and ESEA Title I — critics of compensatory education programs were claiming that the programs had failed due to the limited mental capacities of disadvantaged children, particularly those who were black. It is true that, while the programs of the Great Society offered great promise, positive results were not immediately obvious. The drain of funds to underwrite the Viet Nam war and the election of Richard Nixon were devastating. Over time, the white middle class began to lose faith in social programs and began to withdraw support for social spending. While frustration with a slow pace of change is understandable, it should have been obvious that the educational deficit was the result of a complex problem and that there could be no quick fix.

The Environment, the Schools, and Achievement

It is a weakness in the hereditarian position to ascribe to some innate intellectual deficiency the failure of blacks to gain benefits from compensatory education. First, it should be reiterated that there is growing evidence that compensatory education is having some impact on pupil achievement. But even if there were little evidence of compensatory education's working, it would be of questionable logic to offer a genetic explanation for its failure. For some time now, the research on variations in curriculum or methodology has indicated that, alone, they do not have a significant effect on pupil achievement, regardless of the skin color of the students. [10] [11] Since the lowering of the teacher–student ratio and the increasing of per pupil expenditures for supplies have little or nothing to do with improving white achievement, the "reforms" associated with compensatory education (i.e. small group instruction and increases in a teacher's supply budget) should not have been expected to improve black achievement in any significant manner. It is interesting that the inability of such educational variables to yield gains among middle-class whites is not generally attributed to limited genetic capacities among white students. Consequently, why should it be assumed that the failure of compensatory education to have a profound impact on black achievement must somehow be caused by black mental inferiority?

The research indicates that schools are important to blacks: they are more likely to benefit from instructional variation than are whites; they typically learn more from the schools than do whites. James Coleman, for one, found the highest correlation between school variables and achievement to be among his minority samples. [12] Further, when schools were closed in Prince Edward County, Virginia during an integration dispute and, similarly during the 1968 New York City teacher's strike, black children appear to have suffered significant academic losses. [13] One might argue that in instances of a prolonged school closing, a sizable percentage of middle-class white children receive private tutoring. However, this is surely not the case during the summer vacation when a relatively greater achievement decline seems to occur for blacks than for whites. Therefore, one may conclude that impoverished black children learn most of their academic skills in the schools, while middle-class white children attain a significantly greater portion of their cognitive skills in the home. Thus, if the schools were to close permanently, the achievement disparity between most whites and many blacks would probably be greater than it is today, largely because a greater percentage of whites than blacks reside in an environment that contributes more positively to the acquisition of those cognitive skills that are measured by standardized tests.

Interestingly, many educators who would describe themselves as environmentalists have made an error by overestimating the power of the school in relation to the total environment. While the hereditarian begins with the belief that compensatory education can, at best, have a limited effect, the educational environmentalist believes that a well designed school program can, by itself, bring about equality. The desire to raise the schools to a level where they might substitute for a child's total learning environment has been a frequently stated goal of many compensatory programs. Even today, many people who view the schools as the "great equalizer" expect them to have full compensatory powers, that is to accelerate pupil growth beyond the growth rate of the average child until the disadvantaged children reach the national average. This would require quite an undertaking, since our most extensive compensatory effort, Title I, typically offers pupils less than one additional hour of reading instruction per day. One hour is not likely to change an environment.

Compensatory Education

While the research on compensatory education suggests that programs such as Title I are having an impact, it offers little in the way of generalizations upon which programs can be built to maximize the chances for their success. If one uses short-term achievement gains as the criteria, it appears that a curriculum that embodies specific cognitive objectives is superior to a more loosely structured "whole child" approach. Evidence indicates that strong administrative leadership and high teacher expectations are associated with better basic skills acquisition. However, it is not yet clear whether or not program coordination and parent involvement are related to greater achievement gains. Further, it is only speculative that sustenance of program treatment correlates with sustenance of learning. Consequently, the forthcoming recommendations for compensatory education have been generated more by environmentalist theory than by empirical inquiry.

If it is true that the mean differences between blacks and whites

in measured cognition and school achievement are caused principally by differences in the total learning environment, it should
follow logically that black children who become embued in the
cognitive processes of the larger (or so called white) culture will
have a far greater chance of performing well scholastically than
those children who have a relatively limited exposure to these
cognitive processes. The fact that black and multi-racial children
adopted by white families in Minnesota have been reported to
have significantly higher IQs and achievement levels than similar
children who have attended compensatory education programs is
evidence that, in acquiring the basic academic skills, total cultural
immersion is superior to partial cultural interaction. Since schooling
typically offers disadvantaged children a rather incomplete exposure to the larger socio-cultural milieu, schools that strive for
intensity of educational treatment during the school day and for
the extension of basic skills acquisition beyond the normal school
time will maximize their chances of producing higher achieving
children.

The schools are only one facet of a child's environment and, thus,
in their present form, may not be able to provide an adequate compensation for the exigencies of an economically impoverished
urban environment that has been nurtured by more than 350 years
of racism. One could make the case that total immersion in a new
environment is required. Throughout much of Africa, systems of
boarding schools appear to contribute a good deal to accelerating
and sustaining academic achievement; similarly, the kibbutz in
Israel has enjoyed considerable success in assimilating immigrants
from North Africa and parts of the Middle East.[14] [15] Boarding
schools have been available for centuries in England and North
America for the rich, while the principal residential opportunities available today for America's poor are the armed forces and
the public jails. However, because of the colossal failure of
nineteenth century boarding schools for Indians and the possibility that such institutions could contribute to cultural genocide, as
well as the sheer impracticality of serving large numbers of students, one could not seriously recommend a policy of boarding
schools for impoverished black children. It is not unreasonable,
though, to increase the enrollment of black children on a voluntary basis in existing private boarding schools (or in programs

similar to the ABC program for black high school seniors or the Upward Bound Program, which has placed thousands of black teenagers in college dormitories for the summer). Such an alternative may provide the significant change necessary in the total environment of small numbers of black children to provide them with true equality of opportunity. For the rest, we must focus on improving regular school programs.

Coordination of Effort

Proficiency in the basic skills is strongly associated with educational longevity (particularly beyond high school) and with greater vocational opportunity. Thus, programs for disadvantaged pupils should set as their primary goal a coordinated approach to basic skills instruction. Whether one is building a house or providing educational services, the chances of success are enhanced if the various contributors (whether they be bricklayers and electricians, or administrators and teachers) are in harmonious pursuit of the same goal. Each school must develop an ethos that demands a strong academic orientation and provides a carefully coordinated curriculum designed to enhance basic skills acquisition. Under the close supervision of the building administrator, the teachers and supporting professionals should adopt a common strategy to remediate learning difficulties. A partnership among the principal, the Title I teachers, the regular classroom teachers, and the noninstructional professionals in addressing a particular learning deficiency is superior to an uncoordinated effort in which a child may be confused by conflicting approaches to learning employed by the various staff with whom he/she interacts. Children in need of special assistance are also better served when such efforts are viewed positively by the entire school staff. Too often, the regular classroom teacher views the special needs child in a less than supportive light, and the child suffers for it.

Home Reinforcement

Since the out-of-school environment has a good deal to do with measured cognition and pupil achievement, the school should attempt to exert greater influence on children's out-of-school learning. On the simplest level, homework should be returned to its former level of importance. However, to create an educationally supportive home environment for children with compensatory needs, it is often necessary to develop strategies to involve parents in their child's education. In fact, such participation of parents in children's academic learning is often viewed as an educational imperative for compensatory programs. While there is little evidence that parent involvement *per se* (such as parental classroom visitations and attendance at parent meetings) has much to do with greater pupil learning, greater cognitive benefits appear to be associated with parent education programs that have made specific efforts to modify child rearing behavior.[16] [17] Programs designed to educate the parents of preschool children enjoyed considerable popularity during the 1970s. Over 200 such projects were funded by the federal government during the middle of the decade. A 1980 review of such programs by Alison Clarke-Stewart of the University of Chicago has found them to be generally effective in producing moderate I.Q. gains.[18] However, it is unclear whether working directly with the parent is superior to working directly with the child in a compensatory pre-school program, since parent education programs result in initial I.Q. gains which are generally no greater or longer-lived than those from child training projects.[19]

The U.S. Commission on Civil Rights has concluded that parental involvement has been an important factor in the successful implementation of a school desegregation plan.[20] One must also deduce that such parental participation can promote the actualization of compensatory education goals. Parents can be taught how to supplement that which is provided to the child during school hours. The community control movement provides evidence of the interest of black parents concerning their children's education. While that movement was not successful in wrenching control of the schools from the city-wide school establishment, it did establish a legitimate role for local parents. Schools would be wise to capitalize on that interest. By so doing, perhaps more parents will reach the conclusion that it is necessary for them to turn off the television set and to turn their children on to reading for recreation.

Sustaining Achievement Gains

Test score data indicate that disadvantaged children in regular school programs learn at a constant rate throughout their school career, a rate that is approximately two-thirds that of the "average" student, one who comes from a more academically stimulating learning environment. One of the goals of compensatory education has been to produce a growth rate in excess of the two-thirds ratio by enhancing the educational environment (i.e. including an extra hour or so daily of reading). But although there is impressive evidence that these supplemental services have accelerated learning during a single year, it is not clear whether the gains are sustained in the years that follow.

One thing that is clear, however, is that compensatory educators have not paid much attention to maintaining compensatory treatment over a long period. Originally, Project Follow Through was designed to continue the cognitive growth of Head Start children, but the major federally-sponsored evaluations of Follow Through have not included any longitudinal data that address the issue of preschool to primary school cognitive sustenance. Similarly, in Title I, there appears to be little interest in planning multi-year compensatory services for underachieving children. Seemingly fearful of the "stigma" often associated with Title I and preoccupaied with offering compensatory services only to those with the greatest need, educators have often recommended the termination of program treatment for children who appear to have benefited scholastically in the short term.[21] According to this line of reasoning, children who make progress are "mainstreamed" in order to help them adjust better to the school setting, and to allow the Title I teacher to give greater attention to those with lower test scores. Although Title I rules have permitted certain children to maintain their eligibility for successive years, any child who has reached grade level (not an uncommon attainment for many Title I first or second graders) would generally no longer be considered "educationally deprived," and, therefore, could not legally continue in Title I.[22]

If additions to the educational environment are to produce enduring benefits, educators must give greater attention to planning for the sustenance of those additions. Since it is known that

Head Start can raise measured cognition (but that "wash out" does occur) and since it is clear that compensatory programs such as Follow Through and Title I can improve achievement (but that the gains may be short lived), it would appear prudent for educators to give greater attention to offering continuity of compensatory services from the preschool through the secondary levels. When it is feasible, multi-year plans for remediating individual learning problems should be developed. Educators should also be leary of removing pupils from compensatory programs simply because they have made impressive gains over a short period.

It would seem reasonable that by enrolling underachievers in summer school programs, the relative losses in reading and math that occur among compensatory education pupils during the June to September recess would be reduced. However, the research on the effects of summer school raises serious questions about its cognitive benefits: there exists little or no evidence that summer school improves the reading or math achievement of pupils. When one realizes that there is also little evidence that significant reading or math instruction typically occurs in summer school, there is reason for hope. Apparently, in their desire to make summer school as attractive as possible, teachers have tended toward abandoning the basics, and have leaned toward providing more experiential learning or other activities they believe will be fun. Unfortunately, those activities most likely to lure children to attend summer school may also be most likely to yield the least cognitive benefits. Further experimentation with summer schooling for underachieving pupils is imperative, and particular attention must be paid to making it attractive while simultaneously emphasizing reading and/or math instruction.

Sustained exposure to a learning experience is related to the degree of endurance of that experience. Thus, the more years of enriched schooling (with active parental involvement throughout this period), the more enduring the influence of compensatory programs. Schools must be careful not to withdraw children from special programs too soon and must be ever vigilant that students whom they determine to be no longer in need of compensatory assistance do not fall back into their previous state. It is better for us all if schools err on the side of too much compensation than on not enough.

Desegregation and Educational Outcomes

Christopher Jencks believes that "If we are to have an integrated society, we should have integrated schools."[23] For millions of children, school desegregation has afforded the first opportunity for regular interaction with children of the other race. Not only is an integrated education a constitutional right, but it also provides an environmental change that can promote academic achievement.

In most instances, however, the reported scholastic gains for blacks in desegregated educational settings have been slight. But, given the socio-economic and political factors mitigating against integrated schooling and the fact that formal education is but a part of the learning environment, it should come as no surprise that school desegregation has not had a profound effect on black achievement. A review of the desegregation literature indicates that significant achievement gains can be made given the right conditions. Foremost seems to be the absence of conflict in the community and of racial hostility among the students; thus, there may be little, if any, progress made in the initial year of a controversial desegregation plan. It also appears that the presence of middle and upper income students in the class helps to raise the achievement levels of low income students. Further, the younger the child when desegregation begins, the greater the likelihood that there will be educational gains. Additionally, sensitive and accepting administrators and teachers have been shown to have an influence on achievement levels of desegregated blacks.[24]

Beyond its impact on achievement, desegregated schooling has been shown to have an effect on such indices as educational longevity and eventual vocational status. In the longitudinal area, the research on desegregation is in its infancy, and the available data is far from conclusive. Most of the existing multi-year data suggest, however, that multi-racial schooling is positively associated with attendance at predominantly white four year colleges. Since a college degree is related to access to higher occupational status and greater earnings, it may be concluded that desegregated schooling has contributed to greater economic and career opportunities for many blacks. Their children, in turn, enter the schools with middle-class backgrounds.

Implementing Desegregation Plans

While desegregated schooling and compensatory education have failed to revolutionize American society during the twenty-five years of their existence, one should not conclude that we should abandon our efforts to integrate our classrooms and to erradicate our children's learning problems. While desegregated education has made some contribution to improving black achievement, to promoting higher educational attainment, and to fostering elevated earnings and vocational opportunities, one should not be lured by what Willis Hawley and Ray Rist describe as the "simplistic notion . . . that the mixing of races *in itself* will invariably have positive educational and social consequences." [25] It is reasonable to ask the question whether or not it is always wise to push for greater desegregated schooling for the estimated one-half of the black population that still attends majority black schools. After a comprehensive review of the desegregation research, Hawley and Rist suggest "that when a school district is legally found to be in violation of the fourteenth amendment to the constitution, the remedy [should] be strongly situation-specific." They contend that "greater attention should be given to meeting the educational and social needs of a particular community" which may result in "only partial desegregation, different strategies to be adopted in different parts of the district and the implementation of experimental programs in some schools." [26]

While flexibility in addressing local needs may be a noble goal, one must also recognize that there is a fine line between policies that permit partial segregation to increase the chances of a plan's success and locally tailored strategies that continue to permit segregated schools in order to accommodate racial prejudices and to maintain the *status quo*. One must also wonder (as do Hawley and Rist) whether inequities in desegregation enforcement will not lead to even greater reservations about the fairness of the courts. The continuation of several segregated schools in one city and the elimination of all predominantly black schools in another will not likely lead to greater acceptance of desegregation. Hawley and Rist state it nicely: "The moral force of the law exists only so long as those to whom it applies believe they are justly treated." [27]

Our metropolitan areas provide a good example. School desegregation plans that focus only on the central city have done little to promote harmonious relations between city dwelling and suburban residing whites, particularly when higher income white liberals are championing integration while sending their children to lily white schools far from the central city; their support for desegregation often ends at the city line. Similar problems arise when integration within a school district affects only blacks and working class whites but does not involve the children of wealthier whites. Opponents of school desegregation are more likely to be appeased by comprehensive plans in which the perceived burdens of desegregation are seen as being equally shared.

Miami and Boston, two cities ridden by racial strife in recent years, can serve to demonstrate that the desegregation in big city school systems can be accomplished. Dade County, a metropolitan area that includes Miami, has experienced rapid absorption of culturally different and racially diverse populations during the last two decades. Since 1970, court ordered busing has provided the impetus for the widespread desegregation of the Dade County School System, one of the nation's largest. It has never experienced serious racial conflict due to busing and has had no history of "white flight."[28] (The Dade County School System was, for some reason, not included in Coleman's study, which erroneously concluded that busing-related white flight was a common occurrence.) It should be noted that the bloody 1980 riots in Miami's Liberty City section had nothing to do with school desegregation, but were triggered by an insensitive court ruling that acquitted several police officers who had allegedly beaten a black insurance executive to death following his refusal to stop for an apparent traffic violation. Underlying that community's rage were depression-like conditions that resulted in high unemployment rates and continuing economic insecurity. Hopefully, strong educational programs will assist that city's recovery.

Despite the bleeding that was Boston in the mid-1970s, it was Jonathan Kozol's observation in 1980 that "the schools are working better now than ever before in Boston's history." It was Kozol's contention that busing has largely been responsible for a "dramatic upgrading" of Boston schools, with such additions as instructional technology, greater parent involvement, and better pre-college programs. Even at South Boston High School, the scene of one of the nation's most virulent racial confrontations, the college attendance rate has increased from 10 percent before busing to 37 percent in 1980. [29]

Thus, busing for racial balance can produce results in a most resistent city. Busing is well worth the controversy if it provides blacks with the same high quality educational experiences available to whites. However, gains would occur more quickly if the controversy can be minimized. Thus, desegregation plans should be comprehensive, including options such as magnet schools that encourage voluntary integration. They should be seen as affecting all people equally. Further, there should be active parental involvement in monitoring the implementation and effectiveness of the plan. Whenever possible, the entire metropolitan area should be included in the plan in order to minimize white flight and to insure that there will be economic integration as well as racial integration in the classroom.

Higher Education and Affirmative Action

America cannot afford to wait until desegregation programs and compensatory education programs raise the academic achievement levels of low-income blacks to that of the white middle class before it expands the black middle class. Thus, collegiate affirmative action and special admissions programs have sought to promote equality by providing a greater proportion of blacks with greater access to the gateway to the professions, even though the measured scholastic achievement of these students may have fallen short of that of many of their white colleagues.

American higher education has made major strides in opening its doors to blacks in recent years. In the late 1970s, blacks constituted nearly 10 percent of the total enrollment. In 1967, they had been only 5.8 percent. [30] Testimony presented at that time to the National Commission on Civil Disorders indicated that less than 1 percent of the youth in Harlem went on to college. [31] Today, blacks attend college in proportions close to their share in the population, though they still tend to be clustered in the less elite institu-

tions and still have lower graduation rates than whites. The enrollment imbalance is evident when one understands that despite
their proportionate presence in the higher education aggregate,
blacks constituted fewer than 4 percent of the student bodies at the
state universities and land grant colleges in 1978. [32] These institutions still have a challenge ahead of them, particularly in the area
of graduate and professional school enrollments.

Nevertheless, the pool of blacks qualified for entry level
professional positions has been increased as a result of their
expanded access to higher education. Between 1960 and 1970 there
was a dramatic increase in the number of recruitment visits made
by corporate representatives to predominantly black colleges and
universities. What was a paucity of corporate contacts in 1960
became a pilgrimage in 1970; the average number of annual visits
to twenty-one black colleges grew from four to 297 during that
decade. Similar efforts to recruit black graduates were undertaken
at the historically white institutions as well. This activity has
given blacks greater opportunities in the white collar world of
private industry. Sociologist William Wilson observes that the
"vigorous recruitment of the best black talent by corporations is
probably one of the reasons why the proportion of black male
workers in white collar positions increased from 16 to 24 percent
from 1964 to 1974." Wilson also notes that "The bulk of this
increase occurs in the higher professional, technical and administrative positions" and that "the proportion of white males in white
collar positions remained slightly over 40 percent during this
period." Wilson suggests, however, that black gains in white collar
jobs were primarily the result of the expanded public sector,
which has employed a significant number of blacks to administer
social service programs. [33]

Affirmative action has also resulted in modest increases in the
proportion of blacks on the faculties at colleges and universities.
In 1974, 3.5 percent of college and university faculties were black,
and it has been projected that by 1990 the proportion may increase
to 5 percent. Affirmative action programs have made greater gains
for women than they have for minorities. The University of California at Berkeley provides a good example. From 1973–74 to
1979–80, the proportion of women on the faculty increased from

6.4 percent to 11.1 percent, while the minority faculty employment rose from 5.7 percent to 8 percent; blacks were only 1.9
percent of the faculty.[34] The experience of public higher education
in New Jersey is equally telling. Between 1975 and 1979, the
number of women faculty in that state's public colleges and universities increased by 216, growing from 28 percent of the total to
31.1 percent; blacks, on the other hand, decreased by 22, declining
from 5.8 percent to 5.4 percent of the total.[35]

It is likely that blacks will remain underrepresented on college
faculties, and that they will continue to be nearly nonexistent in
some fields of study for some time to come.[36] A report published
in 1978 by the National Center for Educational Statistics shows
that a proportionately far greater percentage of blacks than whites
are at the lower faculty ranks, and that black scholars are also
much more likely to be clustered in education and the social
sciences than in the "hard" sciences.[37] Between 1958 and 1977, 50.4
percent and 16.6 percent of the doctorates awarded to blacks were
in the fields of education and the social sciences, respectively,
whereas only 7.8 percent of black doctorates were in the physical
sciences and math and a meager 1.9 percent in engineering.[38] An
examination of the doctoral recipients in 1977 and 1978 indicates
that this trend has not been halted. Of the 2,286 doctorates earned
by blacks during those years, 56 percent were in education; nearly
19 percent were in the social sciences. All of the sciences accounted
for approximately 12 percent of the degrees. In that two-year
period, blacks received slightly more than 4 percent of all doctorates awarded. Their share of education degrees was over twice as
high, while they garnered only 0.8 percent of the doctorates in
engineering, 1.9 percent in chemistry and 2.3 percent in the
languages and literature.[39] Accordingly, these data suggest that
affirmative action strategists have a sizeable hurdle to overcome
if blacks are to attain proportionate representation on higher education faculties, particularly in the areas of science and technology.

The Challenge Ahead

Despite the maintenance of black underrepresentation as college and university scholars, there seems to be little question that

affirmative action has had a positive impact on the educational and vocational attainments of blacks outside of academe. Wilson argues that "affirmative action programs have benefited those blacks who are able to qualify for the expanding white-collar salaried positions in the corporate sector." Typically, these are "positions that have higher educational and training requirements than those associated with blue-collar employment."[40] For those blacks, however, who have serious educational deficiencies and, therefore, are unable to compete for white-collar jobs, affirmative action appears to have very little effect. According to Wilson, "As the black middle class rides on the wave of political and social changes, the black underclass falls behind the larger society in every aspect."[41]

It is Wilson's contention that the American economic and political systems have "shown persistent rigidity in handling the problems of lower class blacks." For example, in 1954 black teenage unemployment approximated that of whites, but from 1966 to 1974 the unemployment level of black teenagers has more than doubled the recorded level of their white counterparts. Wilson attributes these black unemployment increases principally to the swelling of the black central-city teenage population (between 1962 and 1969 there was a 75% increase among sixteen-to-nineteen-year-old blacks compared to a 14 percent rise among whites of the same age), to the lack of inner city industrial growth, and to the declining demand for unskilled and semi-skilled labor.[42] Although the percentage of blacks below the poverty level has declined in recent years (down from 55% in 1959 to 33.5% in 1970) a disproportionately high, one-third of the black population still belongs to the economically impoverished underclass. Since 1970 there has been little change in the percentage of blacks victimized by poverty, and it is this group, seemingly unaffected by desegregation, compensatory education, and affirmative action, that should constitute one of our nation's greatest domestic concerns.[43]

Research and Future Policy

The issues of race and education must continue to be addressed throughout the 1980s and the remainder of this century, and greater attention must be paid to the growing body of educational and social scientific research. Back in the early 1960s a model of "cultural deprivation" was accepted, and educators throughout the land made bold promises that ego development and motivational strategies, language training sessions, and an extra hour of reading could serve as the "great equalizer." There was, however, little or no scientific evidence that indicated that blacks had lower aspirations than whites, that they spoke a deficient language, or that the lack of middle-class amenities or the bombardment of slum sounds had anything to do with depressing cognition in any absolute sense. There also existed a paucity of evidence that could be interpreted as suggesting that short doses of environmental medicine during a "critical period" could provide a life-long remedy for social ills, or that schools, independent of more fundamental social changes, could overcome environmentally determined learning deficiencies.

Today, we are still unsure of the precise effects of poverty on measured intelligence, but there is evidence that experiential differences, rather than genetic deficiencies, have isolated blacks from the cognitive processes of the larger American culture, that separate racial development largely explains the existing racial differences in academic achievement levels. The research since 1965, the year that Title I was legislated, has generally contradicted many of the assumptions of the early 1960s. On various affective measures, blacks have been shown to have self-concepts as high as or higher than whites, and to have aspiration levels that parallel the white norm. [44, 45] Similarly, the data collected over the last few decades refute the contention that blacks are culturally deprived or that they suffer from stimulus deprivation. As empirical studies prove old concepts inaccurate, programs based on those concepts must be changed or even discarded.

Research in the behavioral sciences and education is still a developing field, and, thus, it is possible that powerful effects of schooling exist that have been inadequately measured to date. For example, after hundreds of studies that have concluded that class size makes no difference, Colorado's Gene Glass has created a research analysis that apparently permits much greater sensitivity to the effects of instruction, and it is now Glass's contention that small classes do correlate with greater learning. [46] Employing the Glass design, Herbert Walberg of the University of Illinois has reported similar findings regarding the positive academic effects of open education. Since the schools may be capable of making profound changes in the educational attainment of black underclass, and because the pursuit of any contribution to greater educational quality for blacks is an extremely worthwhile endeavor, policies that have demonstrated success should be promoted, and experimentation with many of those have promise but have not yet demonstrated effectiveness should be continued.

A Conservative Trend

While political and economic scholars would generally characterize the last half century as being one driven by liberal policies, it must be remembered that since the 1968 election of Richard Nixon, the national mood has become increasingly conservative. This trend culminated in the 1980 landslide election of President Ronald Reagan. It was an election in which the Republican Party stepped back from its traditional support for the constitutional equality of women and in which the Democratic Party stepped back from its traditional support for federal jobs programs as a remedy for high unemployment. The campaign was also marked by the activity of ultra-conservative groups, such as the Moral Majority and the National Conservative Political Action Committee, that contributed millions of dollars and thousands of campaign workers to conservative candidates. Six of seven liberal senators targeted by these groups were defeated, and control of the United States Senate returned to the Republicans for the first time since 1952.

This unexpected turn of events in the Senate, combined with the Reagan win, could spell trouble for those who support such initiatives as busing, affirmative action, and federally supported social programs. In the days following the election, the lame duck session of the Senate added a rider to the Justice Department's appropriation bill that would prohibit that agency from initiating or participating in court actions intended to support school desegregation programs, which include mandatory busing. [47] However, such a measure, if enacted into law, would probably be found unconstitutional, since it would preclude the government from seeking to carry out a constitutional obligation.

There are, however, several possibilities that would accomplish that same goal. The new chairman of the Senate Judiciary Committee, Strom Thurmond of South Carolina, a long-term opponent of civil rights legislation, has called for constitutional amendments that would prohibit forced busing and, even more drastic, would remove education from the purview of the Supreme Court. Similarly, Senator Orrin G. Hatch of Utah has proposed another amendment that would forbid affirmative action.

While these proposals would take the better part of a decade to be enacted and ratified, a more immediate impact might be felt. Of the nine justices seated on the Supreme Court at the time of Reagan's election, five were over seventy years old, three of that group (including the two leading liberals) were ill. Thus, it is possible that during his term, Reagan could appoint a court that might steer a conservative course for the following thirty years. (It must be noted, however, that the conservative Eisenhower appointed liberals Earl Warren and William Brennan and that liberal John F. Kennedy appointed conservative Byron White. Thus, presidents often fail in their desire to place philosophical compatriots on the court.)

November, 1980 did produce one bright spot for supporters of desegregation and equal education opportunity. A study conducted by Diana Pearce of Catholic University indicated that cities with metropolitan busing plans are experiencing faster rates of residential integration than are cities without area-wide plans. While she found greater desegregation in all of the cities she studied than was present in 1970, she found that parents in communities involved in metropolitan busing plans become more open to integrated neighborhoods when it would not be necessary to bus their children out of the neighborhood. Pearce found, for example, that Charlotte, N.C., was 32.7 percent more integrated in 1980 than it was ten years earlier, while Atlanta was only 9 percent more integrated. Thus, she has concluded that metropolitan plans, in the long run, minimize required busing.[48]

Continued Controversy Ahead

Perhaps the most important reason for the continuation of the commitment to desegregated schooling, affirmative action, and compensatory education is the fact that there are proportionately as many black heads of household out of work today as there were during the Great Depression.[49] As Lyndon Johnson put it, blacks have been moved "from D+ to C−."[50] American education appears destined to retain its historic role as the primary civic institution for the promotion of upward socioeconomic mobility.

For as long as our neighborhoods remain segregated, there will be a need for busing to achieve the integration in schools that the Supreme Court has said is a constitutional right for all Americans. For as long as there remains a large underclass population that suffers an educational disadvantage in addition to its economic disadvantage, there will be a need for compensatory programs. For as long as the schools fail to provide blacks with adequate preparation, there will be a need for special admissions programs at the college level. For as long as historically white colleges fail to meet the educational needs of their black students, there will be a need for black colleges. For as long as there continues to be a paucity of qualified black professionals, there will be a need for affirmative action programs at the graduate school level. For as long as there continues to be discrimination in employment, both in academe and beyond, there will be a need for affirmative action hiring programs. And, if the last twenty-five years are any gauge, the next twenty-five will be full of controversy.

REFERENCES

1. *Report of the National Advisory Commission on Civil Disorders.* New York, Bantam Books, 1968, p. 1.
2. Nelson, L.: *Cuba, The Measure of Revolution.* Minneapolis, MN: University of Minnesota Press, 1972, pp. 44–49.
3. Conant, J.: *Slums and Suburbs.* New York, McGraw-Hill, 1961, pp. 36–37.
4. Anderson, R.: *Liberia.* Chapel Hill, N.C., University of North Carolina Press, 1952, p. 99.
5. Elkins, S.: *Slavery.* Chicago, University of Chicago Press, 1959, p. 63.

6. Leonard, I.: Colonial Society. In Wilgus, A. (Ed.): *Studies in Hispanic American Affairs*. Washington, The George Washington University Press, 1936, p. 249.

7. Haring, C.: *The Spanish Empire in America*. New York, Oxford University Press, 1947, p. 218.

8. Klein, H.: *Slavery in the Americas, A Comparative Study of Virginia and Cuba*. Chicago, University of Chicago Press, 1967, pp. 194–195.

9. Ibid., p. 57.

10. Gage, N. (Ed.): *The Handbook of Research on Teaching*. Chicago, Rand McNally, 1963.

11. Stephens, J.: *The Process of Schooling*. New York, Holt, Rinehart and Winston, 1967.

12. Coleman, J. et al.: *Equality of Educational Opportunity*. Washington, U.S. Government Printing Office, 1966, p. 22.

13. Jencks, C.: *Inequality, A Reassessment of the Effects of Family and Schooling in America*. New York, Harper and Row, 1972, p. 87.

14. Stickney, B.: Boarding schools: An alternative educational experience for disadvantaged children. *Education and National Development*. Amherst, MA, University of Massachusetts, 1977.

15. Miller, H. and Woock, R.: *Social Foundations of Urban Education*. Hinsdale, Ill., Dryden Press, 1973, p. 293.

16. Wellisch, J. et al.: *An In-Depth Study of Emergency School Aid Act (ESAA) Schools: 1974–1975*. Santa Monica, Cal.: System Development Corporation, 1976, pp. VIII 2–3.

17. Irvine, D. et al.: Parent Involvement Affects Children's Cognitive Growth, Albany: The University of the State of New York, 1979.

18. Clarke-Stewart, A.: *Avenues, Answers and Assumptions in Parent Education*. Paper presented at the Annual Meeting of the American Educational Research Association, Boston, MA, 1980.

19. Ibid.

20. U.S. Commission on Civil Rights: *School Desegregation in Ten Communities*. Washington, U.S. Government Printing Office, 1973, p. 3.

21. U.S. Office of Education: *Title I Workshop on Draft Regulations*. March 10–12, 1980.

22. *Public Law 95–561 Title I — Amendment I of the Elementary and Secondary Education Act of 1965*, November 1, 1978, pp. 12–13.

23. Jencks, op. cit., p. 106.

24. Persell, C.: *Education and Inequality, The Roots and Results of Stratification in America's Schools*. New York, Free Press, 1977, p. 145.

25. Hawley, W. and Rist, R.: On the Future Implementation of School Desegregation: Some Considerations. In Levin, B. and Hawley, W. (Eds.): *The Courts, Social Science and School Desegregation*. New Brunswick, N.J.: Transaction Books, 1977, p. 413.

26. Ibid., pp. 424–425.

27. Ibid., pp. 425.
28. Pettigrew, T. and Green, R.: School desegregation in large cities: A critique of the Coleman 'white flight' thesis. *Harvard Education Review, 46(1):*33, 1976.
29. Kozol, J.: The rebirth of education in Boston. *American Education, 16(5):*13, 1980.
30. Brown, F. and Stent, M.: *Minorities in U.S. Institutions of Higher Education.* New York, Praeger Publishers, 1977, p. 37.
31. *Report of the National Advisory Commission on Civil Disorders,* op cit., p. 452.
32. Scientific Manpower Commission: *Professional Women and Minorities, A Manpower Data Resource Service.* Washington, Scientific Manpower Commission, 1980, p. 8.2.
33. Wilson, W.: *The Declining Significance of Race.* Chicago, University of Chicago Press, 1978, pp. 102–103.
34. *Chronicle of Higher Education,* September 29, 1980.
35. New Jersey Department of Higher Education: *Ethnicity and Sex of Employees of New Jersey Institutions of Higher Education: 1975, 1977 and 1979.* Research Note 80–8, 1980, pp. 1–2.
36. Fleming, J., Swinton, D., and Gill, G.: *The Case for Affirmative Action for Blacks in Higher Education.* Washington, Howard University Press, 1978, pp. 77–78.
37. National Center for Educational Statistics: *The Condition of Education, 1978 Edition.* Washington, U.S. Government Printing Office, 1978, p. 194.
38. Scientific Manpower Commission, op cit., p. 67.
39. Ibid., p. 26.1.
40. Wilson, op cit., p. 10.
41. Ibid., p. 22.
42. Ibid., pp. 89–97.
43. Ibid., p. 154.
44. Soares, A. and Soares, L.: Self-perceptions of culturally disadvantaged children. *American Educational Research Journal, 6(1):*31–45, 1969.
45. Gottfredson, L.: *Racial Differences in the Evolution of Educational and Occupational Aspirations.* Paper presented at the Annual Meeting of the American Educational Research Association, San Francisco, 1979.
46. Glass, G. and Smith, M. L.: Meta analysis of research on class size and achievement. *Educational Evaluation and Policy Analysis, 1(1):*2–16, 1979.
47. Chicago *Tribune,* August 3, 1980.
48. New York *Times,* November 14, 1980.
49. New York *Times,* November 17, 1980.
50. Kearns, D.: *Lyndon Johnson and the American Dream.* New York, Harper and Row, 1976, p. 305.

INDEX